What others are saying about

THE SECRETS OF WEALTH

"This book can change your financial life! It gives you a proven blueprint to fast-start your journey to financial independence."

— **Brian Tracy**, Author, *Goals!*

"If you could just take the best chapters from all of the personal finance classics like ***Think and Grow Rich*** and ***The Richest Man in Babylon*** and roll them all into one perfect book, then *The Secrets of Wealth* is the book you are looking for."

— **Thomas J. Vilord**, Author,
1001 Motivational Quotes for Success
Financial Advisor, Morgan Stanley

"Finally, a clear and concise book that's for the beginning wealth builder. A **MUST READ** for anyone looking to build wealth and improve their lives."

— **Mary Goulet**, Talk Show Host, Visionary, and Author

"Here's the stuff you WISH they taught you in high school. Marciano teaches what you need to know about achieving wealth and does it with an incredibly fun story."

— **Mark Farmer**, Founder, TotalLifeSuccess.com

"I've interviewed quite a few millionaires and this book blew me away. It offers a simple to follow, step-by-step roadmap you can use to build wealth…TODAY!"

— **Mike Litman**, Co-Author of the #1 Bestseller
Conversations with Millionaires

Also by Fabio Marciano

The Wealthy Pauper

A little book
detailing the amazing life
of one man
and how he went from
nothing to million-dollar status
in three short years.

THE SECRETS OF WEALTH

The Beginner's Guide

to

Financial Freedom

FABIO "fabman" MARCIANO

FOUR GREEN HOUSES PRESS

NEW YORK

Published by Four Green Houses Press, Harrison, NY
Division of The Wealthy Pauper, LLC, P.O Box 676, Harrison, NY 10528
www.thewealthypauper.com

Printed in the United States

BOOKS ARE AVAILABLE AT QUANTITY DISCOUNTS.
PLEASE SEE OUR WEB-SITE FOR HOW TO ORDER.

The Secrets of Wealth, The Wealthy Pauper, and the Wealthy Pauper Logo are trademarks of The Wealthy Pauper, LLC

10 9 8 7 6 5 4 3 2 1
First Edition

Cover design by Cathey Flickinger
Edited by K&K Design Group

Library of Congress Cataloging-in-Publication Data
Marciano, Fabio
    The secrets of wealth : the beginner's guide to
financial freedom / Fabio "fabman" Marciano. -- 1st ed.
    p. cm.
    Includes index bibliographical references and index.
    ISBN 1-932515-03-8

    1. Finance, Personal. 2. Investments. 3. Success I.Title.

HG179.M268 2003   332.024
                             QBI03-200545

DEDICATION

To my parents, my friends, and my loyal subscribers.
To my wife Amy for all the encouragement.
To my money and real estate mentors
who taught me how to build wealth,
the right way.

But mostly for Big Al,
this book is for you.
I only wish that its Secrets
had found your hands sooner.

TABLE OF CONTENTS

FOREWORD

Over the last 5 years I've had the unique opportunity to interview some of the most successful people alive today. Individuals such as Tony Robbins, Robert Allen, Mark Victor Hansen, Les Brown and many others. Nine of them were featured in our #1 best-selling book *Conversations with Millionaires*.

Because I'm exposed to so much information, I'm not easily impressed. But when I came across Fabio and saw how he was changing so many lives from his website and beyond, he instantly caught my attention.

Fabio brings information to his audience in an simple to understand manner which makes applying it successfully very easy. In his book The Secrets of Wealth he's done it again.

The Secrets of Wealth is not only a book, but a guide for those of you out there looking for the answers to your questions on how to build wealth, achieve financial independence and get out of the rat race for good. Fabio will show you how to increase your cash flow, get out of bad debt, and start investing the right way today. He'll show you how to figure out how much money you need to retire AND he'll show you how to get the money you need to retire.

This is a book you'll want to re-read once a year.

Enjoy!

Mike Litman

Co-Author of the #1 Bestseller *Conversations with Millionaires*

"Keep away from people who try to belittle your ambitions. Small people always do that, but the really great make you feel that **you, too, can become great**."

-Mark Twain

How this Book was Written – and Why

I'm Obsessed with Becoming Financially Free. Aren't You?

Are you longing for a better life? Are you sick of working 40 or 50 hours a week with nothing to show for your hard work? Then this book is for you. This book is for ambitious people who want to build wealth and achieve Financial Freedom. The ideas and strategies in the pages ahead will save you time and money and help you build wealth the *right* way! If you're not committed to getting more out of life, then put this book down and buy another one. I'm serious.

Do You Want MORE from Life?

This book is for those that are longing for a better life and haven't given up on their dreams. This book will show you how to build wealth the right way in an easy-to-read, simple format.

I have been fortunate to have found great mentors for all areas of my life. Thankfully, they've taken the time out of their busy schedules to teach and guide me. The story that follows is a fictionalized version of my life story. The story you are about to read focuses primarily on the teachings of three of the most important mentors I've had in my life: one is a financial planner, one a real estate investor, and the other a family friend. All three are millionaires and soon I will be one as well because I'm putting their simple plan to work for me.

Through the eyes of my mentors and through hearing about their successes and mistakes, I have learned a great deal about investing, living, and getting ahead in life. Many of the thoughts and ideas in this book did not come to me or my mentors in a dream, nor were they part of a series of scrolls buried for centuries. What they are is a combination of time-tested and battle-tested tenets for building wealth. In short, the Secrets will form the basic building blocks of your wealth-building machine. Perhaps you've come across a few of them while reading other books or listening to tape programs. All the better since you'll be familiar with what I'll be discussing. What my mentors did was distill the information into simple Secrets or rules as I sometimes call them, which are easy to follow.

Why I Wrote the Book and How it Came into Being

I want you to **achieve the peace of mind** that comes from having a solid plan to become Financially Free and this book will show you how to do just that – become Financially Free and escape the Rat Race.

I'm sharing these Secrets with you now due to both a sense of duty and a sense of guilt. The sense of duty comes from my belief in the universal law of helping others. My real estate mentor freely offered me the opportunity to learn what would have cost me thousands of dollars if I had paid for the books, seminars, and mistakes I would have surely made along the way. During this time, I have put in place the Secrets he taught me and have realized considerable gains in my income and wealth (as well as peace of mind).

My sense of guilt comes from the fact that I kept my sessions with my various mentors a secret from my friends and family for all these years. I kept my lessons a secret because I was afraid that they would not support me or would poke holes in the theories my mentors spoke of. Often times family members, not knowing any better, did not support my "crazy" ideas regarding investing in stocks, real estate, or business ventures. The truth is that they just didn't understand how to make money work for them. You see, all my life my friends and family worked hard for money, but had they known how to make money work for them, I'm sure they would have lived much easier and happier lives. When I began to see the pain on my friends' faces or the stress they carried with them, I couldn't take it any longer. So I decided to start helping them; one at a time.

This book began with a simple email I sent to a friend outlining the Secrets. I then began sharing them in online forums. When the demands became too great to handle the requests one-on-one, I created a web-site (www.fabmansecrets.com) to give them away. There were usually questions about how to incorporate the rules into their lifestyles, so I wrote a little more about each of the rules and expanded on the topics. Eventually, the notes, letters, and e-mails became quite an extensive amount of writing. The result of all that material is the story, about a boy named David Allen and his mentor Mr. Mathers, you're about to read.

Disclaimer for the Get-Rich Dreamers

This book will not make you rich overnight, but will help you lay down the foundation upon which to build your Financial House. I can't promise riches, but I will guarantee that if you follow the Secrets contained in this book you will take back control of your money and your life. This book will show you how to clarify what your retirement and other financial goals are and show you how to manage your money so that you can afford today's needs *without* sacrificing the needs of tomorrow.

Don't worry if you've tried to save or invest money in the past and haven't stuck with it. Hopefully my story will help you make saving for retirement and other goals a habit that you will never break. I'll teach you how to make your money work for you regardless of how many years you have until retirement. The thing that I hope you come away with most from this book is the fact that you can become Financially Free if you're determined and willing to learn and work hard. Saving money will become a habit and with the right financial plan guiding the way, you'll realize how quickly you'll be in control of your finances and your life.

You'll need equal parts determination, imagination, and most of all *persistence*. **Getting rich isn't a game of chance**. It's a game of learning how to block and tackle, learning how the game is played, and going out and actually playing! If you have no cash or your credit is less than perfect, don't worry, you can fix that. If you have a full-time job, screaming kids, and a demanding spouse, you can still manage your finances and handle the rest of your duties. What you can't change, we'll find a way around. The bottom line is that getting rich is easy if you're willing to take that first step, then follow that step with another and another. Once you get moving in the right direction, armed with the knowledge contained in this book, you'll be unstoppable.

So let's clean up your financial situation, get you educated, and put you on the path to Financial Freedom. **Let's do it!**

"If one advances confidently in the direction of his
dreams, and endeavors to live the life he has
imagined, he will meet with a success unexpected
in common hours."

– Henry David Thoreau

"The only thing that stands between a man and
what he wants from life is often merely the will to
try it and the faith to believe that it is possible."

- Richard M DeVos, Co-Founder, Amway

Author's Note (or My Plea to You)

It's been estimated that only one in ten Americans who are 65 or older are financially independent. That means that even though they've reached the so-called retirement age, **nine out of ten Americans really can't survive** on the wealth they've accumulated from over 40 years of working. **Forty years of blood, sweat, and tears and they still have to work, day in and day out!**

How old are you? Do you love your job or do you keep working at a job you have because "you have to?" Whatever the reason, imagine doing what you're doing for the rest of your life. Is that something you *want to* be doing or is it something you *have to* do to make ends meet? Chances are if you're reading this book, you're at the point where you're fed up with your financial life and you're looking for some answers. This book contains the answers you're looking for, but you will not find any get rich quick schemes or information on how to build a business overnight or buy real estate with no money down. I'm not knocking any of these strategies or individuals who write about these topics. I just know that **if you can't learn how to balance your checkbook or manage your own debt, how the heck are you going to learn how to manage a business or buy real estate?**

This book offers a very simple plan for setting the foundation of your wealth-building machine. The one thing all my mentors taught me is that **getting rich is simple, but not easy**. It's simple because all you have to do is follow the plans that the rich have used for centuries. The reason it's not easy is that the majority of people just don't follow through. Get the difference?

Please Take ACTION!

Here I am writing this book that will improve your financial lot in life if you follow the Secrets, but my question to you is "what will you do with the information once you've read this book?" All too often, we buy books or tapes on losing weight or building wealth and we don't act on the information.

> "If you choose not to decide, you still have made a choice."
> –Rush, the band

Does the quote above make sense? Let me explain a little. By choosing not to do something with the information in this book, you're actually making a choice. Making a decision is normally a good thing, but in this case it's definitely the wrong one to make. Those that choose to do nothing with the information in this book or any of the other thousand or so books on this topic are still waiting to find Financial Freedom. That waiting *is* the problem. If you don't get started on something, how can you succeed? My life changed the moment I decided to stop waiting for something to happen and decided to just do something and deal with the consequences. My life changed completely from that moment on.

Read *The Secrets of Wealth* and the Action Plans that appear throughout the book, then **put the ideas I'm sharing with you to work for you**. Please don't just read the information and do nothing. Worse yet, don't read half the book and discard it for the TV or some other distraction. My real money mentors forced me to learn and experience the rules over a period of time. They wouldn't teach me the next lesson until I acted on the lesson they had just taught me. It was a good strategy and one that will work for you. Read one Secret at a time and please take the time to reflect on how you can incorporate the Secrets into your lifestyle. Then move on to the next Secret.

Take ACTION today! And maybe I'll be writing about you one day.

Good Luck and Enjoy!

Fabio Marciano
Harrison
2003

Chapter 1

You Should Write a Book

How I Started Writing this Book

Did you read the Introduction to this book? If you did, great. If not, please go back to the Introduction. **Do not pass GO** until you've read it. I know, I know. I hate reading those things too, but it's important. I wrote the introduction to give you a sense of where I've been and why I'm writing this book.

All right if you're that lazy, here's the quick synopsis. I learned all the Secrets of Wealth from three main mentors. I implemented what they taught me and people began to take notice. Friends of mine asked for help. Co-workers constantly came up to me asking for advice on all aspects of life, especially financial decisions. After one particularly long session with a co-worker, she said, "You should write a book."

At first I balked at the idea. "I'm not a Certified Financial Planner. I don't have an accounting degree," I said. "Who's going to listen to me?"

"I will and I know there are people out there that need practical advice. Those books you gave me to read are great, but I never know where to begin. The books don't offer any 'next steps' or action plans like you wrote out for me. That's what people need, not reams of hard-core data or useless examples with hypotheticals. You've helped me by explaining in plain language why it's so important to get control of my financial life and get out of the Rat Race."

"But I'm not a millionaire yet. Why would someone want to listen to me?"

A smile came across her face. She started shaking her head at me.

"What?" I asked. "What's so funny?"

"Do you realize that you said 'yet,' as in you know you're going to be a millionaire, but aren't one yet."

"So? What's your point?"

"Don't sell yourself short. That's my point. You can do it. You already know the Secrets of Wealth and they have to be shared with as many people as possible. You can't keep them to yourself."

"But...."

"No 'buts' about it Fabio, just do it."

I began writing that night.

What you are about to read is a fictionalized account of how I learned the Secrets of Wealth from my mentors. They may seem simple, but believe me, if you implement all of them in your life, you will become an unstoppable force to be reckoned with.

Chapter 2

Summertime Blues

Do you know what a millionaire looks like? I thought I knew what one looked like, but I was way off. I'm sure if you've read any of the latest books on millionaires you know that they aren't the flashy types, they don't drive sports cars and they've been married to the same person for thirty years. Exciting stuff, right? It was for me. The first time I read about them I was blown away. Of course when I first read The Millionaire Next Door by Thomas J. Stanley and William D. Danko, I had already met my 'millionaire next door.' It was a chance encounter with my first money mentor on a rainy Saturday morning that forever changed my life.

"How Can I be Broke?"

I graduated college and promptly got a job as a temporary employee or 'temp' for short. If you've ever been a temp you know how demeaning the job can be. I spent my working hours trying to get my work done, take on extra assignments, and play the office politics game with the hopes of trying to impress my boss in order to get hired. Two hiring freezes and nine months later I was hired as a full-time employee. I celebrated by staying late to finish a paper I was writing for my MBA class. I think my dinner was a stale back of pretzels and a Pepsi. Not exactly the celebratory dinner I had envisioned.

During the summer, my friends mentioned that they wanted to go away on a vacation together. Everyone had been working for over a year after graduating from college and was anxious to have some fun. The decision was made to take a trip to Florida for some fun in the sun. The total cost of the trip would be $900 including the flight, food, and the hotel. I didn't think it was much until I realized that I didn't have $900! "How can I be broke?" I thought to myself. I had just maxed out one of my credit cards paying for my summer tuition. It would be two months before my company would reimburse me. Not wanting to tell my friends my situation, I lied and said that I couldn't go because I had a paper to write and an exam during the vacation week. That was the first time in my life that my debt made a decision for me.

That was truly a low point for me. I worked so hard and it seemed like I never went out or bought things for myself and yet I had no extra money. When I had finally had enough of feeling sorry for myself, I decided to do something about my situation. I wanted to figure out how I could make some extra money.

Searching for Answers

One rainy Saturday morning I sat down for breakfast at the kitchen table with the morning paper. I opened up the *Business* section and began to read a story about some guy who had made it big in the stock market despite investing during a bear market. The story got me thinking of ways that I could get the same results. Shortly thereafter, my father came downstairs for breakfast.

"I must be dreaming. You're reading the *Business* section and not the *Sports* section. Are you feeling okay?" he asked.

"Fine," I replied.

He poured himself a cup of coffee and walked over to the table. "Since when have you been interested in the *Business* section of the paper?"

"Just trying to learn a little about investing. I have to find a better way to invest my money versus the way I've been doing it to date."

"I'm glad you're taking an interest in the stock market," he told me.

"But before you go searching for stock investing tactics, you really should know the basics of investing and you're not going to learn it from the newspaper because there's a lot to investing. I suggest you go to the library and see what books you can find on investing before you invest one red cent."

I looked up from the paper. "Can't you just tell me what I should do?" I didn't want to spend my day off going to the library to look up books when my dad could just tell me what to do. I didn't know where to begin and I had never read a book on investing. The guys at work were always talking about the stock market. Perhaps one of them could help me.

"No, I think it's important for you to learn a little about investing before you go putting your money into any investment," he said. "The more you learn, the better you'll be at making investment decisions."

He finished his coffee and got up from the table. "Don't worry, before you go putting your money into anything, I'll make sure to take a look to see that you're not doing anything foolish."

"Thanks," I said half listening. I folded the *Business* section and threw it on top of the table. "I guess I'll be at the library."

As I said, the thought of spending my day off at the library was definitely not appealing. But since it was raining, there really wasn't anything better to do. I found my book bag under the mess in my closet, grabbed a notebook and pen and shoved them inside my bag. I took a granola bar and a bottle of Pepsi with me just in case my little journey to the library took too long. As I walked out the door, I thought about heading over to the mall to take a look at some new CDs and sneakers I needed to buy, but decided that I might as well go to the library since most of my friends were still sleeping. I'm glad I did. The decision to go to the library on that rainy Saturday morning changed my life forever.

Meeting My Money Mentor

I spent a half-hour at the library just looking at various books on investing and personal finance. I couldn't believe how many there were. It was tough selecting which ones to read, but I chose *One Up on Wall Street* by Peter Lynch, some stock picking strategy book that looked good, and some book about picking mutual funds. I chose an empty table by the magazine racks and sat down. I pulled out my notebook and pen just in case I needed to take notes, opened up Peter Lynch's book, and started reading.

After an hour, I needed a little caffeine lift so I grabbed my bag and walked outside. When I came back, the seat opposite mine was taken. As I walked toward the table I noticed that it was Mr. Mathers. Mark Mathers was one of the nicest guys in town. He was always smiling and his clothes never deviated from his uniform of jeans, a flannel shirt, and work boots. At one time or another he had worked at the local pizzeria, the car wash, and the laundromat. I think he was presently doing carpentry work for Grbec Industries, a local construction firm. I saw him at the country club once in a while playing golf with some of the other members. I caddied for him several times, but he wasn't a member at the club, always a guest. I didn't think he had any more money than the next guy did. How was I supposed to know otherwise? I always saw him around town driving his old Ford pickup with a lawn mower and his tool chest in the back.

"Hey Mr. Mathers, how are you?" I asked, sitting down in my seat.

He removed his glasses and looked up from his magazine. "Oh, hi David. Just fine thanks and you?" he replied.

"Can't complain. Just doing some reading."

"On a Saturday morning? Shouldn't you be out on the golf course or in bed like the rest of the kids your age," he said in a serious tone. A smile cracked his face.

"Yeah, I suppose, but it's raining and there's not much to do, so I figured I'd come here and do some reading."

"Reading when you could be sleeping?" he said in a questioning manner. "Must be some interesting stuff."

"Well, to be honest, I'm looking to learn how to make some real money in the stock market."

"Most kids your age are partying rather than learning about investing and financial planning. Why the interest?" he asked.

"Well I do my fair share of partying, but I want to get out of debt and it seems as though despite the amount of hours I work, I never have any money. I want to learn how to make more money."

"Make more money? So the secrets to making more money are in those books?" he asked, pointing to the stack on the table.

"Well, I asked my dad to help me this morning, but he told me to go to the library and read up on investing before he would help me."

"Your father is a smart man. This library is filled with so much information and you're lucky that Woodbridge's library happens to have the best personal growth and finance section in the county." He looked at me and then at the books. "I noticed the books when I sat down. Some pretty interesting ones you got there."

"You've read them?" I asked.

"Sure, all of them. But let me ask you this, what are you trying to accomplish by reading those books?"

"Isn't it obvious?" I responded.

"No, not really. I guess I'm wondering what you're trying to get from those books. What is it that you want to achieve? What are your goals?"

"To get rich, I guess."

"Ahhh," he said, leaning back while placing his glasses on the table. "To get rich. I guess that's what most people are looking to do."

"Aren't you?" I asked.

"I suppose, but let me ask you this, when you say rich, what do you mean?"

"Mean? Well I guess to have a lot of money and a nice car and a big house."

"So that's your definition of rich: a lot of money, a nice car, and a big house?"

"Yeah, I suppose."

"Next you'll tell me you want to be a millionaire, right?"

"The thought crossed my mind," I said with a grin. "Don't we all."

"Hmm, I suppose so," he said, resting his chin in his hands. "Well then, your goal shouldn't be too hard to reach," he said matter of factly. He put his glasses back on and began reading again.

"If it's so easy, then how come you're not a millionaire?" I blurted out.

He looked up from his magazine and removed his glasses. I instantly regretted what I had said and was about to apologize, but he spoke instead.

"David with the way the stock market is going in the past decade even with the recent downturn, with interest rates low enough that anyone can borrow money, and the enormous amount of books on personal finance and real estate investing, it's getting easier and easier to become a millionaire. Already, the aura of the millionaire is dying and now people are obsessed with billionaires like Bill Gates and Warren Buffett. You don't need the right six numbers in tomorrow's lottery or thousands of stock options to do it. You don't even have to give up life's little luxuries that we've all become accustomed to. You don't even have to clip coupons or shop at discount stores."

Insert Foot in Mouth

"And for just $9.99 a month, you too can be a millionaire in as little as a year," I said in an announcer's voice. Looking back, I can't believe I said that, but I'm glad he got a laugh out of my comment. He kidded me about it every chance he got.

"Well, it cost me a bit more than $9.99 and it took a lot more than a year," he replied.

"Say what?" I said, a bit dumbfounded. I was literally shocked. "C'mon, you're a millionaire?" I asked, knowing the answer couldn't possibly be yes. Here was this man, pushing 40, dressed in faded jeans and a golf shirt. His watch was plastic and even his boots were a little past worn down. No way is he a millionaire I thought to myself.

"Well, I don't like to discuss my net worth with strangers, but since I know your father and you'll probably ask him yourself, I guess I can tell you that the answer to your question is yes."

"But…" I started to say, but didn't really know what to say. He didn't have a high paying job and he didn't look like the guys at the club. I wanted to tell him that he was a liar, but I couldn't muster the strength.

"You see, the majority of millionaires in this country aren't the flashy Donald Trump types that you read about or that are glamorized in the media. We're the common folk that you pass by day after day and would never guess that we're wealthy. We're the small business owners or landlords that you pay rent to. We're the ones driving the Fords and Toyotas, not the BMWs and Porsches."

The Money Pact

That's when I came up with the idea to have Mr. Mathers help me. After all, if he had done it, why couldn't I do it as well? I looked down at the book I was skimming through and closed it. "Can you help me? I'll pay you that $9.99 a month," I said half-jokingly.

"Sure I can show you what I call the Secrets of Wealth, but my advice is free on one condition."

"My first born?"

"No, nothing that dramatic. I must have your promise that you will put the Secrets of Wealth into action immediately."

"That's easy enough. I promise."

"Easy is an understatement. Procrastination has killed many a good idea David. But again, I will share them with you only if you promise to use them. You see David these rules or Secrets of Wealth are more about a way of life than they are about getting rich in some get rich scheme. Embracing the Secrets means that you will work consistently toward your goal of accumulating wealth without having to obsess over it day in and day out."

"I think I can get used to the rich life," I commented. "Where did the Secrets come from?"

"A wonderful man by the name of Simon Phillips was kind enough to offer me a job as his assistant. Simon was a financial planner and knew everything about managing money and making it grow. I only worked for him for two years, but I learned a great deal by listening to him talk to his clients and coach them about money matters. He gave me the bug and throughout college I read just about every book I got my hands on. The Secrets of Wealth can be found in dozens of books that line the personal finance section of this library."

"So the rules are in these books I have here?" I said, pointing to the stack of books I had brought over to the table.

"Yes, I'm sure some of the Secrets are in those books and I'm sure there are some rules that can be added to this list, but these Secrets of Wealth have served me well and they served my mentor well."

"So what are the Secrets?" I asked, grabbing my notebook. I was anxious to get working on my first million.

"Slow down. I think if you're really committed, you can hold off on getting them all at once. In fact, I won't tell you all of them up front."

"Why not?"

"Well to do so would be pointless. **The rules and what they mean to you won't sink in unless you really take them one step at a time. Each Secret builds on the previous one.**"

I sat back in my chair. I was so eager to start today and I wanted to know the Secrets NOW, not tomorrow.

"I can tell you're disappointed," he said, noting the change in my demeanor. He stared at me deeply. "Do you really want to be rich? I mean is this just the dream of the month like the way some people go from one hobby to the next or **are you committed**?"

"Mr. Mathers, I want to be rich," I replied. "I've wanted to be rich ever since I can remember."

"The quality of a person's life is in direct proportion to their **commitment to excellence**."
— Vince Lombardi

"Good, because that's really the first step; really committing yourself to the Secrets I'm going to give to you. **If you're committed and you follow the Secrets, you will be rich**. It's also important to accept the fact that **you and you alone are responsible for your Financial Freedom**. You alone got yourself into debt and you alone can rid yourself of that debt."

"I take full responsibility. After all, I'm the one who ran up the bill on my credit cards. But can I ask you something, how rich is rich?" I had to ask because I still was a little skeptical. He didn't look like the other millionaires whose golf bags I carried at the club on the weekends. Maybe he had a lot of money built up in a retirement account and couldn't touch it for another 20 years. I was wrong. Really wrong on that one.

"As rich as you want, but we'll get to that later," he replied. "For now I'm content with your response and I believe you're really committed to being wealthy. But I've got one disclaimer for you before we get to our lessons."

Diets, Ab Bustin' Contraptions, Pyramid Schemes and Other Get-Something Quick Failures

"What I'm going to teach you isn't some 'Get Rich' scheme, but a proven method for building wealth. The 'how to's' in life are no real secrets. In fact the Secrets I'm about to teach you over the next few weeks aren't really secrets. They've been used by the wealthy for decades, even centuries. George Clason wrote about them in *The Richest Man In Babylon*, as did Napoleon Hill in his classic *Think and Grow Rich*. If you read the biographies of Andrew Carnegie, Henry Ford, Bill Gates, Nelson Rockefeller, or J. Paul Getty, you'll see the Secrets in bits and pieces throughout their lives. What made the super rich get all their money is that they had a clearly defined picture of what they wanted to become. They knew where they were going and who they wanted to become before they began their journey. This was the first step they took. For some it was to get rich, for others it was to revolutionize the auto industry or the computer industry. Some like Ted Turner had a grand vision of an all news network. It started with what Napoleon Hill called a '**Definiteness of Purpose.**' Hill studied the most successful men around him and determined that **those who succeeded prioritized their time, money, and effort in order to reach their definiteness of purpose.** One of the main reasons I have the wealth I have acquired is that I first determined what I wanted and *why* I wanted to get it. I had clear goals so I understood *why* I was spending less than I earned, or socking away money every month. **Everything I've achieved in life is according to my plan, which is an outgrowth of the goals I've set for myself.** The dreams I put to paper are slowly becoming reality."

There are <u>NO</u> Shortcuts

"Again, I want to re-emphasize that there are no shortcuts in the path you will walk down. The journey may take you 30 years or it may take you 20 years. Some become Financially Free in less than 10 years, but those are the truly exceptional students that want it bad enough and put all the Secrets to work for them at the same time. They're the ones that are willing to work hard and stick with it through the ups and the downs of the wealth-building process. **Most people aren't willing to make the necessary sacrifices to become rich.** Most want to find the next Microsoft or Dell, invest $1,000 and have it be worth $1 million in 10 years. They might as well be playing the lottery because the odds are better. What I will be teaching you is how to work hard for a short while and how to structure your spending and investing in order to get paid for the rest of your life. Are you up for the challenge?"

"I am. I'm willing to work hard and do what it takes to become Financially Free."

"Good. Glad to hear that," he replied.

"Great. So when do we begin?" I was anxious to get started. It was already getting late and I was starting to get hungry.

"I can tell you're excited, so I'm willing to come back after lunch. I have to go to the office for an hour to meet with my attorney."

"You're not in trouble?" I asked before I realized what I said.

"Heavens no. I'm meeting with my attorney to discuss a building I'm buying."

"Phew. I didn't want to be taught by a criminal," I kidded.

"While I can almost guarantee that you will become a millionaire if you follow the Secrets closely, there's nothing illegal about what I'm going to teach you." He looked down at his watch. "How about we meet at one o'clock sharp."

"Works for me," I said rising from my seat to shake his hand. "Thank you Mr. Mathers."

"Don't thank me yet David. You've got a lot of work ahead of you, but if you stick with it, you'll definitely become wealthier financially and mentally. Anyone who follows the Secrets can become wealthy."

He was so sure of himself. That's what impressed me the most. It was as if he knew that his Secrets would lead me to wealth. I watched him walk through the double doors of the library. I could hardly contain my excitement.

As I walked to my car, I noticed his pickup parked in the shade underneath the big oak tree that sat at the corner of the parking lot. There was a little rust forming on the back. I shook my head. Mr. Mathers' truck had to be 10 years old and although it looked like it was in decent shape, it had to be on its last legs. How was this guy going to teach me about money and investing? Maybe I should ask one of the other members at the club for some advice instead. I'm sure Mr. DeLin or Mr. Orlando would be willing to help me out. They always tipped well and had to be worth big bucks and know how to make money.

As Mr. Mathers pulled out of the parking lot, I noticed the license plate read '10PRCNT' and wondered what it meant. I'd find out soon enough.

Know that you can achieve anything
you put your mind to.
You just have to take action
in order to realize your dreams.
There's no better time than today
to stop kidding yourself
and take **MASSIVE ACTION!**

Secret #1:
SET GOALS FOR YOURSELF–

THE POWER OF WHY?

"If one advances confidently in the direction of his dreams, and endeavors to live the life he has imagined, he will meet with a success unexpected in common hours."

– Henry David Thoreau

Chapter 3

Secret #1: SET GOALS FOR YOURSELF - THE POWER OF WHY?

Are you living the life you imagined?

The bottom line is that you're either living the life you've imagined or you're not. If you're living the life you've imagined, congrats. You probably don't need this book as much as someone else. If you're not living out those daydreams of yours, you've got two choices: make some changes and work toward your dreams or keep dreaming. What's it going to be?

The First Lesson

It was almost one o'clock when I re-entered the library. I didn't see Mr. Mathers' truck outside and I was a bit anxious. I hoped his meeting with his attorney wasn't running late. He wasn't sitting at the table where we met a few hours before, so I checked the personal finance section, but couldn't find him. I threw down my backpack on our table, sat down, and began to read one of the books I had selected earlier. Just then, Mr. Mathers walked into the library.

"Seems like we were just here," he said as he sat down across from me. He reached over to his briefcase and pulled out a binder. "I grabbed my notes on the Secret we'll cover today," he said. "We should be able to finish our discussion in less than an hour."

"Sounds good to me," I said.

"Good, but before we get into the lesson, let me give you some background information. The Secrets of Wealth are simple and easy to follow. They have worked for those starting out with nothing to their name and no previous investing experience, to those who already have started investing but find themselves constantly struggling to make that next jump in net worth. The Secrets will progress in difficulty as we go along. By difficulty I mean that the first couple are easier to implement and can be done within a few days or weeks, while the last few Secrets may require some studying and experience before putting them to use. Remember, the Secrets I'm going to share with you will not make you rich overnight. They will make you rich over a lifetime if you practice them and incorporate them into your life."

"So I won't be an overnight millionaire. I understand, I truly do. So what's the first Secret?" I got my pen ready and turned to the first page in my notebook. I was anxious to begin and couldn't wait to hear what the first Secret was, especially since it was the most important.

"I can see you're getting anxious," he said, noting my enthusiasm. He reached into his briefcase and handed me a sheet of legal sized paper. This is what it said:

The 5 Stages of the Game called Life

1. **Struggling** (Clueless) – At this stage you're having trouble making ends meet and sometimes you have trouble providing the basic needs of food and shelter for you and your family. You have no luxuries, perhaps no car or other assets. Chances are you rent, rather than own your home. Perhaps you're stuck in this stage because your expenses exceed your income. Chances are that your income is not sufficient to get you out of your predicament so you fall deeper and deeper into debt. You blame your small paycheck, but the real culprit may be your spending habits.

You're not alone: **over 50% of Americans are in the Struggling stage** of the Game, with no hopes of ever getting out. They're trapped like you and living paycheck to paycheck. Your main concern at this level is to create a plan to get out of debt and to create an Emergency Fund. If you have the desire and will, attempt to increase your means while decreasing your expenses, but first start by examining your spending habits.

2. **Surviving** (Concerned/Complacent) – At this stage the basic needs in life are provided for and you're able to afford a few luxuries for yourself and your family. You focus your attention on providing for your children's education, building up your retirement accounts, and investing some money for short-term goals. You could do more, but you're content...and that's dangerous!

You need the motivation to take it to the next level. Often people become complacent because they're making a good living at their job, their mortgage isn't too unwieldy, and their debt-to-income ratio is under control.

You're comfortable where you are, but your plan may not be aggressive enough to account for life's unexpected twists (divorce, heart attack, sickness, layoffs, etc.). In reality you're really one small disaster or accident away from financial ruin. Excessive spending and shopping habits can wreak havoc on a family in this stage of the Game.

3. **Striving** (Confident) – At this stage you are not content to just make due with what life has 'given' you. You wish for more and so you begin to enter the stage of striving to improve your lot in life. You have sought the advice of the rich, read books, and attended seminars to increase your knowledge. From this knowledge and experience you have put together a plan for investing that will get you to where you want to be in life.

You're proud of where you are and what you have achieved. You've taken control of your debt and your expenses. You have a positive cash flow and while still a novice investor, you've gotten your feet wet and want to learn more.

Over time you put your plan into action, but you still have the debts that gave you the assets to get you to the next stage of the Game. You actively are looking for ways to continue building your assets and investment base in order to finally be secure so you can weather any financial storm.

There are **3 Levels of Wealth Builders**[1] at this Stage:

Beginning Wealth Builders have their plans in place and have either started the process of creating their business or are learning how to build their businesses.

Junior Wealth Builders have their first business or real estate investment under their belts and are actively looking for new opportunities to expand their budding empire.

Master Wealth Builders have reached a point where they need 'one more deal' to get them to the next stage of the Game.

Create a plan that focuses on acquiring wealth-building assets and PIGs (Passive Income Generators). Wealth building assets are defined as assets that generate a positive cash flow, a reasonable rate of return on capital invested, and a good likelihood of appreciating in value.

---

[1] Many, many, many thanks to Robert G. Allen and his books for first putting the idea of wealth builders and phases or stages of one's investment career into my head. I highly recommend his book *Creating Wealth* for help with creating the wealth-builder mindset.

4. **Capitalist** (Comfortable) - You've been working hard and investing so that you don't have to work hard for the rest of your life. You've either gotten to this stage in life by playing great defense (cutting expenses, living below your means) or by playing great offense (high income, solid investments). You should have a large asset base and a steady stream of passive income flowing every month into your bank account. You can do whatever you want with the money since your income far exceeds your expenses.

Your wealth building assets and PIGs (Passive Income Generators) are in place. Your main concern is protecting them and living life to the fullest. Read up on financial planning and get a team of capable professionals working for you.

5. **Charitable** (Caring) – When you've accumulated enough wealth and your wealth-building machine is on autopilot, you've reached the point where money is no longer as strong a motivator. Your perspective on what's important in life changes and your focus changes as well. Barring any unforeseen catastrophe, you're so rich that you can give most of your money away and still live the high roller lifestyle for the rest of your life. Carnegie, Rockefeller, and Ford all reached this level. It's something to aspire to in your quest to get rich.

BEWARE! The transition from one stage to the next is not something that happens overnight. It involves changing your mindset, as well as changing your spending and investing habits. There is no set or average time that it should take to get from one stage to the next. Some can do it in a few years, while others need several decades. It goes without saying that some unfortunate souls are unable to pull themselves out of the hollow pit that is the Struggling stage of life.

Decide today what you will make changes in your life in order to create your wealth-building machine and change your destiny in the process. Set goals for yourself, create the plan to achieve your goals, and act on your plan. Everyone stumbles and makes mistakes on the road to Financial Freedom. All the world's riches are available to those who persevere and forge on in the face of adversity!

"That's amazing stuff. I'm speechless," I revealed.

"The Great David, King of Sarcasm, speechless?" he said in mock disbelief.

"The ending is kind of hokey isn't it?" I offered as a reply.

"It was written 50 years ago David. The language was quite contemporary at the time, I can assure you. Any questions?"

"Where do I stand?"

"You're somewhere between the Struggling and Surviving stage, which is right where 90% of kids your age are situated."

"So when do I learn how to get to the Capitalist or Charitable stages in life?"

"Ah, that's my 'Get-Rich Quick' boy," he remarked, with a trace of a smirk on his face. "I'm afraid you're not ready for the Secrets that get you to stages three, four, and five in the Game of Life. We're going to stick to the tools that deal with the first two 'S's' in our discussions. The third 'S' or Striving stage and the two 'C's' (Capitalist and Charitable) are reserved for those who have passed through the first two stages of the Game."

"What do you mean 'not ready?' I'm here aren't I?"

"Yes, you're physically here," he said extending his arms, gesturing to the library, "but you're not mentally or financially at the point where you're ready to make it to the third stage."

"I don't get it."

Don't Build Sand Castles, Build Brick Houses

"Let me ask you a question," he said. "Would you build a house without a foundation?"

"No, of course not. That's silly."

"Then why would you jump from one stage of the Game without first laying down the foundation of your Financial House? You have to get your finances in shape before you're ready to invest in real estate or build a business. Without further delay, I think its time we started talking about your goals."

I pulled out my notebook and pen and got ready to take notes.

"You're not going to need that notebook Mr. David," he said, pointing to my book.

"But how am I going to take notes?" I inquired.

"I provide all my first-year students with their very own **Financial Freedom Workbook**." He reached into his briefcase and pulled out one of those plain white binders. It was filled with several pages of loose leaf paper and dividers.

"You will take all your notes in this one binder. If you come across articles of interest on topics of wealth-building, stocks, finance, etc., you are to put them in here. The idea is to have it all in one place for easy reference, inspiration, what have you. Plus, since it's a plain-looking binder, you can carry it around at work and people won't question you or wonder what you're doing."

"Wow, you must have done this quite often to have a book ready."

"Thirty-six times to be exact. You'll be thirty-seven," he replied.

"Thirty-seven! You've had thirty-freakin'-seven students!" The number struck me hard. I felt honored that he would help me. "Thanks for teaching me Mr. Mathers."

"Thank me by paying attention and following the Secrets. Now, where was I?" He rubbed his chin, stared at the ceiling and pondered a moment. "Ah yes, let's talk about roadblocks to your success."

Chapter 4

Eliminate Your Negative Beliefs and Roadblocks to Success

The Power of Beliefs

"We're going to start by eliminating all your excuses and fears, then get into the process of goal-setting."

"I'm ready," I said, obviously anxious to get started in my quest for riches.

"Good. Let's go for a brief walk, shall we?"

"But how can I take notes?" I asked, pointing to my new binder.

"Don't worry David. What I'll be covering is already in there."

BELIEFS and EXCUSES

Mr. Mathers' walk was more of a slow stroll through the trails by the library, than a brisk walk. Every so often he would pause, gather his thoughts and continue on.

"**Success is not a random occurrence**," he said as we crossed the street and headed toward the railroad station. "You have to believe you will be successful before you take that first step. I know how hard this can be, especially in this cynical and pessimistic world we live in. At some point in your life, there's bound to be a teacher or a friend or worse yet, a family member who told you that 'you can't' do something or 'you'll never' reach a particular dream of yours. The truth of the matter is that **you CAN do anything you put your mind to**. You need to take a hard look at the limiting beliefs that you hold. Once you know what they are you can work toward changing them."

"Mr. Mathers," I said, interrupting him. "But what if you don't have the ability or don't have the money to start investing? What do you do then? You can believe you're going to succeed, but if you don't have the money, you can't start investing."

"David, **successful people don't make excuses**. They operate from a positive mental attitude and they believe they can succeed. They don't let the roadblocks in life stop them from reaching their end destination. How about we take a look at some of the most common excuses people have for why they're not successful in life. Then I'll let you decide if you think everyone can be successful in life or not."

"Sounds fair," I replied.

ELIMINATING ROAD BLOCKS:
YOUR NEGATIVE BELIEFS

NO MONEY

"'I don't have money to invest right now.' That's probably the biggest investing EXCUSE people tell themselves.** In fact, you'll come to understand that the size of your salary doesn't necessarily correlate with your level of wealth. You don't need your own money to get rich in life. In fact, **the rich have been getting richer using other people's money for centuries**. Not every person who started a business or struck it rich had money when they started. Andrew Carnegie, the famed head of U.S. Steel worked as a telegraph operator and worked his way up the ladder. Steve Jobs started Apple Computer from a garage with no real investment of his own. Jobs and his partner went out and found someone who was willing to invest money in their dream. Michael Dell started his company out of his dorm room."

"But doesn't it take money to open up a brokerage account? What if you don't have the minimum amount?"

"Yes there are minimums, but **you can invest as little as one percent of your salary in your company's 401(k) plan**. So if you make $800 every two weeks, that's only $8.00 that you would be investing every two weeks or $4 a week. That's all it takes to get started. Now in addition to your company's 401(k) plan, there are numerous other options including Direct Reinvestment Plans (DRIPs) and mutual fund direct investment programs out there where you can get started for as little as $50 a month. That's a little over a dollar a day. That's why this excuse of not having money just doesn't hold up. That's why the first thing I ask people who say they don't have money is 'do you smoke?' because if they do, they can literally save hundreds of dollars just by cutting back on their smoking."

"But how far can $50 a month get you? That's only $600 a year. How can you turn that into a lot of money?"

He laughed at my question. "Ah David. You'll learn soon enough how quickly small amounts of money can grow to big amounts over time. Plus once you start investing, you're not going to stop there. Soon that $50 a month will become $60, then $70, then $100 a month. Once you see your money growing, once you see your account value rising in your monthly statements, you're going to find a way to invest more. I've seen it happen to people dozens of times. Most of them had lower paying jobs than you to start, but they found a way to invest and so will you. **You just have to decide to start today, not tomorrow.**"

TOO YOUNG

"Another excuse people have is that they're too young. You're young, but that doesn't mean you can't start a business. Steven Jobs revolutionized the computer industry and became a millionaire by the age of 23 and he did it in a time where it was harder to build a business. Today's technology makes it easy to start an Internet business or part-time business. When you're young you haven't had time to build up your assets, which might make it difficult to get a loan from a bank, but there are lenders out there that will take a chance on you. You just have to go to bank after bank until someone says yes. Besides, being young means you have a great asset in your corner."

"What asset is that?" I asked.

"Time, David. Time. You see time is one of the greatest allies of an investor. The earlier you start, the better off you are because time can help make up for the mistakes all beginners make. How many guys in this town or this country do you think would change places with you? How many people want to go back to their youth and start all over? We all do, even me. **The truth is that you're never too young to start.** Once you turn 18 in this country you can open your own investment account. If you're under the age of 18, your parents can set up an investment account for you."

He stopped walking and turned to face me. "And as for you," he said, pushing his index finger into my chest. "You're already working and just like everyone else in this country, once you're of age and begin working at a company, you'll be able to take advantage of your 401(k) plan, but we'll get to your investing options another day."

TOO OLD

"The flip side of the 'too young' excuse is the 'too old' excuse. Granted, some people may be older than you and may regret not having started when they were 20 or 30 or 40 or 50 years old, but they should not compound the problem by not starting at all! While time may be an important factor in your success (money is the other, remember) and time may not be on your side, that doesn't mean that you can't learn enough or invest enough in the coming years to impact your retirement years by starting today. Colonel Sanders got his first Social Security check before he even conceived of the idea of hitting the road to sell his famous chicken recipe."

His eyes narrowed and he moved closer to me and began jabbing at the air with his finger. "**The reason age is such an excuse for people is that in their minds they're too old to change**. Changing their daily routine and their lifestyle is a hassle. They've been accustomed to their standard of living and don't want to part with that first $50 it takes to start investing. They've resigned themselves to a life of poverty. They think they'll go on working at their current job forever and haven't planned for a potential disability or layoff. They're living paycheck to paycheck and they're one missed paycheck away from disaster."

"I know what you mean," I said. "I know a couple of people who are afraid to invest and they don't want to start investing because they'll have to cut back their expenses in other areas."

"And they're not likely to change because of fear of losing money, so they never start an investing program or look into investing in real estate. For someone who is 30, 40, or 50 and has not done much investing, they shouldn't compound their mistake by putting off the starting of an investment program. They can still make up for the past by beginning today. If you're 45 and you invest $100 a month for the next 20 years you'll have $76,000 when you retire, assuming a 10% annual return. If they invest $200 a month instead, they'll have close to $152,000. It might not sound like much, but it's better than hoping you'll win the lottery or your kids will take care of you when you're too old to work."

NO KNOWLEDGE

"The next excuse people have is that they don't know much about investing or saving money, so they don't ever do anything about it. That's pure silliness. When I first started out I had no idea about stocks and investing. I did know that GE was a market leader and so was Exxon. I just started putting my money into these stocks. I kept investing in them whenever I could. As I started to read the Wall Street Journal and other investment magazines, I began investing in other market leaders. It was a simple strategy, but I will share with you an even easier way to invest in a couple of weeks. The point I'm trying to make is that even if you truly know nothing about investing, it shouldn't stop you from starting. **Not starting is a bigger mistake than making a bad investment**."

"So where do I start learning about investing?" I asked.

"There is so much information out there today, you'll probably drown yourself in it. Books, videos, magazines, newsletters, seminars, continuing education classes, and the Internet are all sources of information. You should start reading magazines like Money and Smart Money. Fortune and Forbes magazines will give you some great insight into business trends and great profiles on companies. I'll even give you a list of the best books by the time we're done."

NOT SMART ENOUGH

"One of the excuses people often tell me as to why they're not rich is that they're not smart enough. They point to the fact that they don't have a college degree or that they dropped out of high school. I tell them they're just making excuses for themselves. Bill Gates dropped out of college. Ben Franklin dropped out in his teens, as did Edison. But thankfully, it doesn't take an advanced degree to learn about the stock market or building a business."

"So school education isn't important?"

"I will never say that. Never! It is important to be educated and if you have the opportunity to go to college, nine times out of ten, you'd be foolish to waste the opportunity. There's no denying that higher education pays dividends down the line. But more important for our discussion today is your **financial degree in money**?"

"My 'financial degree in money?' What's that?"

"The course you're starting now with me. It's about taking responsibility for your future by learning as much as possible about investing, budgeting, assets, and liabilities. All this knowledge comes with a small price tag, but will pay for itself many times over in the future. You know better than most the size of this library's personal finance section. All those books about investing in stocks and bonds, about real estate and foreclosures, about budgeting and saving money, not to mention the various magazines like Money, Smart Money, Kiplinger's, and Worth all waiting for you. They're free here. Most of these magazines have annual or semi-annual 'investment guide' issues or 'retirement' issues. These issues will take you through the basics of getting started and how to set up an investment plan. The bottom line is that you and only **you are the best person to manage your money**. You may not have all the knowledge of a certified accountant or financial planner, but you are the best person to look out for your best interests."

"But shouldn't professionals manage my finances since they know best?" I asked.

"I actually encourage you to use a certified financial planner. However, educating yourself and learning about investments will help you to better make decisions regarding the advice your planner or accountant discusses with you. In other words, you're becoming financially literate, understanding what the numbers mean, and how everything fits into your plan."

NO ONE TO HELP ME

"Next up is the 'I wasn't born with a silver spoon in my mouth' excuse, or 'I grew up in the ghetto' excuse, or 'I didn't have a father around' excuse and so on. In other words, it's the 'let me figure out who to blame other than myself' excuse."

"Quite a lengthy name," I remarked.

He ignored the comment and continued on. **"People have a bad habit of comparing themselves to others around them**. When they see someone who is doing well they either try to put that person down and or justify why they themselves are not as successful as the other person."

"I know what you mean," I said sheepishly. "I guess I'm guilty of doing that at times."

"We all do it at some point David, but if you don't stop it, you will always come up with excuses for why you won't succeed and you'll never take action on your goals."

"So what do I have to do?"

"Just stop comparing yourself to your sister, your mother, your neighbor, and your best friend. One of the biggest excuses that comes out of people's mouths when you're talking about why someone is successful is, 'yeah, but he/she got help from their _____ <insert name of benefactor>. 'If I was given _____ <insert name of resource> like they were, I'd be rich too.' I usually respond in one of two ways. If the person is thick-headed, I just nod my head and say 'pass the chips.' If I can get through to the person, I usually point out the other things the successful person had to do in order to become successful. Sure Donald Trump got help from his father, but he still had to go to Cincinnati and work his plan. Sure Bill Gates came from a wealthy family, but did that mean he was handed Microsoft? No, he built it from the ground up. The majority of millionaires in this country started with close to nothing and no inheritance. So you *can* start from nothing and become something. Just stop making excuses, find the mentors and resources you need, and put your plan into action. Period. End of story. Let's move on to the last excuse: not enough time."

NO TIME

"We're all busy. We have work to do, friends to hang out with, loved ones to spend time with, and errands to run. These are important things, but if you analyze how you spend your time in a given week you'll realize how much time is wasted on non-productive things. How much time do you spend each week watching television? **The average adult spends over 24 hours a week watching TV.** That's over a day a week, dedicated to the mindless absorption of sitcoms, sports, and commercials."

"I guess I'm guilty of watching too much TV as well," I admitted.

"It's not the TV that's killing you. It's how you're choosing to spend your time, your precious time that's the real issue. Putting the Secrets of Wealth to work for you doesn't require that much time, but it does require some dedicated time during your week, especially in the beginning. Investing isn't a full-time job, nor should it be. Once you learn the basics and get your investing and savings program set on autopilot, you don't need a lot of time to monitor how your portfolio is doing. Plus the majority of people out there are spending more time than ever in front of computer monitors, which means you can easily jump on the Internet and quickly log into your investment account or visit a site dedicated to teaching you the basics of building wealth.[2] The bottom line is that **we're all busy, but if we wanted to, all of us could find the time to set aside for investing and educating ourselves**."

"Okay, I got it," I said. "Stop making excuses and just do it."

"That's the attitude you need to have. If you just get started today, you'll reap the rewards for the rest of your life."

Stop Being a Victim

"I've got one more roadblock that I almost forgot about," he said. "Let's just call it a plea to stop being a victim. What I mean is that you have to stop blaming your parents, stop blaming your boss, and stop blaming everyone else but you. **The only reason you are where you are in life is because you chose to be where you are**."

"Sounds a bit philosophical," I commented.

"Maybe it is and maybe it's not, but the reality is that we choose to react to every situation in life. Okay, maybe you were dealt a bad hand in this Game called Life. Complaining about it isn't going to change your present circumstances, is it? Why not decide that you don't want to keep living the way you've been living thus far in life? If you've been given lemons, make lemonade! Stand up and take action. Turn back to the dreams you wrote down for yourself. Think hard and ask yourself 'How can I realize these dreams if I keep doing what I've been doing?' The answer is that you can't, which is why you need to stop making excuses and take action."

---

[2] Might I suggest www.fabmansecrets.com?

Take Responsibility

"Stop playing the role of a victim and take responsibility for what you have accomplished or failed to accomplish in the past. Your future success is in your hands and no one else's. The moment you accept this as the truth, you will take that first step toward creating your future and living the life you've imagined. Resolve to begin again this day and never look back. Stop dreaming and start doing. Tomorrow will _not_ be filled with happiness or luxury or wealth if you do not actively work for it today. Why not begin that journey today?"

"Awesome information Mr. Mathers," I said. "You really got cooking there."

"And the best part of the lesson is coming up right now," he replied.

"Up to a point a man's life is shaped by environment, heredity, and movements and changes in the world about him. Then there comes a time when it lies within his grasp to shape the clay of his life into the sort of thing he wishes to be. Only the weak blame parents, their race, their times, lack of good fortune, or the quirks of fate. Everyone has it within his power to say, **'This I am today; that I will be tomorrow.'"**

- Louis L'Amour

Chapter 5

GOALS – THE POWER OF WHY?

I know how you feel and I know what you're thinking. Another book touting the importance of goals. Where's the investing stuff you ask? That stuff is coming soon enough. First you have to realize the importance of goal setting. You have to be able to know what you're working toward in order to start your journey. As Yogi Berra once said, **"If you don't know where you're going, you'll end up someplace else."**

We had just finished our loop of the park and had arrived back at the library. We took our seats at our table and began the second part of my lesson.

Keep the Future in the Present
"When I got here you had your head buried in that Peter Lynch book. You were like many people who want to get rich. You go off and immediately get a book on **'How To'** do it."

"What's wrong with that?" I asked.

"You're jumping a step. Instead of focusing on 'WHY' you're going after the 'HOW.'"

"Huh? What's the difference?"

"There's a big difference David."

First WHY, Then HOW
"If you skip the 'WHY' as in 'Why am I investing,' you'll never get rich. You'll never be committed to the plan we're going to create for you."

"But I am committed. You yourself said that you felt I was committed when we first met."

"Don't misunderstand me. I know you're committed today, but unless you figure out what your goals are, you'll never stick to your plan. **You need a compelling reason to stick with anything in life**, especially when it comes to building your financial future. **I can't tell you where or how to build wealth unless we know where you want to end up."**

The Power of Goals

"Cherish your own vision and your dreams as they are the children of your soul; the blueprints of your ultimate achievements."

– Napoleon Hill

"In numerous books that I have read on the subject of wealth-building, there is often one study that is quoted regarding the power of setting goals. Humor me if you know it already. In 1954, the graduating class at Yale University[3] was polled and each student was asked if they had specific, written financial goals? Only 3 percent did. At the 20-year class reunion it was revealed that the 3 percent of students who had clear written goals had acquired more assets than the **other 97 percent combined**!"

"Than the other 97 percent! That's amazing."

"But not improbable. That's the power of goals. Once you set your written goals, it's almost guaranteed that you will achieve them. If you want it bad enough but don't get me wrong. **The road to riches is simple, but not easy.**"

"What's the difference?"

"A big one," he replied.

Simple, Not Easy

"Any undertaking that one chooses can be broken down into simple steps, that when followed, can result in tremendous achievements. But it's not easy to follow those steps, especially in the face of a little adversity or a setback. It's difficult to stay focused and stay motivated with all the noise and naysayers around you. **Achieving your goals will require some sacrifice on your part and some of your precious time.** In a few short moments you will set goals for yourself. Whether you achieve them or not is up to you. I will provide you with the knowledge, but it's up to you to take action."

He paused, flipped a page in his binder and continued. "**Goals are the guideposts in our lives**. Our goals help shape our decisions regarding what our course of action will be. If we know that we want to save enough money for our kids' education, we will find ourselves cutting back on frivolous expenses in order to use that money to build up their education fund. If we have a Christmas or Vacation fund set up, we'll put those extra dollars in the fund rather than spend it. Why? Because the reason we're doing it is front and center in our minds," he

---

[3] For more on this study, see the end of this book.

said placing his hands directly in front of his face. "We have a purpose, a plan, and ultimately goals that we want to achieve."

Three Types of Goals - Setting your personal goals

"There are basically three types of goals we're concerned with:

- **FINANCIAL**
- **ACHIEVEMENT**
- **IMPROVEMENT**

"But what does goal setting have to do with investing?" I asked.

"Did you just miss what I said about the students at Yale? Setting goals has everything to do with investing," he responded. "Investing and goal-setting are intertwined. You shouldn't do one without the other. Whether you're buying a car or a house, or planning for your children's college education or your retirement, these goals all involve money in some way. What you want to achieve in life has a tremendous impact on how you invest and what you invest in."

"So my goals dictate how I structure my investment portfolio?" I asked.

"In fancy words, yes, your goals will help shape your plan and drive the decisions you make in your portfolio of investments. **As any good financial planner will tell you, start with your end goals and work backwards from there to develop your financial plan.** Let's take retirement for instance. Everyone will eventually retire or die trying. The real question isn't if you can retire, but when and what lifestyle will you have when you finally get there. Saving for your retirement is not the same thing as planning for your retirement. Planning means you're taking an active role in the process. Simply putting money away into your 401(k) and an IRA might not be enough."

"I get the difference, but can you go over what the three types of goals mean? I get the financial part, but what's the difference between Achievement and Improvement goals?"

"**Improvement goals** are simply the things we want to change or get better at, as in losing weight, learning a second language, quitting smoking, and so forth. **Achievement goals** are the things we want to achieve or accomplish in life. Goals in this category would be your desire to be promoted, to be the employee of the month, and so on. Financial goals typically have a specific dollar amount attached to them, but can also encompass that Porsche that you want so badly."

"I think I get it. Am I ready to set goals for myself?"

"Just about. A couple more things first."

A Sense of Urgency and Focus

"Self-discipline and persistence are probably two of the most important qualities that you need in order to become wealthy. Without self-discipline, you will never make the sacrifices necessary to build a solid investment portfolio. Without persistence you won't stay the course. You need to have a sense of urgency about you when you're setting goals for yourself and going about your days. Goals keep you disciplined and keep your eyes on the prize. By having your goals front and center, you'll be able to avoid the temptations of instant gratification and opt for behaviors that will lead to long-term prosperity."

"Do you mean that by having clear written goals I'll think about my goals often enough to avoid buying new CDs, magazines, and silly status gadgets in order to save and invest my money?"

"Yes," he replied. "That's correct. As I was saying, after learning the Secrets of Wealth and putting them into action, you will have control over your life, which is something that the majority or workers in America do not have. Because they didn't know better or just 'went with the flow,' they have to live the rest of their lives according to someone else's rules, not their own. That's tough to swallow, but the majority of people just accept their current situation as reality and don't question it. They don't seek out ways to get out of the Rat Race. They just continue to go to work at a job they hate, spend more than they can afford to spend, then cry the blues because they don't seem to 'get ahead' in life. They never look for solutions, just go along working until the day they die; broke, emotionally spent, and never having realized their true potential."

> **"The secret to making the right decision every time is to determine what will take you closer to your life-time goals.** Did you notice I wrote 'life-time goals' and not 'long-term goals'. The difference between to two is vast. **Long-term goals are things you would like to accomplish, while life-time goals are a must**. These are goals that must be achieved no matter what it takes.
>
> - Andrew LaPointe

Goals Have the Power to Motivate

"And the reason 95 percent of the people in this country fail to achieve true wealth is that while they'd like to have more money, **they're just not motivated enough to do what it takes to get rich."**

"That doesn't make sense," I said. "You're saying that the idea of getting rich is not motivation enough. How's that possible?"

"The unsuccessful people in life never take the necessary steps because they have to make short-term sacrifices in order to learn how to manage their finances. They have to spend time to learn how to pay less taxes or how to reduce their debt. Spending the time and putting forth the effort to learn is something people just don't want to do. They'd rather look for ways to get rich quick."

"And those get rich quick schemes don't work, right?"

"No, they DO work…for the people selling them to the suckers out there looking to take short cuts to the Promised Land. These same people who are willing to buy book after book, tape after tape on how to get rich, never follow through. Why? Because they view a savings plan or investing plan as too much work. They'd rather sit in front of the TV with a beer and chips or sleep or hang out with their friends. In reality, their lot in life has been determined by them 100 percent. These folks don't have goals. They have pipe dreams that they never follow through on."

"You know Mr. Mathers, I never thought of it that way. I guess you're going to give me the tools that I will need to improve my Financial House, then it's up to me to follow through."

"That's right. **The goals you set for yourself are at the heart of this financial planning process. It's the fuel for your daily actions.** Those big dreams of yours are what is going to keep you motivated to make those everyday sacrifices in order to make those dreams of tomorrow a reality. Once you have a set of written goals, every time you're presented with a situation, you can't help but ask yourself 'will this take me closer to my goals or farther away?' This is why it's so important to keep your goals in front of you."

"What do you mean by in 'front' of me?" I asked.

Keep Your Goals in Front of You

"What I mean is that you must make sure that you constantly look at them. Lee Iacocca, the former head of Chrysler, used to carry around an index card with him when he worked at Ford with the promotions he wanted and the dates he wanted to achieve them by. Imagine that? Carrying around the same index card year after year, checking off the positions every time he achieved his goal."

"But why do I have to carry it around?"

"Because if you don't carry them around, you may forget why you're working so hard. You may forget the reason you're not splurging your money, buying that new jacket, or going out to dinner every night when you can *afford* to."

"Can I ask where you keep your list?"

"Sure. I actually have them in three places. I have a computer file titled 'Goals.' It automatically pops up every time I log onto my computer, so I can't help but see my goals every morning."

"And the other places?"

"On the bureau by my bed so I can read them when I wake up in the morning and right before I go to bed. I also carry a copy around with me just like Lee."

"Wow. You really make sure you keep them in front of you," I said, amazed that even after all these years, Mr. Mathers still followed the same routine of reviewing his goals daily.

> "You become what you think about all day long"
> - Ralph Waldo Emerson

"By keeping your goals in front of you for the next couple of months, you're going to know exactly why you're following the Secrets of Wealth. That's why I recommend you post the list next to your computer, on your refrigerator or next to the mirror in the bathroom. This way you can't help but see it every day"

The Unemotional Investor

"Goals **provide long-term vision in our lives**. We all need lots of powerful, long-range goals to help us get past short-term obstacles. Life is designed in such a way that **we look long-term and live short-term**. We dream for the future and live in the present. Unfortunately, the present can produce many difficult obstacles.
But fortunately, the more powerful our goals (because they are inspiring and believable) the more we will be able to act on them in the short-term and guarantee that they will actually come to pass!"

– Jim Rohn

"Writing your goals down and keeping them in front of you helps to take your emotions out of the process. You become what's called an 'unemotional investor.'"

"How so?"

"Because once you have a set plan, just stick to it. If the market dips or you get a pay raise, you already know what you're going to do before it happens. You don't base your short-term actions on emotions, rather you act based on the long-term plan you've put together for yourself. If you have those goals of yours at arm's length every day, you can refer to them whenever you're struggling to follow your plan. Being totally objective or unemotional about your investments is a difficult task, but the closer you get to being this way, the better off you are in the long-run."

"Okay, I understand the importance of setting goals, but how do I figure out what I want out of life?"

"Easy. You take the Rocking Chair Test."

"Why is it that you have all these funny names for things?"

"How else would you remember them?"

"Touché."

The Rocking Chair Test

"The Rocking Chair Test is a technique that I learned from Anthony Robbins. All you do is imagine yourself as an old man, sitting on your front porch in your trusty old rocking chair. There you are rocking back and forth, reflecting back on your life. Remembering all the things you did and didn't do. The things you could have done but didn't because you never seemed to have enough time or were afraid of doing it. Think about the things you should have done, but never got around to doing. Think about the things you would have done had you not been so busy, tired, broke, or lazy. **What would you be most proud of accomplishing? What would you regret not having done?** Both questions are equally important. The things you're proud of can help you realize what's truly important in life. You should set your goals based on achieving those things that you would regret not having done. Things like traveling more, retiring early, having more time to spend with your kids, giving more to charity, picking up a hobby, or whatever your heart desires."

"So it's those big things that I wish I could have done in life, but didn't?" I asked.

"That's correct. The reason the Rocking Chair Test is so powerful is because it identifies the things that mean the most to you. Once you identify what your regrets are, you need to make changes. You need to stop making excuses and start shooting for that brass ring. A pupil of mine didn't like the rocking chair analogy because for him it wasn't severe enough. So he came up with the 'if you died tomorrow…' question."

"As in if you were to die tomorrow, what one thing would you want to do before dying?" I asked.

"I see you've played the game before," he commented. "They both work the same way; which is to try and get at what would be your biggest regrets in life be? What could you have done, but never did because you didn't have the money, or the energy, or the countless other excuses you concocted through the years? If you died tomorrow David, what would you most regret not having done or accomplished? Think deeply about it and write down a list of goals for yourself."

Your Top 50 Goals

"There's another technique that I borrowed from Anthony Robbins that I want you to use when we're done today. I want you to sit here and think about what you want to accomplish in your life. Think of every dream you've ever had and don't start trying to figure out if accomplishing one of them is realistic. Just pick up your pen and write them all down. I want you to sit here and write down at least 25 goals that you want to accomplish over the course of your lifetime."

"Twenty-five goals! That's a tall order."

"No buts about it David. The exercise is actually to write down 50 goals, but I'll let you finish another day."

"By recording your dreams and goals on paper, you set in motion the process of becoming the person you most want to be."
 - Mark Victor Hansen, Author, *Chicken Soup for the Soul* Series

Focus on the Important Areas

"When you're done with this exercise, you'll be staring at a piece of paper filled with a wide range (not to mention long list) of goals. This is why you should group your goals into a few key areas of your life. There are many aspects of life where you can set goals, but these are the six main areas:

- Physical
- Financial
- Professional
- Intellectual (incl. Personal Development)
- Relational
- Spiritual

"Most people only think of the first two or three areas, but they're missing out on the other major areas of their lives. I believe you need to have goals in all areas to be truly wealthy in life. After all, what's the point of being in great shape and having a lot of money if you aren't emotionally satisfied and don't have anyone to share the wealth with?"

MY TOP 50 LIFETIME GOALS
Financial, Achievement and Improvement Goals

1. _____	26. _____
2. _____	27. _____
3. _____	28. _____
4. _____	29. _____
5. _____	30. _____
6. _____	31. _____
7. _____	32. _____
8. _____	33. _____
9. _____	34. _____
10. _____	35. _____
11. _____	36. _____
12. _____	37. _____
13. _____	38. _____
14. _____	39. _____
15. _____	40. _____
16. _____	41. _____
17. _____	42. _____
18. _____	43. _____
19. _____	44. _____
20. _____	45. _____
21. _____	46. _____
22. _____	47. _____
23. _____	48. _____
24. _____	49. _____
25. _____	50. _____

"But I don't know where to begin," I said.

"Setting goals for yourself should not be a daunting task. It's as easy as writing down your dreams or examining your life and determining what you want to change. Just dream of what your ideal life would be like, then pick up a pen, and start writing down the things you would like to do and what you would want to accomplish."

Where Have You Been?

"So what about setting deadlines for your goals? I heard that it's important to have a timeline when setting goals," I said.

"You're absolutely correct. Setting a target date or deadline by which you want to achieve your goals is absolutely essential, however we're not going to set deadlines right now."

"How come?"

"I'll answer your question with a question. How much money are you saving a month and how much extra cash do you have at the end of each month?"

I stared at him with my trademark skeptical look. "Extra cash? If I had extra cash I wouldn't have debt."

He smiled and let out a laugh. "Typical," he said shaking his head. **"If you don't know where you've been, how do you expect to know where you're going?"**

"Huh? What's that mumbo jumbo mean?"

"Just trust me on this one. We'll go through the rest of the Secrets and come back to the process of goal setting and you'll understand."

"All right, but if I don't get that Porsche, I'm blaming you."

"Excellent, blaming others. You're right on track for life in squalor."

"'Squalor'? Don't you use words from the 21st century?" I said, shaking my head.

"David, why for art thou so derisive? You should truly fix that."

"Fix that? I don't even know what derigible means," I replied.

"And you can't even say it right. Oh my, we're in for some long days aren't we?" he said jokingly. "But before we handle your Porsche request, we have two more things to cover: focusing only on a few goals and breaking your goals down into manageable pieces."

FOCUS on a Few Goals

"You have to narrow your goals down to the vital few because it helps you to focus on what's important. Muhammad Ali didn't want to become the heavyweight champion of the world, a great businessman, a race car driver, and an author. No. He wanted to become the heavyweight champion of the world and that's it. All too often in life we lack the focus necessary to accomplish our dreams. We waste our efforts on numerous undertakings and don't focus on our biggest goals. **If you give priority to your most important goals and put most of your effort toward achieving those goals, you have a better chance of succeeding.**"

Break Them Down into Manageable Pieces

"Don't view your big dreams or goals as impossible. The key is to break down your goals into small, easily reachable goals that will bring you closer and closer to those big goals. Becoming a millionaire doesn't happen overnight, but you can get there if you set aside your money every month and invest it. **The trick is to keep your eyes on the prize**, figure out the intermediate goals and tasks that need to be accomplished, then take action!" He closed his binder and stood up. "I think we're done for today David. Now it's time for you to write down your 25 goals and by the end of next week, I want you to write out your top 50 goals," he said, putting his binder in his briefcase.

Before I could say anything, he said "One more thing. I want to recommend two books that should help you. One is *The Richest Man in Babylon* by George Clason and the other is *The Millionaire Next Door*."

"Did you write the second one?" I joked.

He laughed. "No, but I wish I did. Buy the books and add them to your Library of Knowledge. Next week we're going to cover the First Law of Gold, which is in the Clason book."

"Alright!" I said, slapping my hands together. "Now we're talking."

He shook his head at me and said, "Let's see your face next week when I explain Secret #2 to you."

He got up and walked out the door, leaving me with my blank sheet of paper to fill out.

Setting Goals - COMMENTS

The successful people in life set goals and they create a plan to achieve them. They realize that they have to focus on where they want to go first, then manage their time, money, and efforts toward actions that take them closer to realizing their goals. They're able to better prioritize their daily activities, weeding out the things that don't bring them closer to fulfilling their dreams. It's a great habit to have and truly vital if you're going to learn to focus on what's truly important in your life.

I know you're sitting there wondering how you can achieve any goals when you have so many other financial issues to deal with at the moment. If you are like I was, you're probably trying to pay for a car, pay down debt, and pay for a vacation on top of handling your daily living expenses. If you have kids, the task seems even more daunting. Perhaps you've tried to build wealth before and failed. Put all that behind you. For now, lets focus on your future and figure out what you want to achieve in life.

Setting Goals (Part One) – ACTION PLAN

Evaluate Your Beliefs: If you have any negative beliefs like you're too old or you're not smart enough, you'll never succeed in life. You need to get rid of those self-limiting beliefs and create new empowering beliefs. Lose the emotional baggage that's holding you back. Leave the past in the past. You need to start focusing on your future.

Begin with the End in Mind[4]: The best way to start this whole goal setting process is to set aside a half hour to reflect on the type of person you want to become over the next 20 to 30 years. Who do you want to be in 30 years? What do you want to own? Where do you want to live? What will your house look like and what kind of relationships will you have with your family, your friends, your co-workers (or employees), and your community.

Dream Big. Write it Down. Get Specific.

Create Your 50 Goals Wish List - Take the Rocking Chair Test!: Now that you have the vision of what you want to become, go back to the Top 50 Goals list in this book or take out a sheet of loose-leaf paper. Now write down the goals that will get you to that end state. Need a starting point? Ask yourself:

> **"If you knew you couldn't fail,
> what would you attempt in your life?"**

THINK BIG and just write them down. **Don't think "HOW" just yet**: Don't think; just write them down. There are no limitations on what you can do or what you can be. Just write what's top-of-mind. Don't worry about *reality* or how you're going to achieve them, just write everything down. I'll show you how to realize your dreams later on.

Think of All Areas of Your Life and Don't Just Focus on Your Financial Goals: Perhaps your goal is to one day travel the world. Maybe it's to own homes in several countries or states. Perhaps you never want to work again after the age of 50. Perhaps you want to become a real-estate mogul. What do you want to accomplish? Do you want to be a manager, director, or vice-president where you work? Do you want to be able to quit your job in 7 years to do volunteer work? Just open your mind and imagine.

Get Specific: Make your goals as specific as possible. Getting rich is not specific: becoming a millionaire by age 50 is.

---

[4] The Second Habit from Stephen Covey's book *The 7 Habits of Highly Effective People.*

Get Leverage on Yourself: Find out WHY you want to accomplish your goals. For instance if your goal is to become a millionaire, why? Because you want a lot of money; you can be wealthy enough to retire early; you want to be secure and free of worries. If you have a big enough 'why' and you attach it to your goals, you're going to pursue your goals until you achieve them. Not achieving them would give you more pain than doing what needs to be done in order to realize your dreams.

Create a Short-Term Goals List: Based on your Top 50 List, create your Top 5 List of Goals to achieve in the next one to three years. This is an important step because you need to **Focus Your Efforts**. By focusing on these key goals that support your lifelong dreams, you'll find yourself rapidly getting closer to achieving your big goals.

Break Down Your Goals into Baby Steps: Take a look at those Top 5 Goals and break them down. Some might seem impossible, but by creating little mini-goals, you'll find yourself motivated because it's a lot easier to reach a small goal. For instance, the goal of becoming debt free might seem like a monumental task, but if you break it down into smaller detailed steps like paying just $20 extra every month, then it might not seem so daunting a task to undertake.

Keep Your Goals in Front of You: Keep your long-term and short-term goals in front of you by either placing them in a goal planner or posting them in your bathroom so you can't help but see them daily. I keep a 3"x5" index card with my goals by my bedside and look at it when I rise in the morning and when I go to bed at night.

Review Them Often to Reinforce Them: By keeping your goals in front of you, you're subconsciously programming your mind. I highly recommend *Think and Grow Rich* by Napoleon Hill to learn more about the whole process of reprogramming your subconscious mind.

Now you're ready to take ACTION!!!

Do Something Every Day: Ideally you should do something every day that will move you closer to your Top 5 goals. You need to discipline yourself to take action on a consistent basis. If you do something every day, you will virtually guarantee that you will achieve your goals. Always ask yourself, "**What can I do today that will take me one step closer to reaching my goal?**"

Celebrate: Once you've achieved one of your goals, celebrate. You're that much closer to living the life you've imagined over the course of your life. It doesn't matter how big or small the goal you achieved was, you need to acknowledge that your concentrated efforts and determination have paid off.

Are You Making a Living or Living a Life?

"If you go to work on your goals, your goals will go to work on you. If you go to work on your plan, your plan will go to work on you. Whatever good things we build end up building us. We all have two choices: **We can make a living or we can design a life."**

– Jim Rohn

Just a Few Assorted Goals You Might Have

- Pay off my credit card debt
- Pay down my mortgage
- Buy a used car once the lease is up
- Get back in shape/ Lose 20 pounds
- Save for a downpayment on a house
- Take a two week vacation every year
- Ensure that my kids' education is provided for
- Retire with a million dollars in the bank
- Do community work for the homeless

Additional Resources

Books:
Smart Women Finish Rich by David Bach
Think and Grow Rich by Napoleon Hill
GOALS! by Brian Tracy

Web-Sites:
For a helpful Goal-Setting tool, check out:
"MY GOAL SETTING WORKBOOK" at www.fabmansecrets.com

Game of Life Grid
When you're done with this book, take a look at Appendix C and check out the Game of Life Grid. See which Stage of the Game you're in!

Secret #2:
SAVE TEN PERCENT OF WHAT YOU MAKE –

PAY YOURSELF FIRST

"The spendthrift cannot succeed, mainly because he stands eternally in fear of poverty. Form the habit of **systematic saving by putting aside a definite percentage of your income**. Money in the bank gives one a very safe foundation of courage when bargaining for the sale of personal services. Without money, one must take what one is offered, and be glad to get it."

— Napoleon Hill

Chapter 6

Secret #2: SAVE TEN PERCENT OF WHAT YOU MAKE

Pay Yourself First

My Second Lesson

I spent the better part of the next week revising and categorizing my goals. I put them in priority order and I determined that getting rid of my credit card debt was priority one. I was anxious to begin my next lesson and got to the library early on Saturday. I was almost done with *The Millionaire Next Door* at that point.

"Morning, junior wealth-builder. I see you're enjoying the book," Mr. Mathers said as he sat down across from me.

I looked up from the page I was reading. "Hey Mr. Mathers. Yep. It's a great book and really challenges some of the things I thought about the rich."

"Glad to see you're enjoying the book, but set it aside for now and let's get started on Secret #2."

I put the book to the side and opened my binder. "Okay. I'm ready for my second lesson."

"It's going to be a quick, but powerful lesson today."

"I'm ready," I said, pen in hand.

That Can't Be the Second Secret of Wealth!

"The second Secret is to Save Ten Percent of What You Make."

I stopped writing and looked up at him. I was a little confused. "That's it?" I stammered. "That's the second Secret of Wealth? The Golden Rule that's supposed to make me a millionaire?" I found it hard to believe. I did some quick calculations in my head and that amount of money would be less than $3,000. He didn't respond. Just kept smiling at me. "That's only $3,000 and like $120,000 over the next 40 years! How can that make me a millionaire?" I asked.

"Your reaction is the same as everyone before you. No one understands it's power, but if you give me some more time, I think I can explain why it works. The Secret was first written more than 70 years ago by George Clason in his book called *The Richest Man in Babylon*, the very same book I recommended to you last week. The

Ten Percent rule was listed as Clason's first cure for a lean purse and his first law."

"A purse?"

"Not a purse like women carry today, smart Alec. Here, copy this down," he said, turning his binder around so I could copy down what he was pointing to. It said:

First Cure for a Lean Purse
"For every ten coins thou placest within thy purse take out for use but nine. Thy purse will start to fatten at once and its increasing weight will feel good in thy hand and bring satisfaction to thy soul."

When I was done he began speaking again. "Just in case you didn't catch it, the rule is telling you to set 10% of your money aside before you do anything else. In other words, you will **Pay Yourself First regardless of what bills or obligations you have**. Think of it as the **'save it before you have a chance to spend it'** rule. Once you follow this Secret, you will begin to accumulate a substantial sum of money and thus you will feel the satisfaction that comes with having money in the bank."

I was frazzled. I wanted to know now how I could make money. I tried asking again, but he refused to discuss the method of making money. I relented. "Okay, but I still think it sounds too easy."

"If you think about it for a while, you'll see why the Golden Rule is just that, the Golden Rule. It's also probably the one that is easiest to implement when beginning down the road to wealth, but the reason that it's one of the first few Secrets is because it helps you to become more disciplined immediately."

"I don't know," I said with a note of skepticism in my voice. "If that's all that's involved, how come everyone doesn't do it?"

Harder than it Seems?

"Remember when I told you that the first few Secrets were easier to implement than the last few Secrets?"

I nodded.

"Well the second Secret is perhaps the easiest to understand, but it's not easy to implement for some people. In fact, several of my students have taken several months to reach the 10% level."

"But why? It doesn't seem that hard."

"Okay then. Reach into your pocket and take out your wallet."

I raised my eyebrow at him, but did as I was told.

"Now open your wallet and take out all your money." He could see me hesitating. "Go on, do it. You'll see why in a second."

I pulled my money out of my wallet and put it on the table.

"Now count it," he instructed.

"I've got $34."

"Okay, now take $4 and leave it on the table. Then put the rest of your money back in your wallet. That wasn't so hard was it?"

"No, not at all. That's why I'm wondering how people have a problem..."

"Hold on, I'm not done yet," he said. "You see that was simple because it was only $4, but what happens when it's $20 or $40 or $100? It gets harder and harder to stick by the rule. Think about it. Every paycheck, every month, month in and month out, you have to immediately set aside 10% of your salary, then live off the other 90%. Some people have trouble doing that."

"I guess it would get harder to put larger sums of money aside."

"Right. And if you don't constantly remind yourself and make it a habit to set aside that 10%, you'll never remember to do it. That's why I try to remind myself as often as possible to pay myself first."

"Is that why you're license plate reads '10PRCNT'?" I asked.

"I see you're very observant," he replied. "Yes, that's what it stands for. I put it there to serve as a constant reminder."

"But why do you need a constant reminder?"

"I don't get a weekly paycheck. My tenants usually pay me on time, but sometimes they're late. As for my businesses, as hard as I try to forecast my monthly cash flow, it's hard to know what your revenue will be any given month. In short, I don't exactly know what I'll be making month to month, so it's hard to establish a specific automatic withdrawal amount. So when I do get something in my hands, I usually go to the bank and deposit a little over 10% in one account and the rest in my checking account."

"Sounds like a lot of work to me." I couldn't see why he didn't just put all the money into one account then at the end of the month add up what he made and put ten percent of that amount into his 10% account.

He gave me a funny look. "A lot of work to see my money grow and honor my self-promise to save 10% of what I make? I don't think so," he replied. "No, it's more a sense of satisfaction. I really enjoy doing it, plus **I tried waiting until the end of the month and making my 10% payment, but I found that I never stuck with it**. Some expense would come along and I'd make some excuse not to set the 10% aside. **The best way to pay yourself first is to do it *immediately*, before the impulse to spend the money takes over**. After doing it for a couple of months, it becomes a habit. It's even easier for someone who gets a steady paycheck."

"How so?"

"They get paid the same amount every two weeks. All they have to do is contact their employer or bank and have money deducted from their paycheck or pulled from their savings account and deposited into another account. To figure out how much to pull out, you take your take home pay and multiply that number by 10%. Easy as pie."

"I get it. The money is automatically withdrawn so you didn't have to think about it."

Friendly Advice – It gets easier

"When you first suggested that I save 10% of my paycheck right off the top, I thought you were nuts. But like you said, it definitely gets easier with time. I was tempted a couple of times to take out some money, but I forced myself not to. Well maybe the first month I took out some money. After that first slip up, I'm back on track. It's been great watching the account grow and grow over the past few months. The best part is that I do nothing, nothing at all and it grows. Setting up the transfer with my company took a half hour to fill out the paper work (and find the person who had the form), sign it and bingo, my automatic deposit is set up. In any event, thanks again for the suggestion. I'm trying to increase the percentage over the next few months. By then I'll be ready to talk about investments."

Cheers,
John B., a subscriber of mine from Arizona

But I Don't Have Ten Percent

As he went through the steps to put the second Secret in action, I realized that saving 10% of my pay might be harder than it sounded.

"But I have car payments, car insurance, phone, and school expenses. I can't change any of these expenses. My paycheck is already spent before I receive it. How will I ever be able to put 10% aside?" I wondered aloud.

"Is the money truly spent before you get your check? By that I mean, do you have obligations that you HAVE to pay that are wiping out your paycheck before you can get some spending money?"

"What do you mean have to? Of course I have to pay my bills or they'll take back my car or cut off my phone."

"We'll get to exactly what I'm talking about next week, but in essence you have fixed expenses that don't change every month and expenses that do change every month. Things like food, entertainment, little indulgences, and other miscellaneous expenses, while they are bought each month, the amount you're spending on them varies each month. **The key is to automatically reduce your available cash that you have to spend on miscellaneous items. You do this by paying yourself first, right off the top each time you get a paycheck.**"

"But I can't afford to put away 10% of my take-home pay. That's too much money for me right now. I can't pay my bills off as it is. Maybe I can start when I'm making more money?"

"First off, you have to remove the word 'can't' from your vocabulary. It's a silent killer of your dreams. Second, **it's absolutely important that you start as soon as possible**. The longer you delay, the harder it will be to start saving 10%. We'll get to paying off your bills another time, but for now let's focus on this saving problem of yours. I know what you're thinking David, 'how can I save money when I'm trying to pay my bills?' The truth is that **everyone, and I mean everyone, can find a way to save some extra money.** It's just that you haven't really thought about *how* yet. I'll be up front with you. It's not going to be easy at first, in fact it will be really tough, but I can guarantee that it gets easier with time. You just need to know where to cut the fat from your budget. You also need to develop the self-discipline to keep your plan on track."

"What if I don't have enough money to pay myself first?"

"You wouldn't stop paying the phone bill or not buy groceries because you couldn't afford it, would you? **Paying yourself first is the most important bill you're going to pay every month.** More important than the phone bill, the car payment, or that school loan bill. If something is that important, you're just going to have to find the way to pay the bill. If you can't afford to set aside 10% of your income then you'll have to work on increasing your income or decreasing your expenses. But enough convincing. Let's get to doing."

Getting Started

"For the next month you're going to pretend that you have a very important bill to pay. You're going to be paying the person that's going to take care of you in your later years, the person who is in charge of your financial destiny. That person is you. **You're going to write yourself a check equal to 10% of your monthly income and deposit it into that savings account you set up**. You're going to write this check to yourself *before* you pay your other bills."

The Power of Doing it on Autopilot: The Pay Yourself First Plan

"Let me ask you a question. How good are you at paying yourself first right now?" he asked.

"Not too good," I replied.

"That's because before you have a chance to save the money, you go out and spend it. One way to make sure you stick to your 10% savings goal is to put yourself on a 'Pay Yourself First' Plan. The plan is simple. All you do is routinely set aside some money from each paycheck to be put in a savings or investment account. I can tell by the expression on your face that you don't do this now. Don't worry, you're not alone. Most people starting out straight from college or high school don't know the first thing about finance and investing, so they never set up an **automatic investment plan**."

"So how old were you when you started paying yourself first?"

"I was lucky. I worked in a financial planner's office. After a few days on the job, I wanted to invest so badly so that I could be rich like my boss' clients. Almost everyone in the office was constantly talking about the price of this stock or that one going up a dollar or two. You could literally see the dollar signs adding up in their eyes. So I asked my boss for help. He gave me a sheet of paper to track my expenses on for four weeks. He made me write down everything. I literally carried a pen and that chart around every day. After the four weeks, we sat down to review where I was spending my money. It wasn't pretty."

"So you were wasting your money away?"

"You could say that. I spent a lot of money on sodas and milkshakes and well, beer."

"Mr. Mathers, I'm shocked," I said in mock surprise. We both laughed. "But back to the Secret. So what else did you do to change your spending ways and start paying yourself first?"

"I pretended that I smoked. Sounds silly, but I started pretending that I had to spend $3 a pack every day like my other friends. Of course instead of spending that money it went into my **cash can**."

"What's a cash can?" I asked.

"Literally a used coffee can that I put my change in. But that's not the point. I set aside $3 a day and that $90 a month added up to around $1,000 a year. But where that money really grows is through investing that money I managed to cut out of my budget."

"What did you invest in?" I asked

"We'll cover the investing part later on. Just remember that saving 10% of your income is the second step in the whole building wealth process. But let's get back to you."

Ten Cents on the Dollar

"Somehow you have to find the money for your future and you do that by paying yourself first *before* you pay any other bills. You set it up so that an amount equal to 10% of your take home pay is automatically taken out of each paycheck and deposited into a bank account or your brokerage account."

"I know you just covered this, but what if you don't have 10% to set aside?" I asked.

"David," he said shaking his head at me. **"It boils down to saving a dime for every dollar you make**. Just a dime. It sounds so ridiculous, but the power of this secret is in its simplicity. Strive to make it to that dime and you'll be well on your way to Financial Freedom."

He was right. Saving just a dime sounded ridiculous, but he had already given me examples of how just an extra few dollars a day could add up to quite a bit of money over the years.

"As your income rises through the years, the amount you're putting aside increases automatically. So years from now, you're not putting away a $100 a month or $200 a month, you're putting in many times that amount."

"I understand," I said.

"Good, because it looks like we covered everything we needed to cover today. I think the next step for you is to visit some local banks and check out which ones offer the best rates with the lowest minimum initial deposits that allows automatic transfers. It would be great if you can open the account by next Saturday. If not, start putting aside some money in an old coffee can or piggy bank and open an account as soon as you can."

"Sounds good to me," I responded.

"Good, because you've just completed your second Secret of Wealth. I'll meet you here next Saturday at 9 a.m. sharp."

With that he got up from the table and gathered his things. We said goodbye and he walked away. I was left staring at my $4 on the table wondering how I could find a way to get my hands on more money. I would find out next Saturday.

Save Ten Percent of What You Make - COMMENTS

"**Every large fortune is an accumulation of hundreds and thousands of small amounts of money,** and the place to start is to take any amount of money that you can right now and begin to save it. When you begin to save money, it sets up a force field of energy and it triggers the law of attraction. As a result you begin to attract to you even more bits of money to add to your savings."

ATTRACT RICHES INTO YOUR LIFE
"And I've spoken to many, many successful people and they've told me the same story. That as soon as you start to put savings aside, it starts to attract into your life and into your work all the money that you need to achieve your goals. The reason why most people retire poor is they never put the initial savings aside to start with."

– Brian Tracy, Author, *Goals!*

The goal may be to save 10% of your income, but if you can't afford to save 10% of your take-home pay right now, don't despair. Remember, I couldn't at first either. **Starting a regular saving plan today is more important than the amount you start with**, so begin with an amount you can afford right now. Just realize that if you cannot save 10% of your salary, either of two things is occurring: either your lifestyle is too rich for your salary or your salary is not enough to support the truly essential expenses. Both situations will keep you from achieving Financial Freedom.

If you're saving 10% of your salary already in your 401(k), this amount <u>doesn't</u> count toward your 10% goal. Why? Because you need to focus on what you do with that 100% of your net take-home pay. You need to focus on getting that 100% down to 90%. In other words, **SET A GOAL to save 10% of your take-home salary**. If you can't do this right away, put aside as much as possible now and write down the date by which time you will be saving 10% of your pay. Each week or month you should increase the amount you're putting away until you reach the magic 10% mark.

Death of the Ten Percent Rule?

I've seen so many articles, books, and authors of late trash the Ten Percent Rule. What these authors fail to realize is that the Secret is a **starting block** – the building block upon which to build one's Financial House. It's the catalyst to get people motivated to start saving and investing when they're starting at ground zero. Obviously, if you save more than 10% of your pay you'll be in a better position, but before *you can do that you have to take that first baby step towards Financial Freedom. If you save more than 10%, then of course you'll increase your odds of retiring faster. Duh! But seriously, here's why the Ten Percent Rule is still the place to start...*

The Ten Percent Rule is Alive and Well!

Scott Burns, in his article titled, "Take a Long Look at Returns[5]" did an analysis of the amount of money you would need to save in order to not run out of money by the time we die, assuming we retired at age 65 (in 2040). The conclusion was that we would have to save 34 percent of our income if we planned on living another 20 years after we retired and earned no return on our investments. But you'll earn something on your investments, right? Of course you will. Burns goes on to show that you can save 9% of your income and be reasonably assured a comfortable retirement.

"The 34 percent of income that young people need to save today if they earn no return **falls to 25 percent if they earn the historical 2 percent real return of bonds**.

It falls to 15 percent if they earn the 5 percent real return that a 60/40 stock/bond portfolio is likely to earn.

It plummets to **9 percent of income** if they earn the **7 percent real return of common stocks**."

Sounds like the Ten Percent rule is alive and kicking, but enough about the second Secret. It's time to learn how you can find money. That's right and I'm not talking about the loose change in your couch.

Start with 10%, Then See How Far You Can Go!

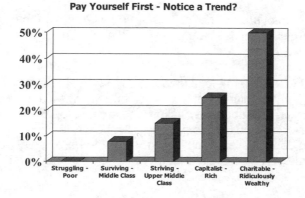

Pay Yourself First - Notice a Trend?

[5] "Take a Long Look at Returns," by Scott Burns, The Dallas Morning News, 11/17/02

Save Ten Percent of What You Make – ACTION PLAN

Step 1: Open a Second Bank Account (or open a first one): If you already have more than one bank account (one with both ATM and money transfer capability) skip to the next step. If not, then you need to contact several local banks and find out the various features they offer for savings and money market accounts. You're looking for a bank with: Low account minimums, free money transfers (unlimited transfers are a bonus), and no monthly account maintenance fees.

Open Your Account. Now you have two separate bank accounts: one for everyday expenses and the other for your **Ten Percent Deposits**.

(Don't despair if you can't find the funds to open a first or second account. We'll work on stretching your dollars later in the book).

Cash Can: If you're not able to get to 10% right away, a helpful idea is to literally have an old coffee can or piggy bank in your room. Dump any loose change or money that's left over at the end of the day from your daily transactions, then deposit the money into your Pay Yourself First (PYF) account every week or month.

Step 2: Set Up Your Direct Deposit from Your Employer: Contact your employer's payroll department and see if they can directly deposit your check into your existing savings account (if you already do this, you're ahead of the game).

Step 3: Set Up a Transfer from Your Existing Account to Your PYF Account: Have 10% (or the amount you can afford right now) pulled from your existing account and deposited into the newly established PYF account (i.e., your 10% account).

Note: Some employers can deposit set amounts from your checks into different savings accounts if you authorize them to do so, which allows you to bypass Step 3.

Bill Yourself?: Another helpful idea is to bill yourself every time you get paid. A friend of mine created a stack of deposit slips, then stapled them in a booklet. The booklet of slips was kept on top of his stack of bills. Whenever it came time to pay the bills, he wrote himself a check and tore off a deposit slip, which he carried to the bank every other Saturday. I guess you can say that he took 'Pay Yourself First' literally.

Secret #3:
BUDGET YOUR TIME and MONEY

"The philosophy of the rich versus the poor is this:
The rich invest their money and spend what is left;
the poor spend their money and invest what is left."

– Jim Rohn

Chapter 7

Secret #3: BUDGET YOUR TIME AND MONEY

"Budgeting Time and Money is a habit that expands exponentially with use. As you become better at budgeting your time, you will accomplish far more because you not only use time more wisely, you use it more efficiently. You find faster, more efficient ways to perform routine tasks, and you become better at establishing priorities."

– W. Clement Stone, Author, *Believe and Achieve*

Wake-up Call

"David!" my father called out from somewhere. "Mr. Mathers is on the phone."

I looked at my alarm clock. It was only eight o'clock. I picked up the phone. "Don't you know that decent people are still sleeping at this hour?" I said, my voice still hoarse from my late night.

"Ah Mr. David, the early bird gets the worm or in my case collects the rent. I'll let you get back to sleep but I need you to bring some information to our meeting at nine o'clock."

"What kind of information?"

"Before you can begin the next step in the process of getting your Financial House in order, you're going to need all your bank, credit card, 401(k), and every other type of document showing what you owe and what you own. I hope it won't be too difficult to find these items in your room."

"Now you sound like my mother," I replied. "I'm sure I can find the information and my room is clean, thank you very much."

"I'm sure it is. Let's just wait and see how clean your finances are before I issue a clean bill of health," he replied.

"Man you can be hokey at times."

"I didn't think people still used the word hokey, Mr. David. Especially at eight in the morning."

"Very funny. Can we get back to me and my millionaire status?"

"Testy, testy aren't we in the morning. I'll see you at nine."

I hung up the phone and promptly went back to bed.

Lesson # 3

"Glad to see you're a bit more chipper at nine than at eight in the morning Mr. David," Mr. Mathers said as he pulled up a chair.

"After more sleep and some coffee, I'm good as gold," I said, pulling my binder from my backpack and putting my baseball cap on the table.

"Ah, our little caffeine addict," he said, tapping the vein on his forearm.

"Very funny. Rather than pick on me, can we start today's lesson?"

"First, I want to ask if you've looked into setting up a separate bank account yet."

"I did. I went to several banks to see what the minimum for their accounts were and what interest rates they gave on their savings accounts. I even went to Westburg and visited some banks there. I decided on Citibank because they had the lowest account minimums and offered me free checking. I opened an account there yesterday and I even deposited 10% of my salary for the week."

"You really are ambitious," he said. "You've done quite well for yourself by trying to save 10% of what you make, but you could have done better."

"But how?" I asked. "How could I have done better?"

"By using the next Secret and taking an active role in lowering your expenses and managing your debt. But before we get into the next Secret, let's talk about that Porsche you've been dreaming about." He pulled out his binder, flipped to a page, and started the lesson.

A Cup of Coffee or a Porsche

"Saving money isn't too difficult. The tough part is not spending it. And do you know how much you can invest with no money in the bank?" he asked.

"Nada!" I replied.

"Exactly. Nothing. You could have the hottest stock tip in the world or come across a great real estate deal, but if you don't have money in the bank, you'll lose the deal. The thing to remember is that **every time you spend money on something or use your credit card, it will have an impact down the line in terms of your lifestyle 10 or 20 years from now.** It will impact what kind of house you will be able to afford or whether you can pay for your kids' education, and when you can retire. It all depends on what you *choose* to do with your money today. Waste it today and you waste your retirement years having to work to make up for your mistakes. Watch it carefully today and you'll never have to worry about money for the rest of your life."

"So I'm supposed to remember every time I want to spend my money that I can be using it for something better 40 years from now? I have some will power, but there is no way that I'll be able to do that. Never in a million years."

"David, I'm not talking about *every* dollar you make, just a few dollars here and there. For example, let's pretend a cup of coffee cost you $2 at Scrappy's Deli and that you drink two cups a day. You pick up one on the way to work and you go to Scrappy's some time during the afternoon for a pick-me-up. But suppose that instead of buying those two cups of coffee you decide to put that money aside at the beginning of each month and invest it in index funds. Those funds do okay and return 10% over the years. After 20 years, guess how much money you will have?"

"No idea, maybe $20,000," I replied.

"Try tripling the number. At the end of 20 years, you'll have enough to buy a Porsche and have some money left over."

"A Porsche! Because I didn't drink coffee every day! That's unbelievable."

"Believe it," he said. He pulled a sheet of paper from his binder and handed it to me. "Here, take a look at this chart which shows you how quickly investing a dollar a day with a 10% annual return can grow into big money," he said.

Figure 7.1 – A Dollar a Day Grows Pretty Quickly!

	$ Saved	1	5	10	# of Years 20	25	34	56
One	$1	$384	$2,367	$6,270	$23,313	$40,801	$105,668	$982,650
Less	$2	$768	$4,735	$12,541	$46,625	$81,602	$211,336	$1,965,299
Expense	$5	$1,919	$11,837	$31,352	$116,563	$204,004	$528,340	$4,913,248
Every	$10	$3,838	$23,674	$62,704	$233,127	$408,009	$1,056,680	$9,826,496
Day	$15	$5,757	$35,511	$94,056	$349,690	$612,013	$1,585,021	$14,739,744
Will	$20	$7,676	$47,348	$125,407	$466,253	$816,018	$2,113,361	$19,652,992
Make	$25	$9,595	$59,186	$156,759	$582,817	$1,020,022	$2,641,701	$24,566,241
You	$30	$11,515	$71,023	$188,111	$699,380	$1,224,026	$3,170,041	$29,479,489
A	$50	$19,191	$118,371	$313,518	$1,165,633	$2,040,044	$5,283,402	$49,132,481
Millionaire	$100	$38,382	$236,742	$627,037	$2,331,267	$4,080,088	$10,566,805	$98,264,962

Note: Money is invested daily at a 10% annual return using Microsoft Excel's "FV" formula. Other calculators might calculate the end result differently, but you get the point. Start investing today!

Do You Value Money?

"Wow! I never thought a dollar a day could amount to that much."

"**That's because you don't value money**. You think a dollar is just a dollar, but it's not."

"So if it's not a dollar, then what is it?"

"**It's your worker**. A powerful worker that will work for you day and night, 24 hours a day, 7 days a week, 365 days a year. There's only one catch. You just have to invest the money, not touch it, and let it work for you."

"So how could a dollar a day possibly grow to a million bucks like your example?"

"Ah easy. It teams up with his buddy who goes by the name of **compound**, the true secret to building wealth. Einstein called it the 'most powerful invention of man' and he was right. Compound interest is like a snowball at the top of a snow-filled mountain. As it rolls down, it continues to gather speed and size. The longer you keep it on the mountain, the bigger that snowball gets. At first it starts out as a small snowball, but after each layer, the snowball picks up speed and soon it's growing faster and faster."

"**So the longer I keep my money invested, the faster the money will grow.** How come?"

"Because at first you only have a little money and you only make a little interest, but that interest earned is added to your initial amount. If you look at that sheet you will see that a dollar a day at 10% interest grows to $6,270 in 10 years. But how much does it grow to after 20 years?"

"The chart says $23,313. Hey, wait a minute," I said. "That's *more* than double."

"We have a winner!" he exclaimed waving his hands in the air. "The reason it's more than simply double $6,270 is because you earn interest on both the principal, or amount you put in, and any interest that you earned in the previous 10 years. In short, your interest will earn interest and that earned interest earns interest and so on. It's an exponential growth thing."

"So how can I get my money to earn 10% interest on my money? My bank only pays me 2% if I'm lucky right now."

"You will learn how in a few short lessons, but the important thing is to learn how to appreciate the beauty of what that chart in front of you says. If you can find a way to scrape together an extra $5 a day, a mere $150 a month, you could have a million bucks in less than 35 years. Sounds very interesting, especially when you'll earn over a million bucks in your lifetime."

Earning a Million Bucks?

"A million bucks? What are you talking about? I make $30,000 a year. How am I supposed to earn a million bucks?"

"Not all at once David, but over time, say the next 40 years, you could earn a million dollars and then some if your average salary is $30,000 a year. You already work hard for those dollars. Why waste that dollar when you can put it to work for you? All it takes is the discipline to set aside a set amount of money each day or month and invest it. Don't touch it and let compound interest work its magic."

Figure 7.2 – You'll Earn a Million in Your Lifetime
How much money is going to pass through
your hands during your working career?

Yearly Salary	10 Years	20 Years	30 Years	40 Years
$10,000	$100,000	$200,000	$300,000	$400,000
$12,500	$125,000	$250,000	$375,000	$500,000
$15,000	$150,000	$300,000	$450,000	$600,000
$20,000	$200,000	$400,000	$600,000	$800,000
$25,000	$250,000	$500,000	$750,000	$1,000,000
$30,000	$300,000	$600,000	$900,000	$1,200,000
$40,000	$400,000	$800,000	$1,200,000	$1,600,000
$50,000	$500,000	$1,000,000	$1,500,000	$2,000,000
$60,000	$600,000	$1,200,000	$1,800,000	$2,400,000
$70,000	$700,000	$1,400,000	$2,100,000	$2,800,000
$80,000	$800,000	$1,600,000	$2,400,000	$3,200,000
$90,000	$900,000	$1,800,000	$2,700,000	$3,600,000
$100,000	$1,000,000	$2,000,000	$3,000,000	$4,000,000
$110,000	$1,100,000	$2,200,000	$3,300,000	$4,400,000
$120,000	$1,200,000	$2,400,000	$3,600,000	$4,800,000

"You've got me hooked. What do I need to do next?"

"Start playing the lottery," he replied.

"Hah! Very funny," I replied, thinking he was joking. By the look on his face I could tell that he wasn't. "You're not serious are you?"

"I'm 100% serious."

Win the Lottery - Guaranteed

"I'm going to teach you how to win the lottery. Now as you know the odds of wining the lottery is something like 76 million to one. I have a surefire secret that will guarantee that you win the lottery."

"How can that be? What is it?" I said grabbing my pen.

"I just taught you David. Weren't you paying attention?"

"What are you talking about?" I asked.

"How much does a lottery ticket cost?" he asked.

"A dollar. Why do you…ohh, I get it."

"'Ohh, I get it'," he said, mimicking me. "Empty your pockets please. Put the contents on the table."

I emptied my pockets. Lying on top of my money was the lottery ticket I had bought that morning. "How did you…" I started to say.

Mr. Mathers was smiling ear to ear. "Relax. I'm not a psychic or anything. I saw you buying it at Scrappy's Deli when I walked by. Not a wise investment is it?"

"It's worth a shot $100 million."

"Perhaps, but I don't think you have a chance. **It's been said that the lottery is a tax on those who aren't good at math.** A 76 million to one shot. Who would like those odds? Yet millions of people line up every week for the lottery. Everyone of them holds the key to winning the Lottery Game of Life in their hands and they don't even know it."

"A dollar bill, right?" I said.

"Yep, that's the real ticket. If you're going to play the lottery, you might as well play your *own* lottery. People find it so hard to save money, but they don't find it hard to wait in line, choose 6 magical numbers and plunk down that dollar. A dollar that will never work hard for them. If they would invest the buck every day, then they'd be staring at a pile of cold hard cash."

Money + Time = Financial Freedom

"**There are two things you need to invest: Money and Time**. The easy part of the equation is the time component. The hard part for most people is finding where to cut the fat in their expenses in order to have the money to invest. Learning to set aside a few dollars here and there and putting them to work for you is the real secret to investing."

"So how do you do it?" I asked.

"Easy David. You do it through learning how to put the next Secret of building wealth into action."

"And what is the next Secret?" I asked.

"**Secret #3 is all about learning how to Budget Your Time and Money**."

"The way to wealth, if you desire it, is as plain as the way to market. It depends chiefly on 2 words: Industry and Frugality. That is, waste neither time nor money, but make the best use of both."

- Benjamin Franklin

Your Financial House

> "If you have built castles in the air, your work need not be lost; there is where they should be. Now put foundations under them."
>
> – Henry David Thoreau

Step 1: Your Net Worth Statement (Where are you today?)
Step 2: Where's Your Cash Flowing? (Know your flow)
Step 3: Create a Budget (Your spending plan)

Step 1. Your Net Worth Statement - Where are You Today?

"In school you get a report card at the end of each semester that tells you how you're doing. In real life you get several account statements telling you what your savings and checking account balances are, how much you have in your 401(k), and so on. You also get statements from your mortgage company, school loan lender, your credit card providers, and so on. These tell you how much you owe. The problem is that all that important information is all over the place on dozens of statements. If you haven't gone through the exercise of looking at everything all at once, you'll never figure out where you stand financially because you'll leave out an IRA statement or forget to put one of your credit card statements onto what is called a **net worth statement**."

"So everything is on one page or something?"

"Right and all you do is add up everything you own (assets) and subtract what you owe (liabilities). **Your net worth makes for an easy way to track how you're doing in this Game of Life**. This coupled with what's called a cash flow statement will tell you how good you are at managing your finances."

"So I go through the process of listing what I own and what I owe, subtract the two and I come up with what I'm worth?"

"Exactly. It gives you a snapshot of where you are today and how you're doing against your goal of building wealth."

"So how do I create my net worth statement? Is that why you had me bring all these statements?" I said pointing to the pile on the table.

He nodded. "We're going to create your net worth statement today if you're ready."

"Sure. Let's do it."

Constructing Your Net Worth Statement
Find the Paperwork

You'll need all of your statements in order to continue with this book. All of the following important information should be at your fingertips to complete your net worth and cash flow statements:

- *Federal and state income tax returns*
- *Insurance Policies*
- *Mortgage, home-equity loan, and property-tax records*
- *Bank Statements*
- *Brokerage, 401(k), IRA and other investment statements*
- *Credit Card Statements – all of them*

Helpful Hint – Get Organized!

If you're serious about getting your Financial House in order, you have to literally get everything on one page and the best way to do it is by keeping everything in one place in your house. I recommend a filing cabinet next to a good-sized desk, preferably with a computer nearby. Make sure the desk has drawers so you have a place to put your stamps, envelopes, pens, and paper. If you don't have them already, go out and buy some manila folders and hanging folders. Label each of the manila folders – one each for each category of bills or statements. The idea is to get everything in one place, which is literally what a net worth statement does. It organizes all your assets (what you own) and all your liabilities (what you owe). Ooops, I'm getting ahead of myself.

It's an Easy Process

"You'll be happy to know that creating a net worth statement isn't that hard. It just takes some simple math and about 30 minutes of time and presto, you've got your first net worth statement."

"So what do I do with all this information?" I said pointing to the statements I had brought with me.

"You're going to organize all that information into two buckets: one pile will be assets or what you own and the other will be liabilities or what you owe."

Assets

"Assets are the things you own. List out everything you can think of and worry about their value after you've completed the list. You include things like cars, houses, stocks, savings accounts, and retirement accounts. Once you're done listing everything, you need to go back and assign a value to each of the items. Now **you're not going to put down how much you paid for the items**, rather you're going to put down what you could sell the item for today if you had to."

"Why do you do that?" I asked.

"Because that car of yours that you bought a year ago is now worth less than you paid for it, while the house or stocks that you bought are hopefully worth more today. Planners call this your assets fair market value or FMV for short. **It's important to use the fair market value for your assets so you don't overstate the value of your assets**, which a lot of people have a tendency to do."

"Makes sense. So for my stocks or savings accounts I can just go to my monthly statement and write down the latest balance?"

"Correct. Stocks and savings accounts are easy to quantify because you have a statement telling you the net value of your accounts. For assets like real estate, it's much harder to put a value on because there is no set price for them. In those cases, you can make an estimate based on what other houses in your area have sold for or you can contact a real estate agent in your area and ask for their estimate."

"What other assets are hard to put a price tag on?" I asked.

"Well, some of my students have jewelry, computer equipment, and unvested options from their companies to name a few other types of assets. I tell them not to put these items on. **In my mind it's better to *underestimate* your net worth, rather than overestimate it**."

"Why would you do that?" I asked.

"All too often, when your net worth starts to rise you get a false sense of prosperity thanks to your increased paper wealth and stop watching what you're spending your money on. You begin to spend your money on foolish things because you have this false sense of security."

"But if your assets are climbing, how can it be a false sense of security?"

"Put it to you this way, just because your stocks are worth X today, doesn't mean they will be worth that next month, let alone next year. The same goes for that house you're living in. Get the picture?"

"Crystal clear," I replied.

Liabilities

"On the other hand, liabilities are what you owe. They include your mortgage, home equity loans, student loans, car loans, and any credit card balances you have. If you've sold stocks and have capital gains for the year, try and figure out the estimated taxes you owe. And if you were self-employed, you probably would owe estimated income tax every quarter. But enough talking," he said. "Let's get busy on your statement before it gets too late." He reached into his briefcase and handed me my first net worth statement.

How it Works

"As you can see, I break out my assets into different buckets. I like to know what my cash or short-term equivalents are so I can figure out how much money I have easy access to if an emergency came up. Then I look at my short-term investments, my long-term or retirement assets, as well as my personal assets. Then all you do is total up your assets and liabilities columns and subtract the liabilities total from the assets total and presto, you have your first net worth statement."

When I finished, I just stared at the page.

"Let's see what you've got," he said, pulling the paper from me.

Ouch!@#!@#&%!

"So I have a **negative net worth**," I stated.

"Don't worry about it David. Most people your age don't have assets beyond their cars and by the time they're done with college, they've accumulated so much debt that it will take over a decade or more to break even," he said.

"Gee, that's comforting. Go to college for four years and then work ten-plus years to pay it off. That doesn't sound fair to me."

"We'll cover off on the subject of your student loans in another lesson, but realize that you're not alone in Debtor's Prison."

The Debtor's Prison

"For people in their thirties, the debt most likely came from a first mortgage, a new car, and wedding costs. For people in their forties, expenses can come from selling their first house and moving to a bigger one, to having and raising kids and the added food, electricity, and heating expenses that come along with raising kids. Of course by the time you make it to your fifties, you generally have to start paying for your kids' college education and start thinking about your retirement and how you're going to pay off all the debt you've accumulated through the years."

Figure 7.3 - Create Your Own Net Worth Statement
The below net worth statement is NOT the one I had at the time,
but I've included it as just an example to work off of.

Assets		Liabilities	
TAXABLE INVESTMENTS		**PERSONAL**	
Savings Acct	$ 4,500	School Loans	$ 12,000
Investment Club	$ 2,432	Car Loan	$ 10,234
Fidelity Acct	$ 11,889	Credit Cards	$ 11,325
Sharebuilder	$ 8,111	Personal Loan	$ 4,353
37 Sunset Lane	$ 200,000		
Subtotal	**$ 226,932**	*Subtotal*	**$ 37,912**
TAX-ADVANTAGED INVESTMENTS		**REAL ESTATE INVESTMENTS**	
401(k)	$ 30,000	37 Sunset Lane	$ 155,421
IRAs	$ 5,000		
Subtotal	**$ 35,000**	*Subtotal*	**$ 155,421**
PERSONAL PROPERTY		**PERSONAL PROPERTY**	
Home	$ 185,000	Home Mortgage	$ 134,231
Vacation Home	-	Vacation Home	-
Car	$ 8,925		
Subtotal	**$ 193,925**	*Subtotal*	**$ 134,231**
a. TOTAL ASSETS	**$ 455,857**	**b. TOTAL LIABILITIES**	**$ 327,564**
		c. NET WORTH (a – b):	**$ 128,293**

Fill Out Your Own!
*You can fill out your own Net Worth Statement by taking out a
piece of paper and folding it in half length-wise. On the left side list all
your assets and on the right side, list all your liabilities. Subtract the
liabilities number from the asset number and you have a quick and easy
net worth statement. Should you want an even easier method to use,
just go to my web-site and download the Microsoft Excel File titled:*
NET WORTH CALCULATOR – Short Form
It can be found at <u>www.fabmansecrets.com/downloads</u>

NOTE: Not all Assets are Created Equal

I don't want to go into too much detail on the net worth statement, but I did want to mention the difference between good assets and bad assets. You see, there's a difference in the quality of the assets you can invest your money in. Just because you have a high net worth doesn't mean that you are doing a good job managing your finances.

A simple definition that I modified from the RichDad^{TM} definition is:
Assets: Feed You *– put money in your pockets*
Liabilities: Bleed You *– take money from your pockets*

Expensive homes, cars, and other depreciating assets all take money out of your pocket. For instance, a car will show up under the asset column of your net worth statement, but you still have to pay for gas, insurance, and repairs down the line. A boat will do the same, as does home furnishings. Good assets like stocks, real estate, and businesses put cash in your pocket. To become rich you need to focus on building up assets that put money in your pocket, rather than those that take money from you.[6]

Back to our story…

Call it a Spending Plan

"Imagine living for 30 years with all that debt, living paycheck to paycheck, covering your short falls with credit cards or home equity loans? Worrying you'll be downsized with no cushion to fall back on, all because you don't have a budget and didn't plan properly for all those expenses."

"No thanks," I replied. "Can you help me create a budget?"

"I'd rather teach you how to spend your money."

"What's the difference?"

"It's all psychological. That's why I call budgets **spending plans**. **A spending plan is like creating monthly saving and spending 'less than' goals**. At the end of the month you know if you've succeeded in meeting your targets. If you 'win' enough times throughout the months and years, that is save more than you're supposed to and spend less than you planned to spend, you're that much closer to Financial Freedom. **You won't become financially secure through budgeting your money alone, but having a budget is one of the building blocks for becoming truly wealthy**."

---

[6] Still scratching your head on the subject of good assets vs. bad assets? Read *Rich Dad, Poor Dad* by Robert Kiyosaki and Sharon Lecter. They do an excellent job of explaining the differences. I'd get into it, but I can tell you're anxious to get on with this process.

Step 2: Know your Flow - Cash Flow Analysis

"The net worth statement is a great starting baseline to figure out where you are financially, but it doesn't tell the whole story, which is why we have to look at your current budget. Before we create your new budget, we have to look at your current budget."

"But I don't have a current budget," I interjected.

"Not a formalized one, but you technically have one already. To find out what your current budget is you'll have to do a cash flow analysis. This simple statement will show you how much money you are taking in and how much is going out on a monthly basis. **People get into trouble when they don't know how their cash is flowing.** As I've said before, it's not how much money you make that will determine whether you'll be rich, it's how much you keep and a cash flow analysis will tell you how much you're keeping."

A Net Worth Statement Tells You Where You Are
A Cash Flow Analysis Tells You HOW You Got There

"A cash flow analysis will help identify your spending patterns and you can see if you have bad money habits that are hurting your chances of becoming wealthy. I've known too many people who were millionaires on paper, but were struggling to make ends meet every month because they were operating with a negative cash flow. Each month they were digging a deeper and deeper hole for themselves. But they had lots of assets so they thought they could spend money because they were making so much of it."

"I never looked at it that way."

"Most people don't. Everyone is concerned with their net worth, but not many people look at their cash flow. They don't realize that the sooner their annual passive income from their portfolio surpasses their living expenses, they can retire!"

A light bulb went off in my head. "So it doesn't matter when you reach that level of passive or portfolio income? You could retire at 30 when you reach that level instead of 65?"

"More or less, yes. **As soon as your passive income coming in exceeds your expenses, you get to quit your job.**"

"Tell me more." Retiring early was a definite goal of mine.

THE CASH FLOW CALCULATOR [7]

He reached into his briefcase, opened a folder and pulled out a sheet of paper. "Before we go any further, I'd like you to fill this out. It's a CASH FLOW CALCULATOR that will help you determine where your money is disappearing to every month. For the monthly expenses like phone bills and car payments, you can just look at the past bills you brought with you. As for the other expenses you don't know off the top of your head, **I'm going to make you track your expenses for 30 days to find those miscellaneous ones that are eating a hole in your pocket.** You're going to carry around a piece of paper or note pad and write down everything you spend money on."

"Seems like a lot of work. Can't I just estimate my expenses?"

"No. **The majority of people *underestimate* how much money they spend** on things like food, clothes, and miscellaneous items. These are the categories where you can easily turn up a few extra dollars a week just by watching your wallet closely. More on this later. For now, just fill out the sheet," he instructed, "and we'll see how you do."

I thought it would be a difficult process to fill out, but it turned out to be relatively easy. Of course there were areas that I was clueless as to how much I spent in a given month, but for those items I guesstimated.

Is Your Cash Flowing?

"Not bad," I said when I finished. I had a positive cash flow of close to $300 a month.

"Let me see," Mr. Mathers replied, grabbing the paper.

"Hmm, not bad, but you're not paying rent right now and your entertainment and food expenses look a bit low. Did you include your trips to the coffee shop and bars?"

"Bubble officially burst," I said. I took the sheet back and made some adjustments. "I net $135 bucks! That's it. How am I supposed to get rich on $135 bucks a month?"

"Patience David, patience. You only have a $135 positive cash flow a month because you never set up a budget for yourself. In fact, most people don't set up a budget until they're so far in debt and have to take drastic measures!"

"Okay, I'm sold," I said. "How do I create my budget?"

---

[7] A version of this is available in Excel on my site: ww.fabmansecrets.com/downloads.htm

Figure 7.4 – The CASH FLOW CALCULATOR
Use the below calculator to figure out your MONTHLY Cash Flow

	Estimated	Actual
Monthly Income		
Net Salary (after taxes)	$_____	$_____
Other Income	_____	_____
Investment Income (incl. dividends)	_____	_____
Other	_____	_____
Other	_____	_____
A. TOTAL INCOME	$_____	$_____
Monthly Expenses		
Pay Yourself First	$_____	$_____
Mortgage or Rent	_____	_____
Utilities	_____	_____
Telephones (incl. Cellular)	_____	_____
Groceries	_____	_____
Dining Out	_____	_____
Car Loan + Insurance	_____	_____
Tolls, other commuting costs	_____	_____
Loan Payments	_____	_____
Health Insurance	_____	_____
Life + other insurance	_____	_____
Home maintenance	_____	_____
Dry cleaning/Laundry	_____	_____
Childcare	_____	_____
Cable TV + Internet Access	_____	_____
Books, Music, Movies	_____	_____
Other Entertainment	_____	_____
New Clothes	_____	_____
Vacation (can average yearly costs)	_____	_____
Gifts (incl. Wedding gifts)	_____	_____
Subscriptions (Newspapers and magazines)	_____	_____
Pet Care (incl. Food)	_____	_____
Gym	_____	_____
Other Memberships	_____	_____
Donations/Charity	_____	_____
Miscellaneous	_____	_____
Other	_____	_____
B. TOTAL EXPENSES	$_____	$_____
C. CASH FLOW (A-B)	$_____	$_____

Note: This is just a quick and easy CFC. The above categories can be added to and changed to meet your needs.

From Cash Flow Analysis to Your Budget

"Your cash flow analysis essentially becomes the basis for your budget. If you did it accurately, the cash flow sheet should be what you typically spend in a given month. Now you need to decide where you can cut some of the 'fat' from your budget."

"Sounds like fun."

"Okay Mr. Sarcastic, let's start the fun," he said, pulling a sheet of paper from his notepad. He drew three columns down the page.

"In column A you write down your fixed expenses like rent, school loans, car payments, and insurance. In the next column you write down those variable expenses like phone bills, electric bills, credit card minimum payments, subscriptions, and food expenses etc."

"Isn't my phone bill a fixed expense?"

"Some would argue that, but I put it under variable because it's not a fixed amount every month. Depending on usage, it could be more or less than planned. Make sense?"

"Got it."

"Good. Now in column C you write down those miscellaneous expenses like gym memberships, trips to the coffee shop, and every other expense."

Figure 7.5 – Fixed, Variable or Misc. Expenses?

Column A		Column B		Column C	
Fixed Expenses		**Variable Expenses**		**Misc. Expenses**	
Item	Amt	Item	Amt	Item	Amt
Total		Total		Total	

"You then total up each of the columns and fill in the lines below:

$ for Fixed Expenses _____

$ for Variable Expenses _____

$ for Misc. Expenses _____

Total Expenses [ ]

How it Works

"This exercise can be a real eye-opener for folks. I like to do it this way rather than the straightforward cash flow statement because it helps people focus on cutting expenses better. You know for instance that you've got a lot of miscellaneous expenses in column C, then you're going to have to watch those discretionary expenses. If too much of your money is being spent by the time you reach column B, you probably should look for cheaper housing or a less expensive car. If your school loans are too much, maybe you should refinance. In my experience, the best way to start is to attack expenses in column C, then column B, and finally column A which brings us to our next topic."

Needs versus Wants

"Before we move on, you need to determine which expenses are needs and which are wants. This is difficult as you know because **if you don't watch it, everything becomes a need over time**. By figuring out what expenses are needs and which ones are wants, it will be easier to cut back. Now I'm not saying that you have to cut back in all areas of your life, just focus on cutting out some of those wants that you really don't need. The 50% off pants you never wear or the $15 CD that you listen to once and then add to the pile of other depreciating goods in your closet. Learn to think of your money as the precious commodity that it is and you'll soon change your spending ways."

Mad Money

"But am I cutting my expenses to the bare bones here?" I asked.

"No David, that's not what I'm saying. **I'm not advocating saving every penny you make and living a Spartan life**. You should splurge here and there on those little indulgences that can bring temporary joy to your life. I'm a realist David. You need to have fun and spend a little of that hard-earned money, especially when you're young. That's why I suggest you budget in some mad money into your budget."

"'Mad money'? What's that?" I asked.

"Mad money is money you set aside in your monthly budget that you can spend on whatever you want. The better you are at managing and limiting your expenses, the more mad money you will have. It's just a way to make sure that you have money in your budget to do those things that you want to do without having the guilt associated with spending money that could be invested."

"So I do get some fun money to spend," I stated. "That's cool, but what if I have extra cash after I've allocated money to my mad money fund? Am I supposed to invest the money that's left over?"

Create an Emergency Fund

"No, your first move should be to create a 'cash reserve' or what most financial planners call an 'Emergency Fund' for yourself. **The money is to be used only if you lose your job, are unable to work, or have unforeseen expenses** that can seriously impact your finances. Your see, no matter how good your budget is, it's difficult to anticipate unforeseen expenses. If you don't have money set aside for these expenses, you'll have to borrow money from a credit card and then you'll get into that vicious cycle of never-ending debt. You'll try to pay it off, but it keeps coming back again and again."

"Enough," I said, waiving my hands in the air. "I get it, I get it."

How Much Do You Need to Set Aside?

He smiled at me. "As you can see, there are many reasons to have an Emergency Fund. Now the money should be put into an account that you have quick access to and where you don't pay a penalty for withdrawal. So this eliminates CDs or certificate of deposit accounts. As for how much you need to set aside, most financial planners out there recommend at least three to six months of your living expenses as a general rule."

"That's a lot of money to tie up in a savings account."

"It might seem that way, but if you've been through a short-term financial crisis, you'll know it might not be enough."

Having an Emergency Fund is Mandatory

"But what if I don't have much left in the way of savings right now. Is it absolutely necessary to have an Emergency Fund?"

"A lot of beginning investors try to get around this step because they know it will take time to build up their Emergency Fund. Don't assume that you'll always be working. You could lose your job or you could have an accident that leaves you unable to work for several months. It's not a pleasant thought, but it happens to people all the time. If it happens, you need to be prepared."

"That's still a lot of money to save," I commented.

"You're right, which is why I often tell my students with little in the way of liabilities or mortgages to do it Dave's way."

"Dave who?" I asked.

"Dave as in Dave Ramsey, the radio talk show host and personal finance author. In his book *Financial Peace Revisited*, he outlines his 'Baby Steps to Financial Freedom' and **the first step is to save $1,000.** After you do this, you move on to paying off your debts. But he believes, and so do I, that it's a lot easier to save $1,000 than it is to save 3 to 6 months of expenses."

"Sure would be for me," I added.

"Right. So choose what works for you. **I say you should have somewhere between $1,000 and two months of expenses to start, whichever amount is more.**"

Is it Smart to Tie-up Your Money?

"All right, you've convinced me, but is it smart to keep all that money tied up in an account that earns a 2% return?"

He laughed. "That's why I like you David. You're always thinking of how to earn more money. Before you go chasing the highest returns, you should know that it's important to make sure that you put the money in an account that doesn't have too much risk. **You never want to put your Emergency Fund at risk**, because if something comes up and you've lost 30% of the value thanks to a short-term downturn in the market, you're out of luck. Stick to money market and savings accounts. You won't earn a lot of interest, but the money will be there when you need it. If you want to shop around for money market or savings accounts that pay the best interest, just check out www.bankrate.com for a list of the best rates around."

"So, do you suggest a **money market account**?"

"They do pay higher rates of return than savings accounts, but realize that they are not guaranteed by the FDIC, which is the government institution that backs banks, but the chances of losing money are marginal. But yes, I do advocate using money market accounts if you can meet the account minimums."

"What about all those **Internet banks** popping up all over the place?" I asked. "I just read an article about them and a lot of them offered some great rates."

"David, the so-called 'Net' banks are backed by the FDIC, just like the First Savings & Loan down the street in Woodbridge. The difference is there is no physical office that you can go to, which means they have lower overhead and bills to pay. They pass those savings on to you in the form of a higher interest rate on your money."

Creating that Budget (Spending Plan)!

"Got it, so what's next?" I asked.

"Would you believe we're done with your budget?"

"Done? How?" I asked.

"Look in front of you. Without realizing it, you've already created your first spending plan," he said pointing to the CASH FLOW CALCULATOR.

"Hey, you're right," I replied.

"Just work on reducing those expenses we listed in Column C (miscellaneous expenses) a few minutes ago and trim the fat from your budget as best you can."

"But how do I figure out how to cut my expenses?"

He opened his binder again and pulled out a sheet of paper. "Here. This should help you," he said and handed the page to me.

"Wow. You really do think of everything," I said staring at the page titled *"Quick Tips to Help You Cut the Fat from your Budget.[8]"*

"It's just a starting point and we'll reference it again in two weeks, when we cover Secret #5, so just tuck the chart away for now," he said, standing up and shutting his briefcase.

I stood up as well, then thought of something. "Hey are you going to help me figure out how I can pay off my loans and reduce my credit card debt?" I asked. "These monthly payments are killing me."

He swung his briefcase around and placed it on the table then searched through his binder for a sheet of paper. "Thanks for reminding me. I want you to fill out this grid by next week. Just list out your debts from highest interest rate to the lowest rate"

I took the paper and looked at it.

"We'll cover all the ins and outs of debt next week. Right now we're going for a walk and we're going to discuss how to budget your time, so tuck that page with the Debt Repayment Grid away and fill it out later. Sound good?"

"Let's do it," I replied.

---

[8] This chart appears at the end of Secret #5. I didn't want you working on cutting expenses until you read the next two Secrets.

Figure 7.6 – Debt Management Grid

Creditor	Outstanding Balance	Interest Rate	Monthly Minimum	Payment Amount
YOUR DEBT MANAGEMENT GRID				
Non-Deductible Interest				
Subtotals				
Deductible Interest				
Subtotals				

Helpful Hint – Invest in a Computer

A computer is an invaluable investment in your financial future. Not only will it help you create a household budget, but you'll also be able to invest in stocks via the Internet and do research on investments, mortgages, life insurance, and just about everything else you'll need in life. If you don't own one already, you have four options: buy a computer, use your work computer, use a relative or friend's computer, or use the computer at the library. The best option is to own your computer. Once you have a computer, I suggest you look into purchasing a money-management software program to help you get everything organized. One of the best software programs out there right now is Quicken®. Quicken® will help you create your household budget and track everything and I mean everything. It may seem tedious at first, but it's like riding a bicycle. Spend a day learning how to use it and then you'll be on top of your finances in no time.

Budgeting Your Money - COMMENTS

You cannot continue to make bad decisions with your money and expect to retire early or grow your investment account. It's just not going to happen. You need to corral those workers of yours (dollars) and put them to work for you. I'm talking about getting control over your money.

At this point, creating a budget to live by might seem like the most time-consuming task in the world, but it's also one of the most important tasks you'll undertake in life. Yes, you read that right; creating a budget for yourself and sticking to it is one of the most important financial tasks that you will undertake in life. Why? Having a budget for time and money will help you allocate your limited resources in a way that will give you the greatest benefit.

I hope you realize the importance of knowing where your cash is flowing because if you don't, you'll never become Financially Free, which is okay if you want to work for the rest of your life. I didn't think so, so do yourself a favor and do the Action Steps that follow. It will be time well spent!

"The spendthrift cannot succeed, mainly because he stands eternally in fear of poverty. **Form the habit of systematic saving by putting aside a definite percentage of your income**. Money in the bank gives one a very safe foundation of courage when bargaining for the sale of personal services. Without money, one must take what one is offered, and be glad to get it."

– Napoleon Hill

Budgeting Your Money – ACTION PLAN

Cash Can: If you're not at the point where you can put aside $100 to $200 a month for your Emergency Fund, I suggest you start a cash can fund. I use an old coffee can, but whatever you use, just put your spare dollars in it at the end of each night. At the end of the month, deposit the money into your newly created separate account. If you find yourself dipping into the can, start depositing it weekly.

Create an Emergency Fund: We've already talked about why you need an Emergency Fund this is important, but I want to make sure you do it. Start building your reserves today. It sure beats taking out money through a credit card advance at 20% interest! Save that first $1,000, then shoot for having 3 to 6 months of living expenses set aside in a savings or money market account.

Go on a Cash Diet: Stop spending! Yeah, I know, I know. It's not the easiest of things, but put yourself on a cash diet if you have to and you'll see how soon you stop wasting some of your hard-earned money. If you can't do the "paying in greenbacks" thing, use a debit card for <u>ALL</u> your purchases.

Create Your Cash Flow and Net Worth Statements: I have Excel spreadsheets online (<u>www.fabmansecrets.com/downloads.htm</u>) that can help you or you can purchase Quicken® or Microsoft Money® software packages. Your cash flow statement and your personal net worth statement are important tools for you to keep track of how well you're doing in the Game of Life, so take the time to fill them out.

Create a Budget: Review your cash flow statement and find out where your cash is currently flowing and determine where you can 'cut the fat' in your current budget. If your budget is too strict, loosen it up a bit. If you find that it's easy to live within your new budget, cut some more.

Budget Tips:

Break Down Your Expenses: Use the example from the chapter and put your expenses into fixed, variable, and miscellaneous buckets. Figure out where you can cut your expenses the most and start cutting!

Question Everything: Even your fixed expenses like rent or car payments can be changed. Question every line item in your CASH FLOW CALCULATOR and see what you can cut out and reduce. Even something as simple as calling up your insurance agent and getting a better rate can save you hundreds of dollars a year.

Don't Cut Too Much: Make sure you budget for some luxuries and take it slow. Don't put yourself on a "crash diet" because you're not going to stick to it. Put in money for those lattes and trips to the convenience store, but don't go overboard.

Mad Money: Set aside some money every month, perhaps $20 to $50 (or more) in a little fund or a second cash can. When you want to buy something on impulse, if you have the money in your "mad money" fund, then go for it. You deserve it…I mean you saved for it!

Save Your "Found" Money: An unexpected refund, bonus, or money from a garage sale, etc, gets cut in half. Half goes toward your savings and paying down your debt, while the rest goes toward your short-term gratification.

One last thing that may help motivate you…

Your Daily Cash Flow:
How much you <u>don't</u> make can inspire you!

Want to get some leverage on yourself and instantly make yourself think twice before you frivolously spend your money on that must have item? Just figure out what your daily cash flow is. It's easy to calculate. Just take your monthly cash flow and divide the number by 30. Now you know how much you have left over at the end of the day after working a day in the life of you. If the amount is only a couple of bucks, it should be all the motivation you need to ignore the triple-shot, mocha blast no cream no whip coffee you buy every day. I know that if you start thinking in terms of "it costs me three days of work to buy this gadget," you'll find yourself resisting temptation and putting more money into your bank account every month.

Chapter 8

Managing Your Time

"You have to exchange a certain number of hours, weeks and even years of your time in order to generate a certain amount of money for savings or investment. That time is irreplaceable. It is a part of your precious life that is gone forever."

– Brian Tracy, Author, *Fat that Frog*

Successful People Increase the Value of Their Time

"If you're going to be successful and get the most out of your life, you're going to have to learn how to manage your time better. Time is your most precious asset besides what's inside that head of yours, so you need to learn how to maximize the time you have available and how to get your work done as efficiently and effectively as possible. Today we're going to go over some great tips, strategies, and techniques for saving hours a day," he said.

"Hours?"

"Yes, hours. I know there are only 24 hours in a day, but I bet you're wasting most of your waking hours and don't even know it."

"I don't know about that one Mr. Mathers. I'm working pretty hard these days."

"Two thoughts on that. First, I know too many people who do nothing for most of the day, then have to scramble to get things done. Often they work late into the night, when they could have easily avoided the situation by planning ahead. Procrastination is a silent killer of dreams. Second, how many hours do you spend watching TV or reading sports and other magazines?"

"I dunno? I couldn't even fathom a guess."

"Most people couldn't. Time flies you see. So it's important to get your priorities straight. There are only 24 hours in a day and 8 hours are spent sleeping and 8 hours or more are spent working. What you do with the remaining 8 hours is what will separate you from everyone else, the wannabes that want to be rich, but never seem to find the time to act on their dreams. You need to learn how to structure your free time so that you can learn and invest your time instead of wasting it."

"Invest my time? How do you do that?" I asked.

"Investing your time is similar to the process of investing your money. If you learn to invest your free cash flow wisely, it will grow and work for you. The same can be said of your time. If you learn to invest your time wisely by reading, learning, and doing instead of wasting it on non-value adding activities, you will see your wealth multiply almost overnight. This may mean sacrificing some of your free or leisure time for self-improvement and other activities."

"So I have to give up having fun in order to get rich?"

"No, not at all. Don't look at it that way," he said, quick to defend his point. "However, **if you are unwilling to set aside 30 minutes a night or a couple of hours on the weekend to read up on important issues or listen to self-improvement tapes, you will never reach your full potential**. All successful people from Henry Ford to Andrew Carnegie to Bill Gates had to sacrifice *some* of their personal time in order to build their businesses. These titans spent some of their precious free time learning more about the areas that they would soon dominate: mass production, steel, and software."

I nodded in agreement. I could understand the importance of setting aside time to learn, but knew it would take a deep commitment to follow through and read or listen to tapes several hours a week.

"By the end of today, you're going to learn how to discipline yourself to get the things done. You need to put off procrastinating and do what you should do regardless of whether you feel like doing it or not. You need to be proactive and do things ahead of schedule. Stick with what I'm about to teach you and you'll become more productive and efficient and thus more valuable to any employer or yourself if you choose to start a business one day."

He flipped a page in his binder and continued. "You've heard the question, 'How do you eat an elephant?' before right?"

"Sure," I responded. "You eat an elephant one bite at a time."

"Correct and that's how you have to approach your life, one step at a time. Reaching your goals is like eating that elephant, the end result may seem daunting, but if you break it up into small steps, you'll definitely reach your long-term goals one step at a time. The better you plan, the easier it is for you to overcome procrastination, to get started, and then to keep going. So let's talk about how you can get more out of your day."

"The best thing about the future is that it comes only one day at a time."

- Abraham Lincoln

How About I Save You Some Time Right Now?

Instead of going back and forth between Mr. Mathers and our hero David, how about I just summarize all the tactics I learned about managing my time in 21 quick steps? I'm sure you'll appreciate it and you won't have to put up with David's sarcastic comments, just mine.

21 Things You Must Do to Manage Your Time Better [9]

It's a sad state of affairs, but an economic reality that the average worker in the US is working more hours than they did ten years ago, but there are only so many days in a week and so many hours in a day You only got 168 hours to do your work, have fun, spend time with your family, and do all those other things you love. Why not learn to manage your time at work better so you have more time for your family and for other things you've stopped doing because you can't seem to find the time anymore? Read the list below and see if you can implement some of the ideas and find more time for the things that really count in life.

1. Plan the Night Before

This is the starting point for effective time management. Gaining control of your time starts with proper planning. During the workday you're bombarded with putting out fires, handling emails, and phone calls, and other fun stuff. It's tough to focus on what you need to get done. Plan out your days in advance and you won't forget any tasks. Remember that **if you fail to plan, you plan to fail.**

2. Prioritize Your To Do List

Once you have a list of things you need to get done, you have to prioritize that list from most important to the trivial. Jim Rohn wrote of about a method I've found to work best for me. He calls it the "A-B-C-D-E" method. You take your list of tasks and assign each item a letter:

"A" is for "absolutely must do" or "very important" tasks.
"B" is for "basically important" tasks that should be done, but are not as important as "A" tasks.
"C" is for "can wait" tasks that are nice to do, but probably don't add value. In short, you can get away with not doing them.
"D" tasks are the ones you should "delegate." Delegate those unimportant activities or drop them altogether which brings us to the letter "E."
"E" means "eliminate them whenever possible." Eliminate every single unnecessary activity you possibly can to free up your time.

---

[9] The below article first appeared in my newsletter: fabman's Financial Freedom Newsletter. I hope you enjoy it and if you haven't joined yet, what are you waiting for! To subscribe, just send me a note: fabman@fabmansecrets.com

3. Eliminate Tasks
Yes, I know this is included in item #2, but I'm serious. You should evaluate your list often and figure out what you can eliminate. Don't overload yourself or get involved in too many side projects. Your time is too valuable to be spent on items that you can eliminate or delegate. Speaking of delegating…

4. Delegate
You should be constantly asking yourself "Who else can do this task?" This was definitely a hard one for me to learn because I'm a bit of a perfectionist at times, but once I learned to delegate, I found that I could handle more projects and I was less stressed.

5. Collaborate
Not the delegating type? How about collaborating on projects? When you work together with someone you get more done and in most cases, the results are better than you could have achieved on your own.

6. Learn to Say NO
Let's face it, we're all overworked and we have too much to do. If you let your boss or coworkers give you more and more work, you'll never get anything done and you'll soon be sitting in the "burnout" corner pining for your next vacation. The cure is to learn how to say NO. Hey, I'm a corporate ladder climber myself and I've found that you can say no sometimes and people won't look at you like you have two heads.

Some advice on saying NO:
  - Don't say no immediately. This will give the impression that you've thought about it and determined you can't do it.
  - If your "no" is not accepted, you could inform the individual that you really don't think you can get the assignment done on time.
  - If that doesn't work, you could also ask them to take an assignment or two away from you.
  - If that doesn't work, you could ask them to work on the project together.

7. Focus on Major Tasks
So now you have a list of tasks that you pared down and prioritized. Now ask yourself, **"What's the best use of my time and energy right now?"** Get working on those "A" tasks right away because they're the ones that will give you the most "bang for the buck." Most people focus on the low-priority items and never get around to the truly important tasks. When you focus on the important tasks, you get more done. It might take some time to get into the habit of doing the important (read: sometimes unpleasant) stuff first, but you'll get used to it.

8. Break Down those Big Tasks

Sometimes tasks on your list will seem daunting and you'll become overwhelmed at the mere site of the task on your To Do list. Don't avoid doing the important stuff. That's a recipe for disaster. Break down those big overwhelming tasks into smaller, more manageable tasks and then begin working on the new bit-sized tasks.

9. Do One Thing at a Time

Focus Danielson.[10] You must learn to focus on one task and one task only. When you avoid checking your email at the same time you're working on that PowerPoint presentation, you'll get more done. Trust me on this one.

10. Set Deadlines

Speaking of time, a sure-fire way of avoiding the procrastination bug is to set deadlines for yourself. When you prioritize your To Do list, you should also be figuring out how much time each task is going to take to complete. Set deadlines that are actually earlier than when the assignment or project is due. For instance, if you have to hand in your weekly report on Friday at 10 a.m., aim to have it done by Thursday at 3 p.m. to give you some extra time if the unforeseen happens.

11. Hour of Power

While we're on the subject of deadlines and time, let's talk about your hour of power. This is simply setting aside an hour each day to get your work done. Yes, I want you to literally block out the same hour on your calendar each day to focus on those priority tasks. If your energy level is at its highest in the evening, schedule your hour for the afternoon and vice versa. Now, let's talk about what to do when your energy is at its low point in the day.

12. Do Routine Items When Your Energy is Low

When my energy is at its lowest, I check my emails, snail mail, and voice mail. Yes all three "mails" are done during my low energy period. These are the mindless tasks that normally don't require much brainpower. Please note that I do check my voice mail and email at the beginning of each day and periodically during the day, in addition to my energy low points.

13. Get Started Early in the Day

I get to work a minimum of a half an hour to an hour earlier than most of my coworkers. I eat my breakfast at work, read my Wall Street Journal, and then get more done in the next 20 to 50 minutes than most people do all morning. Why? It's *not* because I'm a super-worker. It's because I'm less distracted in the morning and my boss isn't there to give me any new work.

---

[10] I hope you get that movie reference.

14. Get Rid of Distractions

Distractions are part of everyone's routines. They are a fact of life, but there are strategies you can use to avoid them. Let your friends know that you can't be bothered every day at 10 a.m.. This is the start of your hour of power and you're trying to get things done. Another tip is to have your phone go directly to voicemail or turn down the sound on your computer so it doesn't "ding" every time you get a new email. I'm sure that if you monitor your surroundings you'll come up with ways to get rid of your distractions, like say for instance cleaning your desk.

15. Get Organized

Clutter doesn't bring out the best in anyone. You're at your desk for most of your waking hours, so why not make the area clean and neat? You'll spend less time looking through stacks of paper for that one page you may or may not have thrown out. Start by setting up a filing system and then start going through the paper on your desk. Throw away what you don't need, put the "in progress" items in a folder, and file the rest. Get yourself an "in" box and an "out" box. Use them wisely. All you should have on your desk is your daily planner, your To Do list, your "in" and "out" boxes, and any file you're currently working on. Yes, staplers and that sort of thing are okay, but not much else.

16. Organize Your Thoughts and Schedule

This ties into the first thing we discussed earlier: Plan the Night Before. You need to have a schedule for how you're going to spend your days. Get a plan, then work that plan. I suggest you get a notebook or planner and take it to every meeting and use it to take notes on assignments. Why carry around the notebook? Because you won't forget anything that was discussed if you're taking notes and when you're in meetings, you can quickly add items to your To Do list.

17. Be Flexible

Getting rid of the clutter and doing things to minimize distractions is a step in the right direction, but you can't completely avoid interruptions. This is why you need to learn how to deal with them when they occur. The good news is that if you're working on those important tasks, you can afford to goof off or take a break during work. In other words, don't schedule work to be done every minute of your day. You need to plan in advance for the unexpected.

18. Include Fun Time in the Mix

We all need to blow off steam and have fun, so why not plan for it? Maybe it's a daily trip to your company store or a walk around the building with a friend. Or a scheduled call to a friend might do it for you. Whatever it is, schedule some fun time and you'll be refreshed and ready to get more done.

19. Stop Being a Perfectionist
Stop obsessing over every little detail and start looking at the big picture and get the most important pieces of your tasks done. I'm not advocating that you become sloppy with your work, but I *am* saying that you don't have to make the borders on your PowerPoint slides look pretty or have your emails perfectly written before you send them. The idea is to get things done. Don't forget that.

20. Organize Your Meetings
If you have a meeting-hungry organization, you definitely have to learn how to organize your meetings. If you're in charge, create an agenda and stick to it. If you're not in charge, ask for an agenda. If you find that meetings you are attending are constantly getting off topic or running over, leave. I'm serious. Stretch the truth and tell them you have another meeting or a conference call to go to. I just say "I've got to go in ten minutes. What do you need from me?" Just because they're not careful with their time doesn't mean they have the right to steal/waste your precious time.

21. Leave Work Early
I'm serious. If you learn to manage your time effectively, you'll find that you can get more accomplished. Don't feel bad about leaving early (or at 5pm sharp) once in a while. You deserve a break. With all you've done lately, you've earned it!

Okay, back to our story…

In Conclusion…
"Any last thoughts?" I asked when we were done.

"Read the book *The 7 Habits of Highly Effective People* by Stephen Covey. It has some great information and ideas that you can use to improve your effectiveness both on the job and in life."

"Got it," I said, writing down the title of the book.

"As always, it's been a pleasure Master David, but I must run. I've got a barbecue that starts in ten minutes."

"By all means, please go," I replied. "I'm just going to finish organizing my notes."

He got up to leave, but stopped. "Say, would you like to come over for some great barbecue?"

"I'd love to," I said, standing up to put my books and binder away.

"Great," he replied. "I'm sure you'll have a good time."

I did have a great time at the barbecue and I met someone who would become a most-valuable asset to my future. This person was the inspiration for helping me start my business, but more on that another day.

Budgeting Your Time - COMMENTS

You must have been surprised to see the subject of managing your time in a book titled The Secrets of Wealth. Hopefully by now you understand why I've included the section. The ability to manage your time allows you to get the most out of your days and accomplish more than everyone else. Mr. Mathers was very passionate and believed strongly that anyone could improve their efficiency both on the job and during their off-hours. He taught me that even managing your money takes time. You'll see soon enough that even the simplest investment plans will require you to invest your time and effort, as well as your money in order to be successful. The better you become at managing your daily activities, the more time you will have to spend on building your wealth and enjoy life.

Budgeting Your Time: As Important as Budgeting Your Money

*One of your greatest assets is simply the time you have left on this planet. Sadly, the majority of people waste their most precious asset because they don't value it. You need to learn to value the time you have and get the most out of your days. You choose whether to spend it in front of the TV three hours a night or in front of a book that will expand your mind. **You choose whether to waste your greatest asset or whether to invest it wisely**. Every day I ask myself if I'm using my time wisely or if I'm wasting it in front of the TV or on the phone excessively or one of the other hundred or so time wasters that kill any wealth-building plan. Until you value your time and your money, you're not going to make the necessary changes (sacrifices) that are necessary to succeed in the Game of Life.*

To find your niche in this world, to increase your knowledge by reading other books, attending seminars, listening to audio tapes, to build a successful business, to invest in real estate, you'll need to find more time in your already crowded schedule. If you cannot find this extra time, you will not succeed in the Game of Life, because improving yourself and investing for your future both take time. You need time to develop the skills and habits that will make you an unstoppable force.

Okay, I'm done. But I'll leave you with some words from the guy who's on those crisp $100 bills you want to have in your pocket.

"The way to wealth, if you desire it, is as plain as the way to market. It depends chiefly on 2 words: Industry and Frugality. That is, **waste neither time nor money, but make the best use of both**."

– Benjamin Franklin

Budgeting Your Time – ACTION PLAN

Reread the Article: Go back and reread the article "21 Things You Must Do to Manage Your Time Better." Are there things in there that you can be doing that you're not? Seriously, go back and reread it with pen in hand. Find out how you can put the ideas and strategies to work for you.

Value Your Time and Yourself: Begin with the end in mind! Know that you'll be making a lot more money in just a few years because you're actively working on becoming more proactive and getting more done on the job.

Change Your Commute: Speaking of valuing your time, if this is possible you'll save yourself hours a week commuting back and forth from work to home. It sounds like a nice-to-have, but it's a must-have if you're going to squeeze more productivity out of your days. Can you move closer to work? Can you come in an hour earlier and leave an hour earlier or vice versa to beat traffic? Think, think, and think some more and find a way!

Do One More Thing: I can't believe I forgot this important idea in the original article I wrote, but **you should always try to do one more thing before you pack up and call it a night**. Scan through your InBox or look at your "to do" list. Is there something that you can quickly and I mean quickly complete? If the answer is yes, get it done. If you do this every night you'll have completed an extra 200 tasks over the course of a year. Powerful tip indeed!

Come Up with Your Own Stuff: Don't just use my ideas. Come up with your own! Always be on the lookout for ways to save time (and money). Try and learn how to do things more efficient with your work. Ask yourself, "how can I do this with the same level of quality, but faster."

So now you've learned how to budget your time and money. Remember to not focus solely on budgeting your money because your time is one of the most important assets you have in life.

> "How you spend your time is more important than how you spend your money. **Money mistakes can be corrected, but time is gone forever.**"
> — David B. Norris

"The second vice is lying, the first is running in debt."
- Benjamin Franklin, *The Way to Wealth*

Secret #4:
GET OUT OF BAD DEBT NOW!

"You cannot enjoy life if you are addicted to consumption and the use of credit."
— Thomas J. Stanley, Ph.D., Author,
The Millionaire Mind

Chapter 9

Secret #4: GET OUT OF (bad) DEBT NOW

The average college student leaves school with over
$3,000 in credit card debt and several thousand dollars in
school loans. The majority of them will be in debt until the
day they die!

The Biggest Financial Mistake

My last lesson was such an eye-opener for me that I was wondering what was coming next as I pulled into the library parking lot. It was a beautiful Saturday morning, so there was hardly anyone inside the library except for Mr. Mathers who was at our customary table.

"Morning Mr. Mathers," I said as I sat down.

He looked up from the newspaper. "Morning to you too David. Are you ready for another important lesson?" he asked.

"As long as it's a good one, count me in," I replied, pulling my binder from my backpack.

"Today's lesson is important alright. It has to do with one of the biggest financial mistakes people make in their lives: getting into debt. Having easy access to what they think is cheap money in the form of credit cards and home equity lines of credit, most consumers are tricked into believing that they don't have to save for rainy days. So they spend, spend, spend, and have little to show for it. **Getting into bad debt is probably the worst financial mistake someone can make**."

"So how much debt is going overboard?" I asked.

Your Debt-to-Income Ratio: How Much is Too Much?

"It all depends on what stage of life you're in, but there is a rule of thumb that banks use to determine what size mortgage someone can carry. You need to add up all your monthly payments for your car, student, credit cards, mortgage, and other loans. Then divide this amount by the amount you make each month in pay. This will give you what's called a 'debt ratio' or the ratio of your debt-to-income."

"So if I have $300 a month in reoccurring debt payments and I make $1,000 a month, my debt ratio is 30%?" I asked.

"That's right. Three hundred divided by a thousand is 30%."

"Is there an optimal debt-to-income ratio I should shoot for?" I asked.

The Perfect Level of Debt

"I get that question a lot. Most lenders have a rule of thumb when they evaluate you for a loan. They want your mortgage payments and all other loan obligations to be under 36% of your total gross income. In reality, there really isn't a *perfect* level per se, but I think as long as you're below the 36% mark you're in decent shape. **I personally like to see a debt-to-income ratio** *well under* **30%.** Further more, I think if your debt doesn't preclude you from creating an Emergency Fund, negatively impact your cash flow so you can't invest for your future, or keep you up at night, you're probably okay."

Not All Debt is Created Equal

"So you're saying that all debt is a bad thing and I should avoid it, right? Get down to zero debt or something?" I asked.

"No, that's not what I'm saying. **I'm not a 'debt-free monger'** because I know that having debt is not *necessarily* a bad thing. After all, some of the greatest wealth builders of all time took on huge debt to get rich. **Debt is a bad thing when people start spending beyond their means and buying things that; don't provide any financial benefits, are consumed immediately, or are not income-producing assets**. In short, people who take on bad debt buy depreciating assets instead."

"'Depreciating assets'? What are those?" I asked.

"**Depreciating assets** are things you buy that are immediately worth less the moment you buy them or that go down in value over time. Depreciating assets don't put cash in your pocket and they cost money to maintain. The trick to getting ahead in life is to limit your purchases of assets that don't add value to your net worth, let alone subtract from them through reoccurring expenses."

Good Debt vs. Bad Debt

"But let's back up a minute. Essentially there are two kinds of debt: good debt and bad debt. Bad debt will put you in a hole that can sometimes take years to come out of, while good debt can help build your fortune and lead you down the path to Financial Freedom."

"So how do you tell the difference?"

"According to Robert Kiyosaki, author of the best-selling Rich Dad™ series of books, **good debt puts money in your pocket every month, while bad debt takes money out of your pocket every month.** I like to say that **good debt feeds you, while bad debt bleeds you.**"

"Can you go over what you would good debt versus bad debt?"

"Sure I can David. Here goes:

Good Debt
- **A Mortgage**: Owning a home is better than renting 9 times out of 10 in my book. While this "asset" will be gaining in value thanks to appreciation and while you're paying off your loan you're gaining valuable equity in your home, it still costs money to support.[11]
- **Student Loans**: Your education is an investment in yourself. A degree will increase your earning power the moment you graduate college or get your masters degree. Just realize that there are no guarantees in life and you might be stuck with a mountain of loans and a low-paying job.
- **Business Loans**: A business loan can be used to help grow your business and so on, but just be careful to not borrow too much money. Make sure you have the ability to pay back the loan on time through the income generated from the business.

Bad Debt
- **Credit Cards**: This type of debt is one of the most expensive around thanks to the high interest rates and low minimum payments, which lull you into thinking that you don't owe that much. That interest compounds and soon you're drowning in debt.
- **Cash Advances**: Cash advances on your credit card carry a higher interest rate than regular purchases, plus you have to pay cash advance fees.
- **Margin Accounts**: We haven't discussed investing and buying securities yet, but margin is when you borrow money from your broker to buy stocks. The interest rate is relatively low, but buying on margin is not a strategy for the long-term investor.
- **Holiday and/or Vacation Debt**: Yes you deserve a vacation, but you deserve one that you can afford. Yes you should give gifts to the people you love, but you shouldn't go overboard.

Neither Good, Nor Bad Debt
- **Car Loans**: A car loan is considered bad debt if you pay too much for your car, put too little down, and carry a large monthly payment.
- **Home Equity Loans**: These loans are good if you use them to pay off higher-interest rate loans or your child's education. It can be considered bad debt if you use the line to buy more depreciating assets or vacations, etc.

---

[11] Be careful with how you view your home. Some people get into trouble when they take on too much debt by buying a house that's 'too big' for them to handle. A house may be considered an asset by accounting standards, but a mortgage costs you money each month. The bigger the house and the bigger the mortgage, the less money you'll have to invest for your future. Plus you have the cost of taxes, insurance, fuel, electricity, and so on. More on this subject later.

Credit Cards
How Do You Use Your Credit Cards?

"Let's talk about credit cards because they're the reason that many people will never achieve Financial Freedom. If you think about it, credit cards are used for one of three ways; convenience, emergencies or indulgence. By **Convenience** I mean when you have the money to pay for an item but don't want to carry the cash. I don't have to carry around a lot of cash to pay for my business and personal expenses and the statements make it easy for me to track my purchases for tax purposes. Credit cards are also great for **Emergencies**. Major car repairs, towing bills, or any other large unforeseen expense falls into this category."

"Shouldn't you have an Emergency Fund for those expenses?"

"Yes, an Emergency Fund should cover them, but sometimes these expenses are more than the 3 to 6 months of living expenses you set aside," he replied. "In addition, sometimes you can't make it to the bank to get at your money, so that's why you use a credit card."

"Oh. I understand," I said.

"And lastly, there's the category that *most* expenses fall under: **Indulgence**. This is when you don't have the money and don't really need the item you're purchasing. If you're using your credit cards to buy things like clothes, CDs, dinners, and the like, then the extra debt you're racking up every month isn't going to help you with your goal of acquiring wealth."

"How can my credit cards impact my goal of being rich?" I asked.

"The problem is that many people buy things they cannot afford today, but they carry a balance, pay the minimum for years, and never pay off their balances. In short, they fall into the Credit Card Minimum Trap."

"The what?" I asked.

"The Credit Card Minimum Trap."

The Credit Card Minimum Trap

Minimum Payments = Maximum Pain

"Credit card companies and other lending institutions aren't stupid. They know that consumers for the most part don't realize how much money they're throwing away by carrying balances on their credit cards. They also realize that the average person is not going to pay off their debt immediately, but rather get that false sense of wealth and start buying more useless goods just because they can afford a low monthly payment. Then they fall victim to negative compounding."

"'Negative compounding'? What's that?"

"It's the reason you'll never be rich if you're not careful," he replied.

Negative Compounding

"Every time you whip out your credit card to pay for something, you're stealing from your future in order to live the life you want in the present. That stuff you buy on credit cards or through a home equity line of credit doesn't just sit there until you pay off the balance. Those dollars you borrowed grow and grow thanks to interest. Do you remember how compounding interest caused a dollar a day to grow to a million bucks after 56 years?"

"Who could forget," I said.

"Well think of it this way. When you owe money, that money is being charged interest and if you don't pay it off the interest you're accruing gets charged interest and so on and so on. **The interest is compounding, only working *against* you**. All of the sudden that $2,000 balance grows to $6,000 if you're not careful. Think of it this way: **Every dollar you spend on credit today cannot be invested for your future**. **Instead, that dollar is working against you**. So what's it going to be David? Do you want your money working *for* you or *against* you?"

"For me," I replied.

Getting the Best Return

"Well, people come to me all the time and say that they don't want to pay down their debt with their extra money because they're missing out on the stock market or some other investment. They don't understand that credit cards often charge upwards of 20% on balances. **When you pay down those cards, you're getting a guaranteed 20% return on your money.** You see David, if you have $2,000 in credit card bills and you have $2,000 in cash ready to be invested, it's better to pay down your debt. Why? Because if your card has an annual interest rate of 20%, you have to get at least a 13% return on your investment *after* taxes just to break even. And you've probably read that the stock market over the long run has returned just a shade over 11%. So you have to outperform or do better than the stock market has done over the last 80 years just to break even. Can you see the losing proposition yet?"

"You've sold me. I just never looked at it that way before," I said.

7-Step Credit Card (and Other Bad Debt) Repayment Strategy

"So how can I get out from under my credit card debt?" I asked.

"Great question. Here's what you need to do:

Step 1: Get Committed to Being Debt FREE

"The first step in the process is to make the commitment to being debt-free. Don't skip this step and think of it as some wishy-washy step some guru created. You MUST make an emotional commitment to yourself that you MUST absolutely get out of bad debt. Make it a priority in your life. If you don't, you'll never get to step #2."

Step 2: STOP SPENDING

"Did you ever see the I Love Lucy™ episode where Lucy is in a chocolate factory and she falls behind on the line and all of the sudden she's eating the chocolate and stuffing them down her shirt to keep up?" he asked.

"Yeah, I remember the episode. The chocolate on the assembly line keeps coming and coming."

"That's what happens to most people with their credit cards. They try to pay them down, but more expenses and charges keep coming. They pay $100 a month, but spend $200. They never get ahead and…"

"The chocolate keeps coming," I said.

"With interest!" he added. "So step #2 in the Credit Card Payment Strategy is to Stop Spending. Pay cash or use a debit card and you'll see how easy it is to say no to that 50% off shirt or pants that you just *have* to have."

Step 3: Know What You Owe?

"Step #3 involves figuring out what you owe and how much you're paying in interest. Do me a favor an pull out your **Debt Management Grid** from last week and let's take a look at what you have."

I did as I was told and handed him the Grid.

"I hope seeing all your debts laid out in front of you and the total amount outstanding shook you up a bit," he said.

"It definitely did and I still have paying down my debt as my number one priority."

"Good. Creating a debt repayment plan is probably one of the most important steps to Financial Freedom. Once you've created your plan and it's well under way, you'll be able to start investing and doing all the other stuff you can't wait to do in life. But until your debt is under control, it will control you! Now let's go over your grid."

He studied the grid for a few moments, then commented, "Okay good. It looks like you've written out and **arranged your debts from highest to lowest interest rates**."

Figure 9.1 - DEBT MANAGEMENT GRID

YOUR DEBT MANAGEMENT GRID				
Creditor	Outstanding Balance	Interest Rate	Monthly Minimum	Payment Amount
Non-Deductible Interest				
Subtotals				
Deductible Interest				
Subtotals				

Step 4: Lower Your Rates and/or Consolidate Your Balances

"Step #4 involves consolidating your debt. Call up each of your credit card companies and ask about their **balance transfer programs**. Most credit card companies allow you to transfer debt from other cards to their card with the added benefit of a low APR for a set amount of time. **What you're looking for is the lowest rate and the longest period for the balance transfer**. Usually credit card companies will extend you the special rate for six months, but I have come across some ads where they give you up to the time it takes you to repay the entire balance."

"Why would they do that?" I asked.

"Because if they extend a rate to you and it takes you a while to pay back, they keep your balances on their books and they accrue interest while you take your sweet time to pay them back. In the mean time they're hoping you use the card and they hit you with the normal

APR, often over 20% on purchases. Then when you pay them your monthly minimum, they apply that money toward the balance transfer amount with the low interest rate."

"Oh, I get it. Until I pay down the balance on the lower interest rate, they're busy collecting a lot of interest on the debt with the highest interest rate. Then if I buy something with the card, it gets added to the high rate balances. Pretty sneaky."

"But perfectly legal if they explain it in that mouse print legal disclaimer they give you. But to make things worse, most folks get lured by the low APR and end up paying more interest because they keep on spending money they don't have. It's truly sad. But enough on that, let's finish up this step. You need to make sure they're not charging you too much to transfer the money to the card. If they're going to charge you $10 or $25 each time you make a balance transfer, then you're defeating the purpose of consolidating your debt, namely saving money. See if you can negotiate the amount down or eliminate it all together. It doesn't hurt to ask. Also, don't get suckered by an offer or sales pitch if they tell you that your rate will be 5% or 6% over prime. People mistakenly think that the 5% or 6% quoted is the rate they will pay, but its not. It means that you're paying 5% or 6% ABOVE the prime lending rate. Make sure when you transfer balances that you're quoted an absolute rate."

Avoid the Yo-Yo

"Just remember that after the transfer period, usually six months, your rate goes back up. Also, **be careful not to get scammed by those 'convenience' checks** that you'll receive from time to time. They are NOT the same as balance transfers. Often there will be a 2% cash advance fee associated with them and the interest rate may be the same as the one you're currently being charged or more."

Step 5: Pay Them Off Wisely

**Pay the <u>Minimum</u> on the LOWEST rate cards,
then put all the rest of your "Debt Repayment Funds"
against the HIGHEST interest rate card**

"On to step #5. Here's the plan for paying down your credit cards if you can't pay them off in one shot. **Always pay off the highest interest rate cards first**. You're going to pay the **minimum amount on your lowest rate cards** and as **much money as you can afford or have decided to allot to the card with the highest interest rate**. This insures that the total interest that will accrue against all the cards is as low as possible. For example, let's say after doing your Debt Repayment Grid you realize that the minimums on your cards is $250. After doing your CASH FLOW CALCULATOR you know you can put $400 toward your credit cards. You would pay the minimum on all your cards except for the highest rate card. On this card you would pay an extra $150 ($400 minus $250). Then when the card is paid off, you need to apply the money you were paying to that credit card and pay off your next victim, which would be the card with the highest interest rate. Just subtract your new monthly minimums, say $220 from the $400 amount and see that you now have $180 ($400 minus $220) extra to put against that high rate card."

"Easy enough. I just put all extra money against the highest rate card. What if two cards offer the same rate?" I asked.

"Pay off the card with the *smaller* balance first," he replied.

Other Methods Need Not Apply

"There are other methods you can use to pay down debt, things like paying the card off with the lowest outstanding balance first or paying the card with the lowest minimum off first or taking the outstanding balance and dividing it by the minimum to figure out which one to pay off first. I understand the methodologies of all those and the rationale, some recommend the system because it makes you feel better to pay off a card or two faster, but all I care about is cold hard cash. That is cash in my pocket. Bar none, the method of paying off the highest rate card first saves you the most money. Period. End of story."

"So if the other methods aren't smart financially, why are they recommending those methods?"

"To feel good inside. **If you want the psychological benefit of paying off a card as soon as possible, go after the card with the smallest balance.** This is what's called the **snowball method**. You'll feel good knowing you paid off one card, but I'd rather have more money in the bank. I'll feel good when **all** the cards are paid off."

A Little Extra Goes a Long Way

"Speaking of psychology, some people stare at their balances and get emotional and feel disempowered. I say you get mad, not at yourself, but at your credit cards. Get so mad that you stop spending and make it a priority to pay them off."

"But what if you have a lot of debt and only a few extra dollars to put toward the debt?" I asked.

"That's fine David. As long as you're not adding to the debt, you'll find yourself rapidly paying them off. Better yet, if you can find a few extra dollars a month, it'll go a long way. Check this out," he said handing me the below chart:

Figure 9.2 - A Few Extra Dollars Makes a Difference	
How long would it take to pay off the entire balance ($2,000) on a card charging 18% interest if you only make the minimum payments of 2% (or $10, whichever is larger) of the balance?	
Paying just the minimum each month Answer: 370 months or 30.8 years	$4,931.15 in interest paid
Paying $50/month Answer: 62 months or 5.2 years	$1,077.25 in interest paid
Paying $75/month Answer: 35 months or 2.9 years	$573.36 in interest paid

"Wow! All that money saved just for paying $75 a month instead of the minimum? That's unbelievable!"

"No, it's just being smart with your money. You might not have caught this, but the minimum payment of 2% on the credit card is $40 a month to start. **Adding just $10 a month to your payment saves you close to $4,000 in interest payments.** All for a lousy ten bucks. So the moral of the story is, don't add to your debt, get smart about paying it off the right way, and excluding your mortgage **you can easily be debt free in three to five years** if you want it bad enough. Just stop adding to your debt and using the **High Interest Rate Snowball Method** to your advantage."

Emergency Fund vs. Paying Down Your Debt

"One question for you," I said. "We talked about setting up an Emergency Fund during our talk on the second Secret of Wealth. What if we're putting all our excess money toward the Emergency Fund and don't have any extra money to pay down debt?"

"The answer depends on where you are in life, your tolerance for risk, and your goals. In principle it's better to pay down your high interest debt than to put that money anywhere else, but you should have a cash cushion to fall back on. I've read where some financial planners suggest paying off your debt completely before creating an Emergency Fund."

"But what if you had an emergency and needed some cash?"

"They suggest that you use your credit card for the emergency."

"Doesn't that defeat the purpose?" I asked.

"Which is why I tell my students to pay themselves first and then put the rest of their cash toward their debts. As I said last week, you can do what Dave Ramsey, author of *Financial Peace Revisited* suggests, which is to save at least $1,000, then pay down your debt."

"What if you have so much debt that the minimum payments equals your take home pay?"

"Then you're in deep doodoo and need to take drastic measures. We'll get to that in a second, but before we do, I want to make sure you understand the importance of paying yourself first. I say you continue to pay yourself first, then put the rest of your free cash toward paying down your debt. You need a safety cushion in life and if you have an emergency you can tap your Emergency Fund. That fund gives you piece of mind and the knowledge that if you wanted to, you could put the money toward your debt. You'll pay a little more in interest along the way if you put cash in your Emergency Fund and not toward your debts, but you get the psychological benefit of seeing your bank account growing and knowing that you're on the right track to Financial Freedom. Okay, on to step #6."

Step 6: Only Keep (Use) the Best Cards

"Step #6 is to figure out which cards are best to keep and which ones are best put on ice. You should make sure that the cards have a rewards or 'miles' program, as well as have the lowest interest rates around. Money magazine prints a list of the credit cards offering the best rates every month. You can also go to www.bankrate.com for information on the best cards."

"You said cards. How many credit cards should I have?"

"It depends really. For you I would suggest two plus a debit card."

"What about actually cutting up your cards and canceling them?"

Having No Debt Can Actually Hurt You

"Most people think incorrectly that it's smart to cut up their credit cards and never having any loans of any kind."

"Uh and just why would that be a bad thing?" I inquired.

"I don't want you to think I'm advocating going on spending sprees and racking up credit card debt. But you do need a credit card for emergencies and your other loans because they build your credit history. **When you cut up your cards, you're losing your credit history. Cutting up your credit cards could actually LOWER your credit score.** I suggest people just lock them away someplace instead or at least cancel the ones that you've had for the *shortest* period of time and keep the ones with the longest credit history."

Step 7: Take Drastic Measures if Necessary

"The six steps we've discussed should get you on your way to reducing your financial burdens, but for some people they may not be enough. They might have to take drastic measures, which is Step #7."

Use Savings if Necessary

"If you have too much debt, you may consider using some of your savings to pay off your debt. I'm not suggesting that you completely erase your credit card debt and wipe out your Emergency Fund. I'm just saying that if you have some extra cash, investing it in your debt would give you one of the best guaranteed returns around."

Friends and Family

"You can also ask friends or family members for help. Just realize that the last thing you want to do is damage a relationship over money. If you ever owe a family member or friend money, don't take advantage of the relationship and fail to pay them back. Create a payment schedule with an agreed upon interest rate and stick to the schedule. Pay earlier than agreed to if you can."

Negotiate with Your Creditors

"Call up your creditors and tell them your financial situation. Your goal is to renegotiate the terms of your loan. Ask for a new payment schedule that either extends the loan period, lowers the interest rate, or both. It's in their best interest to work with you to repay your debts because they don't want to have to deal with the hassle of going through a collections agency and perhaps not getting paid at all."

Borrowing from Yourself

"You can also borrow money from yourself," he said.

"How can you do that?" I asked.

"From your 401(k), 403(b) plan, or whole life insurance plan. Most employers will let you borrow up to 50% of your 401(k)'s value or $50,000; whichever is the lesser amount. The cost of the loan varies by employer and the terms depend on the reason you're borrowing. If the loan is for a home, you can usually get a 20-25 year term, but if it's something else, usually you have 5-10 years to pay back the money. The rates are very low for these loans, usually only a point or two above the prime rate. Also, every dollar in interest you pay goes directly into your 401(k) account, but I'll talk to you about why **this option is not exactly the smartest thing to do** in two weeks time."

Rolling Your Debt into Your Home

"If you're going to owe money, you might as well get a tax benefit from it. A home equity loan is a loan against the equity in your house. You can also get a home equity line of credit which is kind of like a credit card, but your home is on the line if you fail to repay the loan."

"So how does the line of credit or loan work?" I asked.

"You borrow against a line of credit at a low rate, say 7% interest, then pay off your credit cards that are charging you 18% to 24% interest."

"So you cut your interest payment in half."

"That's right, but the savings doesn't stop there. **Since most homeowners can deduct the interest they're paying on the loan, the actual effective interest rate is much lower**. If you're in the 25% tax bracket, that 7% interest rate has an effective rate of 5.25%."

"Wow, that's an awesome rate."

"Yes, but watch out because people often pay off their credit cards, but get into trouble all over again by shopping, shopping, and shopping. So now not only do they have their home equity loan to pay off, but they have their credit card debt as well. The only difference is that if you don't make your payments, your bank may take your house."

Contact a Credit Counselor

"If your debts are spiraling out of control and the above steps have not worked, you may need some outside advice from a debt counselor. Non-profit organizations like the Consumer Credit Counseling Service (www.cccsintl.org) or MyVesta.org (www.myvesta.org) can help you consolidate your debt and manage your payments. The cost is usually free, except for a nominal donation they might ask you to make. You'll work with a credit counselor who will help you determine if you should use a type of debt management program or not."

"So what do these counselors do?"

"Everything from teaching you the basics of good credit management to negotiating with your creditors for lower monthly payments or interest rates. In most cases these services can help lower your payments and if you've enrolled in one of their programs, all you have to do is make one payment to them and they will make your payments to your creditors for you"

"How can they help lower your payments?"

"Since credit counselors have working relationships with almost every creditor out there, they'll probably make more progress than you could in getting balances consolidated and rates lowered. They may also be able to get some of your penalties or overdue interest forgiven by your creditors."

"Why are creditors so willing to cut you a deal?"

"Because most creditors don't want you filing bankruptcy."

"Credit counseling sounds like a good deal to me."

"It can be since using a service like this will give you peace of mind, but your participation in the program *might* also appear on your credit report. It won't hurt your credit rating, but it can leave an indirect mark because your assets are frozen and it can be noted that you have used the service. If you go this route you should ask up front whether using their services will affect your credit rating."

"Got it," I said. "Hopefully I won't have to use this information."

"I hope you don't either," he said.

Bankruptcy

"David, you have an obligation to repay all of your debts, but sometimes there comes a time in one's life when it becomes impossible. Whatever the reason for your money problems, filing for bankruptcy is the last resort. Depending on what type of bankruptcy is filed, you may be able to shelter yourself from creditors and can, as the cliché goes, 'start to put the pieces of your life back together.'"

"What are the different types of bankruptcies?" I asked.

"There are two types of personal bankruptcy: Chapter 7 and Chapter 13. With Chapter 7, you are released from paying most of your debts except you'll have to continue paying child support, alimony, student loans, taxes, and a couple others. You might have to also surrender your property in order to pay for your debts. With Chapter 13, you get to keep your property but you essentially give up control of your finances to the court."

"So they don't have to pay back all the money they owe? Sounds like a good deal to me," I said.

"Don't be fooled. Like I said, they still have to pay any child support, taxes, student loans, and alimony. In order to pay back these debts they may be required to give up some personal property. On top of that, perhaps even more destructive is the effect on your credit rating. People who file for bankruptcy will have the information noted on their file for 10 years and the fact that they filed for bankruptcy will in all likelihood seriously hinder their credit until the bankruptcy information is removed from their file."

"So they might have a tough time getting a loan for a car or a house 10 years after they filed for bankruptcy?"

"Exactly. What's worse is that they may not be able to do anything in life that requires good credit."

Side Note: Know Your Rights

The Federal Fair Credit Reporting Act and the Federal Debt Collection Practice Act were created to stop credit card companies from harassing you if you're behind in your payments. You need to know your rights and the best place to go is www.ftc.gov for more information regarding what you can do to stop the harassment.

Student Loans

"Thank you for the sobering discussion," I said. "What about paying down other loans like my school and car loans, or mortgage?"

"Some people advocate paying down your student loans, but I'm not a big advocate of the idea of paying down this type of debt until you've paid off your credit cards and car loan."

"How come?"

"Because the interest rates charged for government-backed student loans are probably the lowest you'll find around, plus the interest is deductible, which means you're allowed to deduct the interest you've paid on your student loans when you file your tax return."

Consolidate Your Loans and Save

"Speaking of student loans, when you consolidate your student loans, you get a lower rate than you're currently paying in most cases. Once you've consolidated, you should put your loan on autopilot by having your loan payments automatically debited from your bank account. Aside from helping out your credit rating by always paying your bills on time, under some programs you might qualify for a reduced rate if you've paid on time for more than two to four years. Plus some lenders will reduce your rate a ¼ of a point because you've signed up for automatic payments."

"That is a great deal," I commented.

Mortgages

"As for mortgages, if you prepay some money each month, then you'll shave a couple of years off the term of your loan, as well as save a bundle in interest. For example, if you had a loan for $100,000 for 30 years at an 8% rate, and paid an extra $100 a month, you'd save over $62,000 in interest and pay the loan off in 21 years."

"You save $62,000 just by paying an extra $100 a month?"

"Yep, which is why a lot of homeowners focus on prepaying their mortgage instead of investing. This *might not* be the best use of your extra cash, but we'll get to that issue in a couple of weeks as well."

7-Step Credit Card (and Other Bad Debt) Repayment Strategy

"To recap the steps, you have to:

Step 1: Get Committed to Being Debt FREE

Step 2: STOP SPENDING

Step 3: Know What You Owe?

Step 4: Lower Your Rates and/or Consolidate Your Balances

Step 5: Pay Them Off Wisely

Step 6: Only Keep (Use) the Best Cards

Step 7: Take Drastic Measures if Necessary

Improving Your Credit Rating

"Bad credit makes life harder than it needs to be," he said. "It makes it harder to buy a car, get a mortgage, or even buy a TV on credit. That's why it's important to improve your credit rating."

"Credit rating. What's that?"

What's Your Score?

"Your credit rating or your '**FICO score**' is used by creditors to determine if you're creditworthy. FICO is calculated by software from Fair Isaac & Co and they're pretty much the only game in town. In short, **a credit score measures the likelihood that you'll pay back the money you owe**. The number is calculated based on the information contained in your credit report and the higher the score the better. Your FICO score is very critical to the amount of money you can borrow and what rate lenders are going to offer you."

"So exactly how is it calculated?" I asked.

"The number is the result of some mathematical formula that I can't even begin to explain, but the formula is based on the following things:

Figure 9.3 – FICO Factors

Weighting	Weighting of factors in your FICO score
30%	Amounts owed (balance to credit limit ratio)
35%	Your payment history
15%	Length of your credit history
10%	Type of credit use
10%	New credit

Source: www.myfico.com

What's a Good Score?

"Okay, I understand how important it is, but what's a good score? Is it like the SATs or something?" I asked.

"The high goes a little past the 800 mark, but here's a printout from www.myFICO.com that has current rates. I pulled it for someone looking for a $200,000 30-yr fixed rate mortgage. As you can see, **you're going to pay a lot for <u>not</u> having a good credit score.**"

Figure 9.4 – Your FICO Score Makes a Difference

FICO Score	APR	Monthly Payment	Total Interest Paid
720-850	5.559%	$1,143	$211,477
700-719	5.684%	$1,159	$217,159
675-699	6.221%	$1,228	$241,959
620-674	7.371%	$1,381	$297,090
560-619	8.226%	$1,499	$339,698
500-559	8.719%	$1,569	$364,831

Source: myFICO.com 3/19/03

"Holy cow. That's a big difference! Can you tell me more about my credit report?" I asked.

"Sure. Let's do it," he replied.

Step 1: Get a Copy of Your Credit Report

"Your credit report is kind of like a report card on how well you've managed your finances. You can get your credit report from either of the three major credit-reporting agencies for as little as $8, but **if you've been recently turned down for credit you're entitled to a free credit report**. Regardless, you should still purchase all three reports."

"Why?" I asked.

"Because all the bureaus won't have the same information since some of your credit card companies or creditors might not report your information to all three agencies. Secondly, most mortgage lenders are going to pull all three of your scores and select the middle score, not the average score to figure out if they should lend you money."

"So how do I get my FICO score?"

"Equifax is the only one that allows you to buy your FICO score or you can just go to myFICO.com to purchase your score. For $34.95, Myvesta.org will provide credit reports from all three bureaus. Go to www.myvesta.org or call their toll free number (1-800-698-3782)."

The three bureaus are:

Experian (formerly TRW)
P.O. Box 9600
Allen, Texas 75013
800-311-4769
www.experian.com

Trans Union Corporation
P.O. Box 1000
Chester, Pa. 19022
800-888-4213
www.tuc.com

Equifax Information Service Center
P.O. Box 105873
Atlanta, GA 30348
800/685-1111
www.equifax.com

Step 2: What Does it Say?
Just a few of the items listed on your credit report:
- Who you are
- Your current address
- Social Security number and date of birth
- Employment history
- Your income
- Whether you've had a bankruptcy in the past 10 years
- If you have any judgments against you
- If you have any leans against your assets
- Your credit history

"Your report will show the outstanding balances of your loans and credit cards and how you've paid your accounts over the years. If you have late payments, the information will be lumped into one of several categories. There's a '30-day late,' 60-day late,' and '90+ day late' category. What's the big deal about paying late? Well, would you lend money to someone who has a history of paying other people late?"

"No," I said, shaking my head.

"Banks aren't going to either. They'd rather loan their money to someone who pays on time and has a good credit rating."

"So can anyone get my report?" I asked.

"Not everyone David. Only people with whom you've essentially done business with can get it. People like landlords, credit card companies, and bank loan officers."

Step 3: Is it Accurate? If Not, Fix it Immediately

"The next step is to check your report thoroughly to make sure there aren't any mistakes."

"What kind of mistakes?"

"You want to make sure that your name, address, and other contact information is current. Other things like your Social Security number, marital status, birthday, and payment record should be checked as well. It's critical to make sure that all the accounts listed are correct and that someone hasn't stolen your identity and opened any accounts. If there is are errors or mistakes, then you should contact the credit department of the applicable company immediately. Have them research the error and fix the problem. Then once the problem has been fixed, send a note to each of the three credit bureaus. You should go through this process every year or at minimum, you should review your reports several months before you apply for a loan. Why? Because there are probably going to be mistakes on one or all of the reports. Since it can take a while to fix mistakes, the sooner you start, the better."

How to Improve Your Score

"The good news is that it's not hard to improve a low score. Here are some quick things to do."

1. Reduce your outstanding debt balances: Your outstanding debt shouldn't be more than 75% of your total credit limit on your credit cards. This might mean dipping into your savings to pay down some debts so you owe less than 75% of what you can borrow.

2. Don't take out any new credit: Sounds simple, but you'd be surprised to see how many people mess this up. Don't apply for *any* and I mean any new credit, including credit cards with teaser rates for at least six months before you apply for your mortgage or major loan.

3. Don't cancel any of your credit card accounts: Don't cancel any cards right before applying for their loan. Closing your accounts will cause your debt-to-limit ratio to rise. If you feel the need to cancel a card, hang onto your oldest ones (the ones you've had for the longest time) and cancel those you took out recently.

4. Pay your bills on time: It might be that you're applying for a mortgage in the next few months or the next year, but make sure that you pay your bills on time. A missed payment in the past few months is going to lower your credit score and draw the eye of your lender.

Don't Forget to Celebrate

"Of course things like having a steady paycheck from the same employer for the past few years in a row, your overall employment history, and your list of assets will help matters when applying for a loan, but you should still work on the areas we just covered."

"So once my bad debt is paid off, then what do I do?" I asked.

"Simple," he responded. "You throw a party to celebrate being debt-free. You have to celebrate your little victories. You don't do it by blowing a wad of cash on an expensive dinner, but you should celebrate each time a credit card is repaid. **Frame that last statement and hang it on the wall as a reminder of how far you've come.**"

He looked at his watch, then up at me. "I think we're done Mr. David. Do you have any questions?"

"I think my head hurts," I said rubbing my temples.

He laughed. "I know we've covered a lot, but I saw that you were taking good notes. The bottom line is that **you can either get rich using debt or you can go to the poorhouse because of debt**. Use it wisely and you'll find yourself in an elite circle of wealth-builders."

"Again, thank you so much for helping me Mr. Mathers."

"Please David, no thanks just yet. Just go and apply what we discussed and that will be thanks enough."

With that he turned and walked toward the door. I was left staring at my Debt Repayment Grid. It took me only ten minutes to figure out my repayment strategy. Despite my small salary, I was debt-free within three years thanks to applying the fourth Secret of Wealth.

Get Out of (bad) Debt - COMMENTS

Everyone always wants to know what percentage of their pay they should put aside for debt repayment. They always remark that the secret to getting out of debt should have a set target percentage like the Ten Percent Rule. I always argue that paying down your debt is more of an art than a science with hard fast rules. I will mention that In The Richest Man in Babylon, George Clason recommended that 20% of your income go toward debt reduction. I don't recommend a fixed number because it all depends on how much debt you have, what kind of debt it is (good or bad), and what your goals are (to get out of debt or to build wealth). One more thing...

Where you are today is a direct result of what you did yesterday and in the past. What you will be and have in the future will be a direct result of what you do (or don't do) today. It's up to you to decide if you will take action and create a debt repayment plan. If you're ready, let's do it!

Get out of (bad) Debt: ACTION PLAN

Work with Your Partner: If you're married or have a partner, then this is something you need to work on together. Sit down with each other and go through the ACTION steps I'm going to recommend. Don't place blame, don't fight, just work together, and create a plan of action!

Get Committed and Stop SPENDING!: The first step in your debt repayment plan is to promise and commit to becoming debt-free and the second most important step is to stop adding to your debt. If you have problems doing these steps, it might be that your spending is tied to your self-esteem or feeling of self-worth. Read Secret # 5 and see if your mindset changes.

Go on a Cash Diet: Along the lines of the above, start paying cash for your expenses or use a debit card. When you're forking over your hard-earned cash for the latest gadget, you're going to find it harder and harder to blow your money.

Know What You Owe: Fill in your own **Debt Repayment Grid**. Make sure you place the credit cards and loans in order from highest to lowest interest rate for their respective categories.

Lower Your Rates and/or Consolidate Your Balances: With this list in hand, call up each of your credit card companies and see if they will lower your interest rates or offer you a special balance transfer program. Weigh your options and determine what will give you the lowest interest rate and longest repayment period. Don't forget to include fees for transferring balances and what the rate will go back to when the promotional period is over.

Note: Please be aware of the **Balance Transfer Game**. You don't want to be constantly shifting balances from one card to the next without actually putting a dent in the debts you owe. Every balance transfer costs you money and if you pay late one month, your cards will revert back to the high rate, so be careful.

Find Money: If you've still got some problems with your cash flow after consolidating, see if you can raise some money. Perhaps you can hold a garage sale or sell some of your old stuff on ebay. You'd be amazed how much people would pay for your junk, I mean treasures.

Establish Your Debt Repayment Plan and Goals
- Pay the minimum monthly amount due on all your debts, except for the debt with the highest interest rate.
- Allocate any extra money toward paying down the debt with the highest fixed interest rate first. (Don't forget to put some money toward an Emergency Fund every month as well).
- When you have paid off the debt with the highest interest rate, go after the debt with the next highest interest rate.

As for how long this can take to pay off your loans, just go to my site www.fabmansecrets.com and locate the **Debt Repayment Calculator** that will help you figure out how long it will take to repay your debts. After running the numbers, write your repayment goals down:

I will pay off all my credit cards by: _____

I will pay off my car loan by: _____

I will pay off my student loans by: _____

I will pay off my mortgage by: _____

To Cancel or Not to Cancel: Once you've paid off a few credit cards you'll have to figure out if you should cancel those cards. Remember that having a credit line that is current and has been paid on time can help your credit score. If you do decide to cancel your cards, make sure the three credit-reporting bureaus are notified in writing. After a month or so, double-check to make sure your records have been updated.

Get a Copy of Your Credit Report: Speaking of credit reports, know where you stand with creditors. Getting a copy of your credit report is an eye-opener for most people, because everything is there in black and white.

Fix Any Errors Immediately: If there's an error, send a letter to the creditor or lender and then when it's resolved, notify all three major agencies to correct the problem. Just know that the process can take some time.

Order and Improve Your Credit Score: Get your hands on your FICO score ASAP. If you have a low FICO score, take action immediately. Analyze your outstanding amounts owed and make sure your total balance is below 75% of your credit limit. Make sure you pay on time and don't cancel any cards just yet.

Get Help if You Need it: Sometimes after filling out your Debt Repayment Grid and looking at your total monthly obligations and comparing it to your monthly positive cash flow, you might find yourself in over your head. After exhausting the many ways we talked about reducing your rates and paying off your balances during this Secret, you might look into getting some professional help. Just be careful to choose a good organization that's not going to try and take advantage of you and ruin your credit rating.

Remember Why You're Saving: Whether you have a little debt or a lot, paying it off can be a long and difficult road, but you have to stick with it. Remind yourself why you've stopped your spending ways and are funneling all your extra cash toward paying down those little plastic monsters. Realize that you can become debt-free within 5 years if you want it bad enough. Link your actions today to the freedom you will enjoy later in life and you'll stick with the program. If you're still having problems cutting back on your spending, write yourself a little note and tape it to your credit and debit cards. It should read: **"the less I spend today, the more I'll enjoy tomorrow**."

Be Patient: You didn't accumulate this debt overnight and you're not going to get rid of it quickly either. Just set a realistic timetable for your debt reduction plan and stick with it. As the weeks and months pass, you'll start to see a noticeable difference in the amounts you owe (rapidly declining) and the interest charged each month (going down, down, down).

Celebrate Your Victories: Celebrate your victories. When I finally finished paying off my credit cards, I framed the statement of the last card I paid off. It's a beautiful thing and a powerful reminder of how hard I had to work to pay off that debt.

If you're in debt, making more money isn't going to get you out of debt. You can't get out of debt until you first resolve to stop spending, then commit yourself to getting out of bad debt. Don't wait until your next pay raise or that new job you've been waiting to find. The time to start killing your bad debt it today. Every minute you delay is another dollar in interest that you're accruing. Every day you keep paying the minimum on your bad debts, you'll find yourself deeper and deeper in that hole you keep digging. Please, please, please resolve to do something about your debts today.

If you're having trouble controlling your urge to spend, perhaps this next Secret will help…

"This was the great paradox posed by the material prosperity of the twentieth century: prosperity was conspicuously present, but it was always just out of reach, for nearly **every family defined its standard of living in terms of an income that it *hoped* to achieve rather than the reality of the paycheck**."

- Winifred Wandersee, Historian, writing of 1920s life

Secret #5:
LIVE BELOW
YOUR MEANS

"Most people have it all wrong about wealth in America. Wealth is not the same as income. **If you make a good income each year and spend it all, you are not getting wealthier**. You are just living high. Wealth is what you accumulate, not what you spend. How do you become wealthy? Here, too, most people have it wrong. It is seldom luck or inheritance or advanced degrees or even intelligence that enables people to amass fortunes. Wealth is more often a result of a lifestyle of hard work, perseverance, planning, and, most of all, self-discipline."

    – Thomas J. Stanley, Ph.D., William Danko, Ph.D.,
The Millionaire Next Door

Chapter 10

Secret #5: LIVE BELOW YOUR MEANS –

Choose to Live Simply

We had to start my next lesson a little later than the usual 9 a.m. start. Mr. Mathers had a real estate deal he had to close on, so I slept in that morning. I definitely needed the rest. We were running crazy at work and it was starting to wear me down. Our lesson was supposed to start at 3 p.m., but I decided to go to the library a little early and see if I could find some other good books to read. I finally settled on a book and sat down at our usual table and started reading. At exactly 3 p.m., Mr. Mathers showed up.

Don't Be Satisfied with Saving Ten Percent
"Hey there David," he said as he sat down.

"How did the closing go?" I asked.

"Very good. All the paperwork was in place and I'm the proud owner of a great building."

"Congrats," I said shaking his hand.

"Thank you very much David," he replied, pulling out his binder from his briefcase. "Are you ready for today's lesson?"

I nodded.

"Excellent. Today we're going to learn an important lesson that ties into the past two Secrets we've covered. You're going to be looking closely at your expenses to see if you can squeeze even more money from those buckets of spending."

I shook my head. "I don't know about that Mr. Mathers. I've cut down a lot since we first spoke and I don't think I can even…"

"Listen and learn David," he said cutting me off. "You'd be surprised at how much more you can save just by knowing what to look for. Today we're going to find even more fat in your budget by challenging your lifestyle choices."

"Sounds appealing," I said sarcastically.

"It should be because today you'll hopefully learn how you can save more than 10% of your pay."

"But I thought you said that I could retire if I saved 10% of what I earned." I definitely was confused.

"David, the Ten Percent Rule is a rule of thumb and it's just the first step in your wealth-building plan. Don't get me wrong, saving 10% of your salary should get you to retirement with a healthy nest egg, but it will take you quite some time to get there. In other words, **don't be satisfied with saving *only* 10% of your salary**. By now you know how much an extra $20 a month can grow to if it compounds month after month, year after year until you retire. You've got to learn to tighten that belt of yours so that you can save more."

"But how much can I possibly save? I mean 10% is a stretch right now," I admitted.

"You have to trust me David. Once you put the fifth Secret of Wealth to work for you, you'll find out how."

"Does this Secret of Wealth have a catchy name?" I asked.

"Secret #5 is called **Live Below Your Means**."

"Catchy," I said, jotting it down.

"Enough jabbering. Let's get started."

Needs and Wants

"We briefly covered the idea of needs versus wants two weeks ago, but it's important to cover it in detail during this Secret. **A need is something that you have to have in order to live**. Things such as food, shelter, and transportation are considered needs. **Wants are 'nice-to-haves' that you probably can do without**. There's a gray area on some items such as clothing, shoes, and the like that can go either way. Regardless, in order to come out on top of the Game of Life you need to be able to distinguish between needs and wants."

"I get it," I said. "My lunch is something that I can't live without so it's a *need*, but that CD I bought last week is a *want*."

"That's right. While most people understand this concept, they still have problems when it comes to accurately defining what truly is a necessity or a need in their own life."

"But shouldn't it be obvious which is which?" I asked.

"You'd think so, but it's not always that clear cut. By definition, what is a necessity or need shouldn't change that much over time. On the flip side **it's the wants that change with our incomes, not our basic needs**. Unfortunately, our *necessities* have a funny way of growing out of control to meet our increasing income."

I didn't have to ask what he meant by necessities growing to meet our income. I was guilty of doing the same thing. When I was hired I instantly made a few hundred extra dollars a month. Things that I couldn't afford to buy the month before immediately became necessities and part of my monthly purchases.

99 Times Out of 100, That Need is a Want

"When I was growing up, I stayed over my uncle's house after school because my parents were both working and didn't get home until later in the evening. We played games and had marathon sessions of Monopoly™. Every so often, my cousin would say she needed a new bike or needed a new toy and my uncle would stop her and would ask, 'Do you *need* it or do you *want* it?' and of course, what was my cousin's response 99 times out of a hundred?"

"Want," I answered.

"You bet and if you don't learn the difference, you might find yourself caught in the Rat Race of life."

"The Rat Race?"

"It's how the majority of people live: trapped in the Rat Race."

The Rat Race: Expenditure Rises to Meet Income [12]

"It's time for another history lesson, David," he said.

"You're kidding right?"

"No," he deadpanned, then cracked a smile. "Today you're going to learn about **Parkinson's Law**. The historian Cyril Northcote Parkinson noted that work expands to fill the time available for its completion in *The Economist* magazine in 1955. He wrote a book three years later called *The Pursuit of Progress*, which contained his second law '**Expenditure rises to meet income**.' In essence the more people earn, the more they tend to spend."

"Like we just covered?" I asked.

"Exactly. I think we can revise the law to include the words '*and then some*' at the end, given the increased usage of credit cards and the propensity for Americans to take on more debt than they can handle. Unfortunately, **too many people spend today in anticipation of tomorrow's paycheck, bonus, or raise**. They rationalize their purchases by thinking they've got to 'live the life they deserve.' Well the truth is they haven't earned that next jump in lifestyle yet and **by trying to live the good life today, people are destroying their financial future because they're trapped in the Rat Race**."

"Rat Race? What is this race you keep talking about?"

"Well, take your friends for example. When they go off to college, they receive their first credit card. Instantly they're able to buy things they couldn't afford before because they used to pay cash. So they

---

[12] My 'money' mentor originally called this the Vicious Cycle. After reading books by Robert Kiyosaki, John Burley, Marc Eisenson, and others, it is clear that the term "rat race" better describes the vicious cycle my mentor was talking about (sorry PS). If you want to learn more about the rat race and how we get caught up in it, I suggest you read the books by any of these authors or play Kiyosaki's board game Cashflow 101. ™

splurge and go on a shopping spree, buying things they really can't afford. Since everyone is going on Spring Break, they need to go as well and before they know it, they're $2,000 or more in the hole. But everything is okay because they get a job when they graduate. But before they pay off their credit cards, they move into a new apartment, which needs some furniture and appliances, and since they have a new job, they buy some work clothes. Six months after graduation, they receive their first loan booklet and realize they have to pay $150 or $200 a month for the next 200 or so months. They hadn't planned on it or just forgot, so they just pay the minimum on their credit cards and the minimum on those school loans to afford their rent and nightlife."

"Sounds about right," I conceeded.

"It gets better. So our careless spender soon meets the love of their life and they get married, which means a honeymoon, a wedding, and too many other expenses to mention. But it's okay because now they have two incomes and only one rent to pay for. Soon they're out to dinner and having fun with their friends, but they decide they have to buy a house because it's the next step in life. So they take the next step and buy a bigger house than they can afford. So now they have the house and they have to buy new furniture, so out comes the credit card or maybe the furniture store lets them pay in easy monthly payments."

He paused for a second and I jumped in. "Enough, no mas," I said, waving my hands in the air.

"But wait, there's more," he replied, ignoring my pleas. "They decide to start a family and soon they have their first child and there is joy in the house. He works even harder to provide for his budding family. The extra money they used to have each month is somehow gone before they know it. So she goes back to work after a couple of months because *she has to* and they work hard for the rest of their lives. They barely invest for their retirements and barely save enough for college, but that's okay, they have a big house to re-mortgage and those credit cards come handy in a pinch. Then one day they wake up and realize that **they're only a few months away from bankruptcy**."

Those last words just hung in the air and found a home in my churning stomach. "You're depressing, you know that," I said shaking my head.

"Sorry to rain on your parade, David. I'm just telling it like it is, but the story doesn't have to end that way if you decide to re-write it."

The Balancing Act

"Managing your expenses and your desires against an increasing income is a difficult balancing act. On the one hand, you have the desire to enjoy life right now and to do the things you may not be able to do when you get older and on the other hand you have this desire to achieve Financial Freedom. In order to do both, you're going to have to live modestly or below your current means for now. I'm not suggesting that you live like a miser and not enjoy life, but I am suggesting that you put off some of those fancy investments, cars, and other depreciating assets. **By living below your means now, you actually get ahead in three ways:**

First, you're saving money that you're actually making now. For instance, if you take home $2,000 a month, putting aside $200 a month is money in your pocket, which you can invest.

Second, by not slapping down your credit card or borrowing money each time you want to buy something, you save money on the interest you would pay down the line.

Third, you avoid negative returns on investment.

Negative Returns on Investment

"'Negative returns on investment'? What's that?"

"It's something a lot of people don't even think about. When you buy depreciating assets, you're not just paying for the cost of the thing you bought, you're also paying for it many times over down the line. If you buy a new home you have to pay homeowner's insurance, plus oil and heating bills, plus electric bills, plus new furniture, plus, plus, plus. The bigger the house, the bigger your monthly bills are to keep the place. The same is true for a car. The more expensive that car is, the higher the insurance, maintenance, and other associated costs. You can't bring that shiny new BMW to any old car wash, right? You need to take care of that baby," he said with a smirk on his face. "The same holds for many other depreciating assets. They all require additional gadgets or servicing at some point during the year. Think of it as a **negative return on your investment**."

"I see what you mean, but it's hard to say no to a new mountain bike or new CDs."

"If it wasn't a little difficult everyone would be rich instead of in debt up to their eyeballs. It's called discipline. **You need to have the willpower to say no when confronted with immediate gratification expenses that aren't going to build your assets over the long-term**.

That new bike might sound great, but isn't your old one doing the job now? Remember the rule of Needs versus Wants. You have to figure out for yourself where to cut back on expenses. I can't do that for you. You have to decide if you want to take your lunch to work or stop buying magazines and CDs."

"But what's taking my lunch to work going to do for me?" I asked.

"David, open your eyes. Taking your lunch to work can probably save $1,000 a year. I know it sounds silly, but if you pay even $3 to $5 more per lunch because you're buying it, it adds up over the course of a year."

"Oh," I replied. "I see what you're saying. Every little bit counts!"

"That's exactly the point I'm trying to make. Now that you understand, let's talk about the four step plan for living below your means."

Living Below Your Means: The 4-Step System

"There's essentially four main things you need to do in order to live below your means:

#1: Adopt the Frugal Mindset
#2: Live in a Low Status Neighborhood
#3: Be a Smart Shopper
#4: Make it Automatic

Step #1: Adopt the Frugal Mindset

"Over the past few minutes we've discussed why people get into the rat race and how they spend all the money they make without thinking of the long-term consequences of their actions. The first step in the process of living below your means is simply deciding that you will embrace the philosophy and the lifestyle of living below your means."

A Comfortable, Happy Lifestyle

"Each one of us is challenged to create a balance within this dynamic between allocating our dollars toward "stuff," and using our financial resources in support of our greater purpose in this world. Saving is much more than creating a budget. It is defining and then creating a lifestyle in which you are fulfilled, if not completely satisfied, with where you are at."

- Bill Schultheis, Author, *The Coffeehouse Investor*

He paused, flipped through his notes and pointed at a passage. "In *The Millionaire Next Door*, some of the most important common denominators of the over 1,000 millionaires the authors surveyed were boiled down to just seven. Guess which was the first denominator mentioned?"

"Living below your means?" I guessed.

"That's right," he replied. "In a chapter titled, 'Frugal, Frugal, Frugal,' the authors talk about how millionaires make their money work harder than others do. Like I've said before, rich people get rich because they value money more than everybody else. This is not to say that they worship money, it's just that they understand that cutting back on short-term expenses leads to long-term financial abundance."

"But am I cutting out all the good stuff?" I asked.

"No David. You decide what possessions you want and how you spend your money. **I'm not advocating that you deny yourself some of the finer things in life. Just enjoy them in moderation**. I'm not saying that you always have to dine in or bring lunch to work every day. You don't even have to clip coupons to save money on groceries if you don't want to. **You choose how to find the money in your current budget to invest**."

"And I don't have to clip coupons," I added.

"And you don't have to clip coupons," he agreed. "Yes David. No coupon clipping for you."

Choose Your Financial Destiny

"When we spoke about valuing money, I told you that over the course of your lifetime you will have a million dollars, probably more pass through your hands? Paycheck by paycheck, month in and month out, that's how much your paychecks will add up to. So what are you going to do with that money? How you answer this question determines your financial future. Spend every last cent as soon as you earn it and you'll have nothing when you retire. Worse yet, spend more than you make every month and you'll be staring at a pile of debt, with no chance of retiring, let alone enjoying life. Again, it's all up to you whether you become Financially Free or have to work the rest of your life. You can choose to spend all or more of your money or cut back a little here and there to put that extra money to work for you. What's it going to be: spend or cut back?"

"Cut back obviously," I replied.

"Obvious, but not as easy to do as you know. **Living Below Your Means is a simple concept to understand, but <u>not</u> easy to implement for some people**."

"I understand how hard it can be if you don't want it bad enough," I said, "but I'm willing to delay my short-term gratification for long-term satisfaction."

"Good, because I want you to budget and scrape together as much money as possible to start investing so that you can eventually build a portfolio that you can retire on."

He turned a page in his binder and looked up at me. "Okay, enough about adopting the mindset. I think we've about covered that one to death. Let's talk about your neighbors."

Step #2: Live in a Low-Status Neighborhood

Keeping up with the Joneses

"Keeping up with the Joneses was a full-time job of my mother and father. It was not until many years later when I lived alone that I realized how much cheaper it was to drag the Jones's down to my level."

– Quentin Crisp

"There's a phrase that is often used to describe someone who partakes in a behavior of trying to buy whatever their neighbor buys. Do you know the phrase?" he asked.

"Sure. Keeping up with the Joneses."

"That's the one. That particular behavior is one of the leading pastimes for many Americans. It seems harmless enough, buying what your neighbors are buying, and having the things they have. But this behavior of keeping up with your neighbors and friends is one of the biggest obstacles to building a successful savings and investing plan."

"What's wrong with having what your neighbors have?" I asked.

"I'll tell you what's wrong with it. **We've been conditioned by marketers, friends, coworkers, and family members to overspend**. The products we buy are no longer for pure sustenance alone, rather we buy things to lead a certain lifestyle and of course the lifestyle we choose dictates where we shop and what we buy. We try to act rich by spending money we don't have, thinking we'll have it in the future if we get that raise or change our job or win the lottery. In my opinion, this behavior is crazy. What's the point of working like a dog, then blowing too much money on status symbols if you have to turn around and work harder to pay for them? **There's no point in keeping up with the Joneses when the penalty is that you'll be working hard the rest of your life**."

"Keeping up with your friends and neighbors doesn't make sense when you lay it all out like that," I commented.

"It doesn't make sense and the downside is that the folks that attempt to keep up with the Joneses are working hard to collect more bills and debt. Their attitude is to live life to the fullest, not later when they're too old or have kids or are married. It's just nonsense in the end, especially when **living a modest lifestyle can help you acquire assets that will help you retire early**."

Live in a Low-Status Neighborhood

"Now it's much easier to *not* fall into the trap of keeping up with the Joneses if your neighbors are not extravagant, spend-it-all type of people. One way to ensure this is to live in an area that has a low cost of living or what the authors of *The Millionaire Next Door* call a low-status neighborhood. Living in a less costly area will make it easier for you to afford your mortgage payments, taxes, utilities, and just about every other expense and still have money left over to invest and have fun with. If you live in a more ritzy part of town or neighborhood with folks that earn what you earn or higher, you'll find yourself being pulled upward into their spending circles. That's not a situation you want to find yourself in."

"I remember reading that section of the book," I said, "and I recall the discussion about how you'll pay more for your house and taxes and just about everything if you live in a high-status neighborhood."

"That's right David. Plus you have your neighbors pulling up in their new cars or bragging about their latest vacation or big purchase. You'll just get sucked into the vicious cycle and start spending your money like crazy to compete or live the life you think you're supposed to be living. **All too often people let their paychecks set their budgets**, as in 'We can spend up to this amount [their paychecks] each month.' That's just ludicrous. You have to set aside money for a rainy day, pay yourself first, invest for your future, and a bunch of other things with that money before you spend it on indulgences and depreciating assets. **By living in a middle class[13], low-status neighborhood you set yourself up for a simpler, less expensive lifestyle**. Speaking of spending, let's talk about the third step in the process."

> **"Allocating time and money in the pursuit of looking superior often has a predictable outcome: inferior economic achievement."**
> - Thomas Stanley and William Danko, *The Millionaire Next Door*

---

[13] I say middle class, but the real thing to focus on is 'low status' when choosing where to live.

Step #3: Be a Smart Shopper

A Penny Saved Is Two Pennies Earned

"There's a great book that I want you to read. It's called *The Only Investment Guide You Will Ever Need* by Andrew Tobias. The book covers all the basics of investing in the stock market, plus some items on retirement savings."

My eyes lit up. "Exactly what I want to learn."

"You could say that, but what I want you to concentrate on is the second chapter of the book. The chapter is entitled **'A Penny Saved Is Two Pennies Earned.'**"

"Sounds exciting," I replied sarcastically.

"More than you can imagine David. While the book has some good insights into investing, the chapter on saving money is very important. His lesson about **50% money** is really critical to changing your mindset."

"'50% money'? What's that?"

"Tobias shows you in a couple of paragraphs how **the last few dollars you earn only net you only 50 cents after you pay federal, state, local, Social Security, and Medicare taxes.**"

"So if I make $10 bucks an hour, I'm only really taking home $5 at the end of the week?" I asked.

"More or less," he replied. "So **if you save a buck by cutting back somewhere, its like earning two bucks**. That should be motivation enough not to waste your money."

The light bulb went off in my head. "I never thought of it like that, but it makes sense," I said, finally getting it.

"Good, because I'm already talking too much without having given you the payoff and here it is: **The quickest return you can get is the savings you get from reducing your expenses**. In fact, you automatically double your money."

"I guess Benjamin Franklin was wrong when he said 'A penny saved is a penny earned.' A penny saved is two pennies earned!"

"You've got it David and the point Tobias was making is that each dollar is worth something and every dollar saved through smart spending, the more you'll have to invest. Okay, we've got that point covered, now let's talk about football."

"Alright. With you it gets better and better," I said, pulling my chair closer to the table.

"Calm down David, we're not going to talk about the Giants, but something more important than whether or not they'll make the playoffs this year."

Playing Great Defense

"When we first met you told me you were trying to find a way to make more money so you could be rich. You're probably too young to know that regardless of **whether you make $40,000 or $400,000 a year, it doesn't mean that it's easier to get out of debt**."

"But if I make more money, won't it be easier to get out of debt?"

"It should be, but think back to when you were a temp. How much were you making an hour?"

"About $10 before taxes."

"And you managed to survive on that salary?" he inquired.

"Barely, but yes, I survived," I replied.

"So now how much do you make an hour?"

"A little over $15."

"So after taxes you're making $7,800 more a year. Would you say that you feel like you have more money than you did last year?"

"No, I actually feel like I have less to spend," I replied.

"That's because as we just said, **your expenses have a funny way of increasing to meet your income. You always wind up living paycheck to paycheck**, regardless of whether you make more money or not. You'd be better off improving your defense at this stage than focusing on offense."

"Huh? Now what are you talking about defense and offense for?"

"In football you have an offense and a defense. In the financial Game of Life there are two basic ways to have more money: Earn more or spend less, otherwise known as playing good offense (a big income) or great defense (managing expenses). Most people focus on increasing their income, the harder of the two to change *immediately*. If you think about it, every dollar saved equals more than a dollar earned. Lets say you get a $1,200 raise at work. How much more a year are you taking home?"

"Easy, $1,200."

"Wrong. After taxes you're looking at around $800. Now let's say you start buying your groceries in bulk and you buy one less shirt or gizmo each month. You manage to save $100 a month. How much will that add up to over a year?"

"Easy, $100 times 12 months is $1,200…ohhhh I get it."

"Oh, he says. He's had an epiphany. I take it you realize that **you end up with more cash by playing great defense, than you do by playing great offense.** Learn to focus on both offense and defense and you'll soon be winning the financial Game of Life."

"So can we talk about the Giants now?"

"No!" he said with a shake of his head.

"**Millionaires play both quality offense and quality defense** and quite often their great defense helps them outscore/outaccumulate those who outearn/have superior offenses. The foundation stone of wealth accumulation is defense, and this defense would be anchored by budgeting and planning."
- Thomas Stanley and William Danko, *The Millionaire Next Door*

The Best Way to Save Money – Don't Spend It

"So what's the best way to save my money?" I asked.

"Don't spend it!" he exclaimed.

"Very funny Mr. Mathers. No seriously, how?"

"I am serious David. The best way to live below your means is to take a hard look at where you're spending your money. By examining your everyday expenses and shaving a few cents or dollars from those expenses, you're going to find a ton of money that can be put toward your investment account."

"Sounds like a lot of work."

The Two Magic Questions

"Not really. For the next 30 to 60 days every time you pull out your wallet you should ask yourself two questions:

- **Do I really need this?**
- **Can I get it cheaper somewhere else?**

"I have to ask those questions every time I want to buy something? Then what, I don't buy anything anymore and just deny myself the right to spend the money I worked hard for?"

"David, I'm not suggesting that you give up happy hour with your co-workers or live on bread and water. It's just that you can save a lot of money on every day items if you just took the time to examine how much you are paying for that item and whether you can get it cheaper somewhere else or if you need it at all."

I wasn't completely convinced and it still seemed like a lot of work to do.

"The rich are not shy about asking for discounts," he said. "They actively seek out deals, sales and bargains. They know the value of a dollar since most of them worked hard for their money. They delay purchases they don't need right away until their next shopping trip and often they find that they didn't really need the item."

"But, I don't like to ask for discounts. Don't most stores give you discounts anyway?"

"True, the Wal-Mart's of the world often have the lowest prices posted and you generally can't expect to haggle with your local grocer, but why shouldn't you haggle with your car dealer? You see everyone is conditioned to haggle with a car dealer because they know that the dealer has marked up the car to make his or her cut on the sale, but so has the plumber, the electrician, the repair person, the mechanic, and so on. **Shopping around for the best deal makes sense and saves thousands of dollars.** Insurance premiums, mortgage rates, and the like all vary from company to company, bank to bank. Those extra few minutes of asking around and looking will literally translate into hundreds of dollars of savings."

Do It Once

"Still sounds like a lot of work to be going through every week."

"Look, you don't have to do it *every* day for the rest of your life. Eventually you will learn where to buy the cheapest gas or get the best deals on buying your clothes or food. Once you do the legwork and manage down your fixed and variable expenses, you don't really have to do much except save money."

"So I do it once is what you're saying," I commented.

"That's exactly what I'm saying. Just figure out where to cut back and stick with the plan. Once you get rid of some of those money wasters in your spending plan and put that money toward your financial future, you'll be on the fast track to Financial Freedom."

Side Note: Some Helpful Saving Strategies

Fight the Impulse – Don't buy anything that costs over $100 for 48 hours: *Don't be swayed by the latest sale on a gadget or article of clothing. Leave the store and if you still want the item 2 days later, consider buying it.*

Cut the Cost of Frequent Purchases: *Take a look at the things you buy most often and see if you can get the item cheaper somewhere else. Those extra cents add up to big dollars over time.*

Go Generic: *The premium for brand name items can be anywhere from 20% to 60% more than the equivalent generic product. I'm not saying that you have to buy all generic products, but swapping a few of your brand name products for generics can mean the difference between retiring early or retiring when you die.*

Buy at Warehouse Clubs: For those items that you use a lot of, there's no better place to buy them than at a warehouse club. Just make sure you buy stuff you need and use and don't be swayed by the tremendous savings that 3lb. tub of sugar gives you.

Don't Buy on Credit: Seems like we've already covered this in Secret #4, but it bears repeating. Every time you buy something on credit you pay 50% to 300% more for the item if you carry a balance. You'd be wise to set up a "holiday savings club" type deal where every week you set aside money for your new couch, car, or big purchase.

Avoid the Urge to "Rent to Own": Rent to Own might seem like a great concept: you pay a low monthly fee to rent an item and get the option to buy it when the rental period is over. However, when you do the math you'll find that you're paying 100% to 200% interest to purchase the item. Suddenly credit cards charging 20% interest don't seem so bad!

Back to our story...

Big Ticket Items

"Before we get to the last step in the process of living below your means, I wanted to cover ways to save money on big ticket items. I'll let you figure out how to save money for the smaller purchases because everyone is different (i.e., some people can't give up their lattes, but are willing to give up some other item), but when it comes to the big ticket items there are some things that all millionaires do."

Cars: How Much is that New Car Smell Worth?

"Your car is usually the second biggest purchase you'll make in life. Therefore, whether you're buying your first car or trading it in for a new one, it's best to exercise caution and shop around for the best value. **A car is not an investment. It's a mode of transportation, not an asset that appreciates in value**. The sooner you understand that your car is designed to get you from Point A to Point B and not much else, the better off you'll be."

"You're going to make me drive a Yugo, aren't you?"

"No David, but I am going to make sure you buy the best car for your dollar, which means staying away from new cars."

"Why?"

"Because new cars lose their value pretty quickly, which is why they're considered depreciating assets in my book. In fact, the average car will lose about 20% or more of its value in the first year alone."

"That's crazy! Twenty percent?"

"It all depends on the model, but yes, **you're paying a premium for the benefit of that new car smell** and the right to tell everyone who will listen that you bought a new car. Of course that feeling wears off, but you still have to pay for that *new* car."

"Sounds like quite a premium to pay," I commented.

"It is and it gets worse. Your car will lose another 15% in the second year, 10% to 15% in the third year and 10% to 15% in the fourth year. If you paid $20,000 for a new car, then after two years of driving, it may be worth $13,000. Yes sir, $7,000 vaporized in the thin air of depreciation. That's $3,500 per year or almost $300 a month!"

"That's quite a drop after only three years. I take it you're telling me to buy a used car," I said.

"That's what I recommend and here's why. A car you bought new three years ago for $20,000 is now worth $10,000. **Why not buy that car when it's three years old, save yourself the $10,000, and have a lower monthly payment?**"

"Amazing," I replied, writing the information down.

"Saving money on cars is so important that an entire chapter of *The Millionaire Next Door* was devoted to explaining the types of cars that millionaires drive. Over 50% of millionaires never spent more than $29,000 on their cars and close to 40% of them owned cars that were at least three years old."

"What about leasing?" I asked. "Is leasing a good deal?"

"**Buy your cars, don't lease them.** Over 80% of the millionaires surveyed owned their cars. That should tell you something and I'm guessing that those who leased probably did so because they could write off the lease as a business expense. In short my advice is to buy a used or what they're calling a 'certified pre-owned' car that's known to be dependable. You can save even more money by driving the car for as long as you can. When you buy a used car and keep it for a long time, **every year you delay purchasing another car is money in your pocket**."

"I've got it," I said throwing my hands in the air, frustrated at how hard it was to keep up with all the information. "Anything else?"

"One more thing. Sam Walton, founder of Wal-Mart, used to drive through town in a beat-up old pickup truck. Some folks pointed and laughed, but he was laughing all the way to the bank."

"Sounds like someone I know," I said, nodding in his direction.

Housing: How Much House Do You Need?

"We'll cover the housing issue again in three weeks, but I just wanted to give you a taste of how easy it is to save thousands of dollars from making a few simple choices in life. Your house is the biggest purchase you'll make in your lifetime. Done right, your house can become a wonderful asset in your retirement years. Done wrong, it can mean thousands of wasted dollars and more importantly the lost investment potential of those dollars."

"How so?" I asked.

"I see too many newlyweds buying their dream homes instead of waiting a couple of years. So there they are, with the keys to a big spacious house with three or four bedrooms, a play room, Jacuzzi, garage, and other amenities and it's just the two of them. Now they have to fill that house and decorate it."

"But with the way housing prices have been going up, isn't it smart to buy that house now, while they can afford it?"

"David, **buying in anticipation of future appreciation is not a wise move**. I'm not even going to talk about the likelihood of couples getting divorced these days. Instead, I'm going to focus on the lost investment opportunity and the extra cost of that bigger mortgage."

"I feel an example coming up," I said.

"How perceptive you are," he said, with a slight grin. "Okay, we have David and his brother. His brother John decides to finally leave the house, after marrying the girl of his dreams. John and his wife purchase a cozy little two bedroom house on the outskirts of town. Their mortgage is $200,000. Ten years later, David finally moves out and buys his own place with the girl he tricked into marriage."

"Sounds about right," I said, playing along.

"Now David has his friends to impress so he decides to move into a larger place located closer to town and the school. His mortgage is $230,000. Both mortgages have a 7% rate so guess who pays more over the course of their 30 year loan?"

"I do of course."

"Right, to the tune of approximately $72,000."

"Wow! That's almost a $100,000 difference and I only borrowed $30,000 more."

"Yeah, but you wanted the bigger house, which you'd probably sell after five to seven years to move into something bigger and pay commissions and fees all over again."

"Nope, not me. I'm going to live in a low status neighborhood."

"You'd be in the minority. Most people start looking for the biggest house they can afford. Meanwhile, all that extra money in mortgage payments could have been invested in better places. In short, buy a house you can afford or one that's less than what the bank will lend you. A house that's in a good location can appreciate a lot over the years, but you shouldn't mortgage your future in order to buy a home today. We'll cover more on this in three weeks. Let's move on."

Insurance: Getting the Protection You Need

"Insurance is one of those mid-range expenses. Depending on your line of work and your assets, you may have a hefty amount to pay each month to insure your car, your home, and/or your business. It might make sense to **consolidate your insurance policies under one company** and receive a discount for doing so. I won't get into specifics right now, but you're generally better off buying term and investing the difference. Essentially it's a lot cheaper and the savings for buying term outweigh the benefits of whole life insurance. We'll cover this topic again in four weeks, but it's worth noting during this Secret."

College Expenses: Paying for Junior or Not

"What about college costs?" I asked. "Isn't saving for your children's college costs one of those big expenses?"

"Yep, but it can be managed through a variety of investment vehicles out there that can help. I'm not up on the latest numbers, but a four year public university will cost around $35,000 and a private school will cost close to $100,000 nowadays and depending on the institution, that may or may not include books, room and board, and spending money."[14]

"Ouch!" I said, grimacing at the thought of shelling out all that money.

"Ouch is right and by the time David Junior is ready to follow in his father's footsteps, the price tag is probably going to be much larger thanks to the price of tuition outpacing inflation."

"That's it," I said waving my hands in the air. "I'm not having kids."

He chuckled. "Highly unlikely. Imagine denying the world Davey Junior. Let's deal with reality, shall we?" he said giving me a look. "Those are big numbers, but if you start saving when your kids are born, you've got a pretty good chance of having set aside a decent amount of money to pay for college."

---

[14] Estimated costs in 2001 were $33,880 and $90,164 for a four year stint at a public and private university respectively. Check out www.collegeboard.com for the latest estimates.

"Yeah, but if you have more than one kid, can you realistically save for college *and* save for your retirement?"

"It all depends on how soon you start, the amount of money you're able to set aside each month, and the performance of your investments, but yes, you can save quite a bit by the time your kids turn eighteen. But also don't forget that they will be eligible for financial aid and can take out school loans to help defray the cost."

"It still seems like a heck of a lot of money per kid," I said. "What if you have four or five kids? Should you stop making contributions to your 401(k) in order to save for your kid's education?"

"No!" he replied emphatically. **"You should never jeopardize your retirement or investment portfolio[15] to pay for your kid's college bill**. Most parents think they have a duty to pay for their kid's education, but they're wrong. There's nothing wrong with paying the entire bill if you can afford it, but if doing so jeopardizes your retirement, then you should look at different options. Your kids will have a lot of options that will be available to them to help pay for college. They have financial aid or can borrow money from the government at some pretty low long-term rates. In addition, Uncle Sam has given parents and college kids some interesting options when it comes to saving for college.[16] Just remember: **While they can borrow for college, you can't borrow for your retirement**."

"I come first. Sounds good to me," I said.

He shook his head at me. "We'll see what your stance is when Davey junior is ready for college."

Other Tips

"Another way to live below your means is to not spend your raises. Instead, just put it aside into a savings account or better yet, invest it either in your individual investment or retirement account."

"So I'm not supposed to enjoy the fruits of my labor? What about celebrating? I mean if I work hard for a raise, don't I deserve to …you know, spend some of that money on myself?"

"Yes, you should, but **at minimum, try to set aside 50% of your raise and add it to the amount you pay yourself each pay period**. If you've been getting along fine with the salary you were making, what's the difference really? Your expenses didn't go up, only your means did. Why do you have to automatically spend more money just because you're making more? It gets back to the habit most of us have of

---

[15] Or take out a huge mortgage to pay 100% of the bill.
[16] Check out www.fabmansecrets.com and the article titled "Smart Ways to Cut Down the Cost of College."

automatically increasing our expenses to meet our means. There's no physical need that we have to meet, but somehow psychologically we convince ourselves that since we're earning more, we should spend more."

"I guess I could live with only half the amount to spend," I conceeded.

"Of course you can. Just have it pulled automatically from your paycheck and deposited in your savings account. You'll never miss it."

Step #4: Make it Automatic

The Cash Diet: Just Spend the Rest

"Hey what about the fourth step: Make it automatic?" I asked.

"The last step is an easy concept to understand because it's similar to the second Secret of Wealth. **What you're trying to do is have a set percentage pulled out of your paycheck every month and you get to spend the rest**. In other words, you go through the process of creating a budget for yourself and let's say you determine that you can live off of 70% of your income. You simply have 30% of your income pulled from your paycheck and deposited in a separate bank account or investment account."

"Oh, I get it," I said. "Since you're living below your means, you're not spending your whole paycheck, so you just have it automatically invested or something like that, right?"

"That's it in a nutshell. After you've done the work of determining the most cost-effective way to purchase your groceries and other monthly items, you should have a pretty good idea of what your monthly expenses should be. Have this amount put into a "Spending" Account and the rest of your paycheck should be sent to your Investment Account. This way all you're supposed to spend is what is in your Spending Account. Just make sure to pay for everything with cash, checks, or debit card linked to this account."

"Why?"

"Because **if you're paying for stuff with your credit card you'll end up spending beyond your means**. The idea is to have the money immediately taken from you before you have a chance to spend it. In other words, it forces you to live below your means."

"Automatically," I added.

"'Automatically' is right," he repeated.

Wrapping Up

He smiled at me, closed his binder and put it in his briefcase. "I believe we're done today."

It was getting late by the time we finished talking about the various ways to live below your means. I was getting hungry at this point and my attention span was rapidly deteriorating. I think Mr. Mathers sensed this. "Sounds good to me. I'm getting hungry," I said rubbing my belly.

"You're always hungry David. By the way, did you drive to the library or walk?" he asked. "I didn't see your car in the lot."

"I decided to walk. I need the exercise. I've been working so much and I haven't been to the gym in forever."

"Ahh, the corporate lifestyle. I don't miss sitting behind a desk all day," he said getting up from his seat. "How about I drive you home the long way and we'll finish our discussion on living below your means."

"You mean there's more?"

"I just want to cover one more issue that you're likely to encounter which might make it difficult for you to make the transition from spender to saver."

"Sounds good to me," I said as we turned toward the door.

We got into his truck and he pulled out of the library lot. He made a left instead of a right, easing his truck around the narrow road that bordered the Town Park.

"Well, I think I'll be able to fit the last topic in before we make it to your house," he said.

"What's it on," I asked.

"It's on backlash?"

"Backlash, huh? Is that anything like whiplash?" I asked.

"Funny Mr. David. I know you know what the word means."

The Backlash

"When you begin to live below your means, expect a negative reaction from your friends and family. When I refused to purchase an item that I could afford, but didn't need (usually a luxury item) those who knew how much I was earning would constantly tell me, 'C'mon, you deserve it' or 'you can afford it, just buy it.' Yes I could afford it, but chose not to and they would often get mad. Do you know why they had this reaction?"

"No, why?"

"Because they realized that they were spending and buying things that they didn't need and probably couldn't afford, so they tried to justify it to me, but really to themselves. It's like you're condemning their way of life by choosing to live your life in a manner that's different than theirs. They will call you cheap or a miser. I've been called both by some of my family members and friends. It's not a good feeling and I don't think of myself as being cheap, just smart with my money."

At the time I remember thinking that I couldn't live below my means. It just seemed so drastic. I wasn't making much money and as far as I could tell, I wasn't spending my money that foolishly. The fact of the matter was that there wasn't much money left over at the end of the month and I was a bit skeptical about being able to cut back even more and still have fun and lead a *normal* life.

"It just seems a little tough to adopt this Secret," I said.

"It's a simple enough concept really; 'spend less than you make,' and yet so many people can't do it. Why do you think that is?"

I shrugged my shoulders. "I don't know, too many bills to pay."

"Something like that, but it goes much deeper," he replied. "Our culture has implanted in us the mindset that in order to be successful we have to drive fancy cars and wear expensive clothes, watches, and jewelry, to *show* everyone else that we're successful. **When you live below your means, you're rejecting the frivolous lifestyle. Instead, your life and your spending will have purpose**."

You'll Have Different Values

"Your decision to change your lifestyle and spending habits is a positive thing, not a negative life decision. Remember that and realize that they're just sticking up for the lifestyle that you have chosen to reject."

"What do you mean by rejecting?"

"I mean that you're essentially rejecting them by rejecting the way they spend their money and the way they spend their days and paychecks. People hang out with people they identify with and if all of the sudden you've changed, there will be tension. Going out for drinks three nights a week or an expensive dinner every week is not as important as saving your money. You will no longer share the same values as your friends. You value your future and the peace of mind that will come with paying off your debt and building a secure nest egg. They value depreciating assets and material objects that will not help them get out from under their debt. So of course there will be a clash of values. You are no longer exactly like them. Not better, not worse, just different."

I turned down the radio and nodded. In my mind I could already envision the conversations I would have at some point with my closest friends regarding my *shift* in spending and the changes it was likely to have on my social life. He pulled up to my driveway and I opened up the passenger side door to get out.

"You're right Mr. Mathers. It's going to be tough, but I can see how important this lifestyle choice is to my future. I think I can make the break and start cutting back on my spending."

He smiled. "Welcome to the Millionaire's Club David. If you truly live below your means, you're already halfway to Financial Freedom."

The Joneses Do Enjoy Life...for Now

"One last thing, your friends and others who are irresponsible with their money and their plastic monsters (credit cards) are going to be having a lot of fun right now. They're going to have new clothes, the latest gadgets, and a better car than you. This might be hard to swallow, but take heart, because in a few years they will feel the pinch of their spending ways and you'll be sitting pretty with your retirement accounts well-funded and you'll be ahead of the Game. Perhaps you'll even lend them some money when you've retired early and they're still working to pay off the debts they acquired in college."

"Don't worry Mr. Mathers. I understand the importance of living below my means now," I said. "I'll stick with it."

"Good because it won't be easy David, but if you stick with it, you'll see your net worth and bank account slowly begin to grow and gain momentum. It may even take some time before you see a real difference, but trust me on this one, you'll be the one retiring 10 or 15 years before your friends. That alone will be all the proof you need that your way of life was the right choice for you."

"I totally understand now Mr. Mathers," I said slamming the door shut. "See you next week."

"Until next week," he replied and put the car in drive.

I watched as he drove slowly down the road back toward town. I shook my head and laughed at the site of a millionaire driving a beat up old truck even though he could afford a fleet of new ones.

Living Below Your Means – COMMENTS

*If you haven't figured it out already, one of the things this book is trying to tell you is that **you can get rich simply by investing the money that you're currently wasting**. So STOP wasting your money and put it to work for you. Don't go into debt to support your lifestyle. Make that decision today and stick to it.*

*__Mr. and Mrs. Jones exist in your head.__ Sure there's someone down the street, in your family, or among your friends that you compare yourself to. We all play this silly game. I'm guilty of it myself on occasion. I have three people that I "benchmark" myself against to see how I'm doing in the Game of Life. My advice to you is to stop comparing yourself, your house, your car, or your bank account with someone else. **Choose your own path in life**, one that includes living below your means, investing your hard-earned money, and you'll reap the rewards of Financial Freedom.*

*Let me give it to you straight so you don't fall into the viscous cycle or get caught in the Rat Race. **The appropriate standard of living for yourself is LESS than what you can afford, not more**. What do I mean by less? I mean that you should be spending roughly 60%-70% of your take home pay on your mortgage, car, food, and the rest. The other 30%-40% will go toward investments, charity, and paying down your debt. That might sound like an impossible task, but I know dozens of people who are doing it and sitting on some nice sized nest eggs.*

It's Up to You

- You need to determine what level of spending is right for you.
- You choose if you want to save 5%, 10%, or 20% of your income.
- You get to choose how to invest that money.
- You determine how long you will have to work until you've achieved Financial Freedom.

*Believe me, **living below your means can be difficult at first.** I admit it was tough for me in the beginning, but it's gotten a lot easier over the years. Especially when I saw that every dollar I saved was two dollars that I didn't have to earn. Every dollar you save is a step closer to Financial Freedom. Start walking today.*

Okay, enough yapping. Let's get to your Action Plan.

Living Below Your Means – ACTION PLAN

Step 1: Adopt the Frugal Mindset: Living Below Your Means is 90 percent mental. You have to change your mindset before you even start looking for ways to cut costs and downscale your lifestyle. In short, you need to adopt the Frugal Mindset. Realize that you don't need all the stuff you've been buying and that living below your means is not the same thing as being cheap, it's being smart.

Step 2: Live in a Low Status Neighborhood: You don't have to keep up with the Joneses and you don't have to buy any depreciating assets if you don't want to. In short, you'll be more concerned with living a life than living a lifestyle if your neighbors don't try to "one-up" you.

Step 3: Be a Smart Shopper: Learn where to find the best deals on reoccurring expenses like groceries, clothes, telephone service, and entertainment to name a few categories. Buy the book *Get Clark Smart* for hundreds of ways to save money. You can find some great resources online: www.thefrugalshopper.com, www.frugalliving.com, www.dollarstretcher.com, and www.fool.com. Learn how to fix things instead of running to the store every time.

Step 4: Make it Automatic: If you haven't done it already, set up an automatic withdrawal from either your paycheck or your savings account. Automatically set aside 20% to 30% of your paycheck for your debt repayment and/or your investment plan, then live off the rest. Using this trick you'll automatically be spending less than you earn.

Pay CASH: When you pay with cash it's much harder to overspend because you're literally sitting there with the money you've worked hard for in your hand. If you can't do the "pay with cash" thing, use a debit card. Like cash in hand, it's hard to spend money that's coming directly out of savings.

Delay Making Any Purchase Over $100 for 48 hours: Combat the impulse purchase by waiting at least two days before you buy something. Often you'll find that you really didn't need the item in the first place.

Ask the 2 Magic Questions: For the next 30 to 60 days, ask yourself the following questions when you're about to buy something:

"Do I really need this?"
"Can I get it cheaper somewhere else?"

Be Proud: Explain to your friends that the future is more important than $8 martinis. Don't be ashamed or afraid of suggesting dining in or doing activities that don't cost money.

Additional Resources

Books:

The Millionaire Next Door by Thomas Stanley and William Danko
The Richest Man in Babylon by George Clason
Get Clark Smart by Clark Howard

For tips on how to save money, go to www.fabmansecrets.com and check out the following articles:
"Ideas on How to Cut the Fat from Your Budget"
"Living Below Your Means"

Web-Sites:

- www.clarkhoward.com (Radio host and author Clark Howard's site is a treasure trove of great information on getting great deals)
- www.fool.com (Check out the Living Below Your Means Board)
- www.cheapskatemonthly.com (Enough said)
- www.stretcher.com (The Dollar Stretcher Newsletter and tons of articles on how to save some cash)
- www.allthingsfrugal.com (Home of the Penny Pincher and Tightwad Tidbits)

Cut Out the Small Stuff and Make Big Money!

I know I keep harping on cutting out miscellaneous expenses, but there's a good reason I'm so keen on cutting out those little trips to the coffee shop and why bringing your lunch or breakfast to work can pay huge dividends. When I first did the Money Waster Analysis, I was shocked. Below are the actual five categories that I decided to cut out and the payoff for doing so.

Pennies into BIG Dollars: My Old Money Wasters!

Money Waster Cut Out	Monthly Savings	Annual Savings
Magazines I didn't need	$21	$252
Breakfast at work	28	336
Coffee at the coffee shop	48	576
Afternoon snack at work	35	420
One less dinner out a week	50	600
Total Saved	**$182**	**$2,184**

Investing $182 a month at 8% for 30 years grows to $271,245. Invested for 40 years it grows to $635,363! Just because I lived below my means and cut out some Money Wasters!

The Top 10 Ways I Waste My Money

David Letterman has his Top Ten List. Now it's your turn. Fill out this list of the Top Ten Ways You Waste Money! Add up the monthly costs and you'll soon realize that you could be saving $100 to $150 easy if you just cut out some of your money wasters.

	MONEY WASTER	MONTHLY SAVINGS
1.	_____	_____
2.	_____	_____
3.	_____	_____
4.	_____	_____
5.	_____	_____
6.	_____	_____
7.	_____	_____
8.	_____	_____
9.	_____	_____
10.	_____	_____

Total Savings: [_____]

Just go to any online calculator and figure out how much those savings can grow to if you invested it instead. That "Total Savings" figure should be motivation enough to cut back and live below your means.

Now that you've identified how much you could be saving each month instead of spending it on money wasters that won't put cash in your pocket, let's learn how to invest that money you worked so hard to save.

Quick Tips to Help You Live Below Your Means[17]

Household	Transportation	Groceries & Shopping
• Delay buying your dream house • If you rent, get a roommate • Turn off the lights when you're not in the room • Wash dishes by hand • Buy energy-efficient appliances • Do not use the dishwasher • Dry clothes the old-fashioned way • Turn down the heat • Shut off the A/C when you're not home • Ditch the landscaper • Shovel your own snow • Classes at Home Depot (learn how to fix stuff)	• But a used and dependable car • Don't buy more car than you need • Don't lease • Regular maintenance • Learn to change your own oil • Wash your own car • Raise the deductible on your insurance • Carpool • Use public transportation • Buy cheap gas • Drive the speed limit • Walk to town if you're close enough for regular errands	• Always use a list when shopping for groceries • Buy at discount or warehouse clubs (buy in bulk) • Buy private label brands for certain things • Use coupons and frequent shopper cards • Learn to cook • Don't dine out • Wait until it goes on sale • If it's more than $100 wait 48 hours before you purchase it. You might realize you don't need it. • Wait until it goes on sale • Eat your breakfast at home • ebay

Entertainment	Budgets and Finances	Other
• You don't need the latest gadget, computer system, home stereo, DVD player, flat screen monitor, and anything else the Joneses have but you don't • Eat in more often • Rent movies • Read, Read, Read • Read library books • QVC and HSN are NOT entertainment • Invite friends over instead of dining out • Cut out the trips to the coffee shop and make your own • Use frequent flyer miles to pay for vacations • Go for a bike ride • Family board game night	• You MUST have a household budget • Create a holiday and birthday fund to save money ahead of time • Create savings accounts for future big purchases like cars • Create a household maintenance fund for repairs • Invest in low-cost mutual funds • Say no to ATM fees; plan ahead • Use your debit card and put your little plastic monsters away • Refinance your mortgage • Buy term insurance and invest the difference • Don't carry a balance on your credit cards	• Clear out the clutter – have a garage sale or donate your junk (stuff) to charity • Discontinue gym memberships you don't use • Discontinue subscriptions to magazines you don't read • Wear machine washable clothes to work and save on dry cleaning • Quit smoking • Quit drinking • Quit overeating • Exercise more! • Go to your regular doctor and dentist checkups • Borrow it instead of buying it • Make sure your kids apply for every scholarship and grant

---

[17] This is the chart I called "Quick Tips to Help You Cut the Fat from Your Budget" in Secret #3.

"The main reason people struggle financially is because they
spent years in school but learned nothing about money.
The result is, people learn to work for money...but never
learn to have money work for them."
                    - Robert Kiyosaki, Author, *Rich Dad, Poor Dad*

Now it's time to learn how to make your money
work for you instead of the other way around.

Secret #6:
INVEST NOW
NOT TOMORROW

It's amazing how people tend to complicate
the whole investing process
when success can be found in a few simple steps...

Chapter 11

Secret #6 - INVEST NOW, NOT TOMORROW –
Leveraging the Power of Compound Interest

The Size of Your Salary Doesn't Matter

"In the long run, its not how much money you make that will determine your future. It's how much of that money you put to work by saving it and investing it."
— Peter Lynch, former Fidelity Magellan Fund Manger

For our sixth meeting, Mr. Mathers decided to meet at his house since he was hosting his investment club's monthly meeting and had to prepare his den for their arrival. When I arrived, he was pushing me out the front door.

"Let's go for a walk," he said. "I have to pick up some bagels and we only have a little time before they get here."

"Sounds good to me. I didn't eat breakfast this morning."

We left the house in the hands of Mrs. Mathers who was also a member of the investment club. After some small talk, I got right to the point.

"When are we going to talk about investing or learning how to make more money?" I asked, curious to see when we would begin focusing on making instead of saving money.

"I don't want to burst your bubble, but **the majority of the world's millionaires didn't get there because of their incomes**. They got there because of the appreciation in the value of their businesses, real estate properties, or their stock portfolios."

"Or their inheritance," I jokingly added.

"The percentage of millionaires who inherited their wealth in this country is very small. In fact, the majority of them are first-generation millionaires, which was covered in *The Millionaire Next Door*. You did read the book, didn't you?" he asked.

"Oh, that's right. It was the part I read about where they earned their way to millionaire status without the benefit of an inheritance."

"Careful with how you use the word 'earned.' Stay at your company long enough and you'll see that there are dozens of people working hard to *earn* their paychecks, **but they're earning a living, not building wealth**. They work hard and get that paycheck, pay their bills, spend money on things that depreciate in value, and save what's left over, which isn't much. Then they look at their savings account and wonder why they're always short on money. They can't understand why they're working so hard and still have no money. So what do they do? The only thing they know how to do, work harder and wait for their next raise."

"So what do they do to fix their problem?" I asked.

"Nothing. Most people make it worse by borrowing more money to take care of short-term problems. If something is broke, you don't keep using it. You fix it. Unfortunately, **the vast majority of people never stop to see if what they're doing is wrong**. They never change their strategy, so they end up in the same place, no matter how hard they work. Do you know how hard it is to build a million dollar net worth by earning it? Almost impossible, because Uncle Sam wants a cut of all your income."

"Oh I get it. You're talking about taxes," I said.

"Right. We'll get back to Uncle Sam in three weeks, but for now I want to make sure that you understand that your earnings are only one piece of the financial puzzle, albeit an important one. However **it's much more important** *how* **you choose to invest your income, than** *how much* **you make when it comes to building your wealth.** In other words, **the size of your salary doesn't matter**."

He was essentially saying that it really didn't matter how much money I made when it comes to building wealth. How could that be? It just didn't make sense.

"Wait a minute," I said. "How can it be that your income doesn't come into play when we're talking about building wealth which is all about money."

"I know it's hard to believe David. I can't argue that if you make more money, you'll have a better *chance* of creating a larger next egg. Just remember that **trying to increase your net worth through increasing your income** *alone* **is a battle you'll never win**."

"But doesn't making more money make a difference?" I asked.

The Nail in the Coffin – The Story of Anne Scheiber

He reached into his pocket and pulled out his wallet. He flipped it open and pulled out a small piece of newspaper.

"Read this news blurb and let me know if you still think you need a lot of money to become wealthy."

The piece of newspaper read:

Former IRS Worker Leaves $22 Million to University[18]
By Fabman Vonderhoot

Most people haven't heard of her, but Anne Scheiber is one of the world's greatest investors. In 1932 at the age of 38, Anne gave her brother $5,000, her life savings at the time, to invest in the stock market. Her brother promptly lost ALL of her money. Despite her meager salary of $3,000 working at the IRS, Schreiber was able to save another $5,000 over the course of the next 12 years and put the money back into the stock market. This time she took advice from herself. The results: that initial $5,000 and subsequent additions grew to over $22 million at the time of her death in 1995 at the age of 101.

That's right, $22 million. How did she do it? How did she have the resolve to invest again after losing her life savings? She simply knew that she *had* to invest in the stock market. Scheiber realized during her career as a tax auditor with the IRS that the majority of the wealthiest people in the country had a significant portion of their wealth in stocks. She realized that the majority of these individuals bought shares, but seldom sold them, thus avoiding paying taxes in the short-term. She adopted the buy-and-hold strategy and invested in stocks of companies she knew and understood.

For the next fifty years, Scheiber rarely sold a share. She stuck with them through the crash of 1987, the inflationary '70s and the bear market of 1973-1974. Readers will also note that her first investment was at the height of the Depression and despite having lost it all the first time, she kept on investing. Her determination clearly paid off. When she died she left $22 million to New York's Yeshiva University. We could all learn a thing or two from this savvy New Yorker.

I was speechless.

"Close your mouth David. You're catching flies."

"That's amazing," I whispered. "She turned $5,000 and some additional investment dollars into $22 million in less than 50 years. Awesome!"

"Yes, it is quite remarkable, but I want you to realize that her investment plan was not terribly difficult. She just kept investing in good times and bad and never sold her shares."

"My accounts mostly go down every year," I said with a sigh.

"Such is the case lately, but it won't always be that way. Whether or not the current recession lasts another couple of months or another couple of years, you'd be well advised to start your investing program all over again. This time you're going to do it the right way."

---

[18] Yes, a make believe article, but a true story. Go to www.Google.com and type in "Anne Scheiber" and you'll find dozens of articles verifying the story of this extraordinary woman.

Saving Your Way to Wealth is <u>Highly</u> Unlikely

"Essentially what I'm trying to hammer into you is that **saving your way to wealth just doesn't work**. The key reason is the *cost* of realizing your income. The money you earn at your job is taxed and instantly reduced. The wealthy minimize the amount of taxes they pay by having the majority of their wealth in investments where they control the amount of taxes they pay and when they pay them. They invest in their businesses, stocks held for the long run, and real estate holdings with offsetting depreciation and other tax-saving goodies."

"But I don't have a lot of money to invest right now," I admitted. "I can't even come up with $1,000, let alone $5,000."

"That's okay because if you were paying attention during our discussion of the third Secret of Wealth, you would know how to make a little into a lot."

I was confused. He wouldn't answer his own question though, but made me sweat it out. Then it hit me. "Compound interest, right?" I asked.

"Give the man a cigar. Phew," he said wiping his brow. "Thought all that hard work on my part went for naught."

"Hey," I said, feigning being hurt by placing my hands on my heart. "I paid attention."

"I'll be the judge of that," he said. "If you remember, we spoke about a dollar a day becoming a million dollars in your lifetime. The key was getting started, investing on a regular basis, and keeping the money invested for the long haul."

"I'm sold, I'm sold," I said eagerly. "How do I start."

"Patience David. **Investing is not a sprint, it's a marathon**, but the sooner you start the better. In fact, that's one reason the sixth Secret of Wealth is called: **Invest NOW, Not Tomorrow: Leveraging the Power of Compound Interest.** It truly is critical that you start investing as soon as possible to get the power of compound interest to work for you. But before we get into the nitty gritty, let's get our bagels and get home. You're going to need to write this stuff down."

We were standing in front of the bagel place at this point. After five minutes of catching up with everyone and I mean everyone in the place, we bought our bagels and caught a ride home with one of his friends.

Chapter 12

BEGINNING THE JOURNEY

The Investment Pyramid

Back at his kitchen table, he restarted our discussion. "Before we get into how to invest, let me bore you with a little history lesson."

"You're kidding right? I thought we were going to talk about investing not how Columbus discovered America."

"Patience David. I promise this history lesson will be short. Do you know how the ancient pyramids in Egypt were built?"

"Sure. Thousands of slaves carried huge slabs of rocks and somehow placed them on top of one another."

"Correct. They built it layer by layer. The analogy of a pyramid is a great way to visualize your Financial House. You build each new level only after the previous level has been built beneath it. The same process holds for the investment vehicles you will purchase when you build your Financial House. Let's talk about the different types of investments and you'll see for yourself how important this lesson truly is to your future."

"You're the boss. Let's do it," I replied.

Level One – Security: Cash and Insurance

"The foundation of your pyramid represents your basic need for security: cash and short-term investments like CDs or money market accounts. Now your cash reserve should include your Emergency Fund. Most of the investments at this level are low risk stuff. At this stage, you need to develop your budget and get a handle on your debt before you can move on. You also need to make sure that you have the appropriate level of life and disability insurance to protect you against the unforeseen."

Level Two – Comfort and Shelter: Your Home and Bonds

"The second level is where you get to take on just a little extra risk. While not truly part of your portfolio, your home is your biggest expense/asset at this level. Investments at this level also include corporate, Treasury, and tax-free municipal bonds.

Level Three – Growth: Taxable and Tax-deferred Accounts

"At the third level you're investing for growth. Here you're taking on a little more risk with the hopes of higher returns. The main investment vehicles will be your tax-deferred accounts including your 401(k) and IRAs. Level three investments include growth stocks and growth-oriented mutual funds, but you should focus on index funds, although it's okay to start dabbling with stocks on a small scale."

Level Four – Passive Income: Real Estate Investments & Business Income

"At level four you're looking to invest your money in assets that will appreciate in value and throw off some cash. Investments at this level are investment real estate and businesses."

"What do you mean by 'throw off cash'?"

"As in a positive cash flow or passive income. For example in real estate, it means that after taking in the rents from your tenants and paying all the bills, including the mortgage, you're left with excess money at the end of the day."

"I think I like this passive income stuff."

"Looks like we've got a natural born entrepreneur on our hands folks," he said. "Once you've mastered the first three levels of the Game of Life, we'll get you started on a program to build your passive income portfolio. That's where the real money is made."

Level Five – Swinging for the Fences: Options, IPOs, Hedge Funds, Risky Ventures, Big Businesses, and the Rest

"The last stage or step is for sophisticated investors only. In level five you have the smallest percentage of your total available funds, perhaps 5% to 10% of your assets. At this level you're taking on tremendous risk hoping to really cash in on a high-flying investment. Investments in this level include speculative stocks, high-yield junk bonds, options, futures, gold, and limited partnerships. You really shouldn't be playing around with any of these investments until you've taken care of the previous four levels."

Concentrate on Level One and Two...For Now

"How do I learn more about these levels?" I asked.

"The first two Secrets of Wealth, as well as the ninth Secret I will teach you, will help you build the first two levels of the pyramid. The third level is covered in this Secret and the eighth Secret touches upon levels two and four on the pyramid."

"What about level five?" I asked.

"Level five will never be covered in a beginning wealth building class taught by me. There's simply too much risk associated with those types of investments and they are made for two types of investors: those that know what they're doing and suckers. It's simply easier to make money for the average person through safer investments and real estate rental property than it is through level five investments."

"I understand why you should wait to learn about those more complex and riskier investments," I replied. "So what's next?" I asked.

"Let's discuss the main asset classes to start," he replied

ASSET CLASSES - STOCKS, BONDS AND CASH

"An asset class is a group of investments that have similar risk characteristics. The broad categories of assets are cash, bonds, and stocks. Now you can dig deeper into each of those classes and breakout cash by cash and cash equivalents like treasury bills, money market funds, and passbook savings accounts. Likewise you can divide bonds into short-term and long-term bonds and even then you can break down each of those categories further."

"So stocks can be broken down into small cap, mid-cap, and large-caps?" I said, referring to one measure of the size of individual stocks.

"That's right."

CASH

"Cash includes certificates of deposits (CDs) from banks, money market funds, savings accounts, and US Treasury bills. Cash and cash equivalents have the lowest returns of the three asset classes, but what they lack in returns, they more than make up for in security of principal."

MONEY MARKET FUNDS

"I thought you should know about money market funds which are one of the safest kinds of mutual funds out there. They invest in short term debt obligations from the government and corporations. You'll get a higher rate of return through a money market fund than through the money market accounts offered by your banks. Just remember that money market funds are not FDIC-insured."

"So you can lose your money?"

"That's correct, but highly unlikely. These funds are for those seeking to preserve their current capital and earn a return that matches or slightly outpaces inflation. They can be good investment options for people who want to invest their money for the short-term and get a higher return than offered at their local bank. Plus they're better than CDs since they are very liquid."

BONDS

"When a company or government needs to raise money in order to meet short-term demands or grow the business, build a factory, or build a highway, they will often issue a bond. Getting money through issuing a bond is called **debt financing**. In short, a bond is just like an IOU note. When you buy a bond, you're literally lending money to someone and you're receiving a fixed interest rate in return. Bonds also are referred to as 'fixed-income' investments because the bond's term and schedule of interest payments are fixed."

Returns and Risk - Even "safe" bonds have some risk

"Historically the returns on bonds have been higher than cash, but you're also taking on some extra risk with bonds."

"But isn't the return on bonds guaranteed?" I asked.

"No David, **the return is not guaranteed** if you sell a bond before it matures. A lot of people think they can't lose money in bonds, but they're wrong."

The Perils of Inflation

"First off you have the risk that **inflation will eat away at the value of your fixed interest payments**. As you know, a dollar ten years from now isn't going to buy as much as it did today. Unfortunately, bonds pay out fixed interest payments, which might not keep pace with inflation.[19] The longer the term of the bond, the greater the inflation risk."

There are Plenty of Other Risks

"You also have other risks associated with investing in bonds, but the main one is the risk that your after-tax returns will not outpace inflation. I'm not about to go over all the other risks."

"How come?" I asked.

"My intent today is to give you just the basics of what bonds are, how they work, and how they fit into your overall investment plan. We're not getting into the specifics for two reasons: one you can buy any investment book for that and two, you'll be investing via mutual funds anyway. You're not going to be buying individual bonds for quite some time and even when you're close to retirement, you're probably going to work closely with a financial planner who's going to help you create a portfolio of bonds to live off of when you're rich and retired. Make sense to you?" he asked.

"You're the expert. Whatever you think is best," I replied.

---

[19] Except perhaps for TIPS and I Bonds, which are adjusted for inflation.

STOCKS

"The next asset class is stocks. A stock or a share of stock is a partial ownership stake in a company. When you own a share of stock, you're literally one of many owners or shareholders of the company. In essence you get the perks of being an owner (sharing in the profits or appreciation in the business), with a limited downside (how much you've invested and stand to lose if the stock goes to $0). You also have **limited liability**. This means that you're not personally liable if the company you're investing in cannot pay its bills or there is a lawsuit against it. As such you have a legal claim to everything the company owns. In addition, for each share you own, you get one vote and you help elect the Board of Directors."

How a Stock Market Works

"The majority of stocks are traded on exchanges, which is a fancy word for a place where people meet to buy and sell an item. Now I'm sure you've heard of The New York Stock Exchange, the NASDAQ, and the American Stock Exchange. There are also stock exchanges in other countries like the Hong Kong Exchange or the London Stock Exchange. Each of these exchanges help facilitate the buying and selling of stocks around the world. It kind of works like an auction. Stockbrokers are the ones who bring together the buyers and sellers and the stock exchange facilitates the trades. The selling price is set by the price the buyers are willing to pay. This is why stock prices fluctuate on a daily basis."

Value Investors

"Investors in the stock market fall into one of two main categories: value or growth investors. A value investor is looking for shares of companies that are trading below what they think the company is worth. They want to find a company that is *undervalued* by Wall Street and hope that the price of the stock will appreciate to reflect the true value of the company. I won't get into the nitty gritty, but the main thing to know is that **value investors seek out companies that are undervalued**. Warren Buffett is the most well-known value investor."

Growth Investors

"On the other hand, a growth investor is less concerned with buying undervalued stocks. They're trying to find companies that are able to grow their sales and earnings at an *above average* rate. Growth investors are looking to make money on rapid increases in price of the shares. Peter Lynch is one of the best known growth investors."

The Automatic Investor

"So which type of investor are you; value or growth?"

"Neither. I'm an Automatic Investor," he replied.

"What's that?" I asked.

"It's a method of investing that is based on some pretty powerful research that's been conducted over the past decade. I've found this investing method to be the easiest to follow for the average person and it's great because you don't have to bother with the day-to-day swings in the market. However, I must admit that **I do lean toward being a value investor** when picking individual securities."

"Hey, wait a minute," I said. "So you *do* pick individual stocks? You made it sound like you only invested in mutual funds."

"Hold your horses," he replied. "Yes, I do invest in individual stocks, but I don't expect to beat the market and **I surely don't bank my retirement on my stock picking prowess**. That would be playing the Loser's Game[20] and that's just too risky for me. I put 10% of my investment money into what I call my **Vegas Account**, which I use to invest in individual stocks, but the bulk of my money is invested via a more powerful investing method that I will share with you. But let's first talk about volatility and swings in prices in the stock market."

Short Term Volatility - Long-Term Gain

"Some people can't deal with swings in the market and can't stick with their investment plan, so they sell their stocks or mutual funds and sock their money away in cash accounts. The problem with running for cover every time the market dips is that it's too hard to get the returns you need to retire early by investing only in savings accounts, CDs, and bonds. Most people don't realize how damaging *avoiding* stocks can be. Perhaps this chart might help persuade you to stick with stocks:

FIGURE 12.1 - Over the Long Haul, Stick with Stocks

	Last 50 Years (annual)	Last 20 Years (annual)	Last 10 Years (annual)	Last 5 Years (annual)
US Small Stocks	14.0%	11.6%	11.6%	4.3%
S&P 500	11.1	12.7	9.3	-0.6
Int'l Stocks: MSCI EAFE	N/A	10.5	4.3	-2.6
US LT Corp Bonds	6.7	11.0	8.8	8.3
US LT Gov't Bonds	6.7	9.1	7.3	8.2
US 30-Day T-bill	5.3	5.7	4.4	4.2
US Inflation Rate	3.9	3.1	2.5	2.3

Source: Morningstar.com, Annualized Returns for Periods Ended 12/31/02

---

[20] See the book *Winning the Loser's Game*, by Charles D. Ellis and John J. Brennan

Stocks for the Long Run

"As you can see, despite the most recent bear market and the miserable three years of negative returns, the S&P500 is still up an average of 9.3% over the past ten years."

"Wow!" I exclaimed. **"So if stocks have outperformed bonds and T-bills over the past 50 years, why buy bonds?"**

"Ah, the million dollar question," he responded. "Now's the time for our little discussion on risks versus rewards."

Bonds Have Lower Returns Than Stocks, So Why Buy Bonds?

"You see David, both stocks and bonds have their place in your portfolio and you should already know that stocks don't *always* outperform bonds. In fact, in the three year stretch from 2000 to 2002, bond returns outpaced stocks."

"But over the long haul stocks beat bonds, right?" I asked.

"Based on past performance and historical information, your statement is correct," he said, "but you shouldn't be overly bullish in estimating what return you'll get because it might cause you to save less than you'll need to set aside for your goals and retirement."

Risky Business

"Risk comes from not knowing what you're doing." – Warren Buffett

"Most investors think of investment risk as the chance they'll lose their money, but the concept of risk is much more complicated. It has to do with the **Risk vs. Return Tradeoff.** In simple terms, **in order to get greater returns, you're going to have to take on greater risk.** If you can't accept greater risk, then you're going to have to expect lower returns."

"So there's no way to completely eliminate the risk of losing your money?" I asked.

"Not really because with any financial investment, whether it be a savings account or a speculative stock, there is some sort of risk. If you decide to invest it in stocks, there's a risk that you will lose it in the market. Invest in low-interest bearing investments like CDs and your money won't grow fast enough to meet your retirement needs. Even if you choose to do nothing and put that money under your mattress, you risk losing purchasing power thanks to the effects of inflation. Inflation is the silent killer of many an investment portfolio. Of course it could have been avoided had the investors had the **right mindset.**"

"Okay," I said. "I'm all ears. What's the right mindset then?" I asked.

Overcome Your Fear of Taking Risks and Making Mistakes

"You need to work hard at overcoming your fear of taking risks and making mistakes in order to achieve higher returns. The people that win in the Game of Life are the ones who can stomach a little risk. **There's no guarantee that you will make money in the stock market, but you must get over your fear of losing money and take on some risk to make money in life**. Unfortunately, the people who think they're doing a good thing by protecting their money from the ups and downs of the market by sticking it in a savings account are actually losing money every year."

"Wait a minute," I said, shaking my head. "How could they lose money? Is someone stealing it?" I asked.

He laughed at the comment. "No David. Nothing like that. They could be losing their hard-earned money because it's not keeping up with inflation, one of the biggest risks to nest eggs around the world. We touched upon it briefly, but let's dig a little deeper into the subject."

Keeping Up with Inflation

"Inflation is the rate at which the general level of prices for goods and services is rising and because prices are rising, your purchasing power is decreasing. Purchasing power is a fancy way of saying what you can afford to buy with your money. As inflation rises, every dollar will buy a smaller percentage of an item. For example, if the inflation rate is 3%, then a $1 bottle of water will cost $1.03 a year from now."

"I get it," I said. "And every year into the future, the cost of that water will cost another 3% and another 3% and so on."

"That's right and if you're too conservative an investor, there's a risk that your investments won't grow faster than the rate of inflation."

> **"If your life is without failure,
> you haven't taken enough risks."**
> – Albert Einstein

"The rich get rich because no one else is willing to take risks. They're the ones who come along, assess the situation and determine if the risk is worth the reward. And don't think that successful investors haven't lost money many times before. Making mistakes is part of becoming a true investor. **Successful investors simply learn from their mistakes and make sure they don't repeat them**. You need to take on more risk but in a controlled manner in order to achieve Financial Freedom."

Sleeping at Night – What's your risk tolerance?

"The real question at hand is, '**How much risk should I take on to meet my long-term goals?**' In order to answer this question, you have to figure out what your **risk tolerance** is. Your risk tolerance is nothing more than a gauge of your tolerance for or aversion to risk. But in layman's terms, it's called the '*ability to sleep at night*' test."

"The what?"

"You heard me. It's figuring out how much risk you can take on while still being able to sleep at night and be comfortable with the investment decisions you've made."

"Oh, I get it. So if investing 70% in stocks keeps you up at night, you're probably taking on too much risk, right?"

"Something like that. In the end it's about feeling comfortable about your investment decisions and realizing that how much risk you take on determines the potential reward you will get."

Diversification

"Next up in our discussion is diversification, which in layman's terms means **not putting all your eggs into one basket**. This way if one of those baskets should happen to fall, you still have eggs left in the other baskets. Applied to stocks and bonds, this means you shouldn't invest your life savings into one or two stocks. The idea behind diversification is simply to reduce the risk in your portfolio by buying a variety of investments. This limits the impact any one security can have on your total portfolio, thus reducing the overall risk inherent in your portfolio."

"Can you elaborate on that?" I asked.

"Sure. If you were to invest in only one or two stocks you could have a really good year or a really bad year, but a diversified portfolio should yield moderate gains and moderate losses. You'll lose out on the potential blockbuster gain in a stock had you invested a lot in a single stock, but you will also hedge against losing all your money if that one company goes bankrupt. You'll get average returns instead of returns at the extreme ends. You're not going to have 30% returns, but you're not going to have 40% losses either."

"Because of the risk/return relationship?" I asked.

"Nope, because of asset allocation."

> "Increasing our diversification is close to a free lunch -
> **you can decrease the risk of investing without
> decreasing your expected return.**"
> – William Sharpe, Nobel Laureate

Asset Allocation - The 94 Percent Solution

"Simply put, asset allocation is the process of diversifying your portfolio by placing a certain percentage of your money into different types of investments, like stocks, bonds, cash, and other asset classes. You spread your money across different investments in line with your financial goals, risk tolerance, and return objectives. In other words you're limiting the impact any one asset or investment can have on your portfolio because you're well diversified. But **asset allocation goes one step further than simple diversification and takes into account how different asset classes *interact* with one another.** The end result is that you maximize your returns, while minimizing the overall risk inherent in your portfolio."

"Okay, I think I get it, but why is it so important?"

"Because **studies have shown that asset allocation accounts for anywhere between 90 to 94 percent of your investment returns.**"

"Did you just say '94 percent of your investment returns'?"

"I sure did. The number comes from a study that was done a while ago that concluded that asset allocation determines roughly 94 percent of your return. The other 6 percent was due to individual stock picks and shifting money between asset classes[21]."

"That's amazing," I said, still shocked that such a large percentage of your returns could be determined by one investment technique.

"It is David and what's scary is that asset allocation, despite being such an important determinant of one's portfolio returns, has gotten little coverage by the financial media. I'm not going to cover it in detail, but if you want to learn more about the subject, just look it up on the Internet and you'll get thousands of pages on the concept."

"Okay, but can you tell me how it works?" I asked.

Reducing the Risk in Your Portfolio

"Sure," he replied. "Asset allocation is a risk-management tool that tries to stabilize your returns and limit your potential losses. You do this by investing a portion of your money for growth (stocks), some for income (bonds), and the rest for stability (cash equivalents). These asset classes are further broken down into smaller categories/sectors/classes: small cap stocks, large cap value stocks, short-term bonds, and so on and so on. Each asset class will have a different level of risk associated with it and therefore a different anticipated rate of return."

"So how do I put asset allocation to work for me?"

---

[21] "Determinants of Portfolio Returns" by Brinson, Hood and Beebower; Financial Analysts Journal, July/August 1986

How it Works

"You need to first determine what the ideal mix of stocks, bonds, and cash your portfolio should contain. This is based on your: **personal financial situation, time horizon, and risk tolerance**."

Personal Financial Situation

"First up is your personal financial situation. You need to look at your net worth and cash flow statements and see if you have enough money set aside for emergencies. You also need to determine if you have any short-term liabilities that require your immediate attention, like credit card debt that is spiraling out of control."

"What does credit card debt have to do with how you invest your money?"

"Well David, you might find yourself abandoning your investment plan because you need to pay off some of your debts. Along those same lines, investors should also take into consideration the security of their job. If there is the chance that they could be laid off, they should reconsider the level of reserve funds that they have available. They might also want to reassess the mix of assets they have assembled in their portfolio, perhaps shifting funds among the classes to reduce the overall risk inherent in their portfolios."

Time Horizon

"Next up is your time horizon or in other words, how long will it be until you need your money back. The longer your time horizon, the more you will emphasize stocks in your portfolio."

"Is that because you can deal with the loss of some of your portfolio because you have time to make the money back?"

"Exactly."

Risk Tolerance

"Last up is your tolerance for risk. I won't repeat myself, but the key is to develop a plan that is in line with your risk tolerance. Most financial planners and web-sites have a quiz you take to figure our your risk tolerance. Unfortunately, most people *overestimate* their tolerance for risk and then they spend every waking minute of the day watching CNBC, worrying about losing their investments. **Your risk tolerance is probably one of the most important factors since it determines how much money you will have in stocks and how much you will have in bonds or cash**. The more risk averse you are, the less you will have in stocks, which will cut down on your anticipated returns. This will either force you to lengthen the timeline for your goals, cause you to invest more money, or both."

Your Ideal Asset Allocation

"So after you figure out those three things, how do you create your asset allocation for your portfolio?" I asked.

"The best way is to go to a financial planner and have them plug in your risk tolerance and time horizon into their computer and they can develop a portfolio that's theoretically best for you," he replied.

"Is there a way I can figure out the best asset allocation on my own without visiting a financial planner?"

"Sure. Check out www.morningstar.com for one of the best online asset allocators I've seen around."

How Old Are You?

"Most planners like to create an asset allocation plan or percentage mix between stocks, bonds, and cash based on your current age. This kind of takes into consideration your time horizon and risk tolerance, because **as you get older you have less tolerance for risk**. When you're younger, you have more time to make up for any losses you incur, whereas when you get older you can't afford to lose your money because you're going to need the money much sooner."

The Standard Party Line (Allocation)

"Financial planners used to use the formula of subtracting your age from 100 or 120 and the remaining number was the percentage that you should invest in stocks. But I think the formula is pretty much outdated and you can get better results with an online calculator based on the deadlines (time horizon) for your goals."

Time Horizon and Tolerance to Risk

"I generally tell my students to use this chart," he said showing me the below chart, "which has allocations based on time horizons."

Figure 12.2 - Asset Allocation Time Horizon Guideline

Time Horizon	Equity (%)	Fixed Income (%)
5 Years or less	0	100
6 Years	20	80
7 Years	40	60
8 Years	60	40
9 Years	80	20
10 Years or longer	100	0

Source: *The Only Guide to a Winning Investment Strategy You'll Ever Need*, by Larry Swedroe, Truman Talley, New York, 1998 p 174

"Aren't those allocations pretty aggressive?" I asked.

"That's the typical response from my students nowadays," he replied. He reached into his binder and pulled out the following chart:

Figure 12.3 - Find the Right Mix

Suggested Mixes	Average annual return (1926-2001)	Worst 1-year loss (1926-2001)	Number of years with a loss (1926-2001)
Stability • 10% stocks • 80% bonds • 10% cash investments	6.2%	-6.7%	10 of 76
Income • 20% stocks • 80% bonds	7.0%	-10.1%	13 of 76
Conservative growth • 40% stocks • 60% bonds	8.1%	-18.4%	16 of 76
Balanced growth • 50% stocks • 50% bonds	8.7%	-22.5%	17 of 76
Moderate growth • 60% stocks • 40% bonds	9.1%	-26.6%	19 of 76
Growth • 80% stocks • 20% bonds	10.0%	-34.9%	21 of 76
Aggressive growth • 100% stocks	10.7%	-43.1%	22 of 76

SOURCE: The Vanguard Group, Inc., Reprinted with Permission

"Wow! I never knew I could get those kind of returns from sticking with my investments over time," I said.

"These numbers are the result of asset allocation, David. As you can see, the more risk you take on (as you move down the chart), the better your average annual returns are expected to be. But the tradeoff is that you have the potential for greater losses in any given year increases thanks to the greater percentage of stocks in your portfolio."

"So the more risk you take on, the greater your potential reward. Got it," I said. "And **you should always have a proper asset allocation if you want to get the highest return *and* the most stability possible**, but then what?"

"You create your investment portfolio. I guess it's time we talked about creating your investment portfolio and doing it the right way."

"Really!" I exclaimed. "Let's do it."

Chapter 13

INVESTING ON AUTOPILOT:
Becoming a MILLIONAIRE AUTOMATICALLY

The "Do Nothing" Approach to Wealth-Building

"I call my investing approach the *Do Nothing Approach to Wealth-Building* or DNA for short. The name is a bit deceptive, because **there really is no investment around where you can create significant wealth without some kind of involvement on your part**. The DNA method simply requires you to have your money work for you while you're out working hard at your job. Investing is difficult at first since it takes time up front to figure out what to invest in and how to set up your account. But after your initial time spent setting up your account, it's going to get a lot easier and the time needed to monitor your plan decreases significantly. At least in the beginning getting started is a bit scary, but it's just like running a marathon."

"Running a marathon? You lost me."

"All runners start out running with no major running goal in mind. They just start by running one or two miles, then after a while, they gradually increase the distances they run. Then they hear about a 5-mile road race and they enter. It kind of happens automatically."

"I get it," I said. "So eventually they set their sights on a marathon and train for it and accomplish it, is that the moral of the story?"

"Exactly. Once running becomes a *habit*, they're able to go after bigger and better accomplishments. The important thing to remember is to **make investing a regular part of your life**. You've got to stop making excuses as to why you can't do it or how you don't know enough about investing. What my running analogy was trying to get across was that **investing on a regular basis just becomes part of your life**. Every month you pay the phone bill and every month you send $100 or $200 to your investment account. Every two weeks you get a paycheck and every two weeks part of your salary goes to your 401(k). With that having been said, let's learn about your main investment vehicle: mutual funds."

MUTUAL FUNDS - Instant Diversification

"We just finished a discussion about asset allocation and diversification. Now if you had the time, money, and the stamina, you could build a portfolio of stocks from different sectors and countries, as well as add in a few bonds and short-term cash investments in order to create a well-diversified portfolio. However, most people don't want to bother with picking individual stocks and many more can't afford the risks inherent with investing in only a couple of stocks. Besides, it would take a lot of money to create a perfectly diversified portfolio on your own. This is why most people turn to mutual funds because of their convenience and the instant diversification they provide. Mutual funds are like big baskets of stocks and/or bonds that are managed by a professional fund manager. With a mutual fund, you pool your money together with other investors and then a fund manager invests the money in the stock and bond markets."

I Love Mutual Funds and You Should Too!

"I love mutual funds because you spread out the risk you would have taken on had you bought an individual stock, i.e., you're not putting all your eggs in one basket. I admit that mutual funds are kind of boring but in this case boring works and it works very well. You don't have to research any stocks or decide when to buy or sell. You simply send in your check every month and purchase new shares of the fund."

"So how is the price of a mutual fund determined? Is it like stocks with the supply and demand pushing up the share price?"

"No, it's different. At the end of each day, the fund's accountants will determine the value of the total portfolio of stocks, bonds, and short-term investments the fund owns and divide that value by the total number of shares outstanding. The resulting number is the **Net Asset Value** or NAV of the mutual fund. The NAV is the per share price that you see listed in the newspaper every day."

"What about dividends?"

"Dividends from individual stocks the fund might hold and interest earned on cash are sources of income for the fund. This income is distributed to shareholders."

"So they give you that money?"

"Yes. They distribute it to you, but don't even consider touching the money. Instead you should make sure that all interest earned and dividends received are automatically reinvested into the fund."

"Automatically?"

"Yes, automatically. All you have to do is check the box on your mutual fund application or brokerage account application and instruct your brokerage company to **reinvest your dividends**, which means that the money will automatically go toward buying more shares in the fund."

"Wow. That *is* easy."

"Easy as pie, David. Just check the box and always reinvest your dividends."

Shooting Yourself in the Foot - Load vs. No Load Funds

"Now there are various ways you can segment funds, but the first way to sort them is to separate them into those that impose a sales commission or load and those that do not. Funds that don't charge a sales commission are simply called no-load funds."

"How much is that fee going to run me?"

"It'll cost you anywhere from 2% to 6%. **'Front-end' load funds** charge you when you buy shares and **'back-end' load funds** charge you when you sell."

"So which is better; a front-end or a back-end load?"

"Neither. **Never pay a load for a mutual fund.** There has <u>never</u> been a study that showed that load funds outperform no-load funds, so why waste your hard-earned money on fees? It's just not smart. Another way to segment funds is to bracket them into 'actively' managed and 'passively' managed funds."

ACTIVE MANAGEMENT

"Actively managed funds are, you guessed it, actively managed by a fund manager(s). These poor folks have the difficult task of trying to pick stocks that will be future high-fliers and help them beat their benchmarks."

"What's a benchmark?"

"Fund managers benchmark themselves against baskets of stocks called indexes. For instance, there's the S&P500 index which tracks the largest 500 companies in the US. Now in the short-term, some active managers are able to beat their relative benchmarks, but over the long-haul **most actively managed funds underperform the indexes they benchmark** themselves against."

"Say what?"

"You heard me. The majority of actively managed funds total return, which is their returns less taxes, fees, and other expenses, are beaten by passively managed index funds."

"So you're telling me all those highly paid fund managers can't beat a simple index fund. How can that be?"

"Ah David, welcome to one of the most important discussions of your investing career."

PASSIVE "MANAGEMENT"

"Actively managed funds attempt to beat their benchmarks like the S&P500 by doing tons of research to find undervalued or blockbuster growth stocks. In direct contrast, passively managed funds, more commonly referred to as **index funds**, simply buy all the stocks in a particular index. For instance, an S&P500 stock index fund will only buy the 500 or so stocks that comprise the S&P500. Another point of difference is that most S&P500 index funds don't attempt to beat the S&P500 index, rather they try to just earn the equivalent of the index. In short they're trying to be average, nothing more, nothing less."

"So **index funds only want to be average**? Why would they want that?" I asked.

"Because you'll beat the majority of actively managed funds by being average. Take a look at the following chart:

Why Index Funds are Better than Managed Funds

**Fig. 13.1 - % of Active Funds
Outperformed by Comparable Indexes**

This table compares asset-weighted performance of domestic equity funds against comparable S&P indexes.

5 years annualized as of 12/31/02

Capitalization	Type of Fund		
	Value	**Blend**	**Growth**
Large	46%	62%	68%
Medium	76%	81%	92%
Small	44%	55%	65%

2000-2 (Worst 3-Year bear market in post-Depression era

	S&P 500	**S&P 400**	**S&P 600**
Large	54%		
Medium (Mid)		77%	
Small			72%

Source: The Vanguard Group, Inc. and Morningstar, Inc.

"I knew that index funds were good, but those numbers are ridiculous. Aren't managers supposed to be expert stockpickers? Shouldn't they be able to beat the market?" I asked.

"You would think so, but the cards are stacked against them and here's why," he replied.

Index Funds — The best game in town

"The reason index funds beat the majority of managed funds has to do with the way that returns are calculated. A mutual fund's return is the **total return** of the stocks it holds minus any fees associated with investing the money. Since index funds are pretty much on autopilot, transaction fees and management fees are lower than those of actively mutual funds. In order for actively managed funds to outperform index funds, they have to overcome the burden of higher costs."

I shook my head. "Again, those numbers are amazing. So if I hung with index funds during the worst three-year bear market in the post Depression era, the S&P500, S&P400, and S&P600 would have outperformed 54%, 77%, and 72% of their respective peers?"

"That's what the chart is saying, but those numbers aren't even as high as they will be one day. When you take this analysis out 20 years, it gets worse for actively managed funds. **Only 15% of comparable managed funds beat the S&P500 over that the past 20 years.**"

"How come it gets harder and harder to beat index funds over time?" I asked.

"Because of the burdens placed on actively managed funds."

The Burden of Actively Managed Funds
Higher Costs

"All mutual funds charge an annual fee for their services even index funds. This fee is expressed as an **expense ratio**, which is the average amount that a fund charges its shareholders every year to manage the fund. Actively managed mutual funds charge their investors' average annual fees of 1.5% or more. The fees mostly go toward paying for their frequent trading, advertising campaigns, and overpaid fund managers. Plus you have the costs of running the company, printing the brochures and prospectuses, and mailing them out. All in all, that's a lot of money that's being spent to get your attention."

"I take it you think the expense ratios charged by actively managed funds are a bit high?"

"How did you guess?" he said sarcastically. "I don't like to invest in funds that have high expense ratios because they are a drag on the fund's performance. Why? Because expense ratios matter, big time! In fact, **a difference of just a percentage point can make a big difference over the course of a lifetime**. Take a look at this ad from The Vanguard Group, the biggest seller of index funds."

He turned his binder around and moved it toward me. There was an advertisement from Vanguard that had been clipped from a magazine and placed in Mr. Mathers book. The ad was titled '*Chapter*

16 Controlling Expenses.[22]' I won't go into detail about the ad, but it compared two different funds: one with a high expense ratio and one with a low expense ratio. The one percent difference in expense ratios for an initial $25,000 investment yielding 8% annually over 20 years amounted to a $19,751 difference in the fund balances.

"A $19,751 difference all because of a one-percent difference in the expense ratios? Wow!"

"Now on top of the management fees, funds have **12b-1 fees**, which funds charge you for their marketing and distribution expenses."

"Wait a minute. I'm footing the bill for a fund to advertise?"

"That's correct. They are usually included in the funds expense ratio, but are discussed separately in some instances. Unfortunately even no-load index funds charge you 12b-1 fees."

Higher Turnover – Bigger Tax Bills for YOU

"Now in addition to higher expenses, actively managed funds, on average, have higher turnover than index funds."

"What's turnover?"

"**Turnover refers to how often the fund's manager buys and sells the assets within the fund**. If a fund has a turnover of 100% it means that the fund manager turned over or sold the entire portfolio once during that year. Turnover is important because **all that buying and selling creates capital gains and you've got to pay taxes on those gains**. The higher the funds turnover, the more you're going to pay in taxes.   **Funds with low turnover keep stocks as they appreciate in value so you pay less in taxes**. Guess which funds have the lowest turnover around?"

"Index funds," I replied.

"Index funds is right. Just another reason to buy them."

"So the money I would have paid in taxes stays invested and has a chance to grow?" I asked.

"And since you have more money to invest because you're not busy paying taxes to Uncle Sam, your portfolio should grow faster than if it was invested primarily in managed funds," he added.

"I think I want to learn more about passively managed funds."

"Smart decision."

"Investors need to avoid the negatives of buying fads, crummy companies, and timing the market. **Buying an index fund over a long period of time makes the most sense**."
                                                                  - Warren Buffett

---

[22] Source: The Vanguard Group, Inc., 2003 Advertisement

It Boils Down to Lower Expenses and Lower Turnover

"The reason that no-load index funds are so successful is that you're not paying a sales commission, you have lower expenses, they're more tax efficient, and there's no manager risk[23] involved. But out of all these reasons, the two main advantages of passively managed funds are lower costs and lower turnover. So when all is said and done, **what seems like an average return for an index fund before expenses and taxes will actually be *above average* when compared to the after tax and after expense return of actively managed funds**," he said, reinforcing the point.

Dollar Cost Averaging

"Now lets shift our conversation to the process of buying. Since its too difficult to buy at the guaranteed lows of a market, you should invest on a consistent and periodic basis. The term most frequently used with this investment technique is dollar cost averaging."

"Oh, I've heard of the technique before in some book I must have read on investing," I commented. "I can't remember which one though."

A Little Upon a Little Equals a Lot

"Good, then you should know that **dollar cost averaging (DCA) is one of the easiest and best techniques you can use to build your portfolio**. DCA is the process of investing a set dollar amount into a particular stock or fund on a regular basis. Regardless of the share price at the time of purchase, you put in the same amount of money. When the share price is high you buy less shares and when the price is low, you buy more shares."

"Does the strategy protect you from a loss? I mean could it have helped me avoid losing my money over the past couple of years?"

"No. **Dollar-cost averaging cannot prevent a loss if the fund or stock you choose declines over time**. In fact, there are quite a few so-called experts out there who are against the concept of dollar cost averaging. They call it '*dollar cost losing*.'"

"Why?" I asked.

"They contend that if a stock or fund is dropping in value, you should sell, not buy more. Right now with our current bear market, their argument might make sense to the man or woman who has lost 40% to 50% of their portfolio in the last two or three years, but I think there argument is flawed," he said.

---

[23] The risk that your fund manager makes poor investing decisions.

The Perils of Sitting on the Sidelines

"Why?" I asked. "I mean why would you continue to buy into a losing stock or fund when you can just sit on the sidelines and jump back in when the market rebounds?"

"Careful David. It sounds like you're advocating market timing and **no one has consistently timed the market**. While the market is currently in bear territory, that won't last forever. **People who sit on the sidelines with their cash in hand ready to jump back in when things turn around will _never_ get back into the game.** Instead they'll forget to invest and never will get back in and their hard-earned cash will be subject to the ravages of inflation."

Market Timing Doesn't Work

He flipped through a couple of pages in his binder, found what he was looking for and looked up at me. "And now for the data to back up my statements." He handed me his binder. "Take a look at the following chart and see what missing the ten best days in a given year can do to your returns."

Figure 13.2 - Why Market Timing Doesn't Work:
Growth of $10,000 invested in the S&P 500[24]

1980 - 2002	Account Value*
Stayed in Market Entire Time	$172,436
Minus 10 best days	103,239
Minus 30 best days	51,281
Minus 50 best days	29,232
CDs	41,499

* Source: *Fidelity STAGES*, Spring 2003, Used with Permission

"Wow. You miss out on $70,000 in gains," I said.

"That's right and how do you think you miss those days?" he asked. "By trying to time and beat the market," he said, answering his own question.

"I understand what you're saying, but isn't there something you can do during a bear market to limit your losses?" I asked.

"Well, if you don't believe that the market will turnaround, it's up to you to revisit your goals and allocations to determine whether or not you can move more money toward short-term investments and out of equities. Just realize that if you do shift funds from equities into short-term investments like bonds, the anticipated returns will go down."

"That's like rebalancing, right?"

"That's exactly what it's like," he said nodding his approval.

---

[24] Chart appeared in STAGES Magazine, Fidelity Investments Magazine for Retirement Plan Investors, Spring 2003

"It is always the right time to invest the right way.
The right time to get in the market is when you have money to invest, and the right time to get out of the market is when you need the money. Just make sure that when you invest, your risk exposure matches your risk capacity."
                        - Mark Hebner, Founder, Index Funds Advisors

Rebalancing

"**Rebalancing is the process of shifting your money among assets in order to bring your portfolio back to your targeted allocations.** You can rebalance your portfolio by either selling some of your winners or you can add more money to the funds that have underperformed the market. This will ensure that you're selling high (funds/sectors that have appreciated) and buying low (buying more of the sectors that have gone down) in order to bring you back to your original allocation. It sounds complicated, but it's not. Most people do it once a year and it's a simple enough procedure if you're investing via index funds."

"I think I understand how it works. So if I owned a tech fund in the late 90s, I should have been selling some of the shares to buy perhaps a bond fund, since my investments became so heavily stock-focused."

"That's the gist of it, but you'd be well served to work with a planner or an online tool to make sure you're not going to get hit with too much in capital gains taxes. But before we get off on a tangent, I want you to understand that **DCA can help take the emotions out of investing**. As you've learned, your emotions are what stop you from investing the right way. With my approach you simply put your investment program on autopilot and keep adding to your accounts month in and month out. You check up every so often and tinker with the allocations if need be. That's all there is to it. That's why I call it the Do Nothing Approach to Investing."

Side Note: Taking the Emotion Out of Investing: Why it's so important

My friend Mel Lindauer (CFS, WMS, Forum Leader, Morningstar Vanguard Diehards) sent me a great article called: "Party Like Its 1929[25]*," by Tom Jacobs from the Motley Fool web-site. Tom was gracious enough to allow me to reprint it here for you.*

---

[25] "Party Like Its 1929," by Tom Jacobs from the Motley Fool web-site, www.Fool.com, August 1, 2002

Party Like it's 1929

"Even during the Great Depression, when it took 25 years for the Dow Jones Industrial Average to return to its Sept. 3, 1929 peak, investors who put money into the market regularly had positive returns after only five years. Only those who sat on what they had, scared off by the drop, experienced a 25-year drought. Keep that in mind today.

What if we DCA'd through the Depression?

First...imagine investing a lump sum in all DJIA stocks at the market's high, represented by the DJIA's Sept. 3, 1929 peak of 386. Second, we'll posit investing the same amount of money that day and continuing annually on Dec. 31 from 1930 until the DJIA returned to 386 again in November 1954. (I chose these dates because they're related to the data I could find on the Web.) Here are the compound annual growth rates (CAGRs) after each five-year period until the DJIA hit 386 again in November 1954:

	COMPOUND ANNUAL GROWTH RATES	
	Lump Sum	*DCA**
5 years (1929-34)	-23.1%	**+0.1%**
10 years (1929-39)	-9.0%	+4.4%
15 years (1929-44)	-6.0%	+2.8%
20 years (1929-49)	-3.2%	+3.9%
25 years (1929-54)	0.0%	+7.0%

*Dollar cost averaging

Amazing, huh? The Great Depression was the worst sustained economic catastrophe this country has seen. Unemployment hit 24.9% in 1933. Year-over-year GNP declined from 1930 to 1933, turning up again only in 1934. Yet regular investing still yielded a positive annual compound growth rate after only five years - and that's even without adding in the Dow stocks' dividends[26]."

---

[26] [Note to readers: After publication, we were informed that according to Ibbotson Associates it actually took only until the early 1940s for the equivalent of the S&P 500 - dividends reinvested - total return - to pre-crash levels, but not until Sept. 1954 without dividends. This implies that the Dow Jones Industrial Average returned earlier as well if you include reinvested dividends too. More proof: keep investing, be patient.]

He reached into his binder and handed me a piece of paper. "We're about to get into your starter investment plan, but before you begin to invest, you need to look at a couple of things to make sure you're ready to invest."

Before You Invest a Penny – Your Pre-Investment Checklist

Check Your Reserves
Before you invest, check to see that you've set aside some money in an Emergency Fund. Three to six months after-tax living expenses in a money market account would be nice, but you can start investing if you have $1,000 or two months set aside and a savings plan to get to the 3 to 6 months mark.

How's Your Debt-to-Equity Ratio?
You should figure out what your monthly positive cash flow is and determine what your net worth is currently. Why is this important? You should know how much money you currently have available to invest on a monthly basis and second, you need to determine if you have any liabilities that are going to prevent you from becoming the next Warren Buffett.

Pay Down Your Debt
Not exactly exciting stuff, but it has to be done. If you have out of control debt, the first thing to do is **STOP SPENDING!** Hey, if you can't afford to buy it now (ie, have cash in hand), what makes you think you'll be able to afford it next month when the credit card bill comes? Paying down your credit cards should be priority one. Funding your portfolio is not.

Set up a Debt Repayment Plan
Go back to Secret # 4 and get a debt repayment plan together. You should have this in place before you even think about investing in taxable investment accounts.

Make Sure You're Covered
Make sure you have adequate health, life, disability, and home insurance. You don't want an illness or a disability to wipe out your Emergency Fund and then some. Having adequate insurance is a must.

What are Your Investment Goals and Investment Timelines?
Your goals and how much time you have to reach those goals are two of the most important factors in determining how you will invest your money. Investing in the stock market for long-term goals and in savings and money market accounts for short-term goals.

After I finished reading the checklist, he said, "I believe that you have met almost all of those items on the checklist. It's important to go through them and make sure you're ready to invest before you even consider investing in taxable accounts. With that having been said, let's get into your starter investment account."

Chapter 14

YOUR STARTER INVESTMENT PLAN

Setting up Your Brokerage Account

Full-Service Brokers

"Let's start by talking about setting up your actual investment account. You essentially have three main choices: you can go with a full-service, a discount broker, or you can buy direct from the mutual fund company. Full-service brokers are supposed to give you investment ideas, help you with tax strategies, and almost anything else you can think of regarding your investments," he said.

"Sounds like a good person to call upon when you need advice."

"Yes and no. There are some great brokers out there, but as my friend Tommy calls them, they're nothing but *expensive salespeople*. Some receive a commission on each trade you make so they get paid based on how often you trade, not on how well you do. There's also a big problem with conflicts of interest. Often you'll find them trying to sell you stocks that their company represents[27]. That's a big conflict of interest and there have been several scandals in the past few years involving brokers and analysts pushing stocks their company represents. But mind you, not all full-service brokers are bad. It's just that I believe discount brokers offer you more value for your dollar."

Discount Brokers

"In short, a discount broker provides a more affordable way of executing your trades versus full-service brokers. As I've mentioned before, if you're a buy-and-hold investor you're going to be dollar cost averaging into a small number of funds, so why pay double or triple the amount on commissions? Figuring out which broker to use begins with first understanding your needs as an investor. If you plan on buying stocks in addition to mutual funds, or trading frequently, which I don't recommend, then you're going to look to find one with the lowest commissions. At the very least your discount broker should have both phone and Internet trading capability. A local office is a 'nice to have' option. Also keep in mind where you want to be five or ten years from now. Your needs may change and your brokerage firm has to be able to provide for your changing needs."

---

[27] Represents, meaning a company that the firm helped bring public.

Mutual Fund Companies

"You can also invest directly with the fund companies. Some of them are not going to give you the option to invest in individual stocks[28], but you'll be able to invest in index funds through all of them."

Minimum Account Balances

"A number of mutual fund companies and brokers have minimum account balance requirements that might be *prohibitive* for the new investor, but a way around the minimum requirement is to open an IRA account and/or sign up for an **automatic withdrawal plan** which are also called **automatic investment plans** or AIPs for short. Sometimes mutual fund companies will waive the minimums if you promise to add money on a monthly basis. Here's a list of some no-load mutual fund companies," he said handing me the following list[29]:

American Century 800-345-2021 www.americancentury.com IRA Account: $2,500 Regular Account: $2,500 AIP: $50/month minimum	**T. Rowe Price** 800-638-5660 www.troweprice.com IRA Account: $1,000 Regular Account: $2,500 AIP: $50/month minimum
Dreyfus 800-782-6620 www.dreyfus.com IRA Account: $750 Regular Account: $2,500 AIP: $50/mo minimum (will waive min if you sign up for an AIP)	**TIAA-CREFF** 877-518-9161 www.tiaa-cref.org IRA Account: $2,000 Regular Account: $2,500 AIP: $50/mo minimum (will waive acct min if you sign up for an AIP)
Fidelity 800-343-3548 www.fidelity.com IRA Account: $2,500 Regular Account: $2,500 AIP: $200/mo minimum (will waive IRA acct min if you sign up for an AIP)	**Vanguard** 877-662-7447 www.vanguard.com IRA Account: $1,000 Regular Account: $3,000 AIP: $50/mo minimum

"How do I figure out which one is best?" I asked.

"I tell people to start by asking your friends and co-workers who they use. Ask what they like and dislike about their broker. Also, go to

---

[28] Some firms like Vanguard and Fidelity allow you to invest in stocks via their brokerage service divisions.

[29] Please note that investment companies change their fee structures and account minimums from time to time. You should double-check the above items before signing up with any particular company.

their web-sites and 'test drive' their services. See if you like the site, check out their commission schedules, and find out what types of low-cost index funds they offer. I'd rather you put your money into the Vanguard 500 Index or Total Stock Market Index fund to start, but if you think you've found another good index fund, it's nice to know that your discount broker provides you with easy access to those funds. You also want to cruise around your prospective brokerage firms web site to see if they have good research and investing tools. These tools will help you see how stocks and funds have performed in the past. You should also find out if there's an office near you that you can drive to if you have to deposit money or have any questions."

Reinvest Your Dividends!

"Not to beat a dead horse, but always reinvest your dividends. Some companies don't give you the ability to reinvest dividends at all or some only if the dividend is large enough to buy a whole share at a time. Unfortunately, many brokers do not offer this service, but I know that Fidelity allows you to buy partial shares since I have an account with them."

In short, you're looking for:
- Wide variety of no-load, low-cost index funds
- Low commissions on trades
- Automatic investment option
- Dividend reinvestment
- Good tax software
- A web-site that's easy to use
- Access to help via a toll-free number

Side Note: Investing on a Small Budget

Before we move on to the next section, I wanted to talk about some other low-cost investing options. With companies raising their fees to combat a slowdown in trading, it's tougher and tougher to invest on a shoestring budget. But there are several routes you can take if you want to get started and don't have a lot of money to invest. Your best bet for low-cost investing will always be through setting up an automatic investment plan with a mutual fund company or broker, dividend reinvestment plans, or one of the new types of brokerage services that encourage dollar-cost averaging into individual stocks.

The Index Fund Route

As I just explained, you can open an account with some mutual fund companies and invest as little as $50 a month into an index fund. You should start with a low-cost balanced index fund that invests in both stocks and bonds (more on this later). After you've accumulated a decent amount of shares, you can then look into adding another fund, perhaps a total market stock fund or at minimum an S&P500 index fund.

What About DRIPS?

Dividend Reinvestment Programs or DRIPs for short are programs that let you to buy fractions of shares at a time directly from the company. DRIPs are handled through the company's themselves, so you don't have to pay commissions. The only limitation might be the initial investment amount, but there are plans you can start with less than $200 and the monthly investment can be as low as $20 or $30. These plans also allow you to reinvest any dividends you receive, which is how they get their name. Close to 1,000 companies offer DRIPs and we're talking blue chip names here, not just small and mid-cap companies.

DRIPs are a good option for some, but not me. Why? One of the major drawbacks with DRIPs is the amount of paperwork involved in tracking your purchases. If you have several DRIPs then you're going to receive statements from each of the plans, which just adds to the pile of paperwork for you and your accountant. As a result, taxes become difficult to calculate.

Buy-n-Hold Brokerage Services

BUYandHOLD and Sharebuilder have pretty small requirements to open a brokerage or an IRA account. You can buy fractional shares of stocks or ETFs and both allow you to reinvest all your dividends for free (even in fractional shares, unlike some of the bigger brokerage firms). BUYandHOLD charges $14.99 a month for unlimited trading and $6.99 a trade if you go the pay-per-trade route. Sharebuilder charges $12 a month for unlimited trading and $4 if you go the pay-per-trade route. However, if you want to sell your shares in real-time, it'll cost you $15.95. The downside is that the costs can really add up over time, regardless of how low the cost of a single trade.

These accounts can be great for the beginner, but just make sure to review all the rules and fine print. You could get hit with an inactivity fee if you don't make any trades for a period of time.

Now back to our story...

Investment Choices

"Okay, so I know about the S&P500 index, but what other indexes should I invest in or be concerned about?" I asked.

"There are several, so let's go through the main ones that you need to know about."

S&P500 - The S&P500 is the most popular index out there, despite how often people quote the **Dow Jones Industrial Average (DJIA)** which is comprised of only 30 stocks. The DJIA was the original index and it was relevant when there weren't thousands of stocks that were actively traded. Today the S&P500 is the barometer of how the market is doing. It's comprised of the 500 largest US companies and investing in an S&P500 index fund is going to give you a pretty good amount of diversification.

The Wilshire 5000 Equity Index - The Wilshire 5000 is the broadest US equity index. It was named after the nearly 5,000 stocks that existed when it was first created in 1974, but has expanded to hold more than 5,700 stocks. The index includes not only large cap stocks, but small and medium sized companies as well.

The Morgan Stanley EAFE Index - For international stocks, you have to go with the Morgan Stanley EAFE Index. This index tracks around 1,000 companies that are in Europe, Australasia (Australia and New Zealand), and the Far East. This index would give you an easy way to get some international exposure into your portfolio and give you a little more diversification than if you were investing solely in the S&P500 or Wilshire which track US stocks only.

Lehman Brothers Government & Corporate Bond Index - I'm not about to tell you to go out and buy bond funds for each bond category. Most planners would suggest that you put your money into a fund that tracks the Lehman Brothers Government & Corporate Bond Market. This index tracks the performance of both government and corporate bonds that are issued.

Create the Optimal Portfolio Another Day

"So how do I buy all the indexes?" I asked.

"You're not going to buy all of them right now David. You're going to hold off on creating the optimal portfolio another day."

"Why not start today?" I asked.

"Because in order to build the optimal portfolio, that is one that will perform the best over the long-haul and over any market condition and economic climate, you're going to have to spread your money across seven or eight different stock and bond categories. You can't afford the minimums on all those funds now, so I suggest that you forget about creating the optimal portfolio. Instead, you should start with a balanced fund or S&P500 index fund. Then when you have some extra cash to invest or a decent sized investment in your original funds, you can consider diversifying your portfolio further."

"What's a balanced fund?" I asked.

"**Balanced funds invest in both stocks and bonds**. Depending on your asset allocation target, you can probably find a balanced or lifestyle fund as they're also called to suit your needs. For instance, Vanguard has several LifeStrategy™ funds which have different percentages of assets invested in stocks, with the balance invested in bonds and cash equivalents. So if you wanted an 80/20 mix between stocks and bonds, all you have to do is invest in the appropriate LifeStrategy™ fund and you're done."

"Wow. That is easy," I commented.

Starting in the Right Place

I finished writing down all the information and shook out my hand because it was cramping up. Everything he said made so much sense and I couldn't wait to start investing the right way.

"Thank you so much Mr. Mathers," I said. "I can't wait to start investing in index funds and open my 'buy-and-hold' account."

He smiled at me and shook his head. "I'd hate to burst your bubble David, but you're not going to start your investment program by opening a new account."

"What do you mean? Why not?"

"Because you've got to first optimize something that you're probably not fully taking advantage of. There's an investment that will automatically earn you higher returns than the investment program we just laid out for you."

Over the course of the next twenty minutes I would learn about one of the most powerful investment secrets around.

Chapter 15
START WITH RETIREMENT ACCOUNTS

Bursting My Bubble

"Okay. Let me have it," I said, anxious to learn what this secret to earning high returns was.

"David you obviously don't know that your 401(k) plan at work is probably one of the greatest building blocks of your wealth-building machine. A successful 401(k) plan can mean the difference between life on easy street and a life on government assistance. Unfortunately after the latest bear market, people can't see past their current low balances and many have stopped investing for the future. Exactly the wrong thing to do."

"So what should they do instead?" I asked.

"Before we get into specifics, lets go over what retirement accounts and plans are out there."

What is Social Security [30]

"For the majority of current retirees, Social Security is their main source of income. Social Security is simple enough to understand. Essentially you have current workers paying into the system and you have retirees receiving benefits from the system. If Social Security takes in more in taxes than is paid in benefits, the excess money is put in a Trust Fund. As you work, you earn credits and benefits are paid when you retire at age 65. If you want to begin taking benefits early, say at age 62, your benefits are *severely* cut."

"How do they figure out how much you get?"

"They have a formula that takes into account how much you earned and the number of years you worked."

"So how can I increase the amount I get?" I asked.

"Always looking for a higher income, even in retirement," he commented and chuckled. "You can increase your benefits by earning more during your working years or retiring later. When you delay taking benefits, you'll get a bigger check from Social Security."

"I've read some articles that say Social Security is going to go bust when the Boomers start retiring. Is it true?"

"Don't believe it David and here's why," he replied.

---

[30] Information for this article was sourced from: Social Security web-site articles and Trustee reports; "Tax Report" by Tom Herman, WSJ 10/24/02 and *Your Greatest Retirement Fear*" by Walter Updegrave, MONEY Fall 2002

So How's it Going to Go Bust?

"The argument goes that there will be 70 million plus Boomers retiring shortly and they'll be pulling out in excess of $1,000 a month from the plan. Add on top of that the fact that the number of workers per retiree shrank from 41.9 in 1945 to 3.4 today, which means a lot fewer workers contributing. Add on top of this the fact that people are living longer and will receive benefits for a longer period of time than they did in the past and we've got a recipe for disaster. At least that's what the financial press and authors would have you believe."

"So is it true? Is it going to go bust?" I asked.

"Not in my lifetime David. According to the Social Security trustees report, beginning in the year 2017, they'll have to start relying on the Trust Fund I mentioned earlier in order to keep Social Security afloat. The latest mathematical formulas point to a 1.87% *deficit* in 75 years. Yes, we'll probably be dead by then. In the meantime, there are some solutions and short-term Band-Aids™ that can be put in place. Some of the solutions include; delaying benefits, reducing benefits, raising the portion of income that is taxable, raising taxes, and making employers pay more of the taxes."

"But they're not really appealing, are they?" I said.

The Three-Legged Stool: Start Relying on You

"No, they're not. In reality, **you shouldn't rely too much on Social Security for your retirement income**, but according to their web-site, 8 out of 10 current retirees do. In reality, a comfortable retirement is supposed to be based on the '*three-legged stool*' approach, which says that Social Security, pensions, and your savings (investments) should fund your retirement. Let's see how this plays out:

- You should anticipate getting something from Social Security, but don't bank on receiving all of the benefits that appear on the annual statement Social Security sends you.

- Traditional pension plans are going the way of the horse and buggy unless you're a government employee, so unless you have one of these plans, not much is coming from this leg of the stool.

- What is left? Your savings and personal retirement accounts. In short, the onus is on you.

Defined Benefit Plans

"So let's talk about defined benefit plans or 'traditional' pension plans. Back in the old days, these plans were the standard and companies were on the hook for providing for your retirement benefits. Since they cost a lot to maintain, companies stopped offering them to new employees."

Defined Contribution Plans

"So flash forward a couple of decades and most traditional pension plans are being replaced by 'defined contribution' plans. These plans allow employees to contribute money from their own paychecks and make their own investment choices. The most popular or widely-known defined contribution plan is the 401(k) plan. If you work for a tax-exempt organization, then you probably have a 403(b) plan and if you work for the government, you have a 457 plan."

"What's the difference between all of them?" I asked.

"Not much. They all kind of work the same with perhaps a little twist here and there. Essentially, your employer deducts money from your paycheck and places the money in your account. The money is then invested in a variety of investment vehicles. Any and all interest, capital gains, or dividends received are accumulated on a tax-deferred basis. In addition to these plans, you also have IRAs to consider."

IRAs: Individual Retirement Accounts

"Individual Retirement Accounts or IRAS were created by Congress so that individuals could take ownership of and start saving for their retirements. Traditional and Roth are the two kinds of IRAs."

Traditional IRA

"With a Traditional IRA, you're able to put the full contribution amount into your account and reduce your taxes at the same time. For instance if you gross $30,000 a year, come tax time you would take that figure and subtract your contribution amount, say $3,000 which is the max amount you can contribute in 2003. Thus you would only pay taxes on $27,000 in income if you *qualify* for the full deduction. If you're in the 25% bracket that's $750 in federal taxes you don't have to pay ($3,000 x .25). Of course when you withdraw your funds come retirement, you will have to pay income tax on the money you made. With the Traditional IRA you must begin taking distributions by age 70½, so check with your accountant before doing your taxes."

"What do you mean by 'qualify' for the deduction?"

"There is an income phaseout where you are no longer able to take the deduction, but more on this in a second," he said.

Roth IRA

"Roth IRAs are similar to Traditional IRAs, but **with Roth IRAs you invest with money that you have already paid taxes on.**"

"Why would you do that?" I asked.

"Because you will *not* have to pay taxes when you withdraw the money from a Roth. In addition, there are no minimum withdrawal requirements for Roth IRAs, so you can keep the money in your account and let it compound tax-free as long as you like. Just note that there are income eligibility requirements with the Roth as to who can contribute. Here are a couple of tables that should help you immensely:

Figure 15.1 – Traditional and Roth IRA Annual Contribution Limits

Calendar year	Individuals under age 50	Individuals age 50 above
2002 - 2004	$3,000	$3,500
2005	$4,000	$4,500
2006 - 2007	$4,000	$5,000
2008	$5,000	$6,000

Source: Source: www.irs.gov

Figure 15.2 - AGI Limits for Deducting Traditional IRA Contributions

Tax Year	Single		Married (Filing Jointly)	
	Fully Deductible Up to:	Deduction Fully Phased Out At:	Fully Deductible Up to:	Deduction Fully Phased Out At:
2002	$34,000	$44,000	$54,000	$64,000
2003	$40,000	$50,000	$60,000	$70,000
2004	$45,000	$55,000	$65,000	$75,000
2005	$50,000	$60,000	$70,000	$80,000
2006	$50,000	$60,000	$75,000	$85,000
2007	$50,000	$60,000	$80,000	$100,000

Source: www.irs.gov

"Likewise, you're eligible to contribute to a Roth IRA if your AGI is below certain limits. This chart will help you figure it out:

Figure 15.3 - AGI Limits for Making Roth Contributions (2002)

Income		Income	
Single	Maximum Annual Contribution	Married (Filing Jointly)	Maximum Annual Contribution
$0 to $95,000	$3,000	$0 to $150,000	$3,000
$95,001 to $109,999	$3,000 less $200 for every $1,000 of income above $95K	$150,001 to $159,999	$3,000 less $300 for every $1,000 of income above $150K
$110,000 and up	Not eligible	$160,000 and up	Not eligible

Source: www.irs.gov

To Convert or Not to Convert

"Now one more thing to cover is conversion, which is when you decide to convert a Traditional to a Roth IRA or vice versa."

"Why would you convert one to the other?"

"Uncle Sam and his taxes," he replied. "The Traditional allows you to grow your money tax-deferred, but you have to pay taxes when you begin to make withdrawals. On the other hand, you grow your money tax-deferred with a Roth, but you can withdraw money tax-free. If you convert to a Roth, realize that the money will be taxed when you convert, depending on if the funds were deductible or nondeductible. If you convert a Traditional IRA where the contributions were not tax deductible, only the earnings are subject to tax. However, if you were deducting the amounts you contributed when you filed your taxes, the full amount of your IRA, contributions and gains, are taxable."

I grabbed my head. "Too much information. Can't you just tell me when it makes the most sense to convert?"

"You really should visit with your accountant or financial planner. He or she can help you determine which option makes the most sense. As a rule of thumb, you should convert to a Roth if you have a lot of time to go before you retire, because technically you have enough time to make up for the taxes you pay upon conversion. In addition, if you think you'll be in a higher tax bracket when you retire or if you're able to pay the taxes today without much of a hit to your savings, then converting to a Roth might make sense."

Options for the Self-Employed

"Here's an off-topic question," I stated. "What about my dad? He owns his own business and I don't think he has a 401(k)."

"Self-employed people are generally concerned with the present demands of their budding businesses and don't think about their retirements, but they should. There are several options open to self-employed people and they really should make an effort to understand all of them. If they're uncertain, they should meet with their accountant or a financial planner to determine which option is best for them."

SIMPLE, SEP or Keogh Plans

"They can invest in Keogh plans, Simplified Employee Pension (SEPs) or SIMPLE plans, which are available only for self-employed individuals. Contribution limits vary for the three plans and each have their various pros and cons, so you would be wise to consult with a professional planner or talk with an accountant before choosing an option."

401(k)s for the Self-Employed?

"And there's actually one more type of retirement account for self-employed individuals courtesy of the Economic Growth and Tax Relief Reconciliation Act of 2001. Self-employed individuals can now set up 401(k) plans for themselves. Participants can put aside as much as you can as an employee of a company, however they are also allowed to contribute an additional amount of money based on the net profits from their business. The top contribution amount is up to 25 percent of their compensation. The total set aside cannot exceed $40,000 a year if you're under 50 and $42,000 if you're over age 50. These plans aren't widely available yet, but I'm sure you'll see ads for them on TV in a year or so. It's a pretty good deal and is worth the extra paperwork come tax time. Any questions so far?"

Becoming a Millionaire Automatically!

"Not really at this point. Just taking it all in," I said, looking up from my binder. "Just keep it coming."

"Okay," he replied. "Now the best thing about all retirement plans is that you can set it up so they can be funded through automatic payroll deductions and you never see the money coming out, so you don't have a chance to spend it. That's why I say that these plans help you become a millionaire automatically. On top of that, retirement accounts are one of the best ways to put compounding interest to work for you because they take it one step further."

"How so?"

"Because you don't pay any taxes on the money you put in today *and* the capital gains from your investments grow tax-deferred as well. Pretty impressive, huh?"

"I'll say. Tell me more."

"Before I go into greater detail, let's start from the beginning and I'll explain why retirement accounts are really the first place you should turn to when starting your investment program. I'm focusing on 401(k) plans in particular, but most of the reasons to participate hold true for all other types of retirement accounts, especially those that are sponsored by employers."

Ten Reasons To Participate In A 401(k) Plan
- Starting is Simple
- It's Cheap (the 1% Solution)
- Automatic Savings
- Dollar Cost Averaging
- Tax-deferred Growth
- Higher Contribution Limits than IRAs
- Employer Matching – Free Money
- Portability
- Investment Choices
- Borrowing Money in a Pinch

Starting is Simple
"The sign up process at most employers is so easy. Unfortunately, some companies make you wait a few months or a year before you become eligible for their 401(k) plan, but as soon as you're eligible you should sign up. Delaying investing in the 401(k) plan for even a year can mean big money *lost* down the road."

It's Cheap
"The plans are cheap because most 401(k) plans allow you to start investing with as little as 1% of your paycheck. So if you make $20,000 a year and get paid twice a month that works out to $8.33 per paycheck. You spare an extra $4.16 per week, can't you?"

"I think I can handle that," I replied.

Max it out Baby! – The 1% Solution
"Building on this idea a little, let's say you *think* you can only afford to put away 6% of your salary and you do that mostly because your employer matches your contributions, dollar for dollar up to 6% of your salary. So you're in great shape right? Wrong. It's time to start contributing more, because it makes a big difference. For instance, the difference between two people earning $30,000 and one putting away 6% versus 10% is roughly $100 a month. That $100 a month extra will grow to over $100,000 over the course of 30 years."

"Wow. **So how much should I contribute**?" I asked.

"I tell my students to try and max out their contributions. If you think you can't do this, go ahead and put in at least up to the percentage that your company matches. Then you should steadily increase the contributions by 1% every two months (or less) until you reach the maximum allowable amount. You're probably going to forget so write a note to yourself to increase your contributions on your calendar."

Automatic Savings

"After your initial setup, your 401(k) is literally on autopilot because the money comes directly from every paycheck you get. This way you're likely to forget that the money is coming out and **what you don't see, you don't spend**."

Dollar Cost Averaging

"Next up is dollar cost averaging."

"Oh, I get it," I said. "I'm dollar cost averaging into my funds because I'm adding money into them each pay period."

"Correct and you already know how powerful this technique can be, so let's keep going."

Tax-deferred Growth

"There are many reasons to start contributing to your employer's plan, but one of the best reasons is the tax-deferred growth benefit. The money you're contributing every paycheck is deposited *before* Uncle Sam takes taxes out. This means that if you put away 10% of your $30,000 salary, which is $3,000 in annual contributions, he'll only calculate taxes on $27,000 dollars. So you don't pay taxes on $3,000 which is roughly $750 in federal taxes that you would have paid. Now you get to put that extra $750 to work in your 401(k), but it gets even better. **Taxes are deferred on any and all profits that you make on the money you have invested**."

"So no capital gains taxes on my profits, right?" I asked.

"Right. No taxes on your gains as long as you keep that money in your plan. If you do pull money out of your plan before the age of 59½, you have to pay a 10% penalty tax on top of the income tax on the money you're taking out. The bottom-line is to keep that money in there. These two charts should convince you about the power of starting with tax-deferred plans versus taxable accounts," he said, showing me the following charts:

"As a citizen, you have an obligation to the country's tax system, but you also have an obligation to yourself to know your rights under the law."

- Donald C. Alexander

Why You Should be Maxing Out Tax-Deferred Accounts First!

FIGURE 15.4 - Increase your take-home pay by investing in tax-deferred plans

As you can see, investing on a pre-tax basis versus doing so on an after-tax basis nets you more money in your pocket!

	Pre-tax investment plan	After-tax investment plan
Monthly pay	$3,000	$3,000
Monthly 401(k) investment	$300	$0
Taxable income	$2,700	$3,000
Fed income taxes only (25% rate)	$675	$750
Net take-home pay	$2,025	$2,250
After-tax investment	$0	$300
Net cash in pocket	$2,025	$1,950
Increase in take-home pay after contribution	$75	

"I never thought of it this way before," I commented.

"Most people don't and these two charts are why they should max out their retirement accounts *before* they even think about funding their taxable accounts. If you have one person investing a dollar into a taxable account and someone investing a buck into a tax-deferred account, the person with the taxable account would have to have a return of close to 40% just to get back to a dollar."

I shook my head. "That's unbelievable."

"Which is why I tell people to max out their tax-deferred options first," he replied. "You're able to build wealth faster that way. For instance, take a look at the second chart. It shows the difference between investing $300 a month in a tax-deferred account versus a taxable account. Quite a difference in results."

FIGURE 15.5 - Tax-Deferred Investments mean bigger returns!

If you invested $300/mo into a tax-deferred account vs. a taxable account, over 30 yrs, the advantages of tax-deferred investing becomes clear:

Taxable Account	$98,393.22
Tax-Deferred Account	$142,671.46

Footnote - Note: The above hypothetical situation was calculated using an 8% annual return and a 25% federal tax rate, with no state taxes taken into consideration. Of course you have to pay taxes on the tax-deferred money when you take it out of your account.

Higher Tax-deferred Contributions than an IRA

"IRAs are great investment vehicles, but they do have limitations. One limitation is that Uncle Sam allows you to *only* save $3,000 a year tax-deferred. On top of that, depending on your total income, you may not be able to deduct all or even part of your contributions from your gross income. But with your 401(k) you can save up to $12,000 and your contributions are completely tax deductible."

New, Higher Contribution Limits for Employer-Sponsored Plans

FIGURE 15.6 - Employer Sponsored Contribution Limits: 401(k)s, 403(b)s and 457(b) Plans

Year	Contribution Limits	Catch-Up Contributions (over age 50)
2002	$11,000	$1,000
2003	$12,000	$2,000
2004	$13,000	$3,000
2005	$14,000	$4,000
2006 and later	$15,000	$5,000

Source: www.irs.gov

Making Up for Lost Time

"Another great change in the law from the 2001 Tax Reform Act is that if you're over 50 years of age, you get to make an additional contribution to your plan. They did this so that folks who were close to retirement or had few working years left, could catch-up to their younger counterparts."

"I got it. Because they wouldn't have as many years to contribute at the new higher levels, right?" I asked.

"Well done. That's exactly why lawmakers created the catch-up provision."

Employer Matching - Free Money

"One of the greatest benefits that a company can offer its employees is a matching contribution. Many employers match roughly 50 cents on the dollar, up to your first 6% of pay. How they match your contributions vary, but one of the most common ways they match is with company stock. This may or may not be a good thing."

"How so?"

"Your company's stock my soar and your 401(k) will go along for the ride, but the reverse can happen. You just don't want to take the risk of losing your retirement money by having too much in your company stock. If the company's stock takes a dive, so does your retirement account. Just look what happened at Enron or WorldCom."

"Point well taken. That wasn't cool," I said.

"No, it wasn't cool at all, but that's what happens when you take on too much risk and put all your eggs in one basket."

Portability: You Can Take It with You

"Next up in our discussion is portability, which means your ability to leave your company to go to another company and take your 401(k) money with you. Uncle Sam gives you 60 days to find a new tax-sheltered plan to put your money in if you leave a company and close out your previous account. You can put it into your new employer's 401(k) plan, if the plan allows rollovers, or roll the money into an IRA. If you miss the deadline, you pay taxes on that money and on top of that Uncle Sam charges you a 10% penalty if you are under the age of 59 ½."

"Wow. That's steep all because of a missed deadline," I said.

"Speaking of negatives, a downside of some 401(k) plans is that the company has a long **vesting period**. Most companies require that you work a certain amount of years at the company before the matching contribution actually belongs to you."

"At Acme you get to keep 20% of the matched dollars for every year of service, so you're fully vested after 5 years of work."

"It definitely beats no match at all, but that 5 year vesting period to receive 100% of the money might be an issue for you down the road. Considering the way you kids hop around from job to job, if you leave Acme in 3 years, you only get 60% of the matched money. That's why **a vesting period of 3 years or less is best** when looking for your next job. Otherwise you're going to hop around from company to company and never build up your tax-deferred retirement portfolio. And you'd literally be throwing money away by switching jobs."

Investment Choices

"Next comes the question of what to invest in. You want to make sure you're properly diversified by investing across different sectors and different asset classes, but stock funds should make up the majority of your portfolio for any long-term investment plan."

"Sounds like you're talking about asset allocation," I said.

"Which is exactly what you'd be doing by choosing what assets to invest in. The one benefit of the 401(k) plan is that **you don't have to meet fund minimums to invest** in the funds and you can invest in quite a few of them at the same time, right from the get-go."

Borrowing Money in a Pinch

"The next subject has to do with borrowing money and museums."

"What do the two have to do with each other?" I asked.

"A friend of mine calls his retirement accounts his museum pieces. He doesn't touch them because he doesn't want to ruin what he's created over the years. He knows that if he withdraws from his retirement accounts, he'll be interrupting the power of compounding interest, plus he'll have to pay a 10% penalty for early withdrawal. There is a huge **opportunity cost** associated with pulling funds out early. Currently you can withdraw money from your 401(k) for the following reasons without paying a penalty: to pay for your child's college education, to buy your first home, or to pay for high medical expenses above a certain percentage of your income. For all other reasons, you can withdraw the money, but you pay income tax on it and a 10% 'early withdrawal' penalty."

I wrote down the information, then he continued.

"That's if you want to withdraw the money. You can also take a loan for almost any purpose from your 401(k) if your plan administrator allows it. You borrow money from your plan, then pay yourself back plus interest. Normally you can take a loan out for up to 50% of your account value, up to a $50,000 limit. The term of the loan is usually 5 years or less, unless it's for a home and the interest rates are usually one or two points above prime, which really are great rates."

"Sounds like a great deal. What's the catch? There's always a catch," I said.

"**The catch is your opportunity cost: the fact that the money could have been growing during the entire time that you've borrowed it.** Also, if you leave the company, you're going to have to pay back the loan within 30 to 60 days. If you don't repay the loan it's considered an early withdrawal and the IRS will hit you with the 10% penalty and you'll owe taxes on the amount you borrowed."

"But what if you plan on paying back the money?"

"Most people stop making contributions to their 401(k) because they want to pay down the loan as quickly as possible, so they've instantly derailed their wealth-building machine. Also, **paying back the money you borrowed with *after tax* money is not smart** and unlike mortgages, the interest they are paying is not tax deductible."

"But you're paying yourself interest, which is a good thing, right?"

But You Pay Yourself the Interest Right?

"It's not a good thing. Lots of people who borrow from their 401(k)s love to point out that you're paying the interest on the loan to yourself. What they don't realize is that *they're getting taxed twice*: once when they pay the interest with *after-tax* dollars and twice when they take out the principal they paid back, they get taxed again. **Getting taxed twice is not the way to build wealth**. End of story."

When Not to Contribute

"Is there any time or situation where you shouldn't contribute to your 401(k)?" I asked.

"It really depends on you and your situation. The only time I say to scale back your contributions is when contributing money to your 401(k) hurts you in other areas of your life. If you are struggling to make ends meet and you're under a mountain of credit card debt, it might make sense to lower your contributions and pay down the debt. Just make sure you start contributing money again when you're done paying down your debt or handling the emergency."

"Sounds like a good plan to me: get out from under the debt that's outpacing your potential gains in the market, then get back into the investment game when your cash flow is nice and healthy again."

"Right on David," he replied. "There are three other reasons why you might *not* want to invest in your 401(k) plan: the available investment options are bad (loads, high expenses and fees), there's no company match, and you're in a low tax bracket."

He looked up from his notes and took off his glasses. "Well David, I think we've covered the basics. Now it's time to figure out how much you need to retire."

"Retire *early* you mean," I said, grinning ear to ear.

"Yes, retiring early would be a nice goal to shoot for."

5 Steps to Retiring in Style
Step 1: How much income do you need?
Step 2: How much do you need to accumulate?
Step 3: How much do you have to build on?
Step 4: How much do you need to save each month?
Step 5: How do you need to invest it?

Step 1: How Much Income Do You Need?

"The first step is to calculate how much income you'll need in retirement, which depends on what lifestyle you envision leading in your golden years. The rule of thumb in the financial planning world is 70 to 80 percent of the amount you earned during your working years. I don't like this rule of thumb because it assumes that most people downscale their lifestyles when they retire and I can tell you that this is not likely. I tell people to plan on replacing 100 percent of their income during their retirement. To figure out how much you have to accumulate and how much you have to save to get to your goal, all you have to do is fill out your **Retirement Needs Calculator (RNC),**" he said, passing a piece of paper to me. "There are just twelve quick steps to find out how much you'll need on an annual basis in retirement."

Step 2: How Much Do You Need to Accumulate?

"To figure out how much you need to accumulate, you take the annual amount you just calculated in step #1 of this sheet," he said pointing to the sheet "and you just go about filling it out. When you're done you'll know how big of a nest egg you'll have to create."

Step 3: How Much Do You Have to Build On?

"Step #3 is not too difficult, but it might involve some work for figuring out Item #4 on the RNC, but you can get the information easily enough. The other items, like #8 should be easy enough if you have your net worth statement handy. Just fill in the information, do some math, and you're done."

Step 4: How Much Do You Need to Save Each Month?

"There are several ways you can calculate how much you'll need to set aside each month including; using a financial calculator like my hp-12c, using an online calculator, or filling out your Retirement Needs Calculator.[31]"

Step 5: How Do You Need to Invest It?

"The last step is investing your money according to a well-thought out investment plan that has taken into consideration your age, your risk tolerance, your goals, and your personal financial situation. You know that the two biggest obstacles you will face are the twin forces of *taxes* and *inflation*. The former is taken care of for now thanks to the tax-deferred nature of your retirement accounts, with the exception of your Roth IRA. These accounts allow you to keep your money growing on a tax-deferred basis even after you retire. In order to combat inflation, you need to make sure your nest egg outpaces inflation and you do this by investing for higher returns. You achieve those higher returns by properly diversifying your money across a well-balanced portfolio that's geared for maximum growth in your early years and then shifts to an income portfolio in your later years. As I said before, you can just go to www.morningstar.com[32] and check out their asset allocation tool."

---

[31] Or you can go to www.fabmansecrets.com and check out the "MY FINANCIAL PLAN" workbook.
[32] At last check, this was the link: http://portfolio.morningstar.com/PortAsp/PortOpt.asp

Figure 15.7 – How Much Do You Need to Retire?
The Retirement Needs Calculator

		Example	YOU
1.	Current Gross Income	$30,000	$ ___
2.	Inflation Factor (ex. 3% @ 30 yrs.)	2.4	___
3.	Future Value of Income Needed (multiply item # 1 by # 2)	$72,000	$ ___
4.	Minus Projected Pension and Other Sources of Retirement Income	$ 0	$ ___
5.	Minus est. Soc. Sec. Benefits	$18,000	$ ___
6.	Total Annual Income Needed to Replace	$54,000	$ ___
7.	Total Future Principal Needed to Sustain Income Needs (multiply item # 6 by 20)	$1,080,000	$ ___
8.	Value of Current Investments	$20,000	$ ___
9.	Compound Interest Factor (from table below)	10.1	___
10.	Value at Retirement? (multiply item # 8 by item # 9)	$202,000	$ ___
11.	Total Shortfall (subtract item # 10 from item # 7)	$878,000	$ ___
12.	Monthly Amount You have to Invest? (multiply item # 11 by correct Automatic Savings Factor)	$585.63	$ ___

FIGURE 15.8 Inflation, Savings, and Future Value Calculators
Use the Below Table for Filling in the Above Information

Years to Retirement	Inflation Factor at 3%	Compound Interest Factor at 8%	Automatic Savings Factor at 8%
5	1.2	1.47	0.013887
10	1.3	2.2	0.005430
15	1.6	3.2	0.002871
20	1.8	4.7	0.001686
25	2.1	6.8	0.001045
30	**2.4**	**10.1**	**0.000667**
35	2.8	14.8	0.000433
40	3.3	21.7	0.000285

Note that in Appendix A & B of this book you will see a variety of Automatic Savings Factors and Inflation Factors should you want to be more conservative or aggressive in your assumptions.

"So I can just figure out what the right asset allocation would be for me, then invest in low-cost, no-load index funds, and I'm pretty much set for retirement."

"That's how it works," he replied. "Just monitor your portfolio over time and keep adding to your accounts on a regular basis and you should be fine."

At that moment the doorbell rang. He quickly closed his binder and stood up.

"Looks like it's time for my investment club meeting. Luckily we just covered our last point." He began walking toward the front door than turned around. "Say, would you like to stay and join us?"

"Really? That would be awesome!" I exclaimed. I barely could keep my cool. "Do you think the members would mind?"

"No, not at all. They'd get a kick out of it. Besides, they love helping out others with investing. Now go answer the door while I get the bagels ready."

"Deal," I said.

Invest NOW, Not tomorrow - COMMENTS

Only 5 percent of Americans can afford to retire at age 65!

Yes, you read that right. Currently, it is estimated that only one in twenty Americans will be able to retire with an income in excess of $25,000 according to the folks who run Social Security. I don't know about you, but that's not a great percentage in my book.

The rules of retirement have changed drastically over the past two decades. Today you're more in control of your retirement than you were back in the days of traditional pension plans. With this added responsibility is the reality that you can't just sit back and hope things work out in the future. You have to plan for your future today. If you don't plan for tomorrow today, then you'll have to retire later in life, get a part-time job during retirement, or severely downsize your current lifestyle. I don't know about you but those three options aren't particularly appealing. If you still need some guidance after reading through this Secret and you can't make heads or tails out of the Action Plan, then seek out some professional help. Don't delay. Every moment you wait could be an extra year that you have to work instead of retiring early.

Choose a safe withdrawal rate: The worksheet I developed is based on you withdrawing 5% of your portfolio every year. You should realize that if you were to withdraw more than that each year, you would be in danger of running out of money before you died. The 5% rate is just a benchmark and obviously if you took out less you would have an even greater chance of having your portfolio outlive you. By the way, you don't have to take my word for it on the percentage of your portfolio that can be safely withdrawn each year. There was a comprehensive study that was done on the topic and you can read more about it online. It's nicknamed "The Trinity Study[33]."

"401(k) plans; the best place to start investing? You're crazy!"

That was the reaction of one of my readers after I gave him the advice in this book. My recommendation to begin with your retirement accounts, max them out, then focus on taxable accounts is likely to raise some eyebrows, infuriate others, and fill up my e-mail inbox (fabman@fabmansecrets.com) with a ton of flame e-mails, but I don't care. I still believe that the best way to start investing for the average, beginning investor is through their 401(k) plan. A lot of you want to retire Financially Free and think the way to do it is through real estate or building a business. Well...you're right. But both these paths take time...and money.

I believe that the majority of people are better served starting their wealth-building programs by maxing out their retirement options first. If you're still motivated to invest in real estate or build a business, go for it. I just think the majority of people will never get started on becoming the next Donald Trump. I like to bet on sure things and invest when the odds are in my favor. I say put the odds in your favor by maxing out your retirement plan options first, start that regular, investment account, then give the real estate or business thing a try. If you stick with it, all the better. But if you don't, at least you'll have a safety net. Your safety net is your retirement investments.

I'm not going to drag out my comments in this section. I think you know the importance of saving for your financial future. Please don't delay in setting up your retirement accounts and maxing them out. Not taking action on the principles outlined in this Secret is a recipe for disaster. You have the information in your hands that can help make a big difference in your life. Read through the following Action Plans and take action today!

---

[33]The last link I found for it was "Choosing a Withdrawal Rate that is Sustainable," *Philip L. Cooley, Carl M. Hubbard and Daniel T. Walz,* AAII Journal February 1998, Volume XX, No. 2 (http://aaii.com/promo/20021007/feature.shtml)

Retirement Accounts – ACTION PLAN

Just Do It!: Start funding your 401(k) or 403(b) today! There's no better time to start than today.

At Minimum, Get the Employer Match: If you're struggling to invest your hard-earned money, then you should at least strive to put in enough to get your company's matching funds.

Max it Out Baby!: But I don't want you to settle for 6% or whatever the contribution amount that your employer matches up to. I want you to try and add 1% to the amount you contribute every two or three months. Chances are you won't miss the money and will start maxing out your contributions before you know it.

Choose Your Asset Allocation: Figure out your tolerance for risk, your time horizon, and your personal financial situation. After you've got this all figured out, check out any number of tools online that you can use to figure out the asset allocation that's right for you. Check out the one provided by www.morningstar.com. It's one of the easiest to use that I've seen.

Index Funds: No-load, low-cost index funds are the way to go. More money works for you instead of ending up in the pocket of your plan provider and fund manager.

Keep Going: Regardless of life changes (marriage, kids, divorce, you name it) just keep contributing to your account(s). The more you put in now, the more you'll have later on when you want to stop working and live on a beach somewhere.

Don't Borrow: Borrowing money from your retirement accounts is a slippery slope. Exhaust all other options before even thinking of stealing money from your future to live today. Delay gratification for long-term satisfaction.

Increase Your Knowledge: Don't be satisfied with just knowing the information in this book. Check out web-sites, online discussion forums, other books, magazines, the business section of the newspaper, and TV shows on personal finance. The more you know the better.

Taxable Investment Accounts – ACTION PLAN

Max Out Your Retirement and Tax-deferred Options First!: I'm not kidding. If your main goal is to build a huge nest egg for retirement, this is the way to go. If you haven't done this, then you're not maximizing and stretching your investment dollars.

Set Up Your Account: Do your homework and find the discount broker or mutual fund company that best suits your needs. Make sure they offer no-load, low-cost index funds and allow you to automatically reinvest your dividends.

Invest Money You Don't Need: Go back and re-read the section titled "Before You Invest a Penny." Don't invest money that you can't afford to lose or need to pay down some of your debilitating debts.

Choose Your Asset Allocation: Figure out your tolerance for risk, your time horizon, and your personal financial situation. After you've got this all figured out, check out any number of tools online that you can use to figure out the asset allocation that's right for you. Check out the one provided by www.morningstar.com. It's one of the easiest to use that I've seen.

One or Two Funds Will Do: Once you have your asset allocation chosen and your buy-n-hold account set up, it's time to pick no-load, low-cost index funds that match your asset allocation. As I mentioned earlier, a simple Total Stock Market Index fund or a balanced index fund will do to start. Don't even think of buying managed funds.

Don't Pay Loads: Why pay an extra fee to invest when you can buy a no-load fund instead?

Watch Your Expenses: Expenses matter. A lot! The difference between a 0.18% fee and a 1.8% fee can add up to a tidy sum over your lifetime. But don't buy a fund just because it has low expenses. You need to look at the big picture.

Make it Automatic: Make sure you're investing money every month. If you think you can't find the money to invest, go through your budget again and find a way to invest additional funds on a monthly basis. Set up an automatic investment plan with your account so you can just put your investing program on autopilot.

Set Up Your Vegas Account: If you still have the itch to try and be the next Warren Buffett, set up a separate account for this mistake…I mean test. Start off only putting in 5% or 10% of the total funds you have to invest. If you do well, add more money. If not, stick to index funds. Look for a discount broker with low commissions.

Buy and Hold: Let compound interest work its magic. Don't jump in and out of funds and stocks. Market timing doesn't work for the pros and it's not going to work for you. Don't try it.

Rebalance: Every year you should take a critical look at your account and see if your original asset allocation is out of whack. If it is, you may need to either add money to the funds that have underperformed or sell some shares of the high-fliers to buy extra shares of the laggards in your portfolio. Resist the temptation to "ride the winners." This would be akin to staying with tech funds during the late 90s.

Additional Resources

Books & Magazines:

All About Index Funds, by Rick Ferri

The Only Guide to a Winning Investment Strategy You'll Ever Need by Larry Swedroe

Get a subscription to Money Magazine

Web-Sites:

The Vanguard Group (www.vanguard.com)

Morningstar's Portfolio Allocation Tool - Signing up is FREE
www.portfolio.morningstar.com/PortAsp/PortOpt.asp

Morningstar's Discussion Forums
(especially "The Vanguard Diehards")

www.socialize.morningstar.com/newsocialize/asp/coverpage.asp?topnav=conversations

Altruist Financial Advisors LLC – Reading Room
www.altruistfa.com/readingroom.htm

The Motley Fool
www.fool.com

A year from now you may wish you had started today.
Why not start your investing plan today?
But enough about investing your money.
It's time you learned how to invest in something
a bit more important: Yourself.

Secret #7:
INVEST
IN YOURSELF

"It takes more than a college degree to make one a person of education. Any person who is educated is one who has learned to get whatever he wants in life without violating the rights of others. Education consists, not so much of knowledge, but of knowledge effectively and persistently applied.
Men are paid, not merely for what they know, but more particularly for what they do with that which they know."

– Napoleon Hill

Chapter 16

Secret #7: INVEST IN YOURSELF

Increasing Your Ability to Earn More

Fiscal and Physical Wealth

"We've gone through six Secrets of Wealth so far and they've all focused on investing or managing your money, with the exception of perhaps Secret #1 where you set life goals. I'm sure if you look through your list of goals you'll find that the overwhelming majority of them are financial or of a fiscal nature. Today we're going to shift gears and talk about your physical well being. That's physical spelled with a 'PH.'"

"I'm with you," I stated.

"Good. The subject is an important one and for some reason it often gets ignored. Too many books on building wealth only focus on how to get more money and how to invest that money to get more money. The focus is always on money, money, and more money. It's also important to be mindful of the seventh Secret of Wealth: **Invest in Yourself**. Today we're going to talk in-depth about ways that you can make the most of your time and energy in order for you to become the best person you can be. There will be financial rewards for doing so, but that shouldn't be the sole motivation."

Sharpen the Saw

"In his bestseller *The 7 Habits of Highly Effective People*, Stephen Covey wrote about the habit called *Sharpen the Saw*. In the introduction to the section, Covey tells a story of someone coming upon a lumberjack who is feverishly sawing away at a tree. The lumberjack's been there for five hours and has barely made any progress. The person asks the lumberjack if it would make sense to take time out to sharpen his saw, to which the man responds:

"I don't have time to sharpen the saw. I'm too busy sawing!"

"Now think about that for a moment David. If the man had taken a few moments to sharpen the saw, his work would be much easier. Instead, he'll likely be toiling away for another five hours. It's a good analogy for what most people do in life. They refuse to step back, assess their skills, determine their shortcomings, and go about filling in the gaps of their skill set. Whether it's due to laziness, poor time management, or just plain ignorance, too many people don't sharpen their minds after they graduate high school or college. They get into that vicious cycle in life and just get up in the morning, go to work, come home, and watch TV. Then they go to bed and repeat the cycle the next day. It's just plain crazy," he said, shaking his head.

"I guess I'm a bit guilty of that myself," I admitted. "I often have the excuse that I'm too tired to do anything but watch TV when I get home from work."

"It's not a great habit to have," he replied, "especially when you realize that **99% of people don't feed their minds after graduating from school**."

"Most of our mental development and study discipline comes through formal education. But as soon as we leave the external discipline of school, many of us let our minds atrophy. We don't do any more serious reading, we don't explore new subjects in any real depth outside our action fields, we don't think analytically, we don't write – at least not critically or in a way that tests our ability to express ourselves in distilled, clear, and concise language. Instead, we spend our time watching TV."
– Stephen R. Covey, *The 7 Habits of Highly Effective People*

"You just need to find a way to increase the amount of free time you have and dedicate it to reading quality books on a variety of subjects like investing, working out, managing people, teambuilding, business building, and a host of other subjects."

"Just exactly how many subjects am I supposed to become an expert in?" I asked.

He laughed. "You don't have to become an expert in a dozen areas, David. Covey talks about the importance of renewing oneself in four major areas: **physical, mental, spiritual, and social or emotional. We must strive to ensure that the areas are in balance with one another.** If you neglect to develop one area of your life, you'll feel the negative impact."

"So you're saying that I should concentrate on those four areas when investing in myself?"

"I actually tell people to focus on three main areas: **their mind, their body, and their career**."

"I'm all ears," I said, leaning back in my chair. I was relaxed that day and a bit tired from the night before. I had stayed up late to read a few chapters in *All About Index Funds* because I couldn't put the book down.

MIND, BODY AND CAREER
(and LIFE too!)

"Commit yourself to lifelong learning. The most valuable asset you'll ever have is your mind and what you put into it."

- Brian Tracy, Author, *Goals!*

YOUR MIND

Higher Education
"**If you think education is expensive, try ignorance.** I forget who said it first, but it's some powerful advice because you truly have to be educated to make it big in life."

"So you're advocating college degrees, right?" I guessed.

"No David, I'm not necessarily talking about college degrees. Having a college degree or a high school degree for that matter is NOT a requirement for becoming wealthy in this country. However, **having a college degree will increase your odds of becoming wealthy because on average, college graduates make more money than non-graduates do.** Everything else held equal, when you make more money, you have the ability to save and invest more than someone who earns less money than you do, but of course there are no guarantees."

"I think I understand what you're getting at. An advanced degree alone won't guarantee that you become Financially Free, because that depends on your saving and investing habits. But a degree should guarantee a better paycheck. That makes sense," I said after thinking about what he was saying. "So I understand that *statistically* going to college will mean that you make more money, but you can't mean that *every* college is the same, right? I mean there is a difference between a Harvard and Small Town U," I stated.

"You raise an important question and I don't want to spend too much time on it, but let's see if we can answer your question."

Does Success Depend on Getting into the "Right" College?
"There is statistical data and common wisdom that says that college graduates from elite or Ivy League schools go on to earn more money and fill out the ranks of corporate America's executive cadre. It's natural to assume that it's the result of the teaching methods or the institution itself. But, if you look closer, you'll see one important factor that most people overlook: the prestigious schools are *highly*

selective to begin with and you have to be above average in terms of your skills, intellect, and drive *just to get into* these elite schools."

"Are you saying that **elite schools are starting with the best of the best to begin with**?" I asked.

"That's what I'm saying. While your local college might let in the average Joe, the Ivy Leagues just don't do it. They've created an environment of self-starters and eager little beavers that are very competitive and very talented to begin with and would probably thrive in *any* environment. Regardless, back to the original issue at hand. You'll soon realize that there are thousands of examples of successful people who dropped out of school or went to small schools and have become hugely successful. In short, **you can become rich and successful without going to an Ivy League school**."

Easing the Financial Burden of Education[34]

"But all this education costs a lot," I complained. "I have lots of loans and I'm barely making enough to make ends meet."

"I understand your pain and the cost of higher education can definitely be a burden. The good news is that with proper planning, you can reduce the financial hit by getting financial aid and asking for help from Uncle Sam. There are two tax credits; the **Hope Credit** and the **Lifetime Learning Credit** that can help reduce your tax bill. Check with your accountant or planner for more on these. You can also pay for advanced degrees through tuition reimbursement programs through your company."

"Which is how I'm paying for my MBA classes," I said.

"And saving a bundle in the process," he added.

What About Financial Literacy?

There was still something that was bugging me. I had read a lot lately on the subject of schools not providing students with any knowledge or skills in the area of managing money and had to ask what his opinion was.

"I have a question for you Mr. Mathers. I understand the importance of college, but it doesn't really teach you about finance and investing. **I just finished four years and I learned nothing about investing the right way and I'm a finance major!**"

"Look David, the current school curriculum is concerned with giving students the basics they need to survive in the real world, skills like reading, writing, and critical thinking. Sure they *should* teach you

---

[34] For more ways to save, check out www.fabmansecrets.com and find the article titled "*Smart Ways to Cut Down the Costs of College.*"

something about managing money or not getting into debt, but until they change the system, students are going to have to learn about personal finance outside of the classroom. They're just going to have to create that course for themselves."

"What kind of course are you talking about?" I asked, wondering what he had in mind. "And what about all those people who don't want to go to school again or have children and obligations, but don't have their degree? What are they supposed to do?"

Start Your Own University

"Simple. They should start their own university," he stated matter-of-factly. "It's much cheaper than any four-year college and you'll probably learn more stuff that you can actually use in the real world. The process is not difficult and it's what the rich have done for thousands of years. Let me explain why it's so important to start your own university."

The Book a Week Club? [35]

"**Everything you know has gotten you this far in life. What makes you think you'll be able to go farther down the path to Financial Freedom without learning anything new?** Think about it. You may have learned some things from me in the past couple of weeks that will help, but you're going to have to stay on top of your industry at work in order to outperform your peers. Likewise, you need to stay on top of new investment products and strategies, as well as changes in tax laws, to name a few things."

"Sounds like a tall order," I commented.

"It's really not David. **You just have to make learning part of your priorities and part of your life**."

"So exactly how long of a commitment are we talking each week?"

"Just an hour a day, every day for the rest of your life," he replied.

I raised my eyebrows. Every day was a big commitment. I thought of the long hours I was putting in at work and the difficulty I had in finding time to work out even three days a week. He was asking for a lot. I would soon realize how easy the plan was to stick to.

"The mistake that others make, and that I trust you will never make, is to treat education as a chore instead of a joy; to treat graduation as an end of education rather than as a beginning."
— Arthur Burns

---

[35] Jim Rohn, Brian Tracy, Napoleon Hill and Earl Nightingale all speak of the importance of setting aside time in your day to learn. All four have mentioned that an hour is what would help take you to the top. I'm just not sure which one was the first to teach me this idea. Although I believe it was Jim Rohn that came up with the idea of reading a book a week.

It's Easier Than You Think

"Before you start complaining," he said, "let me explain how easy it is and then if you have questions we can discuss the plan in depth. The plan is an outgrowth of a book I read describing Earl Nightingale's comment that **one-hour per day of study in your field of work is all you need to get to the top of your industry within three years**. That's all it takes. You want to know why? **Because the majority of people are either too lazy or too busy to read or invest their precious time in learning something new**."

50 Books a Year?

"In one week I can read through an entire book if I'm not busy scribbling notes and I stay focused on the book for the entire hour."

"What? That's over 50 books a year. That's amazing!"

"It really isn't. It's just a function of persistence. I read a half-hour before work and a half-hour before bedtime. That's in addition to the time I spend reading my papers and magazines every week. All my reading is paying off both financially and personally."

"What do you mean by 'personally?'" I asked.

"As in expanding my mind, learning about how things work, and learning new things. It keeps me on top of the changes in the world and I think it makes me a well-rounded person. I know an hour a day might seem like a lot, but **you don't have to read every night**. Just make sure you set aside at least seven hours a week. Whether you read an hour a night or three hours plus each weekend day, its up to you."

Active Reading

"I keep a highlighter or red pen at my side when I'm reading a book. I highlight any new information I come across and I take notes in this binder of mine," he said patting his binder. "This way I have the information handy if I ever need it."

"And you're able to read through the binder whenever you want to refresh your memory on some of the ideas and concepts," I added.

"You got it," he replied. "And I also keep a folder of articles that discuss successful people and topics of interest so that I can flip through them to help keep me motivated."

"So just by reading a lot of books I'm going to be able to know how to invest and stuff like that, right?"

"You're not going to just read the books David. You're going to actually study and take action after you've read about techniques and concepts. **You'll never truly learn how to do anything if you don't take action on the stuff you're reading about**."

How Much Will It Cost?

"Hey, how much do you spend on all those books?" I asked. "It's got to add up if you're reading 50 books per year."

"I do spend a good deal of money on books, seminars, tape sets, and other forms of education. That's why **I suggest you begin to set aside some money each year to spend on your personal and professional development**. It will be money well spent."

"That's still quite a bit of money though," I commented.

"It is and it isn't. If you think of it as an investment in yourself, you're likely to spend the money because when you learn something and truly take action on the ideas and concepts you'll come across, you'll be rewarded many times over. Besides, you can always cut down on the cost of those books," he said and stopped.

"How?" I asked.

He raised his hand and pointed to the rows upon rows of books that surrounded the table we were at.

"Oh, I get it. The library," I said.

"You can't highlight or underline anything in these books, but you can take them out for a couple of weeks at a time and take notes in that binder of yours. If a book is particularly valuable, you can buy it later."

"Okay, I get it," I said. "But something's bugging me and I have to ask your opinion on the matter."

"I'm all ears," he said, leaning in closer to the table.

"If college is so important to getting ahead in life, how come the richest man in the world didn't finish college?" I asked, referring to Bill Gates.

He stared directly into my eyes and burst out laughing.

After a few uncomfortable moments I asked him what was so funny.

Bill Gates Didn't Go To College

"I'm sorry to have laughed, but whenever I talk about the importance of going to college and getting advanced degrees, someone invariably brings up the example of Bill Gates. Yes, Bill Gates dropped out of college, founded Microsoft, and became the richest man in the world in the process."

"And that's funny why?" I asked.

"Because **people have a funny way of picking out examples in order to justify their ideas or thoughts**. In this case, the idea that just because Bill Gates dropped out of college and became a billionaire, every Joe Schmoe across America and the world thinks they can skip school or drop out of college and become a multi-millionaire by starting a business. Unfortunately, it doesn't work that way."

"And exactly how does it work then?" I asked.

"Listen David, yes Bill Gates dropped out of college and never went back to school, but he was good enough to get into Harvard in the first place. But that aside, Gates set up his own personal development program without even knowing it."

"What are you talking about?" I asked.

Specialized Knowledge

"I'm talking about specialized knowledge David. Yes, Bill Gates, Michael Dell, Thomas Edison, and Andrew Carnegie never received their college degrees, but they had the drive to learn on their own. **All great successful businesspeople and entrepreneurs commit themselves to personal and professional development in some shape or form. Their education takes place outside university walls, but they never stop learning and striving to learn more.** They seek knowledge and don't stop until they understand how things work and how they can do things better. They're constantly on the look out for developments in their industry and are looking to upgrade their skills. All that reading, learning, and on-the-job training is equal to much more than a college or masters degree. The rest of us sit on our laurels, content to complain about our lot in life rather than pick up a book about our industry and learn how we can improve our jobs, our company, and our lives."

"I guess the average college dropout doesn't go through all the extra effort."

"Exactly. Now let's shift gears," he said.

Like-Minded People

"What kind of people do you hang out with David?" he asked.

"Huh? What do you mean?"

"I'm asking you what kind of people you hang out with. Are they motivated and committed like you to do what it takes to get rich?"

I did a quick mental run-through of my friends. "No, I guess most of them aren't really committed to much of anything except perhaps partying and having fun. Retiring early isn't exactly our main topic of discussion. I mean we talk about how nice it would be to be rich one day, but we never do anything about it."

"It's not a surprise given your age. However, I don't expect the discussions with your friends to ever focus seriously on the issues of building wealth, starting a business, or even retiring early, because 95 percent of the people in the world never focus on these topics."

"But won't my friends eventually settle down and start focusing on building wealth and getting out of the rat race?" I asked.

"Probably not David. The topics of partying and meeting girls will give way to talk of marriage, then the conversation will shift to having kids and buying a new house, then to paying for college and to paying for your children's weddings, then to retirement. By then it will be too late and your friends will have some serious catching up to do."

"So what can I do to bring up these topics and get my friends on the right track sooner?"

"You can lead a horse to water, but you can't force it to drink. The best you can do sometimes is to lead by example and hope they follow in your footsteps. Just don't hold your breath."

Improve Your Inner Circle

"I bring this point up because it's been said that **your income is the average of the six people you hang out with the most.** Do the math and you'll see that this idea holds true. That's why it's important to expand your inner circle of friends and develop some key relationships with some people that are going to help add to your reserve of knowledge and help encourage and motivate you to do more with your life. You need to find people who are going to help you become a better person, not just financially but in all aspects of your life. Find those people and get them into your inner circle as soon as possible and you'll reap the rewards of doing so."

Get a Mentor

"One of the best ways to improve your inner circle is to have a mentor(s). Having a mentor is one of the most efficient ways to achieve anything in life. Nothing beats being able to call someone up and brainstorm potential solutions to problems you're encountering. When you interact with other successful and motivated people, their energy will rub off on you and you'll be instantly energized, ready to take on any challenge."

"So I'm ahead of the game, because I have you, right?"

"That's right. You get to tap into my years of experience and you get to save yourself a lot of time by not repeating the mistakes I made."

"There are two ways to acquire wisdom; you can either buy it or borrow it. By buying it, you pay full price in terms of time and cost to learn the lessons you need to learn. By borrowing it, you go to those men and women who have already paid the price to learn the lessons and get their wisdom from them."
- Benjamin Franklin

Increase Your Investing Savvy

"Millionaires spend significantly more hours per month
studying and planning their future investment decisions,
as well as managing their current investments,
than high-income non-millionaires."
- Thomas J. Stanley and William D. Danko, *The Millionaire Next Door*

"One last thing," he said. "I know this is repeating what we discussed last week, but increasing your knowledge about investing is an important aspect of Investing in Yourself. By learning about mutual funds, asset allocation, and investment strategies, you are better informed about the investments you make. You're better able to determine what you should be investing in and you don't have to rely on anyone but yourself."

YOUR BODY

Love Yourself

"The next topic we're going to talk about centers around how to Love Yourself," he said. "What I mean is that **you need to take care of your personal life** just as much as you need to develop and look after your professional or financial life. Too many times I see executives burn out or have nothing to show for all their efforts except achievements in their workplace or their bank accounts. What I'm getting at is that you need to have fun and enjoy life while you can, because you don't get a second chance to do it again."

Taking Care of Yourself Pays Big Dividends

"Eating right, exercising regularly, getting enough sleep each night, and avoiding bad habits like smoking or too much alcohol consumption will improve your quality of life."

"But what does all that stuff have to do with getting rich?"

"More than you think David. I mean what's the point of being a millionaire if you're overweight and unhealthy? What if you're liver's shot from drinking too much or you die from a heart attack 30 years early because of your unhealthy lifestyle and eating habits?"

"You have a point there," I said, stating the obvious. I mean it sounded like a lecture that I didn't want to hear, but he was right. **What's the point of living below your means, saving and investing all that money, and never being able to enjoy it because you short-circuited your life by not taking care of yourself?**

A Good Healthy Diet

"I'm not about to spend a tremendous amount of time talking about what goes into a 'proper' diet, but I just want to make you aware that the foods you eat and the beverages you consume have a dramatic effect on your energy level. Down the line it will have a big impact on how long you'll live. If you're overweight, your risk of an early death skyrockets. If you drink alcohol in excess, you risk shortening your life. In short, you need to take a hard look at your eating habits and make sure that you're eating well-balanced meals. If you're not eating your fruits and vegetables, then you have to start. Lastly, remember to drink plenty of water throughout the day. It will help keep you hydrated and counter the effects of all that caffeine you consume."

Get Some Rest

"We live in a sleep-deprived nation. If you find that you're tired in the afternoon, it's a sign that you probably didn't get enough sleep the night before, so make sure you're getting the proper amount of sleep. I won't dictate how much that is, because it varies from person to person, but eight hours a night is still the recommendation I see most often."

"What and miss Letterman?" I joked.

"Very funny David," he replied, shaking his head at me.

Don't Smoke

"Don't smoke. You'll live longer and enjoy life more, not to mention the negative health aspects I won't go into."

Just Say No to Drugs

"Along a similar vein, just say no to drugs. You'll live longer and enjoy life more."

Watch Your Weight

"It's a sad indictment on our nation when only one state out of 50 has *less than* 20 percent of its population under the obesity level."

"What? So **in 49 states 20 percent or more of the state's population is obese?**" I asked.

"Yep. In this world of supersizing your meals, where fast food is the norm for our children, as well as ourselves, it looks like our dietary habits are catching up with us. And being overweight has a number of health risks associated with it like an increased risk of having a heart attack or diabetes."

"So being overweight can literally cost you your life," I stated.

"That's what I'm saying," he replied.

Exercise Regularly

"To lose weight most people try and starve themselves thin, but if you know anything about how the body works, that's an uphill battle you won't win. When you starve yourself, your metabolism slows down and your body burns fewer calories. That's why after a certain point, you stop losing weight and hit a plateau. In the process, you're losing your lean muscle tissue and that's hurting you even more because muscle burns more calories than fat."

"So what is a person to do? Work out non-stop?"

"Look, I'm not asking you to work out seven days a week for two hours a day. You just need to work out 30 minutes a day for three days a week to see results. Do whatever exercise it is that you enjoy doing, whether it be swimming, biking, running, or powerwalking. Study after study has shown that regular exercise will improve both your physical and mental health. Exercising gets your blood pumping and helps strengthen your muscles, including your heart. As for working out with weights, I strongly suggest that you incorporate resistance training into your exercise regime. Muscle burns more fat and a sculpted and lean body will make you look and feel better about yourself."

"And throw on top of all that how great you feel when you work out and you're in shape, and there's no reason why you shouldn't work out on a regular basis," I said.

"Exactly," he replied. "Just make sure that you consult with a physician before beginning any diet or exercise program."

A Sensible Diet and Regular Exercise Program

"And speaking of diet and exercise programs, you can lose weight by doing one of three things:

a) Eat Less
b) Exercise More
c) Do both a and b

"The best way to lose weight and feel great for the rest of your life is to combine a sensible diet with an exercise program."

He flipped a couple of pages in his binder, then shifted in his seat. "This next discussion covers your career and how you can get more out of your workday and pardon the expression, 'be all that you can be' on the job. There are a lot of topics to cover, so I'm going to go over them briefly and not spend a lot of time on each topic."

"Sounds good to me. Fire away," I said.

YOUR CAREER

Your Job Should Give You a Sense of Purpose

"Everyone has a set of skills, talents, and abilities that could be put to better use in life. Your task is to find the job that's going to make good use of those talents and give you a sense of purpose in life. More importantly, we need to feel competent. We need to know that we are capable of doing our jobs and that we do them well. By doing things that you are good at or more specifically, things you like doing and doing them well, you set yourself up for success."

"So I need to figure out what I like doing and go find a job that's perfect for me?" I asked.

"Amazing concept, isn't it," he replied sarcastically. "And that dream job will be different for everyone. A job you might think is boring as hell could be someone else's dream job. Some people are creative and others are more mathematical and process-driven. It's the whole right-brain versus left-brain thing. Do what you love doing and work won't seem like work anymore. Work will truly become like play as the tired old cliché goes."

Do What You Love

"C'mon, now," I said. "Do you really buy that work is play stuff?"

"Of course I do, but you don't have to take my word for it. Just read any biography, interview, or story of a successful and/or rich person and you'll see that 99% of the time the person keeps on working long after they've made their millions. So if they're millionaires, why do they keep working?" he asked.

"I don't know, they're stupid," I remarked without thinking.

He shook his head at me. "It's a rhetorical question David. They keep working because they love what they're doing. They think running their business or doing their job is fun."

"Wouldn't hanging out with friends or family or chilling on a beach somewhere be a little more fun than running a business?" I asked.

"No. The successful people in life can't wait to get up in the morning to get to the office and work a long day. Why? Because they view their work differently than you and your friends. They enjoy their work and they feel their work has a purpose and it inspires them. Most workers don't feel that way. Instead they view work as a grind and something that they must do to pay the bills. It's never something that they want to do; it's always something they *have* to do. Do you see the difference?"

I nodded and he continued.

"The greatest fortunes this world has known, those built from the ground up, were built by individuals who loved their work. These fortunes, the companies they built, the people they touched, the lives they improved, all stemmed from individuals following their passions. For Ford it was to make a car affordable for every man, for Gates it was a computer on every desk in the world, for Disney it was the best amusement park in the world. Steven Spielberg started making movies as a kid because he loved scaring his sisters. He just raised the stakes and decided to scare a larger audience. And after all his success as a director, what's he doing today? Directing. Why? Because he loves to direct, it's his passion, his life, and the reason he's been so successful. He dedicated his heart and soul to making movies for us to enjoy."

After a few moments of thought, I responded. "I get it. **You need to find work that inspires you and you'll be richer, if not happier than you've ever been before**."

He smiled broadly. "That's it in a nutshell. **Find your true calling and make it your job in life and you'll be happy for the rest of your living days**."

> "You have to find something that you love enough to be able to take risks, jump over the hurdles and break through the brick walls that are always going to be placed in front of you. If you don't have that kind of feeling for what it is you're doing, you'll stop at the first giant hurdle."
>
> – George Lucas

So What Do You Like To Do?

"So let me ask you a question David. What do you like to do? What gets you psyched and excited?" he asked.

I thought about it for a few moments and then it came to me. "Well, I kind of like learning about investing and stuff like that. I enjoy helping others learn about how to manage their finances and talking about the little tips you've given me over the past six weeks." I nodded my head up and down subconsciously. "Yep, that's it. I like helping people with investing."

"Well there you have it. You could be a financial planner or perhaps a columnist who writes about financial matters. To reiterate, you get wealthy in this lifetime through a mixture of your talent, desire, and discipline. You need to figure out where your talents lie and put them to use and be disciplined enough to work hard and stick to your vision. Most people do exactly the opposite. They never find out what their talents are and they just take the first job that comes along. Usually it's the wrong job for them and they're miserable for the rest of their life."

Finding the Perfect Job for YOU!

"You can find your calling by answering a few questions, like:

- What am I passionate about?
- What are my talents, skills and "hidden" abilities?
- What type of tasks at work do I like most?
- If a genie granted me millions of dollars but said I still had to work for the rest of my life, what job would I pick?

"When you answer these questions, you'll be able to paint a better picture of your ideal job," he said, then waited until I finished copying them down.

Ask Around

"If you have no clue about what you really want to do in life, you can ask for help. Those closest to you should know you best and can help you realize that you're good at negotiating or writing or dreaming up new products. They can help you see what you could become better than you can sometimes. The key is to just ask! If you still have trouble, you can just consult that Parachute book.[36]"

Doing What You Love Even If You Have to Take a Pay Cut?

"What if what you love to do doesn't pay very well?" I asked.

"Great question and it will lead you to some hard thinking and serious trade-offs. Ask the question about earning less money and pursuing what you love and most people will think of struggling artists or musicians working as waitresses or waiters in order to pay the phone bill and put food in their stomachs. But **there are many more people than you think out there who have opted for a lower-paying job for quality of life reasons**. The work you do in life is important, at least it should be. What matters is that you are doing something that you love and when the day is done you feel a sense of accomplishment."

"Yeah, but if you're not making a lot of money and you have no real chance of promotion in your job, doesn't it kind of defeat the purpose? I mean if you don't earn a lot of money, you'll never be able to retire early, right?"

---

[36] *What Color Is Your Parachute?: A Practical Manual for Job-Hunters & Career-Changers* by Richard Nelson Bolles

"No David, that's not the case at all. **If you put the other Secrets of Wealth into action, you don't necessarily have to earn a lot of money in order to retire early.** Just look at Anne Scheiber," he said, referring to the woman who never made more than $50,000 a year and died a multi-millionaire.

Do What Makes You the Most Money?

"Of course there is the other side of the argument," he said, "which is that you should take the job that pays you the most money. The payoff being that everything from bonuses, to raises, to pension plans, to Social Security benefits are all keyed off of how much money you make. If you read the book *Live Rich* by Stephen Pollan and Mark Levine, they tell you that the idea behind 'Do what you love and the money will follow' is bad advice. The authors believe that you should be in business for yourself and you need to identify your best interests and pursue them. You have to be a mercenary and always be on the lookout for the next opportunity and the higher paying job. Don't sacrifice money for work you love they tell you."

"A little bit different than the ideas we've been talking about," I commented.

"Polar opposites in fact. I understand where they're coming from, but disagree with the end result. Even if corporate loyalty is dead, going for the highest paying job just because it pays better isn't always the best option. What's the point of being paid well if the trade-off is that you're miserable for 50 or 60 hours a week like a dog? That's not worth it in my book."

"I agree," I said.

"Good. Let's move on to ways you can add value on the job."

Add Value and You'll Add to Your Paycheck

"When you add enough value to the lives of others and to your job, you're going to be rewarded. If you have a business and offer your customers the best prices or a service they want at a great value, then you'll be rewarded with a larger market share. If you put your heart and soul into customer service, you'll see an impact on the bottom line."

"So these people with specialized knowledge use their talents to stand out from the rest of us and get rewarded because of it?"

"You got it," he replied. "They've figured out what makes them particularly valuable to a corporation and they work hard because they love what they are doing. It's a win/win situation for the company and the employee."

Applying Yourself to Your Work

"Just realize that **having specialized knowledge doesn't guarantee that you will earn a higher income**. Just because you have a law degree doesn't mean that you will earn a lot of money. You could decide to be a lawyer, spend all that money on getting your degree, then go and get a job in a small firm that pays you just enough to put food on your table, pay your rent, and pay off your enormous school loans."

"You're so depressing. Did you know that?" I asked.

"I only speak the truth. I've seen it too many times where a smart kid comes out of college or business school or law school and finds that they can barely make ends meet. They think just because they have a degree and put in four or seven years at school they deserve a job."

"Shouldn't they deserve a job after spending all that time in college and spending all that money?" I asked.

"The simple answer is no. No, they might deserve to have a job but they're not *entitled* to one. **Your boss is there to give you a job and that's it. It's up to you to prove your worth to the company and the only way you're going to get a raise is to prove your value**. Sometimes you have to do more than the status quo, which brings us to our next topic."

Go the Extra Mile

"There's a book I want you to read," he said. "It's called *Believe and Achieve* by W. Clement Stone and it discusses at length one of the most important principles I think I've ever come across."

"And what is that?" I asked, ready to write it down.

"The power of 'Going the Extra Mile.' According to Stone, '**If you do more than you are paid to do, it is inevitable that you will eventually be paid for more than you do**.' Unfortunately, the majority of people don't want to work for a living and most do the bare minimum not to get fired. Yet those same people expect, no in fact they sometimes demand and complain that they never get a promotion or that their raise is substandard. The only thing substandard is their work effort and how much of themselves they give to their jobs. They don't realize how easy it is to go above and beyond the average worker. Going the extra mile boils down to giving better service to your boss or employer than you are paid to do. The businessperson who goes the extra mile will build quite a reputation and people will want to do business with them. Thanks to the power of word-of-mouth advertising they'll soon see an increase in their sales and the number of customer referrals they're getting."

"So does this mean that I'm supposed to do more work than everyone else? Of course I'll get paid more," I commented.

"David, going the extra mile is more about adopting the mindset that you should do more than you're asked to do than it is about doing more work. It means saying hello to people and giving more than your boss or your customers expect. It's about overdelivering and surprising people. Do this and you'll see how quickly it can impact your life and give you a greater sense of satisfaction with your work and your life."

I've kept the words "<u>**Go the Extra Mile**</u>" in my head for the past ten years. It's been a great way for me to shine above the rest. Take the time to write those words down right now and keep them close at hand. They will help you tremendously over the course of your career.

Live Close to Work

"Speaking of miles, you should try and live as close as possible to work," he said.

I shook my head at him. "You know you're corny, right?"

"Yes, I know that. But the reason you should live close to work is that you don't have to deal with the stress of a long commute and you can get home quickly to your children and family and still put in a long day at work. Of course living close to work can help you get to work earlier than you competition and your coworkers. And it will save you a boatload of money in gasoline and car expenses."

"I get where you're going," I said. "What's next?"

Arrive a Half Hour Early and Leave a Half Hour Later

"If you're going to outshine your coworkers, a good piece of advice is to get to work a half hour before them and leave a half hour later than them. I know this advice will make you work more hours than your peers, but the payoff is huge. Senior managers get in early as a rule of thumb, so if you don't want to work investment banker hours (12-15 hours a day), then err on the side of coming in 45 minutes to an hour earlier and leaving with the rest of the crowd come quitting time. Put this little tactic to work for you and you're working an hour more than everyone else a day. At the end of a year you've worked an extra 200 hours which is close to a month of work time."

"Wow," I responded. "So I'll be able to do more than others just by coming in a little earlier and leaving a little later. Not bad at all."

"That's right David and you can understand how fast you can move up the ranks by doing more work than others just by putting in an extra hour a day, the easy way."

How to Be a Professional

"How others perceive you is very important to your ability to get your ideas and your thoughts across to others, but your image is more than just the way you look. It involves your ability to listen effectively and thinking before you speak. It involves your body language and how you speak to others. In short, you need to project the right image and attitude if you're going to climb that corporate ladder."

Dress to Impress

"You want people to think of you as someone who is serious about their work and about getting ahead on the job. A decade ago, my advice was to dress like your boss's boss and that's still my advice to this day. The only thing that has changed is the wardrobe. You're no longer required to wear a suit in this dressed-down world, so it's even more vital that you watch what you wear."

"What do you mean?" I asked.

"I mean that it's too easy to get lulled into dressing poorly or wearing things that are inappropriate for the young (or old) go-getter. You need to dress for the job you want, not for the job you have and your boss will take notice. Wear nice slacks and a pressed shirt instead of the standard de facto golf shirt and wrinkled khaki pants and you'll get noticed. Your attitude toward yourself will also change. You'll feel differently about yourself when you're dressed up and you'll be more professional."

Body Language

"Just as important as your attire, is the message you convey through your body language," he said.

"What do you mean by body language?"

"Body language encompasses your stature, how you stand, or sit when someone is talking to you. Making eye contact is also another important aspect of body language. Actually there's way too much involved, but there's an easy way to figure out the 'do's' and 'don'ts' of body language. When you're in a meeting or just sitting in the cafeteria at work, take a look at the different way the successful people and 'higher-ups' are sitting, talking, and holding themselves. You'll probably see that they don't slouch, they sit up straight, and they're making eye contact with you. You get the point."

Think Before You Speak

"Think before you open your mouth. Before you ask a question, take the time to think it through and see if you can figure it out for yourself. Make sure you're adding to the conversation and not just blowing hot air in someone's face. Prepare ahead of time for every meeting and if you're going to speak to your boss about an issue, plan ahead. Think of all aspects of the problem and brainstorm on some solutions. So you're better prepared to meet with others and they'll thank you for valuing their time."

Learn to Listen and Pay Attention

"To many young guns are way too anxious to hear their voice and show their co-workers and their boss that they're the greatest thing since sliced bread. What they should be doing is keeping their trap shut and focusing on listening to the discussion instead. When you listen before you speak, you fully understand what the other person is trying to say. Don't read into what they are saying. If you're unclear of something, ask. When you ask a question or repeat back to them what they just said, it shows that you are an active listener."

"Whoops. I guess I'm guilty of being a bad listener," I admitted. "My mind tends to wander and if I'm talking to someone on the phone, I tend to check email or sort my mail."

"Those are very bad habits that you need to break. Put your pen down or take your hands off the keyboard and look at the person. Concentrate on what they're saying. It will make all the world of difference."

Put Yourself in the Other Person's Shoes

"When you look at things from someone else's perspective, it's much easier to develop a plan of attack or a method of communication that will connect with them. If you don't press or push someone when they're having a bad day or you backoff when you need to, they'll thank you for it. In the process, you'll be building dynamic relationships that will help you in your quest to climb that corporate ladder."

Be Respectful and Professional

"You've got to have good manners and you've got to be respectful of others. Be professional when answering and talking on the phone. Be professional when writing a memo or an email. Forget those silly smiley faces and forget the abbreviations. Don't impose on other people and don't assume that someone's time is not as important as yours."

Don't Burn Bridges

"You never know when you'll be crawling back to your old job, department, or company, so don't burn any bridges. You also never know when a co-worker or peer might become your boss, so don't burn any bridges with anyone, ever! If you don't have something nice to say or you have the urge to gossip about someone, keep your mouth shut."

Solicit Feedback

"You shouldn't find out how you're doing on the job when it's time for your annual review," he said. "You should sit with your boss at least every six months to go over your progress and cover what your strengths and weaknesses are. This way you'll have at least six months to correct the problem before your official review. On an ongoing basis, you should ask for advice and feedback on assignments to make sure you're meeting your boss' expectations. If you're not, ask what you can do to improve your performance."

Hold Yourself Accountable

"Another key point is to hold yourself accountable for your actions. We've already talked about how people look to place blame on others, but the true leaders in life are the ones that take responsibility and shoulder the blame for their mistakes and failures. You need to ask yourself whether or not you're making progress toward your goals or whether you're just making excuses for where you are in life. You need to decide to become a person of character and someone who people can depend on, so hold yourself accountable for all your actions."

Take Your Vacation

"When you don't use your vacation it's the same thing as giving back your paycheck to your company. Time is money David and your boss planned for you to be out that entire week. When you don't take time to recoup or refresh or relax, you get burned out."

"I know the feeling. I'm a bit burned out most of the time," I admitted, "but I just never got around to planning my vacation last year and then it was the end of the year and my department is very busy because we have to close the books so I couldn't take a vacation."

"Here's some advice for you: **Plan your vacations in advance and you'll be less likely not to take them.** Being too busy is no longer an excuse when you're trying to climb the corporate ladder or build your business. If you were to die tomorrow the work in your inbox would still be there and the same goes for when you come back from your vacation; the work will still be there. And if you've learned anything about being an effective manager or leader in your company, you know that you must learn how to delegate some of your tasks. CEOs of major corporations, emergency room doctors, and even the presidents of countries take vacations. Why can't you?"

Take the Day Off! - Are You Working at Less than 100 Percent?

"If you're sick, stay home. Too many young eager beavers come into work when they should be at home lying in bed and getting better. You're no good to someone if you're operating at 50% capacity for several days in a row. I'd rather my workers call in sick, recuperate, and be back on the job the next day, rested and ready to give me their best," he said. "Now on to one of my favorite topics."

The Power of Networking

"When you work for a big company one of the hardest things to do is stand out and get noticed. The good news is that there are things that you can do to meet people and network like join company softball team or sign on for cross-functional projects."

"But what if you're not a good softball player or you don't have time to do any projects or worse, what if your boss won't let you be on a project team?" I asked.

"David, you don't have to be a star athlete to play on a corporate team. You just have to show up, have fun, and show everyone that you're human."

"Human? Would they doubt that?"

He laughed. "If you're on the fast track, you might be perceived as all business and no pleasure. But the main thing to remember about your work is that it's important to stay focused on the job and remember **the objective of networking isn't to kiss someone's butt** in order to get ahead. The objective of networking is to make contacts that will help you get things done faster in the organization, as well as provide you with a cadre of endorsers who will be able to help steer your career toward the fast track. Besides, if you're kissing too many butts it's going to be obvious to your peers and the person you're trying to impress and you'll get nowhere. **You have to be sincere in your approach to networking and you have to give just as much as you receive**. Understand?"

"Got it."

Look Outside Your Cubicle Walls

"Networking outside of your company is just as important as creating a good network inside your company, especially in today's job world. You should look into professional associations, community organizations, social clubs, and charities because you need a powerful Rolodex® of contacts should you ever need to find a job outside your current company."

"That makes plenty of sense to me," I said. "Any other tips?"

"If you want to learn more about networking, you only have to read one book: *Dig Your Well Before You're Thirsty* by Harvey Mackay. It's priceless for helping to build your networking skills."

Identify Role Models

"Lastly, it's important to look around and identify people that you want to model yourself after. We'll talk about mentors in a moment, but there's no reason that you can't find someone at work who is a level or two or three above you that can help you achieve success in the company," he said.

"So I should just walk up to the person and ask them to be my mentor?" I asked.

"Something like that. Just identify the people and tell them that you admire their work and would like to learn from them. The majority of people will be flattered and would be willing to help you out. Buy them lunch or meet them for an early morning breakfast. Ask them to recommend a book, training program, or tape set that has influenced them. Just ask, ask, and ask some more and you'll be amazed at what they'll give you. Just make sure you're willing to give back in return."

"That's a great suggestion," I said. "I already know one person I'm going to ask to mentor me at work."

"That's the spirit. Identify them and ask them to help share their ideas and thoughts on what has made them a success."

"People seem to naturally divide themselves into two groups: those who cheerfully do their best at their jobs and those who seem to have the attitude, 'When they pay me what I'm worth, I'll give them what they pay for.'"

– W. Clement Stone

"Ours is a society that demands instant gratification. We want what we want, and we want it now. Most real rewards, however, don't come that way. Usually, **you must be willing to do the work, to give more than you are asked, before you begin to collect the interest on your investment.**"

– W. Clement Stone

YOUR LIFE

The Whole Package

"Now on to the fourth area of Investing in Yourself."

"Wait a minute," I said. "I thought there were only three: mind, body, and career?"

"Yes and all those things come together to form your life which is the final area you need to invest your time and effort into improving if you're going to get the most out of life."

"If this is going to be a philosophical discussion, how about a walk around the park to capture the moment better?" I asked.

"I like the idea," he replied. "Let's do it."

We gathered our books and stuff and went outside. It was a cool summer morning, which I was thankful for given the heat wave we were currently experiencing.

Love Your Family

"Life is definitely too short not to spend time with your loved ones. Too often we get caught up in the Rat Race and we put our careers first and our families second. Through the course of their careers, millions of Americans will learn that their jobs are not the first priority in life. Perhaps they'll realize it when they lose their job after 20 years of dedication to one company. Perhaps they'll realize it after their marriage falls apart. Whenever it happens, they won't see it coming. Those money-hungry, career fast trackers often lose sight of what's truly important in life until its too late. Their kids grow up and are out of the house and they realize they never spent quality time with them. They might have provided for them, but in the end they'd gladly trade some of those dollars they made for a chance to buy back some time with their kids when they were growing up."

> "It's good to have money and the things money can buy,
> but it's good, too, to check up once in a while and make
> sure that you haven't lost the things money can't buy."
> - George Horace Lormier

Strive for Balance

"In short, what you're looking to do is achieve balance in life. You want to make sure that you're spending time on improving your mind, body, career, as well as your finances. It might seem like a daunting task at first, but it boils down to creating a plan to improve your life and invest in yourself. Once you get the ball rolling, your efforts become habits and you'll find it much easier to do the things that you need to get done. Just make sure you're improving all areas of your life and not working on your career all the time and forgetting about your family or your health."

"So what you're doing is trying to excel in all areas," I said, "but not overdo it in any one area because you might become one-dimensional or miss out on some of the things that life has to offer."

"Well put," he said. "You see David, **life is about making tradeoffs and sometimes you can't have it all**. There are sacrifices to be made and you alone, along with your spouse, need to make the tough decisions. I'm not going to philosophize about the tradeoffs, but I wanted to make you aware that there are more important things than making money in life. Some people never realize this simple fact, but I hope all my students come to this realization."

> "Perpetual devotion to what a man calls his business, is only to be sustained by perpetual neglect of many other things."
>
> - Robert Louis Stevenson

A Little Fun Never Cost a Thing

"Now let's talk about having some fun, going on vacation, taking up new hobbies, and enjoying life."

"Don't those things cost money?" I asked.

"So what?" he replied. **"If you have your Financial Freedom Plan on autopilot you can spend a little money here and there and still be confident that you're on track**. Besides, having fun in life doesn't have to cost a thing. There are literally hundreds of things that you can do that don't involve spending a red cent or hardly any money at all. Maybe it's going for a run or playing sports with your friends. Maybe it's spending endless hours reading books or perhaps writing one. Perhaps its going camping, fishing, cooking, bicycling, playing with your kids, or going to the ballpark with your friends."

"You're so right. I love playing touch football with my friends, but I haven't made the time to do it lately."

"And all that stuff doesn't have to stop. To take it even a step further, you should definitely **schedule in time to do nothing or to hang out with your friends and family**. Take some time off to decompress and relieve any tension or stress you might have from being on the go so much during the workday. Blow off some steam, have some fun, and spend a little money in the process. Life's too short not to have fun, so lighten up and stop stressing about everything. **As long as you've got your Financial Freedom Plan in place, you can have fun and build wealth at the same time."**

"So I can have my cake and eat it to is what you're saying," I said.

"Exactly Mr. Cliché boy," he replied.

You Control Your Destiny

"I could go on and on about the subject of investing in yourself David, but I think that would be overkill. I think you understand that you alone are in control of your destiny," he said.

There it was again. It was a point that Mr. Mathers would hammer home again and again throughout our talks and lessons. I stood there and just stared back at him. There was so much we had covered and I never thought of the idea of investing in myself by increasing my knowledge on an off the job or sharpening my skills, let alone improving my physical health to become more productive and get more out of life. What he was saying made all the sense in the world, especially taking the time to accept who you are and create the person you wanted to become, the person that you were already but just didn't know it. I think I was daydreaming at that point, because Mr. Mathers was waving his hand in front of my eyes.

"Earth to David. Earth to David," he repeated.

"Huh?" I said, waking from my dream of my future self.

"What are you waiting for? Go do something! Go for a run, read a book, or call up your buddies and throw around the football. Just do it...now!!!"

"Thanks again for another great lesson Mr. Mathers," I said.

"Just apply what I've taught you and that will be thanks enough," he replied.

I shook his hand and hurried to my car. That afternoon I played catch with a friend of mine for the first time in years. Later that night I mapped out a plan to increase my education by creating my own university and listing out the areas I needed to improve in order to become a better person. Now it's your turn to map out how you're going to Invest in Yourself.

"If money is your hope for independence you will never have it. The only real security that a man will have in this world is a reserve of knowledge, experience and ability."

- Henry Ford

Increase Your Ability to Earn - COMMENTS

The seventh Secret of Wealth is an important topic to understand, learn, and adopt into your lifestyle. I first learned about increasing your "ability to earn" from the book The Richest Man in Babylon. "Increase thy ability to earn" is the seventh cure for a lean purse according to Clason's classic tale. In short, the concept is all about becoming more valuable to yourself.

Becoming More Valuable to Yourself

*Jim Rohn says, "**Don't ask for things to get better, ask that YOU get better**." Investing in Yourself is about becoming more valuable to yourself. It's about making a conscious decision to improve your skills and develop the habits that will make you a successful entrepreneur, but this rule is important if you work for a company or work for yourself.*

*Ben Franklin once said that **an investment of knowledge always pays the best interest** and he was right. Why? Because as we've discussed, education and the attainment of specialized knowledge improves the odds of your success in life. Education will help you outshine your coworkers and help you outsmart your competitors. By being knowledgeable of the risks of a situation or the mistakes that have been made by others before you, you can help overcome these fears and you can avoid the risks others have made. You also improve your ability to earn more money. Yes, I'd have to agree with Mr. Franklin, investing in your education (and your mind) is one of the best investments around.*

"If a man empties his purse into his head, no one can take it away from him. An investment of knowledge always pays the best interest."
- Benjamin Franklin

You Need to Sharpen Your Saw!

You have to constantly sharpen your saw as Stephen Covey likes to say. Knowledge is power and it's the key to survival. We are living in an age of unprecedented change and those who don't take the time to learn new skills or keep up with changes in their industries, will be left behind. You have no job security when you don't keep up with changes in your industry. Instead you become a liability to your company and you're writing your own ticket to the unemployment line. Are those enough reasons to take action and begin investing in yourself? Good. Let's do it!

Invest in Yourself – ACTION PLAN

MIND

Start Your Own University: It's much cheaper than most 4-year colleges and you'll probably learn more. Just go to www.fabmansecrets.com for a list of books in various improvement areas. Another suggestion is to ask around. This means your mentors, people you're modeling yourself after, and online forums. Take note of which books pop up frequently and read them.

Tape Sets: If you have a long commute or you go for a run or walk every day or every other day, then you have enough time to pop in a tape set and feed your mind. Whatever the subject, get into the regular habit of constantly feeding your mind with new information.

Keep a Journal: Chances are you're going to forget the stuff you're listening to and reading about unless you create a Success Journal. Write down the most important ideas, thoughts, and concepts from the authors and speakers in your success journal.

Apply Your Knowledge: In other words, TAKE ACTION. Knowledge and skills are nothing unless you put them to use in the real world. Knowledge put into action is power. Unsuccessful people either do nothing at all or they read and read and read some more but never do anything with the information they've read about. The Secrets of Wealth are in this book and many others like it that are probably on your bookshelf gathering dust. My challenge to you is to read through this book and actually put the information to good use.

Harness the Power of the Internet: Do I really need to get into all the countless sites that have information on how to improve yourself and improve your performance on the job and in life?

Find a Mentor: Success leaves clues! One of the best ways to ensure success in life is to learn by doing and by following the path of a mentor. Don't be afraid to seek out a mentor and ask them for help. There are experts out there, perhaps right under your nose, who can help you in your quest for Financial Freedom.

"Read books, listen to tapes, attend seminars they are decades of wisdom reduced to invaluable hours."
- Mark Victor Hansen, Co-author, *Chicken Soup for the Soul* Series

BODY

Get Leverage on Yourself: I learned long ago from Tony Robbins that all humans are motivated by the twin emotions of Pleasure and Pain. We'll do everything in our power to avoid pain and we obviously gravitate toward things that give us pleasure. Let's use the example of wanting to lose 50 pounds. Why do you want to lose the 50 pounds? You need to convince yourself that you must absolutely change or else you will have more pain than if you remained in your current condition. The key to getting leverage on yourself is to create so much emotional pain that you absolutely must change and not changing would mean more pain than staying the way you are.

Create Specific Goals: It's important to know exactly what you want to achieve. To lose weight this year is not specific enough. You have to have a specific goal in mind if you're ever going to achieve your weight loss goals. A goal of losing 50 pounds is specific.

Break Your Goals into Manageable Tasks: Your ultimate goal might be to lose 50 pounds, but that sounds like a daunting task for even the most disciplined superachiever. If you lose a pound or two in your first week, you're probably going to be discouraged and give up. However, if your goal was to lose 50 pounds over the course of a year it works out to be a little over 4 pounds a month, that sounds like a much easier task even though it's technically the same goal.

Avoid Fad Diets: I hate fad diets. My friends, family members, and subscribers have tried them and none of them ever achieve any lasting results. The best advice I can give you is to do a little research into the foods you eat and strive to get a proper balance of carbohydrates, protein, and fat in your diet. Figure out what eating and exercise plan works for you and stick to it!

Ditch the Pills: While the pills might help you in the short-term, you'll never learn how to eat and exercise properly so you'll have to take pills for the next 40 years to maintain your ideal weight. Plus you don't know what the long-term effects to your health will be.

Create a Workout Plan: There are a number of different exercise and diet programs out there. Just create a program that will work for you, then work that plan.

Do Fun Activities: Your eating plan is the most important element to losing weight, but exercise is a close second. If you can't afford to join a gym or have injuries that make it physically impossible to lift weights or run, find a fun activity you love to do. It could be walking around town at a brisk pace or rollerblading. Whatever it is, if you're having fun while exercising and losing weight, you're much more likely to stick to your exercise plan.

Hit the Gym: Yes, you can lose weight by doing fun cardio activities, but after reading up on health, nutrition, and weight loss studies, I can't help but recommend two or three days of lifting weights a week. Muscle burns more calories than fat. Let me say that again, muscle burns more calories than fat.

NOTE: Make sure you consult your doctor and learn how to lift weights from a professional trainer before you start your weight training. It shouldn't cost you much and most of the gyms you'll join will include a free workout with a trainer. After a while, you can do it on your own.

Discipline Yourself: The hardest step you will ever take is actually entering the health club on your workout days. Once you're inside, it's easy to start working out because you have a plan and you'll gain momentum once you start. Discipline yourself and tell yourself that you have to go because of the pain you will feel if you don't go. Again, it's about getting leverage on yourself.

Get a Partner: Having someone go through what you are going through will help keep you motivated and on track. Just make sure your partner is reliable and as committed as you are. If they start saying they're not going to the gym today or they are having a "cheat" day when it comes to a meal, you might feel the gravitational pull back to the dark side.

Don't Sweat it if You Miss a Day: All of us have our days off and it's good to take a day off once in a while. Don't let missing a day get you down. Just make sure you're in the gym or back on your eating plan the next day. One too many days off and you'll be on that slippery slope to flab city.

CAREER
Go the Extra Mile: Create that mindset of constantly thinking of ways to overdeliver on your promises and what you said you would do. Do so because you want to and not because you're expecting something in return.

Find Your True Calling: Now's the time to figure out what you love doing and figure out a way to make it your career. Perhaps it involves taking a hobby of yours and making it a part-time job. Perhaps it means networking with another department in your company to get your foot in the door of an area you'd like to work in. If you're still having problems, ask your friends and family members for help. They know you and chances are they know what you would be great at.

Increase Your Productivity: I've already talked at length about managing your time, but the skill of managing your time to increase your productivity on the job is a key skill you'll need to shine on the job. Just go back to Secret #3 and re-read the article "21 Things You Must Do to Manage Your Time Better" and apply the information to your life.

Networking: Go out and buy the book *Dig Your Well Before You're Thirsty* by Harvey Mackey and read it. Apply what's in the book and you'll become a master at networking! I plan on writing a book on this topic in 2004, so check back with my site www.fabmansecrets.com to see if the book is completed by the time you're reading this!

LIFE
Design Your Life: Start to imagine the life you want to create for yourself. I know we covered this during the ACTION PLAN for the first Secret of Wealth, but I want you to get into the habit of thinking of all the areas in your life and visualizing how you want to lead your life. Think about your life in all six areas:

- Physical
- Financial
- Professional
- Intellectual (incl. Personal Development)
- Relational
- Spiritual

Just write down the things you'd like to do in each of these areas or name people you would like to model yourself after that have achieved Financial Freedom or have an awesome relationship with their spouse and family. What are the things they do that you would love to do as well? What are the things you would like to have in these areas? Don't worry about figuring out the ways to get them right now. We'll cover that in the last Secret of Wealth.

Use Your Spare Time Wisely: Your time is precious, so invest it wisely. Don't waste it on watching the TV, playing video games, surfing the Internet, or yapping for hours on the telephone. Invest in Yourself and don't let temporary setbacks get you down. Learn from your mistakes, rework your approach, and make sure you work that plan of yours. Take action today and let the real you shine through. **Either get busy living or get busy dying**. Why not do the former and live the life you've imagined by becoming the person you daydream about becoming? Start today...

"Anything less than a commitment to excellent performance on your part is an unconscious acceptance of mediocrity. It used to be that you needed to be excellent to rise above the competition in your industry. Today, you must be excellent even to keep your job in your industry. By engaging in continuous self-improvement, you can put yourself behind the wheel of your own life. By dedicating yourself to enhancing your earning ability, you will automatically be engaging in the continuous process of personal development. By learning more, you prepare yourself to earn more. You position yourself for tomorrow by developing the knowledge and skills that you need to be a valuable and productive part of our economy, no matter which direction it goes."

Brian Tracy, Author, *Goals!*

Additional Resources

Books:
Believe and Achieve by W. Clement Stone
The Seven Habits of Highly Effective People by Stephen Covey
Think and Grow Rich by Napoleon Hill
The Purpose-Driven Life: What on Earth Am I Here For? by Rick Warren
Body for Life: 12 Weeks to Mental and Physical Strength by Bill Phillips

Web-Sites:
www.selfgrowth.com
www.tonyrobbins.com
www.TotalLifeSuccess.com

Secret #8:
REAL ESTATE
IS
FREE

"Buy land. They ain't making any more of the stuff."
- Will Rogers

Chapter 17

Secret #8 – Real Estate is FREE

You Have a Partner?

At the end of our seventh lesson, Mr. Mathers and I discussed our next meeting briefly.

"If you come to the library next Saturday at nine, I'm sure we can discuss your budding real estate career. I'll see if my real estate partner can make it," he said.

"You have a real estate partner?" I was surprised because he never mentioned one in the past.

"Of course I do. I can't keep up on real estate and all my businesses by myself. My partner does most of the analysis, I do the upkeep, and we split the profits."

"Sounds like a great partnership."

"It is. Let me see if she's available and I'll call you back." Mr. Mathers called two minutes later to confirm our appointment. He said that his partner was very busy, but was willing to meet and help teach me the eighth Secret. "It's her way of giving back," he said.

Partners in Prosperity

One week later, I showed up to the library and Mr. Mathers and his partner were already at the door waiting for me

"David, this is my partner extraordinaire, Allison Roberts."

"Pleasure to meet you Ms. Roberts," I said, shaking her hand.

"Please David, Allison is fine. Allie is even better," she said.

Allison or Allie was a beautiful woman who clearly looked the part of a wealthy person. Her clothes looked very expensive and her watch must have set her back at least a thousand dollars. But the most striking thing was how young she looked. If she was a day over 30 years old, I would have been shocked.

"Allie why don't you give David your credentials and then we can get started," he said, opening the door to the library.

"It's a beautiful day Mark. Why don't we go for a walk instead of sitting in the stuffy old library? David can take notes as we walk or I'll give him my binder to copy. What do you say?" she asked.

"Let's do it," I replied. I slung my backpack over my shoulder and we headed downtown. After some small talk, she gave me her background.

The Partner

"Straight from college I went to law school and got my law degree, then came back to Woodbridge. I was at the real estate agency looking for a place to rent and bumped into Mark and after an amazing conversation, he convinced me to buy a place instead of renting an apartment. That first purchase got me hooked on investing in real estate and soon thereafter, Mark and I formed a partnership. But even before I met Mark, I knew I wanted to get into real estate."

"So you wanted to get into real estate before you met Mr. Mathers?" I asked.

"Sure. At my firm I worked mostly on wills, estate planning, and real estate closings. After only a few months, it was obvious to me that the majority of **our truly rich clients had two things in common: they owned real estate and/or their own business**. However, the truly secure ones owned real estate without exception. Some of the business owners who didn't own real estate were constantly worried about a downturn in their business, succession of the business to their children, and the sheltering of their income. The real estate owners were more concerned with travelling, buying vacation homes, and donating their money. Quite a difference really. In any event, that's me in a nutshell. But enough jabbering, let's get to the eighth Secret: **Real Estate is FREE**."

So You Want to Be a Renter

"Most people either own or they rent the place they live in. There are pros and cons to each side, but if you go the rental route, make sure that your total rental costs (including utilities, maintenance, etc) is not more than 30% of your gross income. This is just a benchmark and kind of high in my opinion, but **one of the advantages of renting is that you normally pay less to rent than if you were to buy a place to live in**."

"I guess it can be hard to stay under that 30% rule in New York City or San Francisco," I stated.

"It is, but it can be done," she replied. "There are areas that are a little less expensive to live in and no one says you can't rent an apartment outside the city. Just make sure you include the commuting costs into your calculation. In an attempt to live in a cheaper area of town, some people spend a lot of money in tolls, cab rides, car expenses, or subway tolls. Those extra expenses can add up quickly. But lets step back a second. Even before you go apartment hunting, you should look at your budget to figure out how much monthly rent you can afford and once you've figured out this dollar amount, you should immediately begin saving for at least one month's security deposit."

"A security deposit? What's that?" I asked.

"Most landlords want you to ante up at least a month if not two months of rent as a security deposit in case you trash the place or skip town without paying your rent," she replied. "You should also create a checklist that will help remind you about questions to ask regarding parking, appliances, security, who does maintenance, are pets allowed, and anything else you can think of. Usually a call to a friend or two who are renters will turn up a few of their 'nightmares' that will help frame out the most important questions to ask. You should also ask if you have the right to sublease the apartment to someone else."

"I see. So when does it make sense to rent instead of own?"

"I think that the main reason someone should consider renting is when there is a high likelihood of moving within five years. By renting you'll avoid the high costs associated with purchasing a home."

So You Want to Be an Owner

"When you buy a home you obviously stop paying rent, which is a good thing, but some people will point out that home ownership is not all it's cracked up to be. One of the arguments against buying a place is that **the average homeowner moves every 5 to 7 years.** This means that they have to deal with the high cost of buying and selling a home pretty frequently. You get to pay things like agents' commissions, points on your mortgage, perhaps PMI insurance, and other closing and moving costs, not to mention the out-of-pocket maintenance costs."

"Yeah, but I have a friend of mine who made over $100,000 by selling his place after two years. He made out like a bandit," I said.

"David, I have also 'made out like a bandit' during the latest real estate boom, but I don't bank on uncertainty," she said. "I lock in my returns when I buy. If you're buying a fixer-upper and know that you have bought a place at a discount and can fix it up for a profit, that's one thing, but **there are no guarantees that the appreciation in price will be greater than the costs of acquiring the property and the interest you're paying on the property.**"

"Okay, I understand where you're coming from, but c'mon. I mean he made a $100,000 and places in Woodbridge keep going up. Wouldn't your home have appreciated in value, at least to the amount where you can offset some of those costs?"

She shook her head at me. "Careful David. *Past performance does not guarantee anything* about returns in the future. The real estate market has been on fire of late, but historically the rate of appreciation has been in the low single digits. If you add in the cost of buying and selling your home, the gain in value can be virtually wiped out after you've sold your place and bought another one to live in."

"Okay, I give in for now," I said. "Can you tell me about the tax benefits of owning a place? My friends all say they're awesome."

The Tax Benefits of Home Ownership

"Yes, there are some great tax benefits of owning a home and the benefit most people talk about is the fact that you can deduct the interest from your mortgage payments."

"How does it work?"

"It's easy enough to understand," she said. "For instance:

If you have $1,000 in interest payments during the year, and you're in the 25% tax bracket, then you take 25% and multiply it by $1,000 and you get $250. This is what you would get back after itemizing your deductions and filing your federal taxes.

Your $250,000 or $500,000 Gift from Congress

"Another benefit is when you sell a house that was used as your personal residence in any two out of the last five years," she said. "A single person doesn't have to pay taxes on gains up to a max of $250,000. A married couple gets up to $500,000 in tax-free gains on the sale of their principal residence."

"So the $500,000 goes right into their pocket or their retirement fund? That's quite a tax benefit," I commented.

"It is and thanks to a revision in the law, you can use the benefit over and over again, provided you've lived in the place as your primary residence in any two out of the last five years."

Which Option Makes the Best Financial Sense?

"Back to the question at hand: to rent or to buy?" she said. "You need to determine whether it costs more to rent or own in your area and it definitely varies throughout the country."

"Is it hard to figure out how much it costs to own a place?" I asked.

"Nope. You're local bank loan officer is going to have to figure all of that out for you when you apply for a mortgage. He or she will take into consideration the price of the home and your downpayment amount to come up with your monthly mortgage payment. But make sure you add in the taxes and insurance to figure out what the monthly cost of owning the property will be for you. Then compare it to what it would cost to rent a similar house in your area."

"But wouldn't it almost always come out to be less money to rent?" I asked.

"True, which is why I tend to tell people **to rent if the rental amount is 30% to 40% less than the cost of owning a place**. It's just my rule of thumb, but I've found it to be a pretty good benchmark."

Mr. Mathers jumped into the conversation. "Of course I'm from the school of thought that **it's almost always better to buy rather than rent.** Why? Because for me the Game of Life is all about getting money to work for you instead of the other way around. If you're renting an apartment or house, you're paying your landlord's mortgage and making them rich."

"But what about all those costs you guys just talked about just a moment ago?" I asked. "Owning a home can be expensive."

"Sure, if you factored in the cost of furnishing a home and paying for the gas, heat, electric, and water bills, it can quickly add up. There's also the opportunity cost of that pile of dough, i.e. your downpayment that you plunked down on your house. That money could have been growing in an investment account. I still think the calculations under most scenarios will come out in favor of owning rather than renting. I like to think that **it's always better to put your dollars toward paying off something you will own one day versus paying rent** which means you're helping to pay off someone else's asset. In the end, the decision is up to you and your spouse. I know where Allison and I net out," he said. "Owning your home is the way to go."

In Summary - Renting vs. Owning

Some advantages of renting:
- A smaller monthly portion of your budget goes to housing (generally speaking)
- Ability to invest that additional money in equities or even investment real estate properties
- Ability to relocate often without incurring significant moving costs
- No or little maintenance to be handled by you

Some advantages of buying:
- Tax breaks
- Appreciation of property value
- Equity buildup from principal paydown
- Living "rent" free once the mortgage has been paid off
- Pride of ownership
- "Forced" Savings

Downsides of Buying

- **Downpayment:** You have to come up with a lot of cash to purchase a home, even if you're only putting down 5% of the total purchase price.
- **Closing Costs:** There's nothing small about closing costs, especially if you have to pay points.
- **Maintenance:** If you rent, you sit on your butt and do nothing. If you own, this means taking care of the lawn, painting, busted pipes, new boilers, leaky roofs, and a host of other things that will need fixing at some point during your ownership.

The House of Your Dreams vs. The House for Right Now

Allison took over the discussion. "Part of the American dream is to own that dream home with the white picket fence. Unfortunately, too many people buy it too early in their lives."

"'Too early'? What do you mean?" I asked.

"Whenever someone gets that big raise or promotion they've been waiting for, they're suddenly flush with cash. They look at their lifestyle and the things they own and they say to themselves, 'I can afford better than this.' So they go out, buy some new clothes, perhaps lease a new car and spend a little more on furniture, decorations and a dozen other things. If they're newly married or have a budding family, they start looking for their dream house and when they find it, they can't help but buy it even if it's more than they can afford. **Buying a house that you can't afford is a mistake that will keep you in the Rat Race forever.**"

"How so?" I asked.

"I mean that your expenses can drain your cash faster than you could imagine," she replied.

The Cost of Home Maintenance and Other Hidden Costs

"An easy way to get in over your head when buying a home is to not plan for the hidden costs of homeownership. Most people plan for the monthly mortgage amount, the taxes, and home insurance, but they never take into consideration the other 'hidden' cost of maintaining their new home. You've got to add in things like decorating, lawn care, incidentals, unforeseen repairs, and other little 'minor' repairs that can add up to thousands upon thousands of dollars every year. That's not even counting any major renovations or big projects like redoing a kitchen or a bathroom. Those projects can run into the tens of thousands of dollars. And don't forget to set aside money for furniture, home stereos, appliances, and just about everything else you're going to want to buy. If you don't plan in advance for these things, you'll find yourself paying for them with credit."

"But isn't your home a great asset," I said. "My parents get to write off the interest from the mortgage, which puts money in their pockets every April. They're always happy to get the refund."

"David, while it puts money in their pockets, **they just paid a dollar in interest for every 25 cents that went into their pockets.** Does that sound like a good deal?"

"I don't follow," I replied.

"We just went through the math in an example before. You spent $1,000 in interest to get back a $250 federal tax refund."

"Oh I get it," I replied. "You're only getting back 25 cents for every dollar you spend in interest."

"So it's not exactly a smart use of your money is it? I don't know about you, but that's not exactly the stuff of wealth-building champions in my book," she said.

A Note on the Tax Deduction from your Mortgage Interest

Too many people think that they simply take their mortgage interest paid for the year and multiply it by their federal tax bracket to come up with their mortgage interest deduction. They're wrong. ***You actually only get to deduct the amount that is greater than the standard deduction.*** *What this means is that you're entitled to a pretty large standard deduction any way. If you're thinking you're going to get a big deduction from your mortgage interest, you'd better check with your accountant before you buy a house. The mortgage interest deduction also phases out after a certain income level, so the tax benefits will decrease as you make more money. In addition, the longer you own the house, the tax benefit decreases because you'll be paying more in principal than in interest. The bottom line: don't ever buy something just because of a tax break. Also keep in mind that you need to keep the home equity component of the loan under $100,000 to be able to deduct the interest payments. More on this subject in Secret #9.*

See IRS Publication 936 for complete information on home mortgage interest deductions.

Buy the House You Can Afford to Buy TODAY!

"To reiterate, it's absolutely critical that you do <u>NOT</u> overextend yourself by buying a more expensive home than you can afford. The mortgage interest tax deduction is just an excuse to buy a bigger home and forget the other arguments as well," she said. "No, you're not going to be making much more money five years from now, at least there's no guarantee that you will. And no, you won't cut back on your spending to live the same lifestyle as you did before you bought the house. Just buy the house you can afford to buy today and that's it!"

"Got the message loud and clear," I said. "So what's next?"

"Let's move on and figure out how much house you can afford."

How Much House Can You Afford?

"I always suggest you choose a home below your means," she said.

"It's kind of like what Mr. Mathers and I discussed in Secret #5. I get what you're saying," I told her. "Just buy based on today's salary and figure on a mortgage payment that you can *easily* afford."

"That's right David," Mr. Mathers replied. "We touched on it briefly, but Allison here is going to go into it in-depth."

Allison swung into action. "That's right Mark. The first thing you should do if you're in the market for a home is look at your monthly budget to figure out what mortgage payment you can afford. Your local loan officer will look at your income, assets, and current liabilities to determine the maximum amount they will lend you. This is NOT the starting point of where you should be looking at houses."

"Huh? Why not?" I asked.

The Calculation

"If your loan officer says you can buy a $400,000 house, this doesn't mean you should immediately go out and start looking at $400,000 houses. This figure represents the *maximum* you're allowed to borrow, but it should *NOT* be the size of the house that you actually purchase. If you go ahead and buy a $400,000 house, you'll definitely be living at or *above your means*."

"Exactly how do they calculate how much you can afford?"

"It's really an easy process. In general, banks look to see that the total monthly costs of your home, which includes your mortgage principal, interest, taxes, and insurance or PITI as it's abbreviated, not exceed 28% of your gross monthly income. In addition, the sum of all your total monthly debt obligations, things like; student loans, car payments, and your PITI payments, should not exceed 36% of your gross monthly income."

"So that's a rule of thumb right?"

Practically Giving Houses Away!

"Yes, that's the rule of thumb David, but we're in a loose credit environment and banks are competing fiercely for your business, so some are becoming more lenient. However, **if you want to be Financially Free one day, you shouldn't overextend yourself and buy a bigger house than you can afford**. Just because a bank will lend you a million bucks doesn't mean you should go out and buy a million dollar home."

Figure 17.1 - How Much House Can You Afford?

Your income for the most part determines the size of the mortgage banks are willing to give you. The following chart is based on putting 10% down and adheres to the 28% of gross income that lenders use as a gauge as to "how much house you can afford.

	Interest Rate					
	5.5%	6.0%	6.5%	7.0%	8.0%	9.0%
$20,000	$81,538	$77,218	$73,246	$69,587	$63,094	$57,538
$30,000	$122,307	$115,828	$109,869	$104,380	$94,641	$86,307
$40,000	$163,076	$154,437	$146,491	$139,174	$126,188	$115,076
$50,000	$203,845	$193,046	$183,114	$173,967	$157,736	$143,845
$75,000	$305,767	$289,569	$274,672	$260,951	$236,603	$215,767
$100,000	$407,689	$386,092	$366,229	$347,934	$315,471	$287,690
$150,000	$611,534	$579,138	$549,343	$521,901	$473,207	$431,534
$200,000	$815,379	$772,183	$732,457	$695, 868	$630,942	$575,379
$250,000	$1,019,223	$965,229	$915,572	$869,835	$788,678	$719,224

Gross Income (before taxes) (vertical axis label)

Note: The above is based on the 28%/36% rule and not my 20% Solution.

The 20 Percent Solution

"I think an easy way to make sure you buy a house that's 'below your means' is to purchase a home that requires a PITI payment of no more than 20% of your gross income. For example, if you and your spouse make $60,000 combined, that's $12,000 ($60,000 x 20%) a year that you should aim to pay for your mortgage payments, property taxes, and homeowners insurance. Compare that with the $16,800 that banks would say you can afford ($60,000 x 28%) and you can see there's quite a big difference. That difference between the two, which is $4,800 annually or $400 monthly in our example, can then be invested however you choose," she said. "Perhaps it's for your kids' education, your vacations, or your retirement."

"Looks like I've found my extra money to invest for my retirement," I remarked.

"Exactly!" Allison said. "And how much will that $400 grow to in 30 years at 8% interest, Mark?"

"Around $600,000[37] when all is said and done."

"Wow! Just for choosing to buy the house for right now instead of your dream home? That's amazing," I commented.

The Dreaded Downpayment

"Okay. Back to reality," I said. "Regardless of how much they'll lend me, I don't have enough money for a downpayment."

Allison looked quickly at Mr. Mathers and shook her head. "You're pretty good at setting up segues to our next topics," she said to me. "In this case we were just going to get into a discussion about downpayments."

Down Payment Size

"Once you know how much you can afford and want to spend, next you'll need to figure out how much money you want to put down. The standard used to be 20 percent, but there are a lot of programs out there that require a smaller downpayment. Just note the bigger the size of the downpayment, the lower the monthly mortgage payments will be."

"So I should put as much down as possible?" I asked.

"Hold your horses," she replied. "I'm not done yet. Let's finish this discussion and you decide what's right for you."

Small Downpayments

"Right now the housing market is hot and home prices are shooting through the roof. Coupled with a low rate environment, you're looking at bidding wars galore. This is causing the average home price to skyrocket. Luckily there are loan programs out there that require as little as 5 percent and some that require as little as 3 percent down if you qualify for the programs."

"Wow!" I exclaimed. "Now you're talking."

FHA Loans

"The 3 percent loan program I'm talking about is part of the Federal Housing Administrations (FHA) program for first-time buyers. It's a great program if you qualify for it. Of course there are limits on the amount of money they'll lend on a home, but if you stay under the limits it's tough to beat this program. Along a similar vein are VA loans."

---

[37] Around $596,143.78, give or take a few bucks.

VA Loans

"Veterans Administration or VA loans can be made with no dowpayment at all. They offer attractive interest rates, but you have to be a veteran and you have to get a certificate of eligibility in order to qualify for this type of loan," she said. "Obviously, you don't qualify for VA loans."

Other Programs

"Those are the two biggies that you'll read about, but in recent years some banks have created programs of their own that will allow you to purchase a home with 3 to 5 percent down.[38] It's even easier to find loans between 5 and 10 percent down. You just have to ask around and do some homework to find them."

Saving for a Downpayment

"What if I don't have the money for a downpayment?" I asked.

"The first thing you've got to do is figure out what money you *do* currently have for a downpayment. Then you have to figure out your monthly positive cash flow and create a savings plan for your downpayment ASAP."

"So once I have that plan in place, where should I put this money that I'm setting aside?" I asked.

Where Do You Put the Money?

"If you need the money in less than six months, you can forget about CDs and you'll have to stick with money market accounts."

"What about the stock market? Should you avoid it altogether?"

"First off, the stock market is for long-term goals, not short-term ones," she stated. "I've heard too many tales of would-be homebuyers who lost their downpayment in the stock market, so I would advise anyone to not put money that is needed for short-term goals into the stock market. I know Mark probably talked to you at length about the importance of taking on risk in life in order to get ahead, beat the market, grow a business, or what have you, but this is one time where you should NOT take on any unnecessary risk."

> "There is the risk you cannot afford to take, and there is the risk you cannot afford not to take."
>
> - Peter F. Drucker

---

[38] Some will let you borrow up to 100% of the value of the home! My advice is to not burden yourself with these type of loans. One small misstep and you'll lose your house.

No Money for a Downpayment?

"Another way to get some cash for a downpayment is to borrow it from your 401(k) plan," Allison said.

My eyes widened in amazement. I turned to Mr. Mathers. "You said that you shouldn't ever take money out from your 401(k) plan!"

"Calm down David," he said putting up his hands in defense. "I still believe that you shouldn't touch your 401(k), but everybody needs to do what's right for them. If they would be stuck renting for the next five years while trying to save the money, it might make more sense to take some money out of their 401(k) plan and use the money for a downpayment. I mean, why throw money away in rent when the cost of housing keeps going up and the ability to save for that downpayment will take a couple of years. You can also withdraw up to $10,000 from your IRA if you're buying your first home."

Other Options

"Of course there are other options," Allison said. "Like receiving a gift from your parents. Each of them is allowed to give you up to $11,000 a year without having to pay gift taxes."

"So they could lend me $22,000?" I asked.

"That's if they have it David. Unfortunately most parents can't afford that kind of gift. You could also look to take out money from your IRA like Mark just said. When you withdraw money from your IRA, you're allowed a one-time withdrawal of up to $10,000 if the money is going to be used for buying your first house. Just note that you might have to pay income taxes on the money."

Bottom Line: Put down whatever amount will:
a) Give you a monthly payment you can live with (read: really afford)
b) Allow you to avoid PMI insurance, if not from the get go, then a year or two down the line
c) Not jeopardize your Emergency Fund holdings
d) Allows you to continue to put money into your investment accounts according to plan

"We are not free to use today or to promise tomorrow, because we are mortgaged to yesterday."
- Ralph Waldo Emerson

Financing: Types of Mortgages

"Okay, enough on downpayments," she said. "Let's briefly cover the main types of mortgages that you will encounter:

Fixed-rate: A fixed rate mortgage is a mortgage that has a fixed or locked in interest rate for the life of the loan. These mortgages are great for a homebuyer that plans on staying in their home for a long period of time because it offers you a fixed mortgage payment over the life of the loan.

Adjustable-rate: Instead of a fixed rate of interest that spans the life of the loan, adjustable-rate mortgages or ARMs for short have a variable interest rate that can fluctuate up and down according to what the market rate of interest happens to be. ARMs make sense for those that will live in the house for a short period of time.

Convertible: A convertible mortgage is an adjustable-rate mortgage that can be changed or converted to a fixed-rate mortgage. The beauty of this type of loan is that you can start with a pretty low rate and then as interest rates rise, lock in at a favorable rate.

Balloon: A balloon mortgage allows you to make equal payments over the course of the loan's term, then make a large payment otherwise known as a balloon payment at the end. This allows you to pay a much smaller monthly amount over the course of the loan, then make up for it with the large payment at the end of the loan term. This type of loan is more typical for commercial loans.

Which is Best?

"There are many types of mortgages, but you'll probably choose between either a fixed-rate or an adjustable-rate mortgage. You can qualify for a larger house with an ARM than with a fixed-rate mortgage, so be careful. You don't want to fall into the trap of buying more house than you can afford, especially when the rates can jump in a few years. If they plan on living in the home for more than five years, then I tell people to go with the fixed rate loan over an ARM. An ARM might make sense for someone who isn't planning on living in the house for at least five years."

Financing: 15 or 30-Year Loan?

"Next up is the term of the mortgage. The most common term loans are either a 30-year or a 15-year. Which is better all depends on your situation and what you're trying to accomplish, but **I think it's best to go with a 30-year fixed-rate mortgage**. With a 30-year fixed-rate mortgage, you're paying less monthly than a 15-year loan. We'll cover how important the term of the loan can be a little later on."

So How Do You Find the Best Rates?

"For now, let's talk about how to find the best interest rates for a mortgage. You need to check out your local banks, savings and loans, and your credit union. You can use a mortgage broker as well. If you want to look further, check out www.bankrate.com. It also doesn't hurt if you have good credit which would qualify you for the best rates. I'm sure Mark showed you a FICO chart," she said, turning to Mr. Mathers. "Do you have it handy Mark?" she asked.

"You're really working me today," he replied. "Here it is," he said, showing me the same chart from a few weeks ago.

"As you can tell David," Allison remarked, "it's worth it to haggle and get the lowest interest rate possible. You can literally save thousands of dollars every time you shave a half point from your loan."

Figure 17.2 – How Much is that Rate Costing You?

FICO Score	APR	Monthly Payment	Total Interest Paid
720-850	5.559%	$1,143	$211,477
700-719	5.684%	$1,159	$217,159
675-699	6.221%	$1,228	$241,959
620-674	7.371%	$1,381	$297,090
560-619	8.226%	$1,499	$339,698
500-559	8.719%	$1,569	$364,831

Source: myFICO.com 3/19/03 (figures are for a $200,000 30-yr fixed rate mortgage)

Some More Mortgage Stuff

"Now let's get into some more mortgage stuff," she said. "There are several sources to find loans, including: savings and loans, savings banks, commercial banks, mortgage bankers, mortgage brokers, and my favorite, through sellers. The first thing everyone does when they go shopping for a mortgage is look at the interest rates, but you also have to look at the closing costs, including the points you might pay on the loan."

"Points? What's that?" I asked.

Paying Points

"Points are nothing more than a percentage of the mortgage amount that you have to pay up front in order to secure a lower interest rate on a mortgage," she replied. "**One point is equal to 1 percent of the mortgage amount**."

"So if I have a $100,000 mortgage and I'm paying 2 points, I have to pay $2,000 for a lower interest rate, right?" I asked.

"Correct. While I hate paying points, it might make sense to pay them if you're going to stay in your home for a long period of time."

Closing Costs

"Closing costs for homes can vary from state to state and from bank to bank. These costs include things like loan fees, attorney's fees, document fees, appraisal fees, home inspection fees, and title search charges. And that's only a partial list. A good way to find out what your closing costs would be is to contact a mortgage broker or your local bank loan officer. Ask them for a list of the typical fees and charges that are associated with a loan. In general, you're looking at about 2% to 4% of the mortgage amount. Just another rule of thumb."

PMI – Unnecessary Costs

"One fee that I want to cover in-depth is **Private Mortgage Insurance** or PMI for short. This is insurance you pay if your mortgage is more than 80 percent of the value of the home."

"What's it for?" I asked.

"It's insurance to protect the lender in case you default on your loan. The theory is that people who put less money down might not be able to keep up with the monthly payments. Of course you don't pay PMI forever. Thanks to the Homeowners Protection Act, a lender has to *automatically* cancel PMI when you have 22 percent equity in your home if you've got a good payment record.[39] You can also request that they cancel your PMI when you reach the 20 percent equity mark. Unfortunately the law doesn't apply to pre-1999 mortgages."

"So once the outstanding balance is less than 80 percent of the value you don't have to pay PMI anymore, right?"

"That's correct, but there are two major exceptions. The law does not apply to FHA or VA loans, but it still covers the majority of loans. In any event, people should watch their equity levels very carefully because there are thousands of people right now paying PMI that shouldn't because of the increase in their homes value. Your banker is legally obligated to stop charging you PMI, but it never hurts to call them up and make sure they stop charging it, especially since PMI can take a lot of money out of your pocket every month."

"How much is a lot?" I asked.

"It depends on the size of your mortgage and the percentage you put down, but on average, **PMI will cost you about 0.6% of the loan amount during the first year and about 0.5% in subsequent years. On a $100,000 mortgage PMI runs around $40 to $50 a month.**"

"That is a lot of money."

"Worse yet, **PMI is not tax-deductible**," she added.

---

[39] A history of paying on time and you don't have any payments 30 days past due in the year preceding your request or 60 days past due in the preceding two years.

A Necessary Evil?

"While PMI may add to your monthly payment, it might be necessary in order to afford that house of yours in today's market. **Most conventional loans require at least 20 percent down**. That's a lot of money for people to come up with, so that's where PMI comes in. It allows potential homebuyers to get a mortgage with a lot less than 20 percent down. It's really a win-win situation. The potential homeowner gets the house of their dreams and the lender has some protection if the borrower defaults on their loan."

"But they can eventually stop paying their PMI right when they've paid down their loan enough, right?" I asked.

"Yes, but the only problem is that it can take up to 8 years to reach the 80 percent ownership level if you only pay the minimum on your 30-year mortgage if you put 10 percent down on your home."

"Eight years of paying PMI? Any way of getting around it?"

"Well, the 20 percent equity mark relates to your home's *value*, not 20 percent of the mortgage amount. So some of my clients who bought way below market or bought a fixer-upper were able to quickly increase the value of their homes and were able to prove that they had more than 20 percent equity in their homes."

"How do you go about proving that?" I asked.

"In most cases they refinanced their loans."

Refinance Your Loan

"When you refinance, you automatically get a new appraisal and if the value of your place has risen enough, your new loan would be less than 80 percent of the current value. So you wouldn't have to pay for mortgage insurance any more."

Avoiding PMI with a Piggyback Loan

"Another way of avoiding PMI is to take out two loans instead of one. Neither loan is for more than 80 percent of the home's value, so you avoid paying PMI. This will cost you more up front in terms of extra closing costs and interest since second mortgages usually carry higher rates, but a piggyback loan can be a good option for some people. The good news is that you can deduct the additional interest from the second loan, whereas you can't deduct the cost of the mortgage insurance (PMI). Not a huge deal, but it's something to keep in mind when comparing the costs."

Chapter 18

Should You Pay Off Your Mortgage Early?

To Prepay or Not to Prepay

"Next up is a topic that I get a lot of questions about: prepaying your mortgage," Allison said as we headed toward Foley Park. "There are a lot of financial planners and authors out there advocating that you should pay off your house because it will be your biggest asset one day. They advocate paying off your house by sending in extra payments or refinancing to get a 15-year loan instead of a 30-year loan. We're going to go over the basics of prepaying your mortgage and then let you decide what's the smartest thing to do financially. Let's tackle the 15-year vs. 30-year loan debate first."

Which Term is Best for You?
The 30-Year vs. the 15-Year Mortgage

"The easiest way to technically pay off a mortgage sooner is to go with a 15-year mortgage in order to eliminate their mortgage twice as fast." She turned to Mr. Mathers and asked, "Do you have the comparison between a 15 and 30?"

"Of course I do Allison," he replied. He opened his binder and began flipping through it. "I updated the chart to revise the return down to 8%." He walked slightly ahead of us and placed his binder on top of a mailbox. When he found what he was looking for, he waived Allison and I over.

Investing the Difference

Allison and I looked over the numbers, then after a brief moment, she spoke. "You see David, under this scenario the person with the 30-year mortgage is investing the difference between the two payment amounts in the stock market. The person with the 15-year mortgage is investing the amount they were paying as a mortgage in the stock market starting in year 16. At the end of 30 years, the person with the 30-year mortgage has an extra $35,000 in your portfolio. This analysis doesn't even include the *additional tax savings* you would receive in the first 30 years of payments compared to the 15-year mortgage."

"Why do you have more tax savings?" I asked.

Figure 18.1 – 30yr vs. 15yr Mortgage

Comparison between the two mortgage terms using an estimated
8% annual rate of return for both investment portfolios.

	30-Year Mortgage	15-Year Mortgage
Loan Amount:	$150,000	$150,000
Interest Rate:	6.50%	6.00%
Monthly Payment:	$948	$1,266
Monthly investment:	$318 for 30 yrs	$1,266 for 15 yrs
Total interest paid:	$191,317	$77,841
Total amount invested:	$114,366	$227,841
Principal owed after 15 yrs:	$108,839.00	$0.00
Portfolio amt after 15 yrs:	$96,431.07	$0.00
Portfolio amt after 30 yrs:	$473,462	$438,010

"Because you're paying more toward interest in the early years of your 30-year mortgage versus the 15-year mortgage, therefore you have more interest to deduct.[40] But since Mark and I don't like making financial decisions based solely on the tax benefits, he's kept them out of the equation and the 30-year option still comes out ahead."

"But you still have the risks involved with investing your extra money in the stock market," I said.

Some Gurus Go with the 15-Year Mortgage

"We hear where you're coming from David," she said. "In fact, a recent article I saw had a piece on one guru who had a similar comparison between 15-year and 30-year mortgages. In the example, the guy who took out the 30-year invested the difference in his 401(k), but only got a 6% return."

"So what happened after 30 years?" I asked.

"The analysis *only* went to 15 years where both men got laid off and they guy with the 15-year loan came out ahead because he didn't have to make a loan payment. You see David, **you can plug any number or create any scenario to make the numbers work for your side of the argument. Therefore, you need to do what's best for you.** Mark and I are investors, so we'll stick with 30-year loans and invest the difference."

---

[40] Check with your accountant because the amount you can deduct phases out at certain levels.

"But what if the stock market doesn't do well?" I asked. "Then you're in trouble, right?"

They both smiled at me. "You're 100 percent correct about that David. As Mark mentioned, it looks like he revised the expected rate of return to 8% down from 10%. What was the value of the portfolio at 10% Mark?" she asked.

"I believe the difference between the two portfolios jumps from $35k to $193K or close to a $160k increase for the 30-year mortgage because of the higher rate of return," he replied.

"Wow. That's amazing and all because of a two percentage points difference in returns?"

"That's right David," Allison chimed in. "As you've probably learned, a couple of percentage points can make a big difference. But Mark was right to revise his forecast down since 8% is a good estimate of what most people can expect to get from their investments."

Mr. Mathers nodded his head in agreement.

More Flexibility with a 30-Year

"**Even if you opt for the 30-year term, you can still pay the loan off early**," Allison said. "In fact, you can still take the full amount you would have been putting toward other investments, in this example $318 a month, and put it toward paying down your mortgage. You'll pay slightly more in interest charges, but **the 30-year gives you a little more breathing room than the 15-year loan**. In case you get laid off, have a major change in lifestyle (one spouse stops working, etc.), or any number of things, **not having a large monthly mortgage payment to make can be a godsend**. In the end, it will be up to you to decide which term makes the most sense for you financially given your monthly expenses and other obligations. Mark and I like the flexibility that comes with longer term mortgages because we can pay off the mortgages quickly or invest our 'savings' in other properties or investments," she said. "In addition, **a 30-year loan allows me to earn less money monthly and still keep my house should something unforeseen happen**."

Are You Disciplined?

"However," she continued, "none of this will mean anything if you don't have the discipline to stick with investing the additional funds. You need to take a hard look at yourself and be honest with yourself. Answer the question: **'Am I the type of person that will invest the additional savings or will I spend it?'** Once you've answered that question, you'll know which option works best for you."

Don't Get Me Wrong: You save a bundle with a 15-year loan

"Don't get me wrong, a 15-year loan will save you a lot of money versus a 30-year loan. Take a look at the chart Mark just handed you and you can see how much money we're talking about."

Figure 18.2 – 15-Year Loans Will Save You a Bundle

Mortgage Amount	15yr/ 6%	30yr/ 6.5%	Monthly Difference in Payments	Total $ "Saved" w/ a 15yr vs. 30yr
$50,000	$422	$316	$106	$37,825
100,000	844	632	212	75,650
150,000	1,266	948	318	113,475
200,000	1,688	1,264	424	151,301
250,000	2,110	1,580	529	189,126
300,000	2,532	1,896	635	226,951
350,000	2,953	2,212	741	264,776
400,000	3,375	2,528	847	302,601

"But that's a lot of money you could be putting into your pocket instead of giving it to the bank," I commented.

"Again David, it's all up to you. I have a 30-year loan and I invest the difference in real estate. You might choose to do otherwise. You make the call on what's best for you."

Biweekly Payment Plans

"So going with a 15-year versus a 30-year loan is one way to pay off your loan early. However, when you talk about prepaying your mortgage, most people think of the process of sending in more than the mortgage payment amount each month. There are two main ways to prepay your mortgage: Make an extra payment every year or make biweekly payments. Banks have programs set up for their mortgagees to make payments every two weeks. Essentially you're taking your monthly mortgage payment, cutting it in half, and paying that amount every two weeks. So if your monthly mortgage was $2,000, you'd pay $1,000 every two weeks."

"What's the difference?" I asked. "You're sending in the same amount, right?"

"Wrong David. Since there are 52 weeks in a year, you'd be making 26 half-payments a year."

"Which is thirteen full payments a year," I added, "not twelve. So you're making one more payment a year this way. I get it."

"Exactly. Making that extra payment helps to cut the amount of interest you'll pay over the life of the loan. On a 30-year loan you'd pay it off in about 23 years."

"How does the other method work?"

Extra Payment a Year Method

"For the extra payment method, you simply send in an extra payment each year. You can do it at the end of the year if you get a bonus or perhaps when you get your tax refund from the government."

"That's it? That's all there is to it?" I asked.

"Yes, it's not too complicated. Just do it as early as possible in the year to really save on interest."

"Why?"

"Because if you make an extra payment in January, you reduce the total principal owed for the whole year. The interest charged each month is calculated based on your outstanding principal amount, so you've instantly reduced the interest you're paying over the course of the year. The savings from making the extra payment in the beginning of the year instead of the end can really add up over time."

Don't Pay to Pre-Pay

"Before we move on, I want to **make sure you don't pay for the right to prepay your mortgage.** Some banks will charge you a one-time setup fee and a reoccurring fee to make your payments on a biweekly basis. Don't fall for it. If you're disciplined enough there's no reason to pay a fee, just send in checks every two weeks or have the money pulled from your account automatically. Just check beforehand with your bank to see if they can process the checks on a biweekly basis. Lastly **check if there is a prepayment penalty**. Most loans don't have this clause, but it's good to review your mortgage documents before you start prepaying."

Prepaying Your Mortgage...or Not
The Argument FOR

"Let's discuss the pros and cons of prepaying your mortgage," Allison said as we stopped to sit on the rocks in Foley Park. It was a welcome break from the heat of the sun. She steadied herself, then began the next part of the lesson.

"Perhaps no book has expounded on the virtues of pre-paying your mortgage than *The Banker's Secret* by March Eisenson. There are literally over a hundred tables in the book that you can use to look up your mortgage amount, how much extra you want to pay, and how much money you'll save in interest." She turned to Mr. Mathers. "Mark, do you have the prepayment sheet in your binder?"

"Right here," he said, handing me a sheet of paper.

The Benefits of Pre-Paying: Cold Hard Ca$h

"Each month, the bank computes the interest due on the outstanding balance of your loan. Pre-paying shrinks that balance- and therefore reduces your interest charge. Once your balance drops, of course, it stays that way. Advance payments stop the bank from collecting compound interest on the amount you pre-pay, not just once, but month after month – year after year. By pre-paying, you invest nothing extra to save thousands. In short, pre-paying saves you the compound interest that you will never have to pay. **By pre-paying, you invest nothing extra to save thousands. Pre-payments are not additional costs**. They are simply advances, small amounts that you pay sooner."

– Marc Eisenson, *The Banker's Secret*

Figure 18.3 – The More You Pre-Pay, the More You'll Save[41]

Down payment:	$25,000
Loan amount:	$100,000
Interest rate:	8%
Loan term:	30 years
Required monthly payment:	$734
Total interest, if not pre-paid:	$164,149
Total outlay without pre-payment:	$289,149

PRE-PAY	SAVE	REDUCE TERM BY YRS/ MONTHS	PRE-PAY	SAVE	REDUCE TERM BY YRS/ MONTHS
$ 15	$15,054	2/03	$ 350	$108,404	18/00
25	23,337	3/07	375	110,719	18/06
50	39,906	6/02	400	112,841	18/11
75	52,484	8/02	425	114,793	19/03
100	62,456	9/10	450	116,597	19/07
125	70,610	11/03	475	118,268	19/11
150	77,431	12/05	500	119,821	20/03
175	83,240	13/05	750	130,930	22/06
200	88,260	14/04	1,000	137,506	23/11
225	92,649	15/01	1,250	141,871	24/10
250	96,524	15/10	1,500	144,986	25/07
275	99,976	16/05	1,750	147,322	26/01
300	103,071	17/00	2,000	149,140	26/06
325	105,866	17/07			

"Now imagine reducing the term of your loan by over nine years because you put an extra $100 a month toward your mortgage."

"But what if you don't have the money?" I asked.

"Use pocket change," she responded and flipped the page over revealing the below chart.

---

[41] Source: *Invest in Yourself: Six Secrets to a Rich Life* (Wiley, www.investinyourself.com), by Marc Eisenson et al., and is reprinted here with permission from the authors.

Pocket Change = Big Savings

Figure 18.4 - A Few Pennies Goes a Long Way[42]
Based on a $100,000 Mortgage at 8% for 30 years

Pre-Pay	Save
10 cents a day	$3,317
25 cents a day	7,986
50 cents a day	15,054
$1.00 a day	27,072

Don't Have Enough Money to Pre-Pay? Nonsense

"Are those numbers for real?" I asked.

"Yes, you're reading those numbers right," she replied. "It only takes 50 cents a day to save over $15,000 in interest. I'm sure you'll be able to find 50 cents a day to save that kind of cash. I run into a lot of people who would like to go the safe and secure route of pre-paying their mortgage, but they complain that they don't have enough cash left over at the end of the month. I tell them to stop kidding themselves."

Forced Savings

"I can't argue with those that say that a mortgage and perhaps prepaying that mortgage is a way to force yourself to save money. For some people, this is the *only* way they will save money. In my mind prepaying your mortgage to save money is not the best way to invest your hard-earned money, but I'll spare you my viewpoint until later. For now just know that I believe that you shouldn't think of it as an investment in the conventional sense. At most, your home should be viewed as a backup safety net."

"A safety net?"

Your Safety Net

"A safety net as in 'just in case' you don't have enough in your nest egg, excluding your home, to generate an income you can live off until you die," she replied. "You see David, when you have a home that has appreciated significantly, you can always sell it and buy a less-expensive dwelling to live in. This is what is meant by a safety net."

"Easy enough to understand," I said.

---

[42] IBID

The Argument AGAINST Prepaying

"Good, because now we're going to get into the argument against prepaying your loan. People make extra payments because they've heard that if they make an extra payment every year they'll pay off their 30-year mortgage in only 23 years. So they quickly realize that not having to make mortgage payments for 7 years means a lot of money saved. So they scrape together any and all extra dollars in order to send it to the bank and pay down that loan. Their hearts are in the right place, but it's not smart in my book."

"But isn't *not* having to pay that monthly amount for 7 years smart?" I asked.

Are You Financially Ready to Prepay?

"It all depends on the situation. In most cases the homeowner that dutifully sends in extra payments does not have an adequate Emergency Fund, does not maximize their investment contributions, or have adequate insurance protection. In most instances they are carrying a balance on their credit cards, student loans, and car loans, which in all likelihood carry a higher interest rate. Paying off your loan might seem like a good move, but if it means sacrificing your retirement plans or paying for your kid's college, it's not a good strategy."

> "By tackling the mortgage issue first, and savings goals second, you fail to consider the role that a mortgage plays in your savings efforts. **Your battle to reduce interest expenses is won, but the wealth accumulation war is lost**. Here's why: You know that by reducing the mortgage payment, or even paying off the mortgage completely, you save lots of money in interest charges. While that is correct, you are ignoring another, equally critical fact: Every dollar you give the bank is a dollar you did not invest."
> – Ric Edelman, *Ordinary People, Extraordinary Wealth*

"You have to look at what your **opportunity cost** is before you decide what to do. Most people think that by saving that money in interest they're being smart, but it's not the same thing as investing that money. Over the course of 23 years our happy homeowner has been diligently paying down their mortgage with extra dollars that could have been used to buy assets that generated additional income; passive income that will feed them when they retire. **Every additional dollar you give the bank is a worker that you didn't put to work for you.**"

"Wait a minute," I said. "But by saving all that interest it's like a guaranteed 7% or more return on your money. Isn't that smart?"

"No, it's not smart and here's why," she replied.

The Opportunity Cost Revisited

"Every dollar you send to your banker in an attempt to save 7% in interest or 5% after the tax benefits, doesn't get the chance to earn 10% or more by investing it."

"Yes, but the 7% or 5% you're paying against your mortgage is guaranteed. You never know what the stock market is going to do. Haven't you seen what's happened lately?" I said, referring to the recent declines.

"While past history does not guarantee future returns, all you have to do is look at the analysis Jeremy Siegel did in *Stocks for the Long Run*. He analyzed every rolling 20-year period of the stock market for the past 200 years. In each of those 20-year periods, the stock market went up an average of 12.6%.[43] While I don't think the market will ever return to those levels, the Vanguard 500-index fund is up over 10% year-to-date.[44] Even if the market only returns the 4% to 7% economists are currently forecasting, that's a lot better than your *guaranteed* return from investing in your house on an after-tax basis. Sure the stock market might go down on occasion, but it's still one of the best places to put your money on a regular, monthly basis. People are just scared right now. Three straight years of declines and they don't think the market will ever come around, but it will. It already has," she said, pointing her finger at me.

"So what *are* you telling me to do?" I asked. "Jump into the market again? I'd rather deal with guaranteed returns!"

> "Although the dominance of stocks over bonds is readily apparent in the long run, it is more important to note that over one, and even two-year periods, stocks outperform bonds or bills only about three out of every five years. This means that nearly two out of every five years a stockholder will fall behind the return on treasury bills or bank certificates. The high risk of underperforming fixed-income assets in the short run is the primary reason why it is so hard for many investors to stay in stocks."
> – Jeremy J. Siegel, *Stocks for the Long Run*

Mr. Mathers jumped in. **"Invest your money where you can get the best return** David. It's easy to see that the highest guaranteed rate or return comes from paying down your credit cards, then any other unsecured high rate debts you might have. It used to be that I could

---

[43] Source: *Stocks for the Long Run* by Jeremy Siegel, p27
[44] Actually +11.7% YTD, June 30, 2003, but why split hairs.

make the argument that your hard-earned dollars would give you the biggest return if you invested it in the stock market, not your house. With projections for long-term rates of return for the stock market anywhere between 4% to 7%, it's obvious to see why many people are leaning toward paying down their mortgages rather than funding their retirement accounts. Allison and I are real estate investors and we think that even the everyday person can earn guaranteed double-digit returns by investing in a real estate property, once they're ready to jump to the Striving stage of the Game of Life."

There is NO Correct Answer

"In the end, it's a personal decision and you have to be comfortable with your decision. Having debt in life, especially good debt, isn't necessarily a bad thing. You just need to know how to manage it. I'm sleeping well at night even though I have a mortgage on my house. To figure out what's best for you, ask yourself these three questions:

1. Can I get a better return somewhere else? It's easy to figure out the after-tax "return" you're getting from investing in your mortgage. Now you have to figure out what kinds of returns you could get elsewhere and compare the two.

2. How comfortable am I with debt? Some people just don't like debt and would sleep better at night knowing their place is paid off. If you don't like the idea of investing your money in stocks or investment properties, while holding a big mortgage, maybe prepaying is the best route for you.

3. Is there a better use for the money? As in perhaps paying down your other debts that don't have tax-deductible interest.

"After you've answered those three questions, sit back and review them. If you think you can do better than 5% or 6% return, try it out. If you fail, pay down your mortgage. It's your choice."

"What about doing both?" I asked. "Is that possible?"

Can You Do Both?

"Yes," he replied. "The choice of whether to pre-pay your mortgage or invest for the future doesn't have to be one of those all or nothing decisions. You *can* do both. Obviously there is a benefit to being debt free and obviously there is a benefit to investing for your future. But enough on this subject. I'll let Allison talk about how your house is a piggy bank."

Chapter 19

Borrowing From Yourself

Your Home – A Giant Piggybank?

"People are running to their bankers and mortgage brokers in droves to take advantage of low interest rates. They're looking to get cash (equity) out of their homes in order to fund their lifestyles or some real needs like; weddings, college expenses, and medical expenses. There are dozens of ways to 'tap the equity' in your home, which is making it easier and easier for people to use the equity in their homes to buy things today they currently can't afford. Others are using loans to help consolidate some other bad debt they might have like credit card balances. Aside from refinancing, the two other popular ways of tapping into the equity in your home is through either a Home Equity Loan (HEL) or a Home Equity Line of Credit (HELOC)."

Home Equity Loan

"A home equity loan is kind of like a mini fixed-rate mortgage. While most mortgages are for 30 years, an equity loan usually has anywhere from a 5-year to a 15-year term. You borrow a set amount of money up front and your payments do not fluctuate and the interest rate charged doesn't change."

Home Equity Line of Credit

"A home equity line of credit or HELOC for short is a credit line that is also secured by the equity in your home. You can borrow up to a set amount for a time limit that is set by the lender. Most HELOCs work just like a credit card in that the interest rate is variable and your minimum payments are usually low, in the 1% to 1.5% of the outstanding balance range (most credit cards make you pay a minimum of 2% of the outstanding balance). With most HELOCs, you get a book of checks or a credit card to use against the line of credit. HELOCs give you the flexibility to borrow only what you need, when you need it, whereas with a HEL you have to take out the money all at once. If you're good about paying down a HELOC, it will cost you less than a HEL or a traditional loan. Unlike the home equity loan or most traditional loans, the HELOC doesn't use an amortization schedule with a set repayment period."

The Downside of HELOCs and HELs

"If you look at the potential savings in interest, then consolidating your debt via a HELOC or HEL is a good idea. But if you're not going to stop spending with your credit cards or spending in general, then you could be in trouble. I've known quite a few people who think that their HELOC is an open invitation for going on vacations or buying new cars and soon they find themselves deeper in debt. But this time your house is collateral for the loan, so the bank will be foreclosing on your home if you don't make your payments."

In Summary...

Home Equity Lines of Credit
Pros:
- **Reusable Credit and Flexibility:** You can open a credit line and use it over and over again.
- **Interest Rates:** The interest rates on HELOCs are often the best around and usually lower than a HEL.
- **Lower Monthly Payments:** Thanks to a lower interest rate and your ability to borrow only what you need, your payments are much smaller.
- **Low Costs:** There are small up front fees and an annual fee, but they're minimal compared to closing costs on other types of loans.

Cons:
- **Fluctuating Payments:** Your payments will depend on the outstanding balance and you cannot plan on them as well as you can with a home equity loan.
- **No Term Limit:** You won't pay off your balance over a set period of time and might find yourself paying for your vacation over the next 15 years.
- **Fluctuating Rates**: Rates are low now, but they could go up from here.
- **Temptation Factor**: Checks in hand and an open line of credit make it easy to run up bills and spend too much money. Don't use a HELOC to pay for day-to-day living expenses.

Typical Uses:
- **Higher Education**: If you need money over the course of several semesters and years, then a HELOC might make sense. Take out money at the beginning of each semester and pay it down over the course of several months until the next semester starts.
- **Emergencies:** People tap their line of credit to pay for those unexpected costs. You should have an Emergency Fund set up for these situations or the right kind of insurance instead.

Home Equity Loans
Pros:
- **Fixed Payments**: You know what your monthly payments will be for the life of the loan.
- **Fixed Rate**: Your interest rate is also locked in at hopefully a low rate and will not rise regardless of what the market rate does.

Cons:
- **One Shot Deal**: Once you take out the loan, you cannot borrow more.
- **Fixed Rate:** This could be a con if we're in an environment where interest rates are falling.

Typical Uses:
- **Debt Consolidation**: You can pay off your credit cards and other debts, but you can't go back and take out more money like a HELOC so you don't run the risk of racking up more debt. Just make sure you STOP SPENDING and don't end up with more credit card debt and less equity.
- **Home Improvements**: Looking to remodel your home? Then your HEL is a good place to get money. If you have cost overruns, tap your HELOC or Emergency Fund. At least you're putting money back into your house.

Tax Deductibility: A benefit for both
"One last thing," she said. "You can deduct the interest paid on both HELOCs and HELs, but you should know that the IRS only recognizes home-equity loans up to $100,000, which means you can't deduct the interest paid on the principal above $100,000."

Refinancing
"Next up is refinancing," she said. "When you refinance your mortgage, you're getting a new first mortgage that replaces your existing mortgage. You typically get a lower monthly payment by either reducing the rate or extending the term of the mortgage. If you're consolidating debt, you can save a bundle. For instance, if you have a 30-year fixed rate mortgage of $150,000 at 8.5% and refinance to a 30-year at 7%, you're looking at a $155 reduction in your monthly mortgage payment. That's a big savings which adds up to over $40,000 in interest payments over the life of the loan. You just increased your monthly cash flow and saved over $40,000 in the process. Now that's being smart about your finances!"

"So when does it make sense to refinance?" I asked.

Cash-Out Refinancing

"If you have a lot of equity in your home and a mountain of revolving debt on your credit cards, it might make sense to take out a home equity loan and pay off your credit cards. Of course you'll have to pay closing costs and other fees up front, but the savings in terms of lowering your monthly payments can be a huge addition to your monthly cash flow. It's a simple enough process, just do what's called a cash-out refinancing: **taking out a new first mortgage that is larger than the balance on your existing mortgage**. The difference between what the old and new balance is cash you put in your pocket and hopefully put toward your other debts."

"Sounds like a sweet deal," I commented.

The Downside of Refinancing (Yes, there is one)

"Yes, refinancing your mortgage is a great option to help get you out of debt, but there's a downside. You have to remember that when you refinance, you're just moving around debt or **you're incurring more debt and in most cases you now have to pay for that debt over a longer term than you would have originally repaid it**. This holds true especially for people who have taken debts like credit cards, auto loans, and personal loans that could have been paid off in 5 to 7 years and are now going to pay them off over 15 to 30 years."

"But wouldn't you be saving a ton in interest?"

"It depends on the differences in the two interest rates, but **you could actually pay *more* under the consolidated, yet lower rate refinancing loan**. I know it's a hard concept to grasp, but if Mark here will give me one of his favorite credit card interest stories from the top of his head, you'll see why you need to think about things carefully before determining which option is best."

Without missing a beat, Mr. Mathers jumped into the discussion. "Let's say you have $8,000 in credit card debt at a 12% APR. If you only make the minimum payments, you're looking at over $7,000 in interest payments made over the next 23 years. If you refinanced your house and rolled that credit card debt into your home mortgage which is at a nice and low 6% for 30 years, you would pay over $9,200[45] in interest on that $8,000 credit card tab."

"That's ridiculous," I said. "I didn't ever think that paying off your high rate debt with lower interest debt would be a bad thing."

"It's not *always* a bad thing David, but you have got to be careful. If you're going to refinance your mortgage and pay down some bad debt, you've got to be smart about it. Do the math before you jump in."

---

[45] Really around $9,267.06 to be exact, but why split hairs.

Know Yourself

"Let's switch gears," Allison said as we crossed Third Street and headed back toward the library. **"You have to know whether you will stop spending money on depreciating assets and unnecessary luxuries for refinancing to work for you**. I've known dozens of people who have refinanced and eliminated their other debts, only to fall back into the spending spree mentality. And now they're no better off than before they refinanced."

"I've got it. I've got it," I said, waving my hands in the air.

"Good. Let's move on to reverse mortgages."

Reverse Mortgages

"A reverse mortgage is when you contract with a bank to convert some of your home equity to cash. So **instead of paying the bank money, the bank pays you money**, hence the name reverse mortgage. It's really a simple process and you can take the money out in a variety of ways: a lump sum, a line of credit, or monthly checks."

"How much can you borrow?" I asked.

"It depends on your age, the current equity in your home, and the interest rate on the mortgage. A reverse mortgage can be a godsend to seniors and future retirees who have not saved enough on their own and can't make ends meet living off their Social Security checks. The income you receive from the bank is considered nontaxable income, but you can't write off the interest you pay on these types of reverse mortgages. But since it's not considered income, the cash you receive shouldn't interfere with your SS or Medicare benefits, but you'd be wise to double-check with a financial planner or accountant before making any moves. Another benefit is that you don't have to pay back the loan until one of the following scenarios occurs: you sell the home, move out of the house on a permanent basis, or die."

So..Exactly HOW is Real Estate FREE???

I stopped walking. "Listen. I appreciate all this information and my head is definitely full of all this stuff, but you said the Secret was called "Real Estate is FREE!" I said pointing to Allison. "Exactly how is it free? When are we going to talk about it?"

"How about now?" Mr. Mathers responded. He turned to Allison and said, "Why don't you give him the five-minute synopsis of how you found out that real estate could be free?"

"It would be my pleasure," she replied.

We were maybe five minutes away from the library and I was seconds away from one of my most important lessons in life.

Allison's No Money Down Deal

"When I got out of college, I came back and lived at home. It was fine for a while, but let's just say that I had a problem with my dad's curfew, so I started looking for a place to rent. I happened to meet Mr. Mathers at the real estate agency and he asked me why I wanted to rent when I could own a place instead. I told him that I didn't have any money for a downpayment and he said that I didn't need one."

"How can that be?" I asked.

Mr. Mathers answered for her. "I told her there was a four-family house I was looking into buying and it needed a lot of work. If I bought it I would have to put down 25 percent, but since she was a first-time buyer, she could qualify for an FHA loan. To make a long story short, she borrowed $10,000 from her parents, which she later repaid, and put down $6,000 for the place and the rest went toward closing costs and fixing the place up a bit. The house had three apartments rented and even with Allison living in the fourth, it had a positive cash flow."

"So let me get this straight," I said. "You bought a home by borrowing $10,000 from your parents, put it down on the place, and all your expenses were covered? That's crazy."

"Not just covered David. **I made $247 a month profit on the investment**. Not too shabby, but you've got to know that this type of thing happens every day," she replied. "Every day, David. You just have to find the deals. I think it was two years later that I realized I could pull out quite a bit of equity from the place and buy another one. This time I called up Mr. Mathers and asked if he wanted to partner up on something."

"We've been partners ever since," they said in unison.

"But..." I stared to say, but didn't have a comeback.

"There are no 'buts' about it David," she said. "I've got dozens of stories like this one where people borrowed the downpayment from a credit card or their 401(k) plan or a family friend in order to get something without taking cash out of their own pockets. I even have examples of people who saved for five years to buy their first property. It doesn't matter how they got the money. In all those cases they bought either two-, three-, or four-unit places that would still qualify for a residential loan. Most times they qualified for an FHA loan or a 3 percent down loan program. The key was to run the numbers and lock in their gains when they bought."

"**So when you say real estate is 'free' you mean that the total costs of acquiring the property and running the place is offset by the rental income coming in**, right?"

"Bingo," Mr. Mathers said. "Most people don't want to deal with living in a two- or three-family home. They'd rather own their white picket fence dream house and don't like the idea of having neighbors so close to them or the hassle of collecting rent and fixing things. What do you say to that Allison?"

"**I'm 27 years old and I'm financially free 38 years early** because I was willing to do all those things Mark just said," she replied.

I shook my head at them in disbelief.

"C'mon Donald[46]," she said. "Let's stop by my office before we turn you lose on the world."

The Mark Mathers Real Estate Seminar

We cut across the small park in front of the library and then crossed the street. Allison's office was a stones throw from the library.

"Come in and I'll get your first book for you," she offered, as she opened the front door.

The office was spacious and filled with dozens of books and pictures of homes on the wall.

"Are all these your…." I started to say.

"Yes, they're all her properties," Mr. Mathers answered for her.

"Yes, they're *ours*," she corrected him. "I like having pictures of them so I know why I'm working so hard late at night."

"To be Financially Free?" I guessed.

She laughed. "No silly, to buy more and more real estate."

"You'll have to forgive her David. She's a bit ambitious."

Allison walked over to the shelf and looked through the row of books. "Ah yes," she said, reaching for one in particular. She grabbed it and handed it to me. "I want you to read it from cover to cover. It's already been underlined and highlighted several times. Feel free to add anything to the notes in the margin. Take your own notes in that binder Mr. Mathers probably gave you. Once you've finished the book, give either of us a call and we'll give you the next two or three books to read and learn from. Follow the same process of taking notes. Write down any questions and we'll answer all of them after a month. Deal?"

"Deal," I said, shaking her hand, then Mr. Mathers.

She gave me a look and Mr. Mathers winked at me. "What are you standing around for? Don't you have some reading to do?" she asked.

"Aye, aye captain," I responded, clicked my heels in attention and saluted them. "Seriously. Thank you so much. I can't say how thankful I am."

---

[46] As in "The Donald," Donald Trump.

"Don't thank us just yet David," Mr. Mathers replied. "You have a long road ahead of you, but it gets easier with time. Get going before Allison here bites your head off."

"Hey, I'm not that bad," she responded and pushed him out of the way. She shook my hand again. "In all seriousness, read the book and let the information sink in. Follow the path we've already walked David and you'll be buying your first property once you're ready."

"**How do you know when you're ready to invest in real estate**?" I asked.

"When your credit card debt is under control, you've got a healthy cash flow going, and you've got the **millionaire mindset**."

"What's that?" I asked.

"Read the book and you'll find out," she replied. "Now get out of here. You've got some reading to do."

"Okay. I'll get out of your hair," I said. I shook their hands, turned, and walked out of her office and into the lobby.

"Think he'll finish the book tonight?" I heard her whisper.

"I wouldn't be surprised if he called later tonight to ask for the second book," Mr. Mathers responded.

He was right.

Real Estate is FREE: Investment Properties- COMMENTS

I truly believe that investment real estate represents one of the greatest investment options around. From tax benefits, to equity buildup to appreciation, real estate has got it all not to mention a cash flow that you can live off of when you retire...early. For those of you looking to take the next jump from the Surviving phase in life to the Striving phase, investment real estate represents one of the primary financial foundations of successful 'Strivers.' There are literally hundreds of books on the subject of foreclosures, rehabbing properties, flipping, and the hundred other ways to buy real estate investment properties. But please take my advice and get a firm and solid financial foundation under you before you decide to invest in real estate. For now, let's talk about your personal residence.

Real Estate is Free: Your Home – COMMENTS

The idea of **delaying the purchase of your 'dream home' is** **something that can pay HUGE dividends down the line for you.** *Don't believe me? How about believing your fellow millionaires next door?*

"**Living in less costly areas can enable you to spend less and to invest more of your income.** You will have less for your home and correspondingly less for your property taxes. Your neighbors will be less likely to drive expensive motor vehicles. You will find it easier to keep up, even ahead, of the Joneses and still accumulate wealth. It's your choice."
- Thomas J. Stanley and William D. Danko, *The Millionaire Next Door*

Delay Instant Gratification for Long-Term Satisfaction!

If you live in a nice neighborhood in a house that's 'too big' for you, you'll have to make more money and spend more money to live there. In essence, you'd be playing great offense in order to live in a 'better' neighborhood, but not playing great defense. The rich don't do that. They live below their means in a house that's less expensive than they can afford, which means they spend less money every year to pay their mortgages and taxes.

Please note that I'm not advocating that you live in a bad neighborhood or in a shack of a home in order to save money and live below your means. I AM advocating that you choose carefully where you live and what you live in by weighing things like quality of schools, taxes, median cost of homes, and all those other goodies. Take it all into consideration and go smaller than you need..er, want. Once you have your passive income coming in and other investments in place, you can then afford to buy that dream house. **An even better option than buying a house or condo as your first home is buying a two- or three-family.** *I recommend this to* <u>everyone</u> *that asks my advice about their first home purchase because your neighbors (in essence) help pay your mortgage. The fact that you receive rent means that your personal residence has now become an income-generating machine. Welcome to the game the rich play!*

A 15-Year vs. a 30-Year Mortgage

My recommendation to people is that they take the 30-year mortgage and use the additional funds that would have been put toward the 15-year mortgage and invest it instead. Invest it in your credit card debt or your car loan or wherever you can get a better return than if you had invested the money in your house/mortgage (perhaps in other real estate properties). I personally like having options in life and I think the 30-year loan offers borrowers the most flexibility. You can invest the extra money if you like or send in the cash to pay down your mortgage. Most young couples look at the mortgage amount of a 15-year loan and think they will always be able to afford the amount. Along comes junior and the decision for one parent to stay home. Additional and unplanned costs creep in and suddenly they're strapped for cash, barely able to make their monthly mortgage payments. The additional cushion of the lower mortgage amount offered by the 30-year loan would have come in handy.

To Prepay or Not to Prepay: You Decide

Along a similar vein is the discussion on whether you should prepay your mortgage. Bottom line: do what's best for you. If you think you can invest your money and get a better rate of return, go for it. If you're not sure about how to invest for maximum returns, and want to keep your principal relatively safe, and want to go for security instead of freedom, invest in your home.

The Prepay Camp
- You know your guaranteed rate of return up front
- You're building up equity a lot faster
- With your mortgage paid off, you'll need less passive income to offset your expenses and you can retire early

The Don't Prepay Camp
- Pay off all other bad debt first
- Make sure you have an Emergency Fund that's fully funded
- Make sure you have adequate insurance
- Long-term results are what matter and the stock market has returned more than 10% on average for every 20-year rolling period for over a century
- I can buy an investment property and easily earn 20% returns or more on my money

Real Estate is FREE - ACTION PLAN

Start Saving NOW! – If you haven't done so, start saving for your downpayment, closing costs, insurance, taxes, remodeling, furniture, etc, etc, etc.

Set Aside Maintenance Money – Don't let your maintenance kill your budget. Plan in advance. Eric Tyson, author of *Home Buying for Dummies* suggests you set aside at least 1% of the home's purchase price annually. Add that to a "house" savings fund.

Start Eliminating All Other Bad Debt – As I've mentioned before, eliminating your bad debt, or at least putting a plan together to get out of bad debt, is the first item that your financial plan is going to have to address. Focusing on any other area, like your retirement or paying down your mortgage, guarantees that you will not get the best return on your money.

Buy a Small Home – Well not literally a "small" home, but one that is below your means. You'll save yourself thousands of dollars in interest, principal, and other costs associated with maintaining your home. Your neighbors are also less likely to be the "Joneses" so you won't feel the need to buy more useless stuff.

Check Out Multi-Families – After all, multi-families and other investment properties are the reason this chapter is titled "Real Estate is FREE." They're not for everyone, but you might be swayed once you run the numbers and realize you're living for half the cost of a rental in your area.

Security or Freedom? – Determine whether you want to be financially secure or Financially Free. Prepay your mortgage if this makes sense for you. I believe you'll come out ahead if you invest the extra cash in low-cost index funds and/or investment properties, but that's just me.

Refinance or Consolidate Your Consumer Debt – Home equity loans charge lower interest than your credit cards, auto loans, and probably just about every other kind of loan you have. Take a look at your outstanding balances and interest rates and determine if a home equity loan would make sense.

Get the Best Deal – Check out www.bankrate.com and www.lendingtree.com to get the best rates and terms for your loans. If you're going the human route, haggle, haggle, and haggle some more until you get the best loan possible. Every percentage point counts. Negotiate brokers fees if you're using one.

Get Rid of PMI - If you're paying PMI, get rid of it. Prepay if you have to or refinance if it makes sense. Just figure out some way to get below the magic 80% mark.

Home Equity Loan, et al – Please be careful when using these products. Don't consolidate bad debt and then rack up some more because you've got cash in hand. That cash came out of your house and you owe it back to your banker. STOP SPENDING your hard-earned cash. I repeat, STOP SPENDING your hard-earned cash!

Your Investment Property? – If you're looking to get into the real estate investing game, you can do it if you want it bad enough. Make sure you have a decent positive cash flow before you go out and buy a place and have at least two to three months expenses set aside. The last thing you want to do is put your current home or lifestyle in jeopardy because a boiler blows on you.

Additional Resources

Books:
Ordinary People, Extraordinary Wealth by Ric Edelman (This book will elaborate on the idea that prepaying your mortgage is NOT a smart thing to do)
Invest in Yourself by Marc Eisenson, et al (This book will elaborate on the idea that prepaying your mortgage IS a smart thing to do)
The Unofficial Guide to Real Estate Investing by Martin Stone & Spencer Strauss

Web-Sites:
www.creonline.com (this is Carlton Sheets' site)
www.richdad.com (check out the real estate forums)

Mainly because I can't help myself, but I wanted to add one more 'word of caution' about living above your means and buying a bigger house than you can afford…

"Like credit card debt, home mortgages are the subject of a constant hard sell, but homeownership is different in its respectability. Friends are unlikely to send congratulations for maxing out a Visa card, but they will buy a drink to celebrate qualifying for a mortgage on the soon-to-be-purchased dream house. Even in the frenzy of modern credit use, there is a widespread feeling that credit cards are dangerous and that their overuse signals irresponsibility. Buying a home, by contrast, is rarely condemned and often applauded. … Yet homeownership gets people into financial trouble in similar ways: They buy more than they can truly afford and they have too little margin left when disaster strikes."
– from *The Fragile Middle Class: Americans in Debt* by Teresa Sulivan, et al

Secret #9:
GUARD YOUR WEALTH

"You never know what life will throw at you
to cause your well thought out plan and financial
house to crumble. You'd better be prepared for the
unthinkable or soon you'll be living your worst
nightmare."

- Fabio Marciano

Chapter 20

Secret #9: Guard Your Wealth

From Life (Your Health, Your Life & Your Stuff)

From Yourself

From Your Spouse

From Uncle Sam

You Might Lose it All

Over the course of the past two months I had learned what would have taken most people a lifetime. More importantly was the fact that I was taking action on the ideas that Mr. Mathers shared with me and incorporating them into my life. During this time, I had finished reading three books and had started working out again. It's amazing what you could accomplish if you put your mind to it.

For our ninth meeting Mr. Mathers suggested we meet at St. Bonaventure's Retirement Home. It was a strange request, but after two months of lessons, I learned not to question his motives. So promptly at 9 a.m. on a beautiful summer morning, we walked into St. Bonaventure's to begin my ninth lesson. We said hello to the receptionists and walked down the hallway to a little meeting room.

"It looks like you've been here quite often," I said, noting how he made himself at home.

"You could say that," he replied. "I have a few friends here that I visit once a month. I usually meet them at 10 o'clock for a game of cards and we catch a baseball game or two, but more on that later. I'm not going to cover the ninth Secret in too much detail, but we've got a lot of ground to cover, so you might as well pull out your binder so we can get started."

I did as I was told and he poured us two cups of coffee from the coffee maker next to the window, then he got right to it.

Protect Your Financial Freedom

"So let's say you've got all the Secrets of Wealth working for you and you've been diligently saving your hard-earned cash and investing it in assets to throw off a positive stream of cash at some point in your life. You're feeling pretty good with yourself and know that one day you're going to reach that point called Financial Freedom and you'll be able to quit the 9 to 5 rat race and play golf every day or travel the world. If you're not careful though, someone could derail your plan."

"Who would do that?" I asked.

"Who knows. It could be you or Uncle Sam or someone you don't even know. Whoever it is, you should make sure you protect your Financial House in advance."

"What are you talking about?" I asked, confused as to how someone else could take me off track.

"David, so far we've talked about building your wealth and assets, but just as important is learning how to protect your assets. That's what the ninth Secret is all about, the Secret called *Guard Your Wealth*. There are four main people or things you have to guard your wealth from including: Uncle Sam, life, yourself, and your spouse."

Life is Unpredictable, but You Can Plan for the Unknown

"Life sometimes throws you curveballs. Some of them, like a serious car accident, a disability, or the loss of a spouse, can dramatically change your life forever. I'm going to teach you how to protect yourself, to shield yourself against those curveballs through various forms of insurance including; health, life, umbrella, and disability insurance."

"Fun," I said, interrupting his train of thought.

"I agree that insurance isn't the most exciting of subjects, but it is extremely important to your quest to build wealth and protect yourself from any threats to your Financial House. Most people don't want to think about the subject, but avoiding it could create a financial risk for you and your family. So let's get into the ways that you can protect your wealth."

Emergency Fund

Your Emergency Fund: Still the First Place to Start

"We've covered this before, but the first way you can guard yourself from unforeseen expenses and accidents is by having a properly funded Emergency Fund. By having an Emergency Fund in place, you don't have to use your credit card or get into debt if you lose your job, have a car accident, or need major repairs on your home."

"I got it," I said. "I can see how you're guarding your future wealth by not having to use a credit card or some other personal loan for unforeseen expenses, helps keep you from acquiring bad debt."

"Good. Let's move on to life insurance."

Life Insurance

Life Insurance 101: You're Going to Die

"It's guaranteed that you're going to die someday," he said.

"But Elvis is still alive, right?" I joked.

"Elvis withstanding, your death is 100% guaranteed and life insurance is the only insurance that you can carry that you will *definitely* collect on at some point in your life if you keep the policy intact. Everyone buys home insurance, but they may never collect on it. You might have disability insurance, but may never collect on it."

Why You Buy Life Insurance?

"You," he said pointing at me, "are your most valuable asset. More specifically, during your peak working (earning) years, you are at your most valuable stage in life to you and your family. If you were to die during those peak years, your family would be financially devastated. The reason you have life insurance is to protect your family and make sure they are provided for should you die while they still depend on you. Now there are two main life insurance options available: permanent and term insurance."

Term Insurance

"Term insurance is a no-frills, straightforward type policy that just pays out a death benefit if you actually die while you're holding the policy. You're buying coverage for as long as the policy term lasts or for as long as you continue to pay the monthly premium. The length of coverage or term of a policy can be anywhere from 5, 10, 20, or even 30 years and the cost of your coverage will depend on the term you choose. Just note that the longer the period during which your rates can't be raised, the higher the annual premium you'll have to pay. Regardless of what policy length you choose, **the premiums on a term policy are very low compared to other insurance policies**, which is one of the reasons term is more popular than permanent insurance."

Permanent or "Cash Value" Life Insurance

"Permanent insurance or perm for short, is also called 'cash value' insurance. This type of insurance lasts until the day you die or until you stop paying the premiums. With perm insurance, a portion of your premiums goes into a savings account, which is invested by the insurance company. This portion is called the 'cash value' of the policy and that amount grows tax-free and is yours to keep. The beauty is that you can borrow against that cash value with no tax penalty."

"Kind of like your home," I mentioned.

"That's right," he agreed.

Borrowing Against Your Cash Value Account

"The main benefit of permanent insurance in my opinion has to do with the cash value account," he said. The money that you're paying in premiums for your permanent life policy can be tapped to pay for college and other types of expenses. Plus the borrowing guidelines are a little more liberal than your 401(k) plan."

"Sounds like a great deal," I commented.

Cons of Permanent Insurance

"It is a good deal from the perspective of a cheap source to borrow against, but remember that permanent policies have high premiums and the investment portion comes at a price, mainly higher commissions. In addition, permanent life policies generally have high fees and surrender charges should you decide to cancel the policy. As for the tax-free savings component that insurance agents like to tell you about, with the availability of IRAs, 401(k)s, and other tax-deferred savings accounts, you can get the same tax breaks with potentially higher returns and greater portability, for a much lower cost."

Life Insurance is Not a Substitute for a Retirement Plan

"In my mind, life insurance is not a substitute for a well thought out and structured retirement or investment plan," he said. "Hopefully when you reach the age of retirement you'll have implemented all the Secrets of Wealth and have numerous tax-deferred and tax-advantaged assets that you can tap for your day-to-day expenses."

"I'm a little confused," I said. "I thought we were talking about insurance, not investing."

"I brought it up because you're bound to hear a sales pitch from an insurance agent that pushes a permanent policy on you. They'll tell you that you're not just buying insurance, but you're buying an investment. They'll show you the wonderful returns and how much your account will grow over the years and how you can borrow from the cash value. But remember that **life insurance should never be purchased solely as an investment**. It shouldn't be purchased as a way to save for your children's college, nor should it be used as a way to pay for an addition on your house."

"So insurance is for insurance only is what you're saying."

"You got it. Anything else is gravy. Remember that. But before we get into the benefits of the different policies, just take a look at this chart," he said, handing me a sheet of paper. "It covers the major types of perm and term insurance."

Table 20.1 – Term vs. Perm Insurance

	PROs	CONs
Term Insurance	• Much cheaper than Permanent Insurance	• Build up no cash value • Expensive over the age of 65
Annual Renewable Term (ART)	• Cheapest policy around • Good choice for those starting out	• Need to renew every year • Premiums can increase every year
Guaranteed Level Term	• Pay set premium until term of coverage expires	• Costs more than ART • Build up no cash value
Perm Insurance	• Forced savings • You can borrow from the cash value you've built up • Tax-deferred growth of cash value	• More expensive than Term • In general, you pay high commissions
Whole Life	• You build up a cash value that you can borrow from • Fixed premiums	• Conservative investment options • No premium flexibility
Universal Life	• Investment options are a little more aggressive than Whole Life (bonds, money market funds) • Premiums flexibility • Guaranteed rate of return	• Investment options are still a bit tame and the guaranteed return is usually still low
Variable Life	• You can invest in equity funds and more aggressive options • You can apply interest earned toward premiums	• Cannot withdraw the cash value during your lifetime
Variable Universal Life	• You have more investment options (stock funds) to invest in • Interest earned on your investments can go toward premiums, lowering your out-of-pocket costs	• Higher risk associated with investment options • High premiums

Which Permanent Policy? - Rules of Thumb

"That's a lot of permanent policies," I said. "Which is best?"

"It all depends on your situation David. Traditional whole life makes sense if you're a conservative investor. If you're a moderate investor and need premium flexibility in the early years of the policy, a universal policy could be your best bet, because you get a guaranteed minimum interest rate, so no matter how badly the investments in your cash account perform, you lock in a minimum return. Now if you're willing to take on some additional risk, a variable universal policy would be your best bet."

Term vs. Perm

"Now let's get into the 'Term versus Perm Debate',", he said. "**A term policy is *a lot* cheaper than a permanent policy**, but with permanent insurance some money gets socked away every month into an investment/savings account. So after several years of payments you begin to accumulate quite a bit of money in that savings account. Despite this benefit, most **financial gurus will tell you to buy term insurance and invest the cost difference** of the policies in a separate investment account. Just make sure if you go with a term policy over a perm policy that you actually 'invest the difference' and don't spend the extra savings."

Expensive Isn't the Word!

"Got it. I think I've read that advice before, but just how much more expensive is a permanent policy than a term policy?" I asked.

"A perm policy can be anywhere from two to eight times more expensive," he replied.

"Eight times!" I said in amazement. "That's a huge difference."

"It is, but you get the cash value of the policy," he replied.

"**So the cash value is kind of like your *reward* for overpaying all those years**?" I commented.

He laughed. "I've never heard it put that way, but I suppose you're correct. The cash value of the policy and the ability to borrow from it is the incentive to keep your policy intact."

"Gee, some incentive. Overpay for 20 years and you get to keep a portion of what you paid. Why would anyone buy a perm policy?"

Don't Rule Out Perm Policies

"I advocate term policies for almost everyone, but just remember that perm policies can make sense for some people. For instance, it might make sense to have a perm policy if:

- You have 20-plus years "to go" and will need coverage for all those years
- Earn a high income, over $100,000 annually
- Already have maxed out your retirement contributions

"Under these three scenarios some financial planners will tell you that permanent insurance would make sense. In my mind, if I'm earning a ton of money and I've maxed out my retirement contributions, I would look into a living trust which we'll cover later."

Who Needs Life Insurance?

"So how much coverage do I need?" I asked.

"Before I answer that question, you should know that you have little or no need for life insurance right now," he replied.

"How come I don't need life insurance?"

"You don't have any dependants and the debts that you owe, like your student loans and credit cards, can usually be assumed and paid off by your parents if you were to die."

You probably don't need life insurance if:
- You're young, single, and have no dependents
- You're married, but not planning on having children, and your spouse will be well taken care of thanks to your prodigious accumulation of assets while alive
- You don't have a ton of bills and liabilities that you'll leave behind for your heirs

You probably need life insurance if:
- You have dependents that are relatively young and won't be "out of the house" for quite a few years
- You're married and want to leave your spouse in good shape should you die (i.e., with enough money to live off of)
- You have a lot of bills you would leave behind (perhaps a mortgage, credit card bills, tuition, and other loans)
- You're looking for a way to reduce the hit from estate taxes through tax-free life insurance proceeds

How Much Coverage Do I Need?

"Now back to the question at hand," he said. "I can't tell you how much life insurance you need because everyone's situation is different. When an insurance agent figures out your insurance needs they have to factor in your marital status, the number of dependents you have, your current income, the anticipated college costs of your children, and your outstanding mortgage to name a few items. You also need to figure out what kind of lifestyle you want to provide for your family and whether you want your spouse to work after you die."

"But isn't there a rule of thumb or something?" I asked.

"Of course there is. The rule of thumb I've seen is that **you need to carry a policy that has a face value of anywhere from 5 to 8 times your annual income** as a *minimum*. Others suggest even more. My suggestion is that you get your Financial House in order, which means getting your net worth and cash flow statements together, and go talk to a good insurance agent about your needs. They will look at three main categories: funeral and other 'final' expenses, income loss, and your outstanding debts. In short, an agent will total up estimated burial and estate settlement costs, calculate how much your dependants will lose from you not being there to provide a check every two weeks, then add in the cost of paying off all your debts. I've developed this handy chart to use for figuring out how much you'll need:

Figure 20.2 - How Much Insurance Do I Need?[47]

# of Years of Income You want to Replace	Multiply Your Net Income by the following Factor
5 - 9	5
10 - 19	8 - 10
20 - 24	12 – 15
25 - 30	18 - 20

How Long Do I Need Coverage For?

"Okay, we've spoken about how you can keep your whole life policy until you die, but **you might not need a ton of life insurance when you reach a certain age**. If you've got your Financial House in order and your children are out of the house and no longer in need of your support before your term policy expires, you might not need to worry as much about having a life insurance policy."

"Can you elaborate?"

"Sure. Let's say you have twins that are five years old. You also have a life insurance policy that will expire in 20 or 30 years. Chances are that your kids might not need that death benefit on your life insurance policy when they're 25 or 35 years old. Of course they might, which is why you should…"

"Consult your financial planner," I said, finishing his thought.

"Exactly. Because you might want to make sure your spouse is *well* covered if you were to pass away."

"So you essentially want to have a policy that lasts as long as it takes for your kids to move out of the house, but can I renew my policy after it expired when I'm say 50 or 60 years old just in case I still want the coverage?" I asked.

"Technically yes, but there's another reason why you may opt not to carry life insurance at that age: the cost. **Life insurance tends to get very, very expensive the older you get**. As soon as you reach your 50s, you're looking at a huge jump in premiums because the odds of you dying increases. No insurance agency is going to write you a new 30-year policy when you're 65, because the odds of you dying and your

---

[47] Chart is based on several books I've read on the subject, as well as an analysis done on insurance web-sites. Check with a qualified insurance agent or visit www.insure.com for more information on determining your life insurance needs.

heirs collecting on that policy are against the insurance company making money on the deal. This is one of the arguments for having a perm policy: you get to lock in a premium for the rest of your life."

"But it's up to eight times more expensive," I stated.

"Which is why it's difficult for people to afford perm coverage and why I advocate term policies," he replied. "**The idea is to have other assets and investments that your beneficiaries and heirs can rely upon when you die besides your insurance policy.**"

How Much Does Coverage Cost? [48]

"So exactly how much will life insurance cost me?" I asked.

"The easiest way to find out is to go to www.quotesmith.com or www.intelliquote.com. If you're still not satisfied with the information you find, you can always check out some local agents in your hometown. They might not be price competitive, but they can help make sense of the stuff we talked about today. As for the cost itself, the price of your policy depends on a number of factors; your age, sex, and medical history."

"So I should buy life insurance when I'm young?" I asked.

"That's right. **The sooner you buy a life insurance policy, the better**. Now select or preferred rates go to those people who are in good health and don't smoke. If you smoke, have a risky profession, are overweight, or have a family history of some sort of ailment, then life insurance is going to be expensive. So what can you do about it? Control the things you can control. If you smoke, quit. If you're overweight, lose the extra pounds and save the extra dollars."

"Anything else to discuss on life insurance?" I asked.

The Rating System

"Just make sure you buy life insurance or any type of insurance from large and reputable firms. You want a company that is large enough, financially strong, highly rated, and one that's going to outlive you so you know they will be around to pay your claim."

"What do you mean by 'rated'?"

"There's a rating system that exists and essentially the best ratings are AAA, AA, or A+. When you find a company you like, check them out at Standard & Poor's (www.standardandpoors.com), A.M. Best (www.ambest.com), or you can always try Moody's Investors Service (www.moodys.com)."

---

[48] How much you're going to pay varies by state. Why? Because of the McCarran-Ferguson Act, passed in the '50s which allows for the insurance agency to be regulated at the state and not the federal level.

Annuities

"Another way to protect or secure your income stream is through annuities. I'm not a big fan of annuities," he admitted, "but I thought you should know about them. Life insurance companies can sell you an annuity, which will pay you a stream of income to live off of when you retire. Like cash value life insurance policies, you can grow your account tax-deferred. Essentially there are two different types of annuities: immediate and deferred. An immediate annuity will pay you, well immediately upon purchasing it. A deferred annuity will pay you once you retire."

"They sound like a good deal. Why don't you like them?"

"There are a lot of fees and commissions you have to pay with most annuities, although some big name companies are jumping into the game and offering low-cost options. Perhaps in a few years they'll make more sense to me, but right now I'm putting my money toward better investment options."

Life Insurance - COMMENTS

Life insurance is an important part of your Financial Freedom plan. It's sole purpose is to create security for your family and beneficiaries should you die. I think most people would be fine with term insurance, but you need to make sure that it's guaranteed renewable every year. If it's not, you're going to have to get a physical exam every year. Get a policy that takes you through at least the age where your kids are done with college and out of the house. In other words, until your dependants are no longer draining cash from you. If you want to be a little more conservative, you can extend it out so that you can help out with things like paying for a wedding or a downpayment on a house, as well as creating a bigger cushion for your spouse.

I'm not going to drag this out. Let's get to your Action Plan.

"Life is a grindstone. But whether it grinds us down or polishes us up depends on us."
                                                    - L. Thomas Holdcraft

Guard Your Wealth: Life Insurance – ACTION PLAN

Assess Your Life Insurance Needs: Look at your income, future college expenses, other household income sources, and any debts you want paid off should you die (mortgage, auto, credit cards, etc).

Buy What You Need: Calculate your needs and buy accordingly (i.e., buy the longest guaranteed period that you need and can afford).

Buy Early: The younger you are when you buy, the cheaper your premiums will be

Stay Healthy: Life insurance is going to cost you less if you don't smoke, don't drive recklessly, and don't have a gut (I mean you're not out of shape). So kick the habit and drop the weight if you can.

Shop Around: Go to www.insure.com or www.quotesmith.com and find out which insurers offer the best rate. Don't go with the cheapest just because they're the cheapest. You want to make sure the insurance company has a high rating and will be around in 20 to 30 years.

Avoid Commissions: Even if you're buying a permanent policy, you can save on your commissions by buying directly from the insurance company. Do your homework and find out if the provider you're looking into allows this, because it could save you a bundle.

Consider a Supplemental Policy: If you have life insurance solely through your employer, you might not have enough coverage to meet your needs. You also can't take that policy with you should you leave your job or get fired. Look into the costs of purchasing another (supplemental) policy.

Review Your Needs: Your life insurance needs are going to change over time. When you get married and have kids, you're going to need more life insurance. In short, during major life events and changes, review your insurance needs.

Health Insurance

Health Insurance Basics

"Next up is how to guard your health. Right off the bat you should know that health insurance is a must have, no two ways about it."

"I can't imagine not having it," I remarked naively.

"It might seem like a given for someone your age who's got employer-based health insurance, but guaranteed health insurance is not always the case for a lot of small business owners and their workers. Only a little over half of American workers can get health insurance through their employers. An even scarier statistic is that **over 45 million Americans have no health insurance**. Imagine if you're not working or your company doesn't provide health benefits. See how hard and costly it is to get health insurance. Even worse, companies cut back significantly in the '80s and '90s, so the number of companies that take care of their employees after they retire, is declining rapidly."

"What about Medicare? Shouldn't that cover the retirees?"

"**Medicare** only kicks in after you turn 65, which doesn't help all those folks who retired early. If you don't have a high income or if your medical expenses are too high, you might qualify for some sort of federal or state subsidized health coverage. If people don't qualify for Medicare or **Medicaid** coverage, then a public health clinic might be their best option."

COBRA

In my head I was processing what he was telling me, but I was still searching for ways to get health coverage without resorting to public assistance. "But what about COBRA coverage? Can't they do that instead?" I asked.

"If you lose your job or work for a company with 20 or more employees, COBRA[49] requires that your employer let you continue coverage for up to 18 months. COBRA is a great short-term fix, but the idea behind it is for it to act as a kind of a bridge between your old insurance and your new coverage. It used to be that COBRA was the only option for someone who was let go from a company and still needed health care coverage. However, with the passing of the Health Insurance Portability and Affordability Act (HIPAA) there are more options. The act states that no insurer can turn down your request for coverage if you were covered by a group policy within the last 63 days. But the act doesn't put any restrictions on the level of premiums your new provider can charge you so you might be able to get coverage, but

---

[49] COBRA stands for the Consolidated Omnibus Budget Reconciliation Act.

the cost could be a lot more expensive than you can afford. With that having been said, let's move on to the two main types of health insurance: fee-for-service and managed care."

Traditional Indemnity or Fee-for-Service Plans

"Traditional indemnity plans are also called fee-for service plans and you'll have to pay more in premiums than with managed care plans. You pay more because you're more in control with these plans. You choose who your doctors are and you choose where you get treated. These plans are good, but they're going the way of the dinosaur. If you do happen to have an indemnity plan, you've probably found that the insurance company is shifting more and more expenses your way. You pay for the medical expenses up front and once you reach your high annual deductible for out-of-pocket expenses each year, your insurer picks up 80% of the tab for the rest of the year."

"Sounds like a good deal," I commented.

"Yes and no," he said. "Your insurer will only cover 80% of what they deem to be the 'usual and customary' fee for the service in your area, not 80% of the actual bill. So you could get stuck with paying a lot more than 20% of the bill if your insurer feels the cost of service is way out of line with what is customarily charged for that service.[50]"

Managed Care Plans

"Next up are managed care plans which are the HMOs and PPOs of the world. That's Health Maintenance Organizations (HMOs) and Preferred Provider Organizations (PPOs)," he said, looking up from his binder. "If you have one of these plans you know that doctor visits and other services you may require won't cost you much out-of-pocket. Just make sure you use doctors that are part of the network."

HMOs

"With HMOs, you have a monthly (or bimonthly) payment(s) and all your medical care and services are covered. You pay a small fee every time you visit a doctor or get a prescription filled. The downside is that you only get to use the doctors and hospitals that are on the HMO's 'approved' list. If you do go outside the plan list for medical care, you will pay much more out of pocket. The only real issue I've had with HMOs is with the requirement to get a referral before you see a specialist, which is a nuisance but a necessity under plan guidelines."

---

[50] In general, indemnity insurance will only cover accidents and illness, but will not pay for any preventative care like birth control, but it all depends on your policy. Some pick up the cost of prescription drugs, some don't. Bottom Line: if you choose to get an indemnity plan, look over your plan carefully and know what you're covered for upfront and you won't get any surprises if you need medical help or other services.

PPOs

"Preferred Provider Organizations or PPOs for short are somewhere in between traditional indemnity plans and HMOs. You have more flexibility in the doctors you see and where you can go than with HMOs. Unlike HMOs, you can see doctors outside the netowrk and the PPO will pick up some of the cost. HMOs will not. PPOs are a great option if your employer makes them available on your plan."

Self-Insurance

"Of course, you can go the self-insurance route which is a bit pricier, but if your employer doesn't offer a medical plan, you may be forced into this option."

"That's probably pretty expensive, right?" I asked.

"It can be, but you can always get 'stop loss' insurance in which the insurance company will pick up the tab if a claim exceeds a certain amount. In short, you would pay the amount up to that stop point."

Are You in the High-Risk Pool?

"Lastly, if you've been denied insurance or the premiums for these traditional plans would strangle your budget, you might qualify for insurance through your state. Most states offer a high-risk pool that you can get into as a last resort. This might be a good option for someone with few alternatives. Also, if you don't have insurance, are disabled, or you earn a modest income, you might qualify for free or low-cost health care insurance through Medicare or Medicaid."

Flexible Spending Accounts (FSAs)

"One thing I wanted to cover before we moved on is Flexible Spending Accounts. You fund these accounts with pre-tax dollars and you get to use the money throughout the year to cover expenses like co-op payments, day care, and other expenses not covered by your insurance plan. The benefit is that you're doing so with **pre-tax dollars** so you're in essence getting more bang for your buck. If you have an FSA they're a great tool, but be careful and make sure that you use the money by the end of the year. **If you don't use it, you lose it**, since the money doesn't get rolled over into the next year."

"I had an FSA last year but didn't use the money, so I didn't sign up for it this year," I admitted.

"I would take a second look at FSAs David, but if you don't have the discipline to use it, then you shouldn't pay for something you won't use."

Medical Savings Accounts (MSAs)

"Medical Savings accounts or MSAs for short can be a great solution for small businesses and self-employed people looking for low cost health-care. MSAs are only for the self-employed or for people who work in small companies (50 people or less) and in order to qualify you must have a high-deductible individual health insurance policy. If you qualify, you get to put money for medical expenses into an investment account with pre-tax dollars. **The investments grow tax-deferred** and unlike flexible spending accounts, **you don't have to use the funds by the end of the year**. Money that you put in a given year can grow tax free for many years!"

"Wow. That is a great deal."

"If you're self-employed or work for a small company, MSAs are definitely worth a look."

Cutting Costs

"Okay, let's finish up here. Remember that the best 'deal' isn't necessarily the plan with the cheapest premiums or the one with the most benefits. You have to figure out which plan offers you the best combination of flexibility, benefits, and costs. If you're looking to cut your insurance costs, you can opt for higher deductibles. **Higher deductibles will reduce your monthly premiums**. With that having been said, I think we're done with health insurance," he said looking up at me. "I know I flew through this stuff, but you can always learn more by reading through your plan brochure."

"Sounds good to me," I said.

Health Insurance – COMMENTS

I wasn't about to get into all the differences in plans and policies in this book because the topic is beyond the scope of this book.

There is no such thing as standard coverage with health insurance and costs are going to vary a great deal from plan to plan. Most insurance plans will cover your doctor and hospital bills with certain limits, but after that everything is different. So, how do you compare plans? The best way is to list out the services you normally use, as well as the ones that you might need. Then you have to create a chart that lists the coverage each plan offers for these services. The best plan for you is the one that covers all of you normal needs and most of the benefits you might need some day. Don't go for the cheapest plan if it means putting yourself at risk. Be smart and Guard Your Health. After all, you are your most important asset.

Health Insurance – ACTION PLAN

Review Your Plan: Pull out your health care plan materials and double-check your benefits, services, and doctors. Every plan has different rules and guidelines; failure to follow them means you're going to pay more out-of-your-pocket. Know in advance which doctors are in your plan, what approvals you need, and if you're covered for certain medical procedures like laser eye surgery and so on.

Consolidate Plans: If you haven't done so already, see if it makes sense to combine your coverage with your spouse. Sometimes it makes sense to keep two different plans, but that's rarely the case.

Go Generic: If you want to cut the costs of your prescription drugs, always ask your doctor if the comparable generic is just as good. This strategy can save you a couple hundred dollars a year.

Don't Go Cheap: If you picked the cheapest health plan last year because, well it was the cheapest, you need to look at your plans a lot more closely when it comes time to renew. Spend the 30 minutes it takes to make sure you have the best coverage possible.

Raise Your Deductible and/or Co-payment: If you're able to do so, raising your deductible or co-payment will drastically reduce your monthly premiums. By "if you're able to do so," I mean that you have a properly funded Emergency Fund to pay the larger deductible should you require medical treatment.

Band Together: If you don't work for a big company or you're self-employed, see if you can cut costs by banding together with other self-employed brethren. Lots of trade associations, your chamber of commerce, and other community groups offer health insurance plans that are reasonably priced. They get great rates because they have larger groups that belong to an association or network. Ask around, it'll save you a bundle.

Get Physically Fit: Quit smoking and lose weight. There, I said it. Just like with life insurance, you're going to save a bundle if you quit smoking and get down to your ideal weight.

Use your FSA Funds: At the beginning of the year, every one is gung-ho about Flexible Spending Accounts because they like the idea of paying for out-of-pocket expenses with tax-free dollars. Don't lose the money by not using it and make sure you ask for a receipt to file the proper paperwork for the disbursement of funds.

Disability Insurance

What's Disability Insurance?

"Your greatest asset is your ability to earn money over the course of your working career. So it makes sense to protect that ability and you do that through disability insurance. Disability Insurance or DI for short is a type of insurance policy that will pay you if you are unable to work due to a disability or injury. It's like a safety net that protects you in the event that you get hurt and can't work for a period of time or in the worst case scenario, if you can't ever work again."

Your Financial Safety Net

"Let me ask you a question David. If you were a betting man, would you bet that you're more likely to die or become disabled during your prime working years?"

I thought about it for a few seconds. "I'm going to have to go with getting injured on the job for $2,000 Alex.[51]" I replied.

"That's correct. The odds of suffering a disability that lasts at least 90 days is 1 in 8. What's alarming about the stats is that only 15% to 40%[52] of the U.S. workforce has disability income protection. On the other hand close to 70% of individuals have life insurance policies."

"So **more people are protecting themselves against dying, but not protecting their greatest asset, their ability to work**," I observed.

"That's correct and the consequences of not having DI can be dreadful. As you already know, the majority of American workers are living paycheck to paycheck. **If the primary breadwinner is out of work for even a month or two without pay, the family would be wiped out completely.** DI will pay you a monthly amount, the size of which depends on your policy, which will continue to be paid until you're able to return to work.[53]"

"Sounds like a pretty good safety net."

"Compared to digging into your cash reserves or borrowing money to pay for your daily expenses, you better believe it."

Disability Insurance Is NOT Cheap

"So if it's so great, why do so few people have DI?" I asked.

"Because of the cost," he replied. "**The annual premiums for DI can be anywhere from 1% to 3% of your annual salary.**"

---

[51] Yes, referring to the game show Jeopardy's host Alex Trebeck.

[52] Depending on which publication you read.

[53] There are dozens of different types of disability insurance, from just the basics to those with all the bells and whistles. The coverage you choose will determine what benefits you receive, when you receive them, and how long you'll receive them.

"Ouch. Why so expensive?"

"Because the odds of your filing a claim are pretty high and because it costs more to support a living person for the rest of their working life than it does to make a one-time payment if they die."

"Oh, I get it. So if I get hurt and can never work again, they'd have to pay me $30,000 for the next 45 years versus making a one-time payment to my beneficiaries if I die."

"Yep, that's it in a nutshell. If you become disabled, that's $1,350,000 versus say a $200,000 policy you might have on your life."

Don't Skimp On Your Coverage

"To get around the costs of the annual premiums, some people attempt to skimp by buying a cheap DI policy. While that might seem like a smart thing to do when you're healthy and saving money by paying less in annual premiums, you will find out how dumb it was to skimp if you're ever injured and have trouble collecting your benefits. **Those cheap policies have a funny way of excluding certain kinds of injuries**. That's why you need to make sure the policy you buy has a liberal definition of how a disability is defined, which will make it easier to collect should you get injured."

"I know what you're talking about," I said. "My friend is a doctor and he told me that the anesthesiologist in his hospital has her thumbs insured. If she severely hurts a thumb, she's out of work for life."

"And if she has a policy with a liberal definition of injured, they will understand that she is disabled for life because she will never be able to be an anesthesiologist again. She may be able to work another job, but she can't operate the equipment required for her current occupation, so she's technically disabled."

"That's what my friend told me, which is why she pays so much for her insurance."

"That's an excellent segue to our next point regarding disability insurance. Sometimes those that need it most can't get it or can't afford it."

"What do you mean 'can't get it?'" I asked.

"I mean that someone who works in construction is going to have to pay a heck of a lot more than you because you sit in an office all day. Some people just have a higher risk of getting hurt than others. With that higher risk comes higher premiums and lower benefits. Some insurance agencies won't even touch workers who have what are deemed really dangerous jobs: pilots, police officers and coal miners."

"That's rotten," I commented.

"Welcome to life David. It's not fair," he replied.

Don't Just Be Part of the Group

"Now there are essentially two types of DI: group (through your work or a membership in an association or organization) and private (getting a policy on your own)."

"I'm pretty sure I have disability insurance through work, so I'm okay, right?" I asked.

"Yes and no. While it's good that you have some form of DI, there are some drawbacks to only having your DI coverage through your employer. If you leave your job, you lose your coverage. In addition, the coverage you receive might not be enough. There might also be another issue to face with regards to the taxability of your benefits. Normally insurance proceeds are tax-free, but **if your employer provides the DI benefits those benefits are considered taxable distributions**.[54] The typical employer-paid benefits are around 60% to 80% of your pay, which is only 40% to 60% of your current pay after taxes. Do you think you can live on 40% of your pay?"

I shook my head.

"I didn't think so. Most people can't live on 40% of their income, which is why a supplemental DI policy can be a good thing to have."

"So **how do I compare the various types of plans**?" I asked.

"There are a lot of considerations. For instance, you need to find out what portion of your income is replaced, what the policy cap on income replacement is, how long you can collect on long-term disability, and how a disability is defined by your insurer. But let's not get into the nitty gritty because we're running out of time."

"Fine by me, but one more question. Back to those people that can't get coverage or don't work for a big company. Are there any other options for them?" I asked.

Create a Group

"If you're self-employed or your employer doesn't offer disability insurance, you still can get a group policy discount by going through a trade or professional organization. If you don't belong to one or there aren't any around, you can create a group and get a discounted rate. I believe the guidelines want you to have at least 10 people in the group to qualify for the discounted rates."

---

[54] ATTN BUSINESS OWNERS: If you deduct your premiums as a business expense, you'll get a tax break when filing your tax returns, but if you collect on that DI policy, the distributions will be considered taxable income. If you pay for the coverage out of your own pocket, your distributions will come to you tax-free. Check with your financial planner and insurance agent about this for further information.

Cutting Costs

"Unfortunately, there aren't many ways around the high costs of disability insurance, but there are some things that you can do to cut down the cost of premiums, like delaying the start of your benefits by 90 days. The reason the 90-day threshold exists is that insurance companies and their number crunchers have figured out that most disabilities and injuries don't last longer than 90 days. So there's a good chance that you'll be back on the job before you have a chance to collect any money from them. In the meantime, you live off your cash reserves or any sick-leave benefits you might have at work."

Brief Notes on Disability Insurance

- The longer the waiting period for you to receive your benefits, the cheaper your premiums will be. Yet another reason to have an Emergency Fund.
- You want a policy that's "non-cancelable" and guaranteed renewable up to at least age 65.
- Check the fine print to see if your policy excludes any pre-existing medical conditions.
- Look into the cost of coverage for your own occupation.
- Avoid "accident-only" policies. They're cheaper, but if you become disabled in any other manner, you won't get any benefits.
- Also look into getting a cost-of-living rider. This will help protect your benefits from the effects of inflation.
- Where to Shop for Disability Insurance: Here are some long-term disability insurance providers that you can check out: Unum Provident (www.unumprovident.com), Northwestern Mutual (www.northwesternmutual.com), and Mass Mutual (www.massmutual.com). But don't take my word for it. Go to www.ambest.com (the leading evaluator of insurance companies) and check out the ratings for a host of companies.

Long-Term Care Insurance

The "Just-In Case" Insurance [55]

"Next up is long-term care insurance or LTC which will help pay for nursing care and other associated costs of old age, but coverage can be quite expensive."

"So how much is this coverage going to run me?" I asked.

"A policy will cost you anywhere from $500 to $2,000 a year or more, depending on how old you are when you get the policy."

"What! That's really expensive!" I exclaimed.

---

[55] But highly likely that you'll need it someday.

"It is and it isn't. The cost of a nursing home can run you $30,000 to $45,000 a year or more and in-home care costs even more."

I could immediately understand why LTC insurance costs so much. Insurance agencies would have to pay out $45,000 a year over the course of someone's remaining life, which could be 20 to 30 years given the increase in life expectancy over the past few decades.

"What if you can't afford the coverage?" I asked.

"Don't buy it," he said matter-of-factly.

"You're kidding right?" I asked.

"Nope. If you can't afford the premiums you're probably going to qualify for Medicaid. Medicaid will pick up the tab for your home stay if you qualify, which essentially means you have to have almost no assets to your name. On the other hand, Medicare will usually only pick up the first 20 days of an LTC stay," he replied.

I shook my head in disbelief.

"Look David, long-term insurance is good protection against going bankrupt due to the costs of growing older, but financial planners are still divided on whether you need it. If you have a lot of assets and a passive income stream, then you're likely to be able to afford any long-term care when you get older. In that case you don't really need to worry about LTC insurance. But…"

"I knew there would be a but," I interrupted.

Keeping Your Assets Intact

"But some people like to purchase a policy even if they can pay for their own long-term care, because they want to make sure that the costs of that care doesn't eat away at their assets they're planning on passing along to their children and grandchildren."

"So they do it as a hedge to insure[56] that if there are any astronomical expenses, it won't wipe them out," I said.

"That's right and that's why some children will go out and buy policies for their parents."

"So should I buy a policy for myself?"

"Hah," he said slapping his knee. "You're too young David. You should wait until you're around 40 years old to buy a policy, because you don't want to be paying premiums for too many years before you'll actually need LTC. But in reality, each individual is different and therefore should make the decision to either buy or pass on LTC based on their unique situation. If they decide to purchase LTC, the timing of their purchase is also dependent upon their particular financial

---

[56] Pun intended.

situation. Just know that **the longer you wait to get coverage, the more your premiums will likely be.**[57]"

"So I should wait until I'm 40 or so?"

He nodded. "I know it's difficult to even think about making payments on something you might not need for 20 to 30 years after you purchase the policy, especially when you have to pay for your current life insurance and living expenses, but LTC deserves a look. It's a very expensive way to get '*peace of mind*' for knowing that you'll be taken care of until the day you die. Only you can determine if the benefit of '*peace of mind*' is worth the high premiums."

Scary Facts Regarding Long-Term Care Needs
- Two out of five people age 65 or older will need long-term care.
- One in four will spend more than a year in a home at some point in their life.
- The average cost of a nursing home is over $40,000 a year.
- Do I really need to post any other statistics?

Should You Buy Long-Term Care Insurance?

You should _not_ buy long term care insurance if:
- You can't afford the premiums.
- You have limited assets.
- Your only source of income is a Social Security benefit or Supplemental Security Income (SSI).
- You often have trouble paying for basic needs, such as food, medicine, housing, or utilities.

You should consider buying long term care insurance if:
- You have significant assets and income.
- You want to protect some of your assets and income.
- You want to pay for your own care.
- You want to stay independent of the support of others.

Source: The National Association of Insurance Commissioners

Additional Resources
Web-Sites:
The Long Term Care site: (www.longtermcare.com)
LTC Insurance National Advisory Council:
www.LongTermCareInsurance.org
GE Financial: www.gefn.com
Mr. Long-Term Care: www.mr-longtermcare.com

---

[57] I just ran a quote on the Internet and the monthly premiums for a 65-year-old was twice that of a 55-year old. Twice!!!

Car Insurance

Driving Safely

"Next up in our insurance discussion is car insurance, which protects against any potential damage to your car or injuries that are caused by your car. The cost of insurance can vary greatly depending on your age, your choice of coverage, size of your deductible, where you live, what car you drive, and too many other factors. Your car insurance policy is actually a package of several different types of coverage. But thankfully I'm not going to bore you with all the details on the various types of coverage, but you should know that they include: bodily injury, property damage, medical payments, personal injury protection, uninsured, underinsured motorist protection, collision, and comprehensive protection."

"That's a lot of stuff to consider," I commented.

"It is, but your insurance agent or a site like www.insure.com can walk you through all the items. I will cover three kinds of coverage for you today. **Liability Insurance** is required by most states and covers damage done by your car to other people's cars and property. You should have at least a minimum of $50,000 as a starting point, but I recommend you go with a higher amount, anywhere from $100,000 to say $250,000 per individual, $100,000 for property, and between $300,000 and $500,000 per accident. The most expensive part of auto insurance comes from liability insurance, but you shouldn't skimp on coverage in an attempt to lower your premiums."

"Is there any way to reduce your costs?"

"**You can keep auto insurance premiums low by taking the highest deductibles you can afford**. Deductibles are normally somewhere around $500 or $1,000. You can also reduce your costs by receiving additional discounts if your car has a security system, antilock brakes, or air bags. You even save money if you take a defensive driver course."

Dropping Your Comprehensive and Collision Coverage?

"Now **Collision** insurance pays for the damage to your car while driving it, while **Comprehensive** covers non-collision expenses like vandalism, theft and natural disasters. If you're driving a car that's older than five to seven years, then it probably has a low blue-book value,[58] so you might consider dropping your collision and your comprehensive coverage."

---

[58] An industry term for the estimated depreciated value of the car based on the model, age of the car, and mileage.

"But if I get into an accident, then my insurance company won't pay for the damages. Then what?"

"David, if your car isn't worth much, your insurance company is probably not going to give you a lot of money to replace it, but in the mean time you're paying a lot in insurance premiums every month. At that point, you probably could cover the total cost of repairs or replacement out of your Emergency Fund. Okay. Enough about car insurance," he said. "Now let's talk about your home or in your case, your future home."

Homeowner's Insurance

Home Safe Home

"Your house is probably going to be your biggest purchase or 'investment' in your lifetime, so you should protect it. Your lender is probably going to require that you buy homeowner's insurance, but even if they don't, you should purchase a policy because it could cost you a lot of money to replace your personal property and the contents inside if you don't have a homeowner's policy. Now your policy should have dwelling coverage and should include a **guaranteed replacement cost provision** that will ensure that the insurance company will rebuild the home even if the cost of rebuilding exceeds the coverage you purchased. Now most policies don't cover flood damage and a host of other natural disasters, so you may have to seek out separate coverage for these catastrophes."

"What about the stuff inside my house?" I asked.

"Your homeowner's policy should cover most of your personal property. Most policies cover anywhere from 50 to 75 percent of the total dwelling coverage. It's wise to keep an inventory of your valuables. The best way to do it is to list each of the items and how much you paid for them on a sheet of paper. Then, you should walk through your house with a video camera and film all the contents. Keep the tape and inventory list in a safe place somewhere *other than your home*. For expensive assets and items, you should also look into purchasing a rider or what's called a 'floater' to cover your valuables like computers, stereo equipment, collectibles, jewelry, and other expensive items."

"Got it," I said, writing down the information.

"Lastly, homeowner's insurance contains **liability coverage**, which protects you and the members of your household against lawsuits for injuries or property damage that you or your family members may have caused accidentally, but more on this coverage later."

Renter's Insurance

Rental Safe Rental

"As a renter, you don't have to worry about insuring the building you live in. That's your landlord's headache," he said. "However, you do need to buy a policy to cover your possessions. You should buy replacement cost coverage for your valuables and go through the same process of writing out a list of your assets and their value and putting the list in a safe place. You also should make sure you have liability insurance as part of your policy. Most policies have this coverage, but just double-check. The policies are cheap enough, going for as little as $100 per year and they can save your butt should someone get hurt in your apartment."

"That's pretty cheap," I commented.

"It is pretty cheap and even if it was a little bit more than that, you can always save money by seeing if your auto insurer offers renter's insurance. **You should always be able to get a discount by offering all your insurance business to one insurance company.**"

Umbrella Policies & Personal Liability Insurance

Protecting Yourself from Lawsuits and More

"I want to briefly cover personal liability insurance which is insurance that protects you in the event that you are sued or cause damage to someone else," he replied.

"Didn't you just say that most people have liability insurance through their home insurance?" I asked. "Why do you need more?"

"You're right, but **the coverage under your home policy might not be adequate**. If someone slips and falls on your front steps, breaks a leg, or is disabled for life, you better believe they're suing you and can easily win a judgement. Homeowner's insurance policies and auto policies have liability limits. For instance, the typical auto policy would have a liability limit of $300,000 per accident, but it might be close to nothing if you opted for lower coverage in an attempt to save some money on your premiums. Let's say you're sued for a $1 million by someone you get into an accident with and you lose the case. If your auto policy covers the first $300,000, guess who has to come up with the difference?"

"Me," I replied, pointing to myself.

"That's right and it will come out of your assets and if you don't have $700,000 lying around you could be forced to sell your house, your car, your jewelry, your…"

"I get it. I get it," I said, raising my hands in surrender.

"A personal liability policy would kick in after your car or home policy is used up and reached its limit."

"So how much personal liability insurance do you need?" I asked.

"Good question and it depends on how much you have to lose if someone were to sue you. Take a look at that net worth statement you created and if you're looking at quite a few digits, then it might make sense to insure against at least that amount and a little extra. **Some experts suggest that you have a personal liability or an umbrella policy of at least twice your net worth**, but like I said, it all depends on your situation and the likelihood that you'll be sued. Certain professions like doctors and lawyers have a higher probability of being sued than say an office worker."

"How much does a liability policy cost?"

"Liability policies are pretty cheap. For as little as $150 to $200 a year you can get a million bucks worth of coverage. Just note that rates will vary by area of the country and your profession."

"Wow. That is cheap! Especially when you think of how much coverage they give you."

"Which is why every junior wealth-builder should have an umbrella insurance policy. Most people would be good with a million-dollar policy and it will cost them less than $200 a year in most cases."

"Got it. I have a silly question. Why is it called an umbrella policy?" I asked.

He smiled. "Because it covers or extends past what your current insurance (auto and homeowners) doesn't cover and acts like a shield for you. Not a silly question at all. Let's move on."

Estate Planning

Guarding Your Estate

"Estate planning is the management of your assets and valuables so that you can transfer them upon your death to those you wished to receive your stuff. It involves writing a will and setting up different types of trusts if necessary, giving to your charities and your children over the course of several years leading up to your death. In addition, estate planning involves setting up your funeral and burial plans in advance so that everything goes according to *your* plan when you die, not someone else's plan."

"Who else would inherit your stuff?" I asked.

"Try the state. When you die without a will, a probate court will take over and try and determine what you wanted to do with your assets and how you wanted them distributed."

"How can they know what I wanted to do?" I asked.

"Good question. Ponder that one for a while and you'll soon realize why it's so important to have an estate plan, regardless of how much you're worth."

Estate Planning 101

"I'm going to give you a basic overview of the process and what you need to consider, but you should consult with a professional advisor and/or lawyer when it comes time to plan your estate. Planning your estate means taking stock of all your property, assets, heirlooms, etc. and figuring out what you want to happen to them after you die. You should figure out in advance who gets what and you should double-check the beneficiaries on your retirement plans and insurance policies. The easiest way to lay it all out for everyone to see is through a will. Unfortunately, **only one in every three Americans has a will**. At least these people will have their money passed on to their heirs. As for the other two-thirds, who knows who will get their money."

Wills

"A will is literally a legal document or declaration of how you want to give away your assets when you die. The idea behind having a will is to make sure that the people and things you care about are well taken care of when you die. You want your liabilities satisfied or paid off and you want to make sure that the remaining assets are distributed according to your wishes. When there is no will, assets are frozen and the court will pay off the deceased's debts, then the remaining assets will be dispersed according to state guidelines."

"Not cool," I commented.

"It happens more than it should. I've seen widows wind up with close to nothing and money tied up in the legal system for years and years, while the children of the deceased waited and waited for the money their parent wanted them to have. In short, the disbursement of your assets is not something to leave to chance. Fortunately, at least things like your pension rights, life insurance benefits, and IRA or 401(k) assets will be paid directly to the beneficiaries you named while you were alive. Your home, depending on how the property is deeded, will in all likelihood pass on to your spouse if they were a joint owner."

"But everything else could get hung up in court without a will, right?" I asked.

"That's why you need a will David, so the people you want to get your assets will receive them when you die. Another important thing to do is have an **executor** of your estate. This person will help to carry out your wishes. Of course you need to realize that you can't avoid the probate court regardless of whether you have a will or not."

"So what's the point then?" I asked.

"The point is that it will take a fraction of the time to execute and finalize the distribution of your assets when you have a will. It's easy for the court to name an executor because the person is listed in your will. Unless your will is contested by one of your heirs, it's easy for the court to dole out your assets because you've indicated how you would like them disbursed."

"Oh. I get the difference now," I said.

Guardians

"Another thing to include in your will are the names of the individuals who will be your children's guardians when you die. This makes sure your kids will be taken care of by the people you trust and whom you think will do the best job raising your kids. You also avoid subjecting your kids to a drawn-out custody battle between your siblings, parents, or friends. Now your will also tells everyone how you want your assets distributed, but should you get into an accident and slip into a coma, that's another story. This is why you need to have a **durable power of attorney for your health care and finances**, as well as a living will drawn up."

A Living Will

"A living will tells your health care providers how to treat you should you become seriously ill, mentally incapacitated, or become unable to speak for yourself. I've heard it described as a '**letter to loved ones**' that tells them what to do should you become incapacitated. This way they don't have to agonize over any decisions. They just do what you would have wanted done, as outlined in your living will. Make sure your doctor has a copy and keep a copy with the rest of your medical records."

Power of Attorney

"A power of attorney designates someone to act on our behalf should you become incapable of making decisions on your own."

A Health-Care Durable Power of Attorney: A health-care power of attorney is also called a health care proxy. This document assigns someone to act on your behalf on all health care issues. They will make those big decisions on how to treat you should you become incapacitated.

A "Finances" Durable Power of Attorney: A "finances" durable power of attorney handles your finances should you be incapacitated or find yourself on your deathbed. This person will handle your finances, pay your bills, make your deposits, and handle all aspects of your financial house. It's wise to have one of these set up because you don't want to have your unscrupulous nephew handling your finances while you're in the hospital.

Tax Planning

"Not to be missed in all of this is the importance of minimizing the tax hit from settling your estate. In fact, developing strategies to minimize taxes is often the most important part of the estate planning process. Normally your estate pays the taxes and the balance of your assets or what's left over is passed on to your beneficiaries. The first $1 million in assets in 2002 are not subject to federal estate taxes. That $1 million number rises to $3.5 million in 2009 and during this time period, the highest tax rate drops from 50% to 45%."

"What happens in 2010?" I asked.

"After 2009 it's up to Congress to determine new limits."

"Got it. So what exactly makes up your estate?" I asked.

What's Your Taxable Estate?

"Your taxable estate is the sum of all your assets that will be taxed upon your death. In order to calculate your taxable estate, you need to determine the value of all your assets including any life or mortgage insurance proceeds minus the assets that would be given to charity or your spouse. There's an **unlimited marital deduction** which means one spouse can pass an unlimited amount of assets tax-free to the other spouse."

"So you can give your assets to your spouse tax-free and avoid paying taxes, sweet!" I said.

Joint Tenancy

"Yes, but not so fast David. The first $1 million in assets is tax-free, but when you hold assets in joint tenancy your spouse has the right of survivorship and the assets are automatically transferred to them. By giving all your money to your spouse, you just *gave away* your $1 million exemption. That can be a costly mistake, especially since estate tax rates can top out at close to 50%. So depending on your situation, it might make sense to give away the first $1 million in assets in order to avoid your heirs having to pay taxes on the amount in a few years when your spouse passes away. Now let's move on to giving gifts," he said, flipping the page in his binder.

Consider your Gift Giving

"You currently can give away $11,000 a year in cash, stock, property, or other assets to as many people as you want without incurring a gift tax. Based on the current law you can give away a total of $1 million in your lifetime as I just stated. This means that if you've given away $200,000 thus far in your life, you have another $800,000 that you can give away. If you're interested in giving away more money, you'll need a plan. A trust might be the best way to go for you."

"What's a trust?" I asked.

Trusts

"**A trust is a *separate entity* that holds assets and property of yours, but you still get to maintain control over the assets while you're alive**. A trust is great because when you die, these assets will not be considered part of your estate and will not be subject to estate taxes. Any property that you place in a trust goes directly to the beneficiary without having to deal with the trials and tribulations of probate."

"How do you put your assets in a trust and still maintain control of them?" I asked.

"Easy. Make yourself the trustee of that trust. The trustee is the person who oversees how the assets are managed. In the meantime, you can still use your assets for the benefit of you and your beneficiaries. Of course how you use the assets depends on the trust you set up because **statutes may regulate when and how payments can be made out of trusts**."

"Still, it sounds like a sweet deal. You avoid paying estate taxes and you get to provide for your loved ones."

"It is a 'sweet deal' as you put it, but you should definitely read up on them before running to your lawyer to set up one since there are many types of trusts, but your lawyer can help you select the one that makes the most sense for you."

He paused and motioned toward my binder. "Just for your notes," he said, "the most **common trusts include; irrevocable life insurance, charitable remainder, revocable living, marital, and bypass trusts.** To reiterate what we've covered, living trusts are helpful come estate tax time because they help avoid the costs and perhaps reduce the time in probate. In short, a living trust will help shelter your assets from creditors and speed up the transfer of your assets to your heirs."

"Are they expensive to set up?"

"It depends on where you live and the cost of legal advice, but you should be able to set them up for anywhere from $1,000 to $5,000. The money is well spent. I have a charitable remainder trust set up, but you should meet with an attorney to figure out which trust makes sense for you and whether or not you even need to set up one."

"I think the cost would be well justified," I commented.

"When you get to the Striving, Capitalist, and Charitable stages in life you'd better believe the cost is worth it," he replied. "Trusts can save you thousands upon thousands of dollars.

Guard Your Wealth: Estate Planning - COMMENTS

I tried to give you the basics of estate planning and hopefully you understood what I was talking about because this stuff can get complicated pretty quickly. The bottom line is that you need to plan ahead for the day you die in order to make sure that your assets are distributed according to how you would like to give them away. You can go the do-it-yourself route and get many of the legal documents you need drawn up via a software program like Quicken Family Lawyer or www.nolopress.com, but I think it pays to make the investment in having a competent lawyer do the work for you.

Save yourself some time and money when you visit your attorney. Have a list of all your assets and liabilities (in other words your net worth statement), who you want to give your assets away to, your choice for an executor and guardian, and any other thoughts or questions you have. Attorneys charge a lot of money and I'm guessing that you make less per hour than they do. Save yourself some cash and go prepared to your first meeting, but don't be afraid to ask questions.

Guard Your Identity

Protect Your Identity

"In 2002, roughly 160,000 people had their identities stolen and that number will definitely rise with the increased usage of online banking and online purchases, because identity thieves don't need much information to steal your identity. A Social Security number is all you need to apply for credit cards, loans, bank accounts, passports, and just about everything else in this world. You're on the hook for the goods in most cases and have to prove that someone else made the charges. There are services that will monitor your credit for a fee of between $40 and $80 annually. I'd say skip the services and do the job yourself every six months to a year. You already know that you can get all three of your credit reports for under $40."

"What can I do to stop my identity from being stolen?" I asked.

"There are steps you can take to protect yourself. For instance:

- Never leave any passwords lying around and don't use the same passwords for everything.
- Order your credit report regularly and check to make sure the information is accurate.
- Check your credit card statements thoroughly each month to make sure someone isn't charging anything to your account.
- Don't give out your Social Security number if possible. Even if your school or work wants to use the number as your ID number, ask to change it if possible. Banks, your employer, and the IRS are pretty much the only ones that really need to know your SS#.
- Buy a shredder! Don't throw out any bank or credit card statements without shredding them first. Shred those stupid daily offers for new credit cards and loans you receive in the mail.

For more tips, go to: www.consumer.gov/idtheft

"In the course of a busy day, you may write a check at the grocery store, charge tickets to a ball game, rent a car, mail your tax returns, call home on your cell phone, order new checks, or apply for a credit card. **Everyday transactions that you may never give a second thought to are an identity thief's bread and butter**. Each of these transactions requires the sharing of personal information: your bank and credit card account numbers; your income, Social Security number and name, address and phone numbers, to name a few. While you can't prevent identity theft, you can <u>minimize your risk</u> by managing your personal information wisely."

- US Government's Identity Theft Web-Site

Guard Yourself from Yourself

"I'm going to go over the next two sections of this Secret pretty quickly, because I think they're relatively easy to understand, especially when compared to insurance and tax planning," he said.

Your Investments: Diversify or Die?

"As you've learned over the past few years, most investors are very emotional and hurt themselves by selling when they should be buying and vice versa. The only investment strategy that has worked over time is to buy no load, low-cost index funds and continue to buy them on a regular basis. You've also learned to diversify your investments according to a proper asset allocation. Unfortunately, most of us are still looking for the next blockbuster stock and we're not willing to invest the boring, but proven way through index funds."

"But I can have my **Vegas Account** for excitement, right?" I asked.

"Correct. You can try to beat the market in that one *small* account and leave the *majority* of your money in index funds."

The Wealth Effect

"In the late '90s, there was a lot written about something called the wealth effect. In a nutshell, what happened was that a bunch of regular Joes and Janes, bolstered by soaring stock and 401(k) accounts, began spending like drunken sailors because they were rich on paper. As you know, that bubble burst and those folks were left with a mountain of debt. I'm bringing this up because if you put the Secrets of Wealth to work for you, you'll see your net worth growing and growing over time. Don't let it go to your head. Keep your nose to the grindstone and stick to your spending and investing plan. **Your end goal is Financial Freedom, not 'Lifestyles of the Rich and Famous.™'**"

"Darn. I really had a dream of being interviewed by Robin Leach," I said, slapping my hands down on the table.

"Spare yourself the scrutiny and stay humble David," he replied. "Now let's talk about your partner in life."

"Discipline comes through self-control. This means that one must control all negative qualities. **Before you can control conditions, you must first control yourself.** Self-mastery is the hardest job you will ever tackle. If you do not conquer self, you will be conquered by self. By stepping in front of a mirror, you may see at one and the same time both your best friend and your greatest enemy."

- Napoleon Hill

Guard Your Wealth from Your Spouse

Spouse Support

"Your spouse is an important ally in your quest to become Financially Free. Unfortunately for some, their spouse isn't supporting their efforts. I've heard it all before:

"All the other wives get to stay home with their kids. How come I have to work?"
"They get to go on vacation to Hawaii, how come we can't?"
"Bob has two cars. Why can't I buy a sports car for myself? I work so hard and I deserve it."
"That real estate stuff doesn't work. How many hours have you wasted looking in the paper?"
"Why don't you get a second job instead of trying to be a landlord?"
"How come you don't buy me nice things?"
"You don't make enough money."
"When are you going to get a real job and quit trying to build that great business of yours? I'm sick of being the sole bread winner in this house."
"This certainly is not the lifestyle I signed up for when we got married."

"These comments and others like them are tiny little daggers that can kill any wealth-building program," he said. "You see David, **the journey toward Financial Freedom is supposed to be a group project for a family, not a one-man or woman solo act.** If you're truly going to build a well-oiled wealth-building machine, you're going to need the support of your spouse in order to put the Secrets of Wealth in place. After all, if you're busy saving and watching your cash flow, but they're out spending like a drunken sailor, you'll never get ahead. Never!"

Share Your Vision of the Future

"Unfortunately, some people never think past their wedding to the kind of life they want to live with their partner. Perhaps they dated for a few years or less and all they've known is their separate lives. Each might have a different view of how they want to live their married life. Sitting down to discuss your finances, how many kids you want to have, how you'll spend your money, and so on are all conversations that should happen *before* you take that walk down the aisle."

"Sounds like a fun conversation to have," I said sarcastically.

"They might not be the most 'fun' of conversations to have, but they are critical to your financial future."

"But how do you know what to talk about?" I asked. "I mean the future is the future and you can't predict how you'll react to job changes and things like that."

"I disagree David. You can plan for your future in advance and you can at least share your vision of how you *think* you want to live your life. You can also discuss what you value most: career, family, security, freedom, adventure, and a whole host of different values and the priority order of your values. The key is to listen openly and not comment while your partner goes through their vision of the future. Then when it's your turn, you go through you envision things and discuss what's most important to you and why. You need to set aside some quiet time where you're not going to be interrupted. Get in a comfortable environment and just start talking."

"About what?" I asked.

"I'm not going to list out all the things you need to ask and go through together, but I will give you a partial list of some things to consider in the area of finances. Just remember that money is often a taboo subject and these questions are personal, so some people might be a little hesitant to start a conversation around the topic of money."

Questions about Finances

- What are your financial goals?
- Do you believe it's important to achieve Financial Freedom?
- Do you think we should live below our means?
- How big of a cash cushion do you feel we need?
- What role does charity play in our lives? Should we give away some of our money each year?
- Who is going to handle the household budget?
- Are we going to have joint or separate credit cards, checking and savings accounts, and are we going to jointly own all our assets?
- How was money handled when you were growing up? Perhaps it was the job of the husband in one family and the mother in another.
- Do we have adequate life insurance?

"The key is to talk about your money habits, which involves your spending habits, credit history, and investment strategies. You need to have an open and honest dialogue to figure out what is most important for the two of you, including what your values are and what your goals are in life. **Through the process of talking, you can align your goals and create a plan of action that both of you can agree on.**"

"You know you could be a marriage counselor the way you talk."

"I doubt I'd give Dr. Phil a run for his money, but finances and married life are intertwined so you need to work together or else the marriage isn't going to go too far," he replied.

More Hard Questions

"I could go on and on about the questions to ask each other and discuss with your future spouse, but all you need to do is go out and buy one little book called *The Hard Questions: 100 Essential Questions to Ask Before You Say "I Do"* by Susan Piver. It's an excellent book and it's the perfect companion for the type of conversations you need to have with your future spouse before you walk down the aisle."

Living Below Your Means

"We've already covered living below your means in Secret #5, but it bears repeating. By now you understand that achieving Financial Freedom is within your reach and you can conduct your finances and life in such a way to increase your odds of becoming Financially Free. You can get there without earning any additional income, but you're going to have to cut out some of your current expenditures if you want to be successful."

"But it's not about cutting everything out, right?" I added.

"Right," he replied. "Remember that **I'm not talking about being cheap or a miser or anything like that**. You work hard so you should enjoy the things that your hard-earned money can buy you, but you need to make sure that you're not going overboard and that you're properly funding your investment portfolio and not collecting a bunch of cash-sucking liabilities that will bleed you dry and put you in hock until the day you die."

"That's a pretty picture," I said, trying to add humor to the dismal picture he was painting.

"It's a grim one indeed and by the time you turn 30 and some of your friends get married and have kids, you'll see how important our conversation today was. You'll see how devastating living above your means can be. I'm not trying to scare you, just show you how important it is to live below your means as a method of guarding your future and helping guarantee that you'll be able to retire in style. **You need to buy into the idea of prudent and smart spending and so does your spouse**. Adopt the frugal mindset and you'll be glad you did."

"I get where you're coming from," I said.

"It's one of the best Secrets to hold close to your heart and take action on David," he replied.

Guard Your Wealth: From Yourself - ACTION PLAN

You Can't Beat the Market. No Really: Set up your autopilot investment plan and stop trying to beat the market. You can do your trading in your Vegas Account if you like, but leave 90% to 95% of your other investment dollars alone and put the money toward no-load, low-cost index funds.

Forget the Luxuries, Gadgets, and Useless Stuff…for Now: Everyone has their vices, be it the latest tech gadgets, exercise tape sets, or latest fashion accessories that they fall prey to. You shouldn't waste your money on this stuff now. You can "invest" your money on these things when you reach million-dollar status, not before.

Living Below Your Means: You should know that this is one of the keys to Financial Freedom by now. As Nike says, Just do it!

Guard Your Wealth from Your Spouse – ACTION PLAN

Create a Budget: But don't let it strangle you. You need some leeway in the amounts each of you is allowed to spend. This could be difficult at first if neither of you have never had a budget. In addition, the both of you will also be encountering a lot of expenses you've never had before. The 30-day journal we talked about in Secret #3 will work for the both of you. Carry around a pad and write down all your expenses for the month. After you include your utilities, car, mortgage, school, and other reoccurring monthly payments, you have yourselves a working budget.

Cut Expenses: This one is self-explanatory. Upon viewing your monthly budget, if the both of you go into cardiac arrest, it's time to question some of the miscellaneous expenses and see if you can trim them. Question everything and be ready to compromise and be willing to give up some of your little "luxuries" for the betterment of your financial future.

Pay Yourselves First: If it's not a habit by the time you get married, then it should become one after you're married. It's too easy to spend every last penny when you're busy redecorating your new place or dining out. Commit to socking away at least 10 percent of your pay into your investment plan. An investment of $300 a month will grow to over a million bucks after 40 years with an 8% annual return. That should be motivation enough to start paying yourselves first.

Create a Debt Repayment Plan: If you have outstanding bad debt, particularly credit card debt, then you should discuss it openly and create a debt repayment plan. Don't place blame if one spouse is coming into the marriage with a lot of debt. It's now a joint problem and both of you have to work together to reduce the debt.

Commit to a Long-Term Investment Plan: If you have one spouse who is an aggressive investor and one who is more passive, then you're going to have to come together and figure out the best way to invest for the both of you. Perhaps it's allowing the aggressive spouse to have their own investing account (read: Vegas account), while the rest of the money is invested in no-load, low-cost, index funds.

Commit to Becoming Financially Free: You're obviously reading this book for a reason.   Hopefully it's one of your goals to become Financially Free and if so, it should be your spouse's goal as well. As part of your frank and open discussion, make the commitment that you're going to arrange your spending, budgeting, and investing habits in such a way to make it easier to achieve Financial Freedom. Commit and take action today!

Review Your Progress Monthly: Usually one spouse gets the financial duties, while the other contributes little to the management of household finances. This is a less than idea situation for the spouse who doesn't handle the finances. Why? What happens to them if their spouse dies or leaves them? They know nothing about finances or how to invest their money. To combat this, set up a monthly meeting to go over the finances and investments. Both of you should know where your money is going and how your investments are performing. Marriage is a team sport. Your finances should be too.

Create a Reward System: You should reward yourselves for following your plan. Perhaps it's a night on the town or a new gadget for meeting an investing goal. Whatever it is, celebrate and have fun. You deserve it. You're in this together, so don't forget that.

One Final Thought
A subscriber of my newsletter sent me the following after I sent out an article about the importance of your spouse to your success in building wealth:

Marrying incorrectly = wealth eater
Marrying correctly = wealth builder

Take a look at the above equations again. Aren't they 100% true?

"No matter what happens the rest of your life you may never again utter these words: "Whatever you want to do, Honey." Wrong, cop-out breath, you have to stick in there and make this work. And as you sit there, you must be a grown-up and realize that we cannot spend more than we make and have financial security or build wealth. Your wants, needs, and desires must be combined with your family's, and the new total must be less than your family income."

> \- Dave Ramsey, from *Financial Peace Revisited*

Chapter 21

Guard Your Wealth from Uncle Sam

I don't claim to be a tax expert, nor would any of my mentors claim to be accounting experts (except for my accountant of course). What follows is a brief overview of definitions, forms, and tax strategies. I tried to give you accurate, up-to-date information on recent tax law changes, but you should always check current rules and work with a tax expert when filing your tax return or making any investment or decision that has major tax implications. Now that the legal disclaimer is done with, let's learn something about taxes, shall we?

The Tax Man Cometh

"Next up in our discussion on how to guard your wealth is taxes. Taxes can have such a debilitating effect on your portfolio returns over the course of time and they effect your ability to build up a sizeable nest egg. Why? Because **every dollar you pay Uncle Sam in taxes is a dollar that will never get to work for you**," Mr. Mathers said, pounding his fist into his hand. "That's a dollar that will never earn a return for you because it's been taken from your wealth building machine. Taxes are an inevitable part of life, but today we're going to talk about ways of reducing the pain of taxes by minimizing your taxable gains and deferring the payment of taxes."

Your Tax Return

"Every year you have to file your tax return by April 15th for the previous years' income. If you're running behind schedule, you can **file for an extension**, which is usually good for another four months. Filing your return is essentially a process whereby you settle up with the Internal Revenue Service to make sure that you've paid all the taxes you were supposed to. Some people actually file taxes on a quarterly basis.[59] Usually these people are self-employed or commissioned salespeople. It's a bit more complicated for them, but for the majority of workers, the process of paying their taxes is quite simple. You get a W-2 form from your employer that details your total wages from your job, as well as any tax-deferred contributions you may have made during the year. You then fill out Form 1040EZ and you're good to go. If you have an investment account, things are a little bit more difficult. You'll receive a Form 1099, which will report the interest you've

---

[59] Quarterly taxes are due on January 15, April 15, June 15 & September 15.

earned, any dividends you may have received, and you'll also receive a form that details your stock purchases and sales throughout the year. You will have to fill out the regular version of Form 1040 or the so-called 'long form.' You might even have to fill out some additional forms or 'schedules' to further detail your income."

"Sounds very complicated," I said.

"It is and it isn't. It all depends on your situation, but the process really is simple. You add up your total income and subtract any deductions to determine what your taxable income is, then apply the appropriate tax rates and then subtract any tax credits you might be entitled to which results in either a tax refund or you owing Uncle Sam money."

"You make it sound so easy," I said. "The last time I tried to do my taxes, I went nuts."

"That's because you had all those stock transactions to sort through, but if you took the time to read through the booklet that accompanies most tax forms, you could figure it out. But at a certain point, usually when you get married or buy a house, I suggest people see a qualified accountant."

"Why do you suggest that?" I asked.

Filing Your Taxes: Man or Machine?

"Well, for those with straightforward tax situations, it makes sense to save the money and file taxes on their own. There are some great tax software packages out there like TurboTax™ that make filing your taxes a snap. However, when you have a little more complexity, it makes sense to see a pro."

"What do you mean by complexity?" I asked.

"When you're self-employed, have a lot of miscellaneous deductions, or if you're going through a divorce to name a few situations, it makes sense to see a professional tax preparer. Another reason to go with a pro is for peace of mind and to save your precious time," he quickly added.

"Okay, so how do you find a good accountant?" I asked.

"Word of mouth works best. Just ask your friends, family members, and coworkers who they use and if they're happy with the results. Just make sure the person is a Certified Public Accountant or CPA for short. During your first meeting, you should ask to see their credentials before you start working with them."

"Got it," I said, writing the information down.

"There's one more reason to go with a pro," he offered.

"What is it?"

The Tax Reconciliation Act of 2001 and
The Jobs & Growth Tax Relief Reconciliation Act of 2003

"In 2001, President Bush signed the Economic Growth and Tax Relief Reconciliation Act of 2001. The Act significantly changed the tax rates and the amount of money you could contribute to your retirement accounts, as well as made some tweaks to various deductions you could take. All in all I believe the law had over 400 changes to the IRS code.[60] Add on top of that the changes thanks the Jobs & Growth Tax Relief Reconciliation Act of 2003 that President Bush signed and you're looking at some serious changes."

"Please tell me that you're not going to go through all the changes to the tax law today?" I said in a moment of desperation.

"Do you really think I would waste my time reading through all the changes in the tax code?" he asked. "Not a chance. That's why I pay my tax advisors. But I will go through the major changes that affect you, namely the reduction in the tax rates and the increase in the amounts you can contribute to your retirement accounts. We'll go through those changes, then I'm going to take you through some basic strategies to reduce your taxes."

Lower Tax Rates

"First lets talk about the changes in the tax rates," he said, then flipped to a page in his binder and turned it around so I could see.

Figure 21.1 - New Tax Rates from the 2001 and 2003 Tax Acts

Old Tax Rate	2001	2002	2003 - 2010
10%	New	Same	Same
15%	Same	Same	Same
28%	27.5%	27%	25%
31%	30.5%	30%	28%
36%	35.5%	35%	33%
39.6%	39.1%	38.6%	35%

Source: www.irs.gov

"The tax rates were lowered in 2001 and then again in May of 2003 as part of a stimulus package. The idea is to put more money in the hands of taxpayers so that they could turn around and spend that money which would help get our economy out of its' current downturn."

"Makes sense," I said. "I guess the more money people have…"

---

[60] The 2001 law is 291 pages long, has 85 major provisions and 441 changes to the Internal Revenue Code. Try keeping up with those changes if you're not a tax pro. I had to rewrite this Secret twice thanks to changes in the tax law.

"The more they spend," we finished in unison.

"Sad, but true," he added. "But that doesn't mean that you have to spend the 'extra' money the government is allowing you to keep."

FICA Taxes – Social Security and Medicare

"Just realize that this tax rate table," he said pointing to the table, "only shows federal rates and doesn't include any state or FICA taxes."

"'FICA taxes'? What's that?"

"In layman's terms, it's money that gets pulled from your paycheck to pay for Social Security. Currently the Social Security payroll tax rate is 12.4%. An additional 2.9% goes toward Medicare."

I did the math in my head. "So you're saying that there is an additional 15.3% tax on top of the state and federal taxes I pay? That's ridiculous," I said.

"Well if you're a wage or salaried employee you only have to pay half or 7.65% of the tax. Your employer picks up the other half. If you're self-employed, you have to pay the entire 15.3% yourself, but you get to deduct half of the taxes paid as a business expense when you file your taxes."

Not all Dollars are Subject to the Social Security Tax

"Just so you know, not every dollar you earn is subject to the Social Security tax. The tax is limited to the first $87,000 you make."

"What a break," I said sarcastically.

"It might not sound like much, but if you've got a high income and don't have to pay a 6.2% tax on any income over $87,000 it's money in your pocket instead of Uncle Sam's. And every little bit helps. Unfortunately you still have to pay Medicare taxes since there are no income limits on Medicare taxes."

Other Types of Taxes

"Of course you have plenty of other types of taxes," he said. "In some states, there are personal property taxes whereby the government requires you to pay tax on certain types of property. For instance, our neighbors in Connecticut have to pay personal property tax on the value of their cars each year. Then you have real estate property tax where you have to pay taxes to your county based on the value of your home and the land its built on. Capital gains taxes are paid on any profit you have on the sale of an investment that is subject to taxes, i.e. held in a taxable account. Of course you already know about sales tax, which is levied on items as varied as soda to the services you use like auto repairs to filling up your gas tank."

"Now I know why they had the Boston Tea Party," I commented.

Three Categories of Income

"Let's shift gears," he said. "There are three categories of income: gross, adjusted gross, and taxable."

Gross Income is income from wages, commissions and bonuses that you earn and have to pay taxes on before you can take any deductions, credits, or exemptions.

Adjusted Gross Income or AGI as it's commonly referred to as, is your gross income minus any losses from operating a business or contributions you make to qualified retirement plans like your 401(k) or Traditional IRAs.

Taxable Income is calculated by taking your income and subtracting all your exemptions and deductions from your AGI.

How to Reduce Your Taxes

"So now you know the different types of income, the next step is to learn how to legally reduce your taxable income. You can do this in three main ways:

- Minimize your gross income through contributions to qualified retirement accounts and other "above the line" deductions

- Use any allowable itemized deductions

- Reduce your taxable income enough to fall into a lower tax bracket

Four Types of Deductions

"Let's tackle deductions first. There are four main types of deductions: business deductions, adjustments, itemized or standard deductions, and exemptions."

Business Deductions: Business deductions, as the name implies, are deductions you take related to your business.

Adjustments: Adjustments cover things like contributions to your IRA or any alimony you may have paid during the previous year. When you subtract your adjustments from your gross income you get your AGI.

Itemized and Standard Deductions: Something a little more difficult to understand is the difference between itemized and standard deductions. A standard deduction is easy to figure out because all you have to do is look at the chart the IRS provides and you're done.

Standard Deductions

"The standard deduction amounts vary by filing type, but your accountant or tax software package can automatically give you the most up-to-date deduction amounts. You should know that the deduction amounts changed recently thanks to the 2003 Tax Act. **The 2003 standard deductions are** $4,750 for single taxpayers; $9,500 for married couples filing jointly; $7,000 for heads of households; and $3,975 for married couples filing separately. Now, the standard deduction for single taxpayers stays the same, but the deduction for married couples filing jointly jumps to $9,500. The deduction for married couples filing separately is eliminated over the next two years and they will have the same deduction as single taxpayers."

"Sounds like **they did away with the 'Marriage Penalty' Tax.**"

"Yes and no. The so-called Marriage Penalty Tax was due to the fact that two single people would be able to have a greater standard deduction than a married couple. Right now the deduction is equal to the deduction two single people receive, but unfortunately, the standard deduction for married taxpayers falls to 174 percent of the standard deduction for single taxpayers, then steadily rises back to double the amount in 2009. With that said, let's dig deeper into deductions."

Above the "Line" vs. Below the "Line" Deductions

"Pretend there is an imaginary line between your gross income and AGI and there are certain deductions that are 'above the line' and others that are 'below the line.'"

"Why the difference?" I asked.

"You calculate your AGI by subtracting 'above the line' expenses from your income. Everyone gets to take the deductions that are qualified as 'above the line' and only some people get to take the 'below the line' deductions. Everyone can take the above the line deductions regardless of whether they itemize or take the standard deduction?"

Above the Line Deductions

- Deductible retirement contributions from Traditional IRAs, 401(k), Keogh, SEP, or SIMPLE plans
- Medical savings account deductions and self-employed health insurance
- One half of your self-employment taxes
- Moving expenses that are from employment reasons
- Alimony payments (your former spouse pays the taxes due)

Below the Line

"'Below the line' deductions are also called **itemized deductions**. These deductions are more personal relating to charitable, medical, or economic items. Economic items are things that help spur the economy or encourage you to buy a house for example, which is why you get to write off the interest on your home. It used to be that you could write off your credit card interest and interest from personal loans, but they did away with that. 'Below the line' deductions include:

- **Certain Taxes:** State and local income taxes, property, real estate, and unemployment or disability taxes you might have paid.
- **Interest payments** on your home mortgage, second home, mortgage points, investment interest paid, and interest on student and business loans.
- **Miscellaneous deductions**[61] can also be included only after they exceed 2% of your AGI, because the government sees this as the cost of doing business. They include things like subscriptions to work-related journals and publications, fees you paid for your accountant, work-related educational expenses, and qualified job-hunting expenses.
- **Expenses for business purposes.** Things like deductions for the mileage driven, meals that are work-related but not reimbursed; business supplies, union dues, and any educational expenses that you have for improving your skills on the job.
- **Charitable contributions** up to certain limits.
- **Medical expenses**: You can deduct unreimburseable medical expenses for you and your dependants that are greater than 7.5% of your AGI. Premiums, copayments, and prescription medication bills are some of the qualifying costs.

I squeezed my head. "Too much information to handle," I said.

Standard or Itemized – Which is best for you?

"Which is exactly why I have my accountant handle things for me. In any event, as you can see, claiming itemized deductions requires a little more work. You have to add up things like medical expenses, state and local taxes, investment expenses, and any mortgage interest you might have paid during the year. **You're allowed to claim either** *itemized deductions* **or the** *standard deduction,* **whichever is larger**. Most people end up using the standard deduction because they don't have many expenses to itemize or write-off. However, you'll find that when you buy a house and your income gets larger or you have more

---

[61] Check out IRS Publication 529, *Miscellaneous Deductions* for more information.

write-offs in general, you may want to start itemizing your expenses. Check with your accountant to see if you should begin itemizing your taxes."

Exemptions

"Last up are exemptions. These are a little bit easier to figure out. They're listed on a chart provided by the IRS. All you have to do to get a personal exemption is be alive. You also get an exemption for every dependent you have. Just look at the chart, figure out what exemptions you can take, and then add up all your exemptions. Just note that the ability to use exemptions phases out at certain (high) levels of income."

"Okay," I said. "Then what?"

"Then you take all your deductions and exemptions and subtract them from your total income. The result is your taxable income. Next you have to take this amount and multiply it by your applicable tax rates."

"Did you just say 'rates?'"

"Yes, as in multiple rates," he replied.

Marginal Tax Rate

"There are multiple tax rates which means **you pay less tax on the first dollars you earn and a lot more tax on the last dollars you earn**. For example, let's say you made $100,000 a year," he said.

"Thanks for the raise."

"Don't mention it," he said, not missing a beat. "The first $7,000 you earn is taxed at 10%, while every dollar after that up to $28,400 is taxed at 15%. The money you earn between $28,400 and $68,800 is taxed at 25%, while dollars $68,800 to $100,000 are taxed at the 28% rate. This 'tier thing' is very important since every time you enter into a new tier, you pay more in taxes in percentage terms. **Your effective tax rate**, the percentage you paid in taxes, is much *lower* than your top marginal rate."

The Alternative Minimum Tax (AMT): The Parallel Tax System

"Now if that didn't have your head spinning, this next topic will definitely get you confused. There is actually a second tax system that can increase your taxes beyond what we have discussed so far. Lawmakers created the Alternative Minimum Tax or AMT system to make sure that the people who claim a large number of deductions pay at least a minimum amount of tax on their incomes. **In layman's terms, it was created to stop wealthy folks from avoiding the payment of taxes by taking an excessive number of exemptions and deductions**."

"So how does the AMT work?" I asked.

The AMT essentially eliminates many of the deductions and personal exemptions that you are entitled to under the regular tax system. You have to calculate the taxes you would pay under the regular tax system and then calculate the taxes under the AMT. Whichever tax amount is *highest* is what you pay."

"Not cool."

"Exactly. Lawmakers need to revise the AMT laws so as not to penalize the middle-class who can have high deductions thanks to mortgage interest and other qualified deductions. The good news is that they're starting to make changes. Under the Jobs and Growth Tax Relief Act of 2003, the amount of income that was exempt from the AMT was raised to $58,000 for married couples and qualifying widows; $29,000 if you're married filing separately; and $40,250 for singles or head of households. However, if your salary is high enough you don't qualify for the full AMT exemption."

"Sounds like it would involve a lot of math to figure all of it out."

"You're right. There's just too many *ifs* and *buts* involved with filing your taxes when you move up the food chain," he said. "Yet another reason I have a pro do my taxes. Let's move on to credits before we run out of time."

Payments and Credits

"The IRS allows you to claim certain credits that will reduce the taxes you owe; dollar for dollar. The biggest credit you have to subtract is the amount of tax your employer withheld from your paycheck, followed by any estimated tax payments you may have made during the year. There are also education tax credits like the **Hope Scholarship Credit** and the **Lifetime Learning Credit**. You can also deduct a portion of childcare costs."

"You can deduct child care?" I asked.

"Yes, you can deduct a *portion* of the your expenses and the size of the credit depends on your income, so ask your accountant if you're able to take advantage of this credit. Like I said, I'm not an accountant and don't pretend to be, but I know the basics. You should check out the IRS web-site for information on the latest tax credits."

I scratched my head. "Credits are easy to understand, but can you explain the difference between a deduction and an exemption? They sound like the same thing."

"They're not," he replied.

Figure 21.2 – The New Tax Rates from the 2003 Tax Act

Single				
Taxable income is over	But not over	The tax is	Plus % on Excess	Of the amount over
$0	$7,000	-	10%	$0
7,000	28,400	$700.00	15%	7,000
28,400	68,800	3,910.00	25%	28,400
68,800	143,500	14,010.00	28%	68,800
143,500	311,950	34,926.00	33%	143,500
311,950	-	90,514.50	35%	311,950
Married Filing Jointly Qualifying Widow(er)				
Taxable income is over	But not over	The tax is	Plus % on Excess	Of the amount over
$0	$14,000	-	10%	$0
14,000	56,800	$1,400.00	15%	14,000
56,800	114,650	7,820.00	25%	56,800
114,650	174,700	22,282.50	28%	114,650
174,700	311,950	39,096.50	33%	174,700
311,950	-	84,389.00	35%	311,950
Head of Household				
Taxable income is over	But not over	The tax is	Plus % on Excess	Of the amount over
$0	$10,000	-	10%	$0
10,000	38,050	$1,000.00	15%	10,000
38,050	98,250	5,207.50	25%	38,050
98,250	159,100	20,257.50	28%	98,250
159,100	311,950	37,295.50	33%	159,100
311,950	-	87,736.00	35%	311,950
Married Filing Separately				
Taxable income is over	But not over	The tax is	Plus % on Excess	Of the amount over
$0	$7,000	-	10%	$0
7,000	28,400	$700.00	15%	7,000
28,400	57,325	3,910.00	25%	28,400
57,325	87,350	11,141.25	28%	57,325
87,350	155,975	19,548.25	33%	87,350
155,975	-	42,194.50	35%	155,975

Source: www.irs.gov, see (http://www.irs.gov/pub/irs-pdf/i1040tt.pdf)

Deductions vs. Exemptions

"**A deduction reduces your taxable income while a credit directly reduces your taxes**. A deduction reduces what you owe by a percentage for every dollar you deduct. So if you have a $100 donation to a charity and you're in the 25% bracket, you will pay $25 less in federal taxes. On the other hand, a credit will reduce the taxes you pay dollar for dollar. A $100 credit reduces your taxes by $100."

"Simple enough," I commented. "What's next?"

"Well," he replied, "after you've gone through the process of figuring out your taxable income, taking any deductions you might have, and then multiplying the applicable tax rates against your taxable income that is subject to taxes, you then have to take the tax amount you come up with and subtract your credits from it and figure out how much you owe Uncle Sam. If the number is negative, this is the refund amount you have coming to you."

"So that's how I got a refund last year," I commented. "I didn't know how it worked, but I was just happy to get a refund."

Refunds are _NOT_ a Good Thing

"Most people think of their refunds as a bonus and they feel lucky to get it, but they shouldn't David."

"How can a refund be a bad thing?" I asked.

"Because **a tax refund means you've overpaid your taxes for an entire year**. **You've essentially given Uncle Sam an interest free loan**. That's not so smart, is it? The average person had a refund of about $2,050 in 2002. That's $2,050 that they overpaid and its money those folks should have been receiving throughout the year. It's money that could have gone into a retirement fund or toward paying down debt. In surveys, only 30% or less of refund receivers said they are going to use the money to invest with or pay down debt. The rest plan on spending it. Not smart tax planning at all."

"So how do you fix it so you don't overpay?"

"If you're receiving tax refunds due to tax credits and the writing off of losses in the stock market, that's another story, but you shouldn't overpay your taxes due to incorrect information on your W-4 form. You fix the problem by making sure that you claim enough exemptions on your W-4 form. All you have to do is talk to your benefits department and fill out a new one. Based on information you provided on your W-4 form, your employer uses tables provided by the IRS to figure out how much of your paycheck goes to you and how much gets withheld for taxes. You can change the form at any time, but most people only bother when they get married (i.e., change their tax filing status). In addition to your filing status, you choose the number of allowances you want to take."

"'Allowances'? What are those?" I asked.

"Allowance is just another word for exemptions or credits you plan on claiming come tax return time."

Strategies to Cut Your Taxes

"Now that the technical stuff is out of the way," he said, "let's get through the various strategies to cut your taxes and put more money in your pocket."

"Sounds good to me," I said. "I can use all the help I can get!"

EMPLOYMENT INCOME

How Much are You Withholding?

"As we just covered, every year you should double-check with your benefits or payroll department to make sure you are taking the right amount of taxes out. Perhaps you got married, divorced, or maybe your checks were being incorrectly deducted from, but if you're constantly getting refunds, then one tactic to solve this could be to increase the number of exemptions you're taking."

401(k)s, IRAs, and other Tax-Deferred Plans

"As you know from our discussion of Secret #6, a great way for employees to immediately reduce their taxable income is by contributing to tax-sheltered retirement accounts. When you make a contribution to your 401(k) or 403(b) plan at work, you are doing so with gross or pre-tax dollars. The money goes straight into your account and you avoid paying Uncle Sam. The money and any subsequent distributions from mutual funds or interest earned will continue to grow tax-deferred until the funds are withdrawn. **You get the benefit of immediately reducing your taxes and you build up your nest egg at the same time.**"

Flexible Spending Accounts

"As we discussed earlier, a Flexible Spending Account is an account where you can put in pre-tax money to pay out-of-pocket health care, childcare, and dependent care expenses. The money just comes out of your paycheck if you choose to contribute and goes into the account. Then when you have qualified expenses, you just fill out some forms and submit the receipts and you get to pay for your out-of-pocket costs from the FSA. But if you don't use the funds, you lose the money because you can't roll it over into the next year."

"Use it or lose it," I said. "Got it."

College Savings Vehicles

"Okay, next up are ways to save on taxes through college savings vehicles and deductions. Some of the ways to save taxes won't save you money up-front, but they will save you money on the back end because withdrawals are tax-free. Let's go through this in rapid-fire motion:

Coverdell Education Savings Accounts: Formerly known as Education IRAs, the contribution limit has been increased to $2,000 from $500 in 2001. Qualified expenses have also expanded to include elementary and secondary school expenses. Another revision is that you're now able to roll over any unused Education IRA funds into accounts for other family members. Contributions aren't tax deductible, but the withdrawals are tax-free.

529 Plans: These plans were also revised under the Tax Act of 2001. Now the distributions you make from them are tax-free which can save you a bundle in taxes when its time to pay for junior's college bill. There are dozens of programs out there since they vary from state to state. Like the Coverdell Accounts, contributions are not deductible, but withdrawals are tax free. Just note that you have to be below certain income levels to qualify for both the 529 and ESA plans.

Education Expense Deductions: You can now deduct up to $3,000 in qualified tuition and fees for undergraduate or graduate expenses for yourself, your spouse, or your dependents. To qualify the courses must be college level and necessary for your degree. (That basket weaving class you took in college wouldn't be eligible unless you became a professional basket weaver). Make sure not to double-dip by counting expenses twice. What I mean is that you need to first deduct from your total fees and tuition any money you got from an Education IRA, to come up with the net expense amount. Sounds complicated, but it's really not. You also can't take the deduction for the **Hope Scholarship Credit** or **Lifetime Learning Credit** if you're trying to use the $3,000 deduction. The Hope Credit is $1,500 and the Lifetime Learning Credit is $1,000. There are also income limits. You can't have made more than $65,000 if you're single or $130,000 if you file jointly. Unlike the other tax breaks we discussed earlier, this one disappears after 2005.[62]

Student Loan Interest: It used to be that after 60 months of paying your school loan that you would be ineligible to deduct the interest paid. Not any more. You can write-off the interest until you pay off the loan.

---

[62] Check out www.fabmansecrets.com and the article titled "Smart Ways to Cut Down the Cost of College" for more information on this subject.

Charity

"The thing I like about donating my money to charity is that while I'm giving, I'm also receiving something in return: a valuable tax deduction. When you make a charitable contribution to a *qualified* organization, you're allowed to take a deduction against your taxes. For someone in the 25% tax bracket, a $100 donation is really costing you only $75 out of pocket ($100 minus the $25 in tax savings they receive). One of the reasons the rich love to give money to their favorite charities is that typically they're in a higher tax bracket, so their after-tax cost of donating is actually less. For instance, someone in the 35% bracket who made that same $100 donation would receive a $35 tax savings for a total out-of-pocket cost of $65."

"Not a bad perk for being rich and giving your money away."

"No, not too shabby at all," he replied. "**It's my hope that you make it a habit to give to charities for a multitude of reasons**. For now, let's just go over some of the basics, because before you give anything away, you need to know if your charity of choice is a qualified recipient.[63] This means that the government recognizes them as a entity being exempt from U.S. income tax. Your contributions are deductible in the year that you made them and donations made via a credit card are deductible immediately."

"Any limitations on how much you can give?" I asked.

"Check with your accountant or tax advisor, but most people won't have to worry about limitations unless they give away more than 20% of their adjusted gross income. There is another cutoff of 50% of your AGI and I personally don't understand all the rules."

"What about donating clothes to the Salvation Army?"

"Right. **You don't have to donate cash to get a tax deduction**. You can donate old clothes, cars, furniture, and equipment to a charitable organization. **Just remember to get a receipt** when you do so or else your accountant is going to throw a fit because you need a receipt in order to claim the deduction. You should always get written proof from the organization, especially if your donation is over $250.[64] **A canceled check isn't going to cut it**."

"What about donating your time like at a soup kitchen?" I asked.

"While your time is definitely money when you're at work, you get nothing in terms of a deduction for your services from the Tax Man."

"Well at least you get a deduction for donating money," I said.

"What's even a better deal is **donating appreciated assets** and getting the benefit of deducting for the market value of the security or

---

[63] See IRS Publication 78 for a list of organizations that qualify.
[64] According to the Omnibus Budget Reconciliation Act of 1993.

assets. If you sell an appreciated asset, you're going to pay capital gains on it. However, if you donate it to a charity, you can take a charitable deduction for the market value of the asset (real estate, securities, etc.) and you thereby pass the gains on to the charity. Then they can sell the asset and not pay taxes on the gains."

"Wow. That's pretty cool."

"Like I said. **You *can* give and receive at the same time.**"

Gifts

"What about gifts from family members. Are they tax deductible?" I asked.

"Nope. A gift between individuals doesn't produce a deduction for the donor or income for the recipient. However, if you give more than the exclusion amount, which is $11,000 in 2002 to someone other than your spouse, things get a little more complicated. Check with your accountant if you plan on giving away anything in excess of $11,000."

"I don't think I'll be doing that any time soon."

He laughed at my comment. "There are exceptions to the limits. You can give an unlimited amount for the payment of medical expenses or education, as long as you pay the money directly to the hospital or university."

"That's understandable," I commented.

"Oh," he said, tapping his finger on the side of his head. "One more thing. There is a lifetime limit on what you can give away. In 2003, the amount or cap was $1,000,000. For tax-planning and estate purposes, you need to keep it in mind."

Estate Taxes

"We just went over this ten minutes ago, but your estate can pass assets on to your heirs free of federal estate taxes up to the $1 million limit. The exemption increases to $3.5 million and then disappears in 2010, but it'll be back in 2011 with a $1 million exemption and a top rate of 55%. After that, it's up to Congress to amend the law. As I mentioned earlier, a living trust can help you avoid the costly and long process of probate. Just thought I'd throw this idea in here because you really can save a lot in taxes if you know what you're doing."

"I've got it," I said, writing down the information. "Perhaps some day I will need to know more about trusts."

"It's almost guaranteed if you follow the Secrets of Wealth very closely David," he replied.

BUSINESS & SELF-EMPLOYED INCOME

Writing Off Your Hobby (wink, wink)

"Do you have a hobby?" he asked.

"Sure, why?"

"Well you might be able to claim some tax losses or write-off some expenses for your hobby," he replied.

"What? How do you do that?" I asked, anxious to know how.

"Well, let's say that you **take your hobby and make it a business**. Perhaps you love writing and so you create a web-site and sell your essays as e-books. If you show a profit in at least three out of every five years, you *might* be able to qualify your hobby as a business."

"Which let's me deduct expenses like web-site management and software for conducting my business, right?"

"Exactly. It's a slippery slope as to what qualifies as a business and what is just a hobby in the eyes of the IRS so you should talk to your accountant before you start taking deductions for buying stamps for your stamp collection."

"Will do," I said.

"And speaking of starting a business," he said. "Let's talk about the perks of owning one."

Mind Your Own Business

"There's no denying that one of the best ways to get rich is to be in business for yourself. I'm not going to get into the ins and outs of building your own business right now because that's the stuff you'll learn when you're ready to jump to the Striving stage of lie. Just write the information down for future reference. You can take a lot more legitimate deductions when you have a business than when you're an employee. You can even hire your children as workers and they don't have to pay taxes on the income up to a certain amount. This way you can give them money for helping you with your business and you get to write off the amount instead of shelling out an allowance and getting nothing for it."

"You think of all the angles, don't you?" I observed.

"I have to David. The more I keep, the more I'm able to invest and give away to my favorite charities. If you're self-employed, it would be wise to get your hands on the IRS Publication 533: *Self-Employment Tax* and Publication 334: *Tax Guide for Small Business* to make sure you're following all the rules. The last thing you want to do is take any chances. Speaking of taking chances, let's cover the area of expenses that people often get into trouble with."

Cars and Other Business Expenses: Meals, cell phones, etc.

"You can also deduct the lease expense for your car, your cell phone, 50% of the cost of your meals, and a ton of other business-related expenses. Just be careful. You should keep your nose clean and not try any funny stuff. A prominent politician's husband in our area got caught writing off his Mercedes and BMW as business expenses and he went to jail."

"I remember reading about that case," I said. "He tried to write off a ton of personal items as business expenses."

"Some people think they got caught because his wife is a high-profile person, but I don't think so. I know of other people who have been audited and gotten into trouble for some questionable accounting practices, so keep your nose clean and pay your taxes is my recommendation."

INVESTMENT INCOME

Index Funds

"Okay. Now it's time to talk about investment income. Can you remember from our discussion on the sixth Secret of Wealth what my favorite investment vehicle is for new investors?"

"Sure I do. Index funds," I answered.

"And some of the reasons were the low costs, low turnover, and the fact that over the long haul most index funds will outperform their more expensive counterparts; managed funds. **Since index funds have lower turnover on average than managed funds, they're highly tax-efficient**," he said.

"By tax-efficient you mean that I pay less in taxes because they should have less capital gains than other funds who might have higher turnover and thus higher capital gains which are distributed to me and are considered income," I said.

"Well done," he said, nodding his approval. "Mutual funds by law have to distribute their short- and long-term capital gains to shareholders who must pay taxes on those gains."

"How do **'tax-managed' funds** fit into the mix?" I asked.

"Tax-managed funds are funds that purposely try to minimize or eliminate all-together any taxable distributions to shareholders. Fund managers who manage these funds will attempt to minimize distributions by buying stocks with no or low dividends, buy and hold a particular stock for a minimum of a year or longer to qualify for a reduced tax rate, or they might even try and sell stocks they are carrying at a loss to offset any gains in other stocks they are holding."

Municipal Bonds

"Tax-free investments like municipal bonds or 'munis' as they're also called are good options for high income-earners. Tax-free municipals, which typically pay less in terms of interest rates, have tax savings benefits that could more than offset the lower interest rates they pay relative to taxable bonds. Due to the high tax bracket of the individuals buying them, these individuals would wind up with a higher return from the tax-free municipals than with a comparable taxable investment."

"A little confusing, but I think I understand," I said.

"Good. Now let's talk about selling your losers?"

Selling Your Losers

"When your stocks go down, you don't have to hold onto them just because you feel bad because you've lost money on your investments."

"I'm guilty of doing that. I've held off on selling my stocks at a loss because I was hoping that they'd come back sooner or later."

"And you probably didn't want to sell any of your winners because you didn't want to pay taxes, right?" he asked.

"How did you know?" I said.

"You're not the only investor who does the wrong thing when it comes to buying and selling stocks. What you could have done is sold those stocks you were carrying at a loss and used them to offset any gains you might have had for the year. **Each year you're allowed to deduct up to $3,000 in losses from your income**."

"Yeah, but what if I had more than $3,000 in losses?"

"You're allowed to carry forward any losses for use in future years. Just make sure that you are using long-term losses against long-term gains first and using short-term losses against short-term gains."

Be Careful of the Wash Sale Rule

"When you sell for a loss, just watch out for the 'Wash Sale Rule.' Essentially what this rule says is that you're not allowed to buy a *substantially similar* security back within 30 days before or after you make the sale. If you do this, your loss will be negated. Make sure that if you buy back the security you do so 31 days before or after you sell it. If you want to somehow get around the wash sale rule, you can buy a *similar, but not substantially similar* security at the time you sell it. This is best achieved when we're talking about mutual funds. For instance, if you sell a Fidelity growth fund and buy a Vanguard growth fund within 30 days, you can legally take the loss[65]."

---

[65] Please triple-check with your accountant before you buy or sell anything that might have tax implications.

Put Dividend Paying Stocks in Tax-Deferred Accounts

"Even though the latest tax bill reduced the taxes on dividends to 15%, it still makes sense to shelter those dividends and delay paying taxes on them for as long as possible. In short, by putting income-producing assets in tax-deferred accounts, you hold off on paying taxes on any interest and dividends and let that money take advantage of the power of compounding interest."

REAL ESTATE

Tax-Free Gains

"Now let's talk about how your home provides you with some great tax benefits. Last week we covered the fact that you get to deduct the interest you pay on your home mortgage. And you already know that you can sell your home for a gain of $250,000 and not pay taxes on the gain as a single person or up to a gain of $500,000 as a married couple."

Debt Consolidation Loan Interest

"And last week we also discussed how you can consolidate your non-deductible interest loans into a home equity loan or line of credit to turn your non-deductible interest into deductible interest. This allows you to write-off all the interest you're paying. If you're going to be smart about converting bad consumer debt to tax-deductible mortgage debt, then you should take it to the next level and STOP SPENDING your hard-earned money on non-value-adding assets like clothes, stereo equipment, furniture, and the like."

I threw my hands in the air. "I got it. I got it," I said, hoping to end the sermon on the perils of bad debt.

You Can Deduct the Points You Paid

"I can't remember if we covered this point last week," he said, "but you should also know that you can deduct the points you pay on your mortgage. They get amortized over the life of the loan and can't be deducted just in the year you get the mortgage."

Wrapping Up

"Okay David. We've covered way too much information today and it's time to call it quits." He stood up and stretched. "Phew. My back is a little tight."

"I know what you mean," I said standing up and stretching a little. "But it was all worth it. I got a lot of good stuff out of today."

I gathered my things and stood up from the table. "As always Mr. Mathers, that was an excellent lesson and I'm going to make sure I review my insurance coverage."

"Don't delay David. It's wise to get your Financial House in order when it's still small and manageable. Unfortunately, most people neglect to put Secret #9 into effect and then someone or something comes along to rock the foundation and they're left penniless."

"Thanks for the cheery picture," I said as we walked outside the conference room. I had almost forgotten that we were in a retirement home.

"Don't mention it," he said and smiled. "Now it's time to visit a few of my friends. The reason I wanted you to come here is to show you what can happen if you don't Guard Your Wealth. A number of my friends here can't afford better health care and they're living off of the government. Some once had businesses bigger than mine, but several missteps or a lawsuit and they were completely wiped out. It's quite tragic and sad to see first hand."

I spent the next hour listening to stories from his friends who reinforced the lessons that Mr. Mathers had taught me that morning. Sobering wasn't the word for them. If you've ever listened to someone who's lost it all, then you know what I'm talking about.

Guard Your Wealth: Taxes – COMMENTS

You pay income taxes, capital gains taxes, property taxes, sales tax, inheritance taxes, Social Security taxes, and dozens of other taxes over the course of your lifetime. While you receive a benefit for those taxes (roads, schools, Medicare, etc, etc, etc.), you don't have control over how the money is spent, but as you've learned in this section on taxes, you can take an active role in managing your own personal taxes. Every dollar you save is another dollar that gets put into your wealth-building machine. Even small decisions like delaying the sale of a stock for a few months to qualify for the long-term capital gains rate can mean hundreds of dollars of savings. Savings that you get to keep in your pocket and not put in Uncle Sam's.

Contributing to your 401(k) or any tax-deferred savings plan is not only good for reducing the amount you pay in taxes, but it helps you build up a sizeable nest egg; a nest egg that you will live off of at some point in the not-to-distant future. That having been said, it should be obvious that tax planning should be a year-round activity, not something that you scramble to complete by April 15th. Proper planning will help you minimize your income and minimize your taxes year-round. Why not start today?

Guard Your Wealth from Uncle Sam: ACTION PLAN

Get Organized: Come tax time you want to make sure everything is in order. You should definitely have a folder in a file cabinet labeled "Taxes." Put in all your receipts for expenses you can deduct, letters from charities you've donated to, and every other form of proof for something going on your tax return. If you're expensing things like mileage on your car or other business expenses, keep track of them in a little notebook.

Max Out Your Tax-deferred Contributions: Set up your retirement accounts and max them out. You defer paying taxes on your gains and those gains get to grow...tax-free! It's like a snowball rolling down a hill and gathering steam.

Buy-and-Hold: Take advantage of long-term capital gains tax rates by buying your stocks, bonds and funds and holding them for at least a year to avoid paying taxes on your gains at your normal income tax rate. Thanks to the 2003 tax bill, you're looking at a 15% capital gains rate instead of 18%. Sounds small, but you already know that a few percentage points will help determine if you're retiring early or flipping burgers when you're 70 years old.

Sell Your Losers: You can deduct up to $3,000 in losses and carry any losses above this amount forward into future years.

Invest in Low-Cost Index Funds: Lower turnover, lower fees, and lower costs all add to your total return allowing you to beat managed funds and should lead to a smaller tax bill because lower turnover leads to lower capital gains taxes all things held equal.

Consider College Savings Plans: If you're saving for junior, definitely check out your long list of plan options. Many plans allow you to sock away money on a tax-deferred basis.

Don't Give Uncle Sam an Interest-Free Loan: If you're consistently receiving a refund from the government, talk to your accountant about a plan to stop overpaying your taxes.

Itemize Your Deductions?: Itemize your deductions and see if they exceed what your qualifying standard deduction would be. Choose the approach that gives you the best answer (read: lowest taxes paid). Consult with an accountant for the best option..oops, that's next.

Use an Accountant: If you just have employment income and not much else, you probably can continue to do your taxes on your own, but I'm in the camp of paying for good advice. In this instance, a qualified and knowledgeable accountant probably can save you a lot more money, especially with all the recent changes in the tax law.

Can You Move?: I just had to throw this one in there. Some states don't charge state income tax: Alaska, Florida, Nevada, South Dakota, Texas, Washington, and Wyoming. New Hampshire and Tennessee only charge tax on interest and dividends.

Give it Away!: Old clothes, cash, stocks, computers, your old car, and much, much more can all be given away for a nice tax deduction. You can get a deduction for the first $11,000 you give away. So you truly can give and receive at the same time.

Mind Your Own Business: If you're self-employed, you've got a lot of things you can deduct. Just make sure you follow the law and work with a competent accountant who knows their stuff. Be aggressive, but not to the point that you'll end up behind bars.

Plan Your Estate: Work with an attorney to set up a trust and get your estate in order if you've got a lot of assets to shelter.

Learn More if You Want: I'm not about to tell you to read up on the tax system and all the ins and outs of it, because it's too complicated after you get beyond the first two stages in the Game of Life. You can always check out the IRS web-site at www.irs.gov for more information. The site has a couple of lesson plans that are great. You can also check out several books on taxes.

Additional Resources

Books:
J.K. Lasser's Your Income Tax by Harold Apolinsky and Stewart Welch
Taxes for Dummies by Eric Tyson and David Silverman
The Ernst and Young Tax Guide by Ernst & Young LLP (editor)

Web-Sites:
The IRS web-site of course: www.irs.gov
www.taxsites.com lists a bunch of different tax and accounting sites

"The life that conquers is the life that moves with a steady resolution and persistence toward a predetermined goal. Those who succeed are those who have thoroughly learned the immense importance of plan in life, and the tragic brevity of time."

- W.J. Davison

"Reduce your plan to writing...The moment you complete this, you will have definitely given concrete form to the intangible desire."

- Napoleon Hill

Secret #10:
CREATE
AND WORK
YOUR PLAN

THE POWER OF HOW?

"If you have built castles in the air, your work need not be lost; that is where they should be. Now put the foundations under them."

- Henry David Thoreau

Chapter 22

Begin with the End in Mind
Identifying Your Goals – Part Deux

"There is no direction other than the one you have set for yourself."

– Author Unknown

A Perfect Ten

It was a beautiful early summer morning the day Mr. Mathers and I had our last meeting. Over the course of the past nine weeks I had learned a great deal and by taking action on the strategies and ideas he had taught me, I felt more in control of my finances and my life. Today was the day we would create my financial plan and then he would send me on my way. It felt like I was about to take a final exam.

What Do You Really Want Out of Life?

"So where do I begin?" I asked, as we settled in at our favorite library table.

"Well, most people have an idea of what they want to accomplish in life, but they've never put it down on paper. **Once those dreams and ideas of yours are put on paper, they become goals. When you have goals, you have a mission and a purpose in life.** With dreams, you're constantly dreaming of building that castle in the sky but never laying that first brick. The trick is to get your arms around those dreams of yours and write them down on paper. Since you followed the Action Plan from Secret #1, you already have your Top 50 goals for yourself. Now you just have to take out that list and review what you wrote down and add anything you might have missed."

"Got it, but which goal do I start trying to achieve first?"

"You need to separate your goals into three different buckets: short-, mid-, and long-term goals, but for now let's take a look at your Top 50 Goals List and see what should be your next steps," he said.

After a quick review, I pointed to my need to fully fund my Emergency Fund.

"You're right David. That should still be your first priority, along with paying down your credit card debt. Let's see if we can't go through the major areas of your life and come up with a list of goals for you for the next couple of years."

We talked at length about the various stages of life and the fact that almost all of them involved money in some way, shape, or manner. I began to realize that it was truly important to have clear goals to shoot for or else I'd be stuck not having the cash to pay for a new car or clothes or a house.

"That should about do it," he said when we were done. We had a short, but pretty in-depth list in front of us.

- Insurance Needs
- Emergency Fund
- Pay down credit cards
- Pay off student loans
- Car loans
- Mortgage payments
- Wedding costs
- Vacation funds
- Children
- Retirement funds
- Long-term medical needs

"So now you have some basic buckets to plan for, but before you do anything you have to figure out where you are in life."

Where are You and Where are You Going?

"You see David, you will have different goals and focus areas depending on where you are in life, which will dictate how you invest your money. In life you're going to go through **several stages**. Each stage dictates what your focus area (funding your retirement vs. paying for college) is. Then based on your goals and priorities, you create a financial plan to help you meet your objectives."

"So which stage am I in?" I asked.

"You're in the '**Just Starting Out**' stage. Why don't you take out your binder and pen, so you can write this stuff in next to those notes on asset allocation."

I pulled out my binder and placed it on the desk. As I flipped through the pages I remembered our previous lessons. I could still picture us sitting at this very table, weeks before, discussing how to save money and live below my means. It was hard to imagine that I had gotten this far without some concrete plans for my goals. That was about to change.

"Life is what happens while you are making other plans."
                                                      - John Lennon

Note - What About the Five Stages of the Game of Life?

When Mr. Mathere spoke to me about the various stages of life, it never occurred to me to ask about how they correlated with the Five Stages of the Game of Life. I called him later to ask that very question. His explanation was that **you can be at any stage in life, but at various stages of the Game.** For instance, you can be a young person just starting their career, but because of careful planning, budgeting and investing, you're rapidly moving past the Surviving stage toward the Striving stage. Make sense? No? Okay then, one more example. Let's say you have kids, a good paying job, and your spouse works part-time. You're making ends meet, but you have credit card debt, a home equity loan, and two car payments that are making things 'tight' every month. You're probably in the Struggling stage of life and don't even know it.

The stages of life are important to plan ahead for because millions of people before you have gone through them and have made mistakes (sometimes many mistakes) with their finances and their lives. Doesn't it make sense to plan for the expenses you know will occur beforehand and plan for the changes to your needs and income along the way? That's what this secret is about, planning for the future…while you still have time to make changes!

"Life is often compared to a marathon, but I think it is more like being a sprinter; long stretches of hard work punctuated by brief moments in which we are given the opportunity to perform at our best."
        - Michael Johnson, multiple Olympic gold medal winner

Just Starting Out

"In the Just Starting Out stage, you're just starting your career or maybe you're still in college and trying to get a jump on your investing career. Whatever the case, **the key is to learn to establish good financial habits and learn to manage your cash flow**. This means you budget for your expenses, try and save 10% of your salary, and start your investing plan. If you're not in credit card debt up to your ears, you're ahead of the game. If you do have a bit of credit card debt, you need to establish a debt repayment plan similar to the one we discussed during the fourth Secret of Wealth: Get Out of Bad Debt Now. It may be tough to start saving and investing at this stage, but you just have to remember how much a tiny sum of money invested monthly can grow to over the course of your life."

"What about real estate?" I asked.

"If you're not living at home, you'll have expenses you never even thought of. Who would have imagined that groceries cost that much or that dining out every night would cause your paycheck to disappear before the end of the month? Focus on creating a budget for yourself and sticking to it. You should definitely include some luxuries, but draw the line somewhere."

"What about school loans?"

"School loans fall in under credit card and general debt. You usually have a six-month grace period after you graduate before you have to begin paying your student loans back. It's important to plan for this expense in advance so that you don't feel the crunch once those monthly payments start."

"And what about investment accounts?" I asked.

"Since you're newly employed, you need to start thinking about the retirement investment tools at your disposal. If you're working at a company that offers it, you need to sign up for the 401(k) plan ASAP. You should aim to contribute at least the minimum percentage to get any company match that may be offered. If you're not maxing your contributions, you should aim to increase the percentage you're contributing by 1% every month or so until you reach the maximum allowable percentage. You should also begin looking at opening up a Roth IRA. If you want the tax deduction you can open a Traditional IRA, but I'd go with the Roth for the long-term tax-free gains benefit."

"Got it."

"Good. Now all these things should take you a couple of months to establish or get under control. It could take longer if you're paying down the credit card debt you accumulated during your spending sprees at college."

"Guilty as charged," I joked, but secretly cringed thinking of the mountain of debt I had to pay down.

"In due time you'll get rid of your bad debt. I'm confident of that David. Now on to the next stage in life."

"Which stage is that?" I asked.

"The Honeymoon Years."

"You come up with some of the most interesting names for things."

"How else do you expect people like you to remember them?"

"Real funny," I replied. "Now that you're done making fun of me, can you tell me what goes on during the honeymoon years?"

"I thought you'd never ask," he replied

I'll Spare You!

Rather than go through a total recount of some of the discussions Mr. Mathers and I had, I thought that you would enjoy (read: be thankful I didn't drag this out) a brief checklist type outline of some points to consider. Please note that this checklist is <u>not</u> meant to be an all-encompassing list of things you should cover, rather a list to stimulate your thinking and planning for things you might encounter in the future in the areas of: savings, spending and credit management, investing, insurance, home/car/other, education/kids and retirement/estate planning. With that having been said, let's get started.

"All high achievers plan their work and work their plan, for they are keenly aware that "luck" is most often the result of being prepared to take advantage of a situation."

- Author Unknown

Just Starting Out

Savings: At this stage, you're new to the world of responsibility and paying for things on your own. You never know what expense will come your way. So plan ahead. If you don't have an Emergency Fund of 3 to 6 months set aside, plan on putting some money aside each month until you get to a minimum of 3 months expenses in the bank.

Spending/Credit Mgmt: Create a budget and stick to it. Curb your spending if you're already out of control. Reduce your debt by setting up a debt repayment plan. Start by putting any extra funds toward the highest rate card or loan and pay the minimum on all the rest. Consolidate your student loans if possible.

Investing: Max out your retirement accounts before you invest in taxable investments/accounts. Open an account if you haven't done so already. Set up your automatic withdrawal (contributions) between your savings account and your brokerage account. Aim to set aside 10% of your income to invest. Invest in low-cost index funds and forget about getting rich quick. That just doesn't happen in the real world.

Insurance: Make sure you're covered through your employer's plan and have adequate life, disability, health, and auto insurance.

Home/Car/Other: Don't get suckered into driving your net worth. Buy a sensible car and forget leasing. Thinking about buying a house someday soon? Plan on setting aside some cash every month for a downpayment and closing costs.

Education/Kids: Consider getting that graduate degree. The sooner you start, the easier it will be. See if your company will pay for it. Not interested in 'higher learning?' That's okay, just make sure you Invest in Yourself and stay current on topics that concern your work and/or company by creating your own university!

Retirement/Estate Planning: As I mentioned earlier, set up your retirement account(s) and begin funding them ASAP, no matter how small your initial contributions are. Harness the power of compound interest in order to retire early.

In-Between Single and Married Life

So you've met the man or woman of your dreams and you're slowly, but surely moving toward the 'til death do us part' vows. Do you know how much weddings cost? Don't get me started. Even I get nauseous at the thought of how much mine cost me. At this stage you're probably moving in together or looking for a new place, perhaps a home. You're just starting out as a couple, so make sure that you review your financial goals and how you view spending money with your spouse. Doing this BEFORE you get married is important. Both of you need to be on the same financial page before marriage. It saves you from a lot of arguments down the road. For more on this, re-read the section titled 'Spouse Support' in Secret #9.

Savings: You should have a minimum of three months expenses (if not more) set aside by now. Start saving for that wedding.

Spending/Credit Mgmt: Cut back on expenses and start saving some more. Unless you're independently wealthy or have rich parents, your wedding will take a serious bite out of your bank account.

Investing: Put half of any of your raises into your investment accounts. Set up an automatic withdrawal from your paycheck so that you don't have to think about it.

Insurance: You probably don't have any dependents, so your need minimal life insurance.

Home/Car/Other: Start saving for that downpayment and closing costs. Think twice before you sign up for a new and bigger car loan or any other major expense/loan before you buy your house. Buying a house will take a serious chunk out of your positive monthly cash flow – plan for it.

Education/Kids: Now would be a great time to go for your graduate degree before you get married or have kids. Get into the habit of reading motivational books and listening to tape sets. Keep feeding your mind and building your library of knowledge.

Retirement/Estate Planning: Are you maxing your contributions to your 401(k) by now? If not, strive to reach that level, just in case you make the mistake of reducing your contributions when junior comes along. If you decide to reduce your contributions years from now, at least you'll have set aside a pretty nice nest egg up to that point.

The Honeymoon Years

This stage is the period of time when you newlyweds enjoy life and live it up before you have kids. This is an important stage because your salary should begin to increase after being in the workforce for several years. You're making more money, which means you should be contributing more to your 401(k) plan. And since you've been receiving some raises, you should be saving at least 50% of those raises and putting them toward your investment account and mid- to long-term goals. Also, since the two of you are living in one place instead of both paying rent, you should earmark that money for investments or debt-reduction, not frivolous expenses.

Up Front: Before you marry, talk to your future spouse about your goals and dreams. Think both short- and long-term (have I mentioned this enough yet?).

Savings: You're going to need a lot of savings to pay for unforeseen expenses. Aim to have more than three months of expenses set aside.

Spending/Credit Mgmt: Revise your budget (or spending plan if you prefer). Stick to it. Determine who is in charge of handling the finances, bill paying, investing, and overall household budget. It's good to have both of you involved, but sometimes it's easier to delegate the tasks and review your progress monthly.

Investing: Initiate a discussion about your future goals (see "Up Front" above) and take a look at both your portfolios. You should determine any changes that need to be made to investment contributions and asset allocations.

Insurance: You now have someone else depending on you, which means you have to make sure you have adequate life and medical insurance. Assess your new needs and add your spouse as a beneficiary to your accounts and assets. If you don't have disability insurance yet, what are you waiting for?

Home/Car/Other: Buy your first home. Go for a 30-year fixed mortgage if you plan on being in the house for a long time.

Education/Kids: Start saving NOW for kids. You'll be surprised, make that shocked at how much money kids cost. I'm not against kids, just plan for them and you can afford to buy little Johnny however many GI Joe's with the Kung Fu grip as his little heart desires.

Retirement/Estate Planning: Create a will. See a qualified attorney to set one up. Revise your beneficiary forms to include your spouse.

The Family Years

Your family years are filled with a plethora of expenses. According to the US Department of Agriculture, it will cost $249,180 to raise ONE kid until the age of 17. Now tack on the cost of college! Your 40s and 50s are your peak earning years, so don't waste your money on fancy cars, bigger houses, and things you really don't need. You might also find yourself caring for both your kids and your parents, so you need to plan ahead (read: set aside a ton of cash now).

Savings: With the addition of kids to the family, you might want to bump up your Emergency Fund to 4-6 months of expenses.

Spending/Credit Mgmt: Still drowning in credit card or other debt? Take a look at the equity you've built up in your home. Now might be a time to consolidate your debt and gain an additional tax benefit.

Investing: Revisit your asset allocation plan. You might not be as aggressive an investor as you were when you were single.

Insurance: Now that you have a family, you have a couple more people depending on your income. Review your insurance coverage, particularly your health, life, and disability coverage. Look into the benefits of getting long-term care insurance for you and your parents.

Home/Car/Other: If interest rates have dropped since your first mortgage, consider refinancing. If you have a lot of outstanding, high-rate credit card debt, consider taking out a home equity loan to pay down these debts. Just make sure you don't fall off the wagon and start spending again. This time your house will be on the line. Drive your cars into the ground. This way it's one less bill to pay each month.

Education/Kids: You should start living below your means so that when junior comes along, you won't feel the hit as much. You also need to start planning for college. Check with your accountant or planner for the college savings plans that make the most sense for you. Look into every grant, loan, and scholarship available when your child finishes their junior year of high school.

Retirement/Estate Planning: Don't stop contributing to your retirement plans. Money can be tight during these years because of the expenses associated with raising your kids, but you can't mortgage your future by living the high life today. Keep your investing plan on track because every dollar invested today really does go a long way. Revise your will to include your children and the names of the guardians for them. Talk with your parents about their estate and make sure they have a will and their desires and wishes are well known and documented.

Empty Nesters

Finally the kids have moved out! At this stage, your expenses should decrease since you don't have to support moochers, I mean children. Retirement is on the horizon and while expenses may decrease, some of you took out loans to pay for your kid's education's or tapped savings or investing accounts. You should take a careful look at your budget and determine what your annual expenses are and what level of income you'll need to provide for your living expenses after you retire. If you haven't done so yet, it makes sense to get in touch with a financial planner. It's important to have a good plan and strategy in place before you retire.

Savings: You need the standard three to six month's living expenses.

Spending/Credit Mgmt: You probably have some debt acquired to help pay for your children's weddings and college degrees. Now's the time to start chipping away at that mountain of debt.

Investing: Assess when you can retire and how much you'll need. Look closely at how you plan on living in your retirement years and how much your vacations, golf, charity, etc. are going to cost you. How close are you to that magical Financial Freedom number? If you're not close, you'll need to increase your contributions or put off retiring early.

Review your portfolios: (taxable and tax-deferred) to see if you should change your asset allocation and keep it in line with your changing risk profile. By this I mean shifting some money from equities into bonds and cash as you get closer and closer to retirement.

Insurance: Work closely with your planner to examine your life insurance needs. Now that you have fewer dependants to rely on (your kids have their own policies and don't rely on your income), you might be able to reduce or cancel your life insurance polices, provided you have enough assets to cover long-term needs for your spouse.

Home/Car/Other: Are you close to paying off your mortgage? If you have a lot of years left on it, it's going to increase the amount of income you'll need to retire. Selling your home to scale down your expenses may be an option.

Education/Kids: Tell your kids to pay their own way or pick up the tab for the loans you've been paying and think twice before providing Economic Outpatient Care (ongoing handouts) for your children to use a *Millionaire Next Door* term.

Retirement/Estate Planning: Your expenses should go down now that the kids are out of the house. Max out your retirement savings and contribute as much as you can to your other investment accounts.

The Retirement Years

The last stage is the stage you've been waiting for: The Millionaire Years. Now it's important to remember that just because you've built that million-dollar-plus portfolio and some online calculator says you can live off you nest egg, it doesn't give you the ability to forget about financial planning, budgeting, and watching your spending. With the average life expectancy increasing higher and higher, you might live to 100. If you retire at 65, that's 35 years left of expenses to pay for!

Savings: You will have a lot more money in savings and short-term securities than you've ever had in your life. Why? Because you're going to be living off of it that's why. It's not unheard of for retirees to have a year or two worth of living expenses in CDs, money market funds, or other cash equivalents.

Spending/Credit Mgmt: Develop your retirement budget and stick to it (most people don't plan for the unexpected (health care costs, emergencies, etc.) and therefore spend more than they can afford to spend, when they really should be saving for the future.

Investing: Take a hard look at your current asset allocation and rebalance if necessary. You shouldn't have too much money in stocks, but if you've got a long time to live off your assets, you're going to have to have a portion of your investments in stocks. Normally at this stage retirees are looking to shift their portfolios from a growth strategy to an income-generating strategy. Determine when and how much you should begin withdrawing from your IRAs. Determine where to roll over your 401(k) (if you decide to do so) and learn about your pension options if applicable.

Insurance: Health care costs and a long-term stay in a nursing home can seriously damage your retirement dreams. If you haven't done so already, you might not be able to purchase long-term care insurance or the premiums might be astronomical.

Home/Car/Other: If you don't have a large enough nest egg to live off the income that it generates and Social Security isn't cutting it, look into a reverse mortgage. It can help provide income to you and you get to live in your house until the day you die.

Education/Kids: Give a little to your kids and grandkids. Life's too short to horde your money and not enjoy life.

Retirement/Estate Planning: At this stage you MUST have a financial planner. You need to discuss how you're going to begin withdrawing funds from your investments. It might make sense to pull money from your taxable or your tax-deferred accounts because it all depends on what your strategy is and the plan you created with your planner. If you have enough money to outlast your needs, you may consider giving away some of your money for worthy causes. Work closely with your estate or financial planner to determine what's best for you and your spouse.

Yes, It's a Lot of Stuff to Think About...But

I know all these items might seem overwhelming and it might be at first, but you don't have to do it all at once. You only have to concentrate on a few key areas for your short-term goals. Just start by going back to the stage of life you're in and figure out your priority areas. Then get to work!

Now back to my dialogue with Mr. Mathers. It's time to create your Financial Freedom Plan!

Chapter 23

Secret # 10: CREATE AND WORK YOUR PLAN –
The Power of HOW?

Creating Your FINANCIAL FREEDOM PLAN

"The majority of people meet with failure because they lack the
persistence to create new plans to take the place of failed plans."
- Mark Victor Hansen, *Chicken Soup for the Soul* Series

I Know What I Want but How Do I Get It?

"Okay lets tackle one of the most important parts of the whole
wealth-building journey. If you recall, the first Secret we spoke about
was the power of setting goals for yourself. We started with setting
personal and financial goals for you over the short-, mid-, and long-
term. Goals as you will recall are the 'why' as in 'Why am I doing all
this planning, budgeting, and sacrificing?' Next I gave you insights
into the tools or strategies of what will get you there. Things like
creating a budget for yourself, living below your means, and investing
the smart way. These tools will help you get there, but you need to do
one more thing. I save this step for last, even though some would
suggest it belongs in the goal-setting section."

"What is it?" I asked.

"It's the tenth Secret of Wealth: **Create and Work Your Plan**.
The Financial Freedom Plan we'll be creating for you in simple terms
is the 'how' as in 'How am I going to reach my goals?'"

"So let me get this straight. I know why I'm doing all this stuff
(following the Secrets), because it will help me achieve my goals. Now
you're giving me the 'how to do it' part of this whole wealth-building
process."

"That's it exactly, so let's get into it," he replied.

Your Goals: Easy as 1-2-3?

"Writing down your goals was the first step, the second step was
learning strategies that will help you achieve them, and the third step is
creating the plan that will help you realize your goals. The reason we
didn't talk about goals and then create a plan to reach them is that you
and I needed to discuss the tools you'd be using to reach your goals."

"You mean the other Secrets, like budgeting, getting out of debt,
and paying myself first?"

"That's right. If you didn't understand the tools and how to use them, what's the use of creating a plan? Now that you have a set budget you can create a plan that involves real numbers. If I told you to save more money than you currently were, you'd argue that you couldn't possibly find money within your budget to invest. Am I right?"

"Yes," I responded. "Before I created my budget, I just spent every dollar and had nothing left at the end of the month. But once I created a budget, I found I could pay myself first and still have money left over to live on and invest with. Now I'm ready to create my Financial Freedom Plan, so let's get to it," I said, slapping my hands together.

"Excellent. Essentially what we'll be doing is working backwards from your goals to determine what actions you need to take on a daily basis to reach your goals of tomorrow. You'll be using the other Secrets when designing a plan that's right for you and you alone. One final word, the longer you delay creating your plan and acting on it, the less time you have to realize your goal and the less time you have to reach your goal the more…"

"Risk you have to take on," I finished.

"Exactly. Which is why starting today is so important."

"Let's do it," I said.

Your Plan: Easy as 1-2-3 and Well 6

"Depending on who you talk to or what book you read, there are six steps in the financial planning process," he said. "You've already done some of them, but let's go through them one by one and you'll see how easy this planning thing can be. I'll cover them pretty quickly, then provide you with the worksheets[66] you can use to quickly run through the steps to create your plan."

Step 1: Where am I Today?
Step 2: Where Do I Want to Go?
Step 3: What Will it Take to Get There?
Step 4: How Will I Get There?
Step 5: What Will I Do?
Step 6: How am I Doing?

> "In the long run, men hit only what they aim at.
> Therefore, they had better aim at something high."
> - Henry David Thoreau

---

[66] These will be at the end of the ACTION PLAN section of this chapter.

Step 1: Where am I Today?

"The first step in the planning process is to figure out where you're starting from. This involves taking inventory of your current assets and liabilities, as well as figuring out what your current cash flow is."

"Didn't I already do all that?" I asked.

"Like I said, you've already done some of the steps. When we created your Net Worth and Cash Flow statements, you immediately figured out where you stood financially. You've also done the next step which is figuring out where you want to go."

Step 2: Where Do I Want to Go?

"Step #2 in the process is to write down your goals, including the timing of when you want to achieve those goals."

I looked down at my Top 50 Goals List. "Looks like we'll be going through this thing again," I said, pointing to the list.

"Exactly, but now you have to attach a cost and a timeline to each of those goals. I'll let you do that later, but the process is as simple as saying that you want a new car in three years that will cost you $10,000. You simply enter that information in next to the goal of 'buy a new (used) car', then create the timeline."

Step 2a: TIMING - One Goal, One Timeline

"There are no unrealistic goals, only unrealistic deadlines." - Unknown

"Since all of your goals won't be achieved at the same time, each goal you set will have it's own timeline. Buying your first house and retiring are not going to be happening in the same year, let alone the same decade, so how you invest for both of them will be different. Sometimes I add in the timeline of 'Immediate Goals' to segment your short-term goals even further."

Immediate Goals (Today – 12 Months)
Short Term Goals (1 - 3 Years)
Intermediate Goals (3 - 5 Years)
Long-Term Goals (5+ Years)

Step 3: What Will it Take to Get There?
COST - How much do you need?

"You now have a list of goals and when you want to achieve them by. Step #3 involves figuring out two different costs: the total cost of your goals and the monthly cost or amounts you'll have to invest to reach the total costs of your goals. If you're not sure what something costs, you'll have to do a little research. Call a friend or acquaintance that has achieved your goal or go to any of the numerous sites on the Internet that have financial 'what if' calculators."

Your Goals: Attaching a Monthly Cost to Them

"The second part of this step is figuring out how much you have to invest on a monthly basis to reach your goal. This will take some time to calculate, but you can use the worksheet from Secret #6 to figure out the monthly investment required to meet your goals."

I thought about it and then it hit me. "Oh, I get it. I can use the '**Retirement Needs Calculator**' to figure out my monthly investment needs."

"That's it exactly and once you've determined the cost of your goals, you have to figure out the return you'll need to get there. One way to do this is to determine what level of annualized return you will need over the course of your plan to meet your goal. Just remember that the higher the return needed, the more risk you will have to take on. It's easy to determine how much you need on an annualized basis to meet your goals."

(Note: Not all your goals will be financial in nature. You may want to learn a new skill or learn how to play the piano. Invariably these things cost money as well, as in tuition at a community college or the cost of piano lessons, so it's wise to plan for them as well).

Step 4: How Will I Get There?

"The next step is to figure out how you're going to invest your money and how you're going to go about creating separate accounts for your goals," he said.

"Separate accounts? What do you mean?" I asked.

"The easiest way to describe it is to liken it to having a Holiday Account at your bank that's used solely for setting aside money to be used during the holidays. Some of my students set aside money for buying a car in a separate bank account or investment account. Others will use different piggy banks for small goals."

"So they keep the money separate this way, right?"

"Yes. This way there's no temptation to dip into the fund and tell yourself that it's for one goal versus another. For long-term goals like retirement, the process is a little more involving. You have to look at your IRAs, 401(k) plans, and other vehicles and put together a truly comprehensive investment plan. Luckily, most goals are short- to mid-term in nature so the plan is simply to set aside funds every month into a separate savings, money market, or investment account."

How to Allocate Your Money

"Now to figure out how you should allocate your money in your portfolio and other accounts, just answer the following questions:

- How much time do I have to reach my goals?
- What kind of return do I need to achieve on my investments to meet my goals?
- What level of risk do I have to take on to reach this return?
- Can I save more money monthly in order to reach my goals faster and with less risk?
- What asset allocation works best given my answers to the above questions?

"You will now have a starting place and a destination, and you will be able to determine what it will cost you to get here... You will be going someplace."

- R. Stanley Judd

Step 5: What Will I Do?

"Step #5 is literally about laying out everything you need to do. You simply map out how much money you'll need to put toward each of your goals. You need to make sure that you commit to putting your plan in motion and stick with it. After you work through the worksheets I'll give you, you might come across a short-fall in the funds you have available for your goals. This might happen because you want to do too many things and you don't have enough cash to fund all your goals, so you have to make tradeoffs. Part of step #5 is **prioritizing your goals** and figuring out what your most important goals are so you can allocate your resources (read: money and time) toward the most important ones. This is why you rank your short-, mid-, and long-term goals in order of importance."

"Why do you do that?" I asked, not quite following what he was saying.

"Let me explain," he replied. "To me this step is a lot like step #4, but the reason you MUST do it is that after taking a look at your monthly free cash flow, you might realize that you've run out of money. In other words, **you might not be able to fund all of your goals, so you have to know which ones are the most important to you**."

"Now I get it," I said. "I have to choose between my goals if I'm unable to set aside the amount needed for each goal. That's got to be tough to do, choose between goals like that."

"Yes, it's not an easy task, but it's something that you've got to do in order to create your Financial Freedom Plan. That's what life is about: setting priorities and making tradeoffs."

> "Making choices. Setting priorities. Accepting tradeoffs. That's what financial planning is all about, whether it's a teen-ager passing on the latest CD or designer jeans to save for her first car, or older adults juggling multiple goals, such as saving for retirement, sending the children to college, or taking a once-in-a-lifetime vacation. For most of us, this balancing act is no easy task."
> – Humberto Cruz, personal finance writer

Step 6: How am I Doing?

"You went through the trouble of setting goals, figuring out how much they cost, and how much you have to invest on a monthly basis, but now you have to make sure that your plan is on track. This is where step # 6 comes in. In this step you're literally checking to see if you're making progress on your goals or whether you're falling behind."

"How do you do that?" I asked.

"You have an annual checkup."

Your Annual (or semi-annual) Checkup

"Every year you go to the doctor's to see how you're doing. Your doctor checks your pulse, your blood pressure, and a host of other things to see if you're healthy. You need to do something similar for your portfolio."

"Sounds easy enough," I commented.

"It's not too difficult to figure out how you're doing compared to your goals. For instance, if you goal is to have $10,000 set aside in two years and you're one year into your goal and you have less than $5,000, then you're probably behind in your goal. You might decide to invest some more money monthly or decide to change your goal's timeline."

"I get it," I said writing down the information. **"You're essentially setting milestones along the way for each goal to make sure you're on track."**

"Well done," he said, nodding his head in approval. "Now you can run through your annual check-up by asking four main questions: how much did I save, what was my total return, could I have done better, and should I make changes?"

Your Annual Checkup Questions:

- **How much did I save?** - You should have monthly savings and investing goals. Did you stick with them? Did you save more or less money? Why or why not?
- **What was my total return?** - You need to determine what your portfolio's total return has been over the last six months or year. Never go beyond this amount of time without reviewing your investments.
- **Could I have done better?** - You need to compare your performance against other investment choices to see if your return could have been better. Choose whatever index or benchmark you want to use and stick to it.
- **Should I make changes?** - Am I on track or do I need to make changes? Is the return on your portfolio satisfactory? If not, you may have to do some work to re-tool your portfolio by carefully looking at some of your investment choices or the amount your investing each month.

Step #2A and #3 Revisited: The cost and timing of your goals determines what you invest in

"Before we move on David, I wanted to cover the topics of the cost and timing of your goals a little further," he said. "You see David, the cost of your goals and the deadlines for achieving them dictate what you invest in. While the *exact* assets or investment vehicles you choose to invest in may be difficult to figure out, the rule of thumb to figure out what type or category of investment vehicle to use is easy. If you need money soon, **think safety**, if you don't need the money in the next couple of years, **invest for growth**."

"I get it," I replied. "It's what we covered in Secret #6 about timelines and your asset allocation. If you don't need the money for a long time, you'll be investing a larger portion of your money in stocks, but if you need the money say in 5 years or less, then you're looking at bonds and safer investments."

"I'm glad you understand that David. It looks like you're ready to fill out those worksheets I gave you."

I picked up the worksheets and looked them over. "Hey. Not too difficult at all," I said.

"Easy as pie, David," he replied. "You just need a calculator and a pencil and you're ready to go."

"I'm game," I replied.

"Good. Let's get to it and create your Financial Freedom Plan."

Create and Work Your Plan - COMMENTS

"Fail to plan and you plan to fail" - Jim Rohn

The financial planning process I outlined has six steps that you must go through. They will help you frame out what you want to achieve in life and how you'll get there. I can't tell you enough how important it is to have compelling goals that motivate you and energize you to save and invest for your future. This last Secret of Wealth is something that you shouldn't take lightly. Proper financial planning will make sure that you will meet your goals in life because you'll have a clear outline of the steps and strategies you need to take and incorporate into your life.

I love having a financial plan because it has helped simplify my life and made it easier to make decisions and tradeoffs in my everyday life. By this I mean that it's easy to put off buying something if it doesn't take me closer to my end goal of retiring early or bring me toward some other goal I've set for myself. It's easy to figure out what types of investment vehicles I should consider because I know what return I need to get and what my time horizons are for my goals. At the end of the year (or even on a monthly basis), I can see how I am progressing toward my goals and seeing myself get closer and closer to realizing my dreams and my goals, makes it a lot easier to stay the course.

Baby Steps

*Success is not measured in big steps or leaps and bounds. There are no overnight successes! Every success in life is the result of consistent action, a series of tiny steps forward and toward your goals. Your success will be measured and achieved by adding up all those little baby steps you've taken along the path to Financial Freedom. Don't get caught up in creating a plan that calls for you to triple your net worth in two months or double your income tomorrow. Take baby steps and you'll soon be amazed at how far you've traveled. Most people think everything in life is just going to work out. Well they're wrong. **Nothing falls into place unless you plan for it**. Figure out what you want to accomplish in life, create your plan, then take action. Remember, you MUST take action to achieve Financial Freedom!*

Strategies for Every Life Stage

Each life stage has their own particular needs in each of the life stages we covered, however, **no matter what stage of life you are in, you need to have the following:**

Savings: You should have an Emergency Fund with a minimum of 3 to 6 months expenses in a money market or savings account.

Insurance: You should have adequate and appropriate levels of health, life, disability, liability, and home insurance. You need to guard your wealth regardless of where you are in the Game of Life.

Spending/Credit Mgmt: You need to have a household budget that will allow you to pay for life's necessities and allow you to invest for your future. Aim to first STOP SPENDING if you haven't done so already. Next, create your debt repayment plan. Then work that plan!

Investing: Your first action should be to max out your retirement contributions. After you get to this level, you can begin by opening a brokerage account and funneling your money every month into low-cost index funds according to a properly selected asset allocation.

Insurance: You need to have adequate disability insurance, regardless of what stage you are in. If you have dependants, you're going to need life insurance. Buy term insurance and *really* invest the difference. Health insurance is a must.

Home/Car/Other: Save your dream home purchase for when you've reached million-dollar status. In the meantime, buy an affordable house or a fixer-upper. The same rule applies for cars: don't drive your net worth. Buy, *don't lease*, a dependable used car.

Education/Kids: Start socking away money for junior the moment he/she is born, if not sooner. Don't jeopardize your retirement to fund your kids' education. They can always get loans for their education. No one is going to loan you money for your retirement.

Retirement/Estate Planning: You need to maximize your tax-deferred investment accounts before investing in taxable accounts if retirement is your #1 priority. As for your estate, get your will and estate plans in order as soon as possible. You can probably hold off until you're a parent, so the moment you find out you're pregnant, get in touch with your lawyer and draft up a will and other necessary documents.

Create and Work Your Plan – ACTION PLAN

Top 50 Goals: Take out your Top 50 Goals List, review it, and make revisions or additions. Segment your goals according to short-, mid-, and long-term goals on a separate piece of paper.

Prioritize Your Goals: Go down the list of each of the three buckets of goals and prioritize your list from most important to "nice to have" or least important goals.

Attach Costs to Your Goals: You might need to do some detective work in order to find out how much each of your goals will cost. You can use the resources on the Internet, Consumer Reports, or ask a friend.

How Much Do You Need to Save: Take a look at Figure 23.2 the "Goals Cost Estimator" at the end of this section and use it to figure out how much you'll need to set aside every month to reach your goals.

Set Up Different Accounts: This step might get cumbersome if you have 15 goals you're saving for, but most people will have three or four accounts they will use in addition to their 401(k)s, IRAs, and 529 Plans.

Set Up a Funding Plan: Using Figure 23.4 the "My Monthly Action Steps" worksheet that follows this section, figure out how much you need to allocate to each goal, and start funding your goals on a weekly or biweekly basis.

Your Annual Review: This step is critical. You need to review your progress every six months or at minimum, once a year. If you need to make adjustments (such as reducing your anticipated rate of return, increasing monthly contributions and so on), then do it immediately! No sense in finding out ten years from now that you've been underfunding your retirement accounts. The time to find out if you're off track is today, while you still have time to make changes.

Get Help: If you need help with the process and feel overwhelmed, don't sweat it. It might be time to check into using a financial planner. A professional will be able to create a custom-tailored plan that's right for you. The next chapter will help you figure out how to find a planner that's right for you.

But for now, let's go through a case study of how you could put a simple Financial Plan together.

JUST A QUICK, OVERSIMPLIFIED CASE STUDY
(or really just a more in-depth look at the 6 Steps)

Step # 1: Where am I Today?

Fill out your net worth and cash flow statements to determine your current assets, liabilities, and monthly free cash flow.

Step # 2: Where do I Want to Go?

Review your Top 50 Goals List and make sure you break your goals out into short-, mid-, and long-term goals. You can use the chart in Figure 23.1 "Your Goals: How Much Do You Need?" for this process.

Step # 3: What Will it Take to Get There? (Cost of your goals)

In this step you figure out how much you need to invest monthly to reach your goals. Figure 23.2 "Goals Cost Estimator" will help you with this process.

Step # 4: How Will I Get There?

This process involves creating separate accounts for your major goals and perhaps lumping a few smaller goals into one or two accounts. Why all the accounts? So you don't steal from one account to fund another account/goal.

Step # 5: What Will I Do?

Compare the total cost of funding your goals to your current free monthly cash flow, because you might not have enough money to fund ALL of your goals. Check out Figure 23.1 for an example of the process. Once you've figured out what goals you can afford, it's time to set the plan on autopilot. Whether it be upping your 401(k) contributions or having money automatically pulled from a savings account to the account for a particular goal, just do it!

Step # 6: How Am I Doing?

Check your progress on a periodic basis. For some that means monthly, for others it's once or twice a year. You need to add up how much you contributed toward each goal, what your total return was, and compare that return to the returns of your benchmarks (i.e., other money market accounts or stock index funds.)

Do you need to make changes? Perhaps your retirement accounts are lagging after a bear market or you weren't able to put as much away in your "new home" account. What do you do? That's up to you, but maybe you could increase your 401(k) contributions or get a little more aggressive with your investment allocations. Perhaps you put off buying a new home for another year or start saving more.

Step #2 - #3
Figure 23.1 - Your Goals: How Much Do You Need?
Note: The amounts entered should be the **remaining** amount you need to save.

SHORT TERM GOALS: 0 – 3 Years

	Goal	Current Cost of Goal	By When	How Much Monthly
1.	Buy a new "used" car	$10,000	3 yrs	$289.72
2.				
3.				

Subtotal

Where to Put Money: Savings, money market accounts, and CDs.
Estimated return on investment anywhere from 1% to 3%.

MID TERM GOALS: 3 - 5 Years

	Goal	Current Cost of Goal	By When	How Much Monthly
1.	Buy a House (downpayment)	$30,000	5 yrs	$529.20
2.				
3.				

Subtotal

Where to Put Money: Brokerage cash accounts, short-term bond funds, and muni bonds. Estimated return on investment anywhere from 3% to 6%. Note: as you get closer and closer to your goals, you should shift funds to cash investments.

LONG TERM GOALS: 5+ Years

	Goal	Current Cost of Goal	By When	How Much Monthly
1.	Retirement	$600,000	30 yrs	$964.80
2.				
3.				

Subtotal

Where to Put Money: Stock index funds and mid- to long-term bond funds.
Estimated return on investment anywhere from 6% to 10%.

(STEP # 1) Current Free Monthly Cash Flow: (A.) $2,050.00

Subtotal of all Monthly Costs for Goals: (B.) $1,783.72

Difference (A. minus B.): = (C.) +$266.28

NOTE: If the amount in "C" is NEGATIVE you will either have to revise your goals by lowering them or extending the timeline you wish to achieve them by. You can also go back to your CASH FLOW CALCULATOR or budget and figure out where you can cut some expenses.

The "**How Much Monthly**" amount was calculated using the chart on the next page (Figure 23.2 – Calculating the Cost of Your Goals).
NOTE: Short-term goal example used 3% return estimate, Mid-term used 5%, and Long-term used 8%. Choose the estimated returns that are right for YOU.

Step # 3 (cont'd)
Figure 23.2 - Calculating the Cost of Your Goals
Note: If you've already saved money for your particular goal, the amounts you enter in really should be the remaining amount you need to save.

The Goals Cost Estimator

		Example	YOU
1.	Cost of Goal	$10,000	$
2.	Inflation Factor (ex. 3% @ 10 yrs.)	1.3	
3.	Future Value of Income Needed (multiply item # 1 by # 2)	$13,000	$
4.	Value of Current Investments	$2,000	$
5.	Compound Interest Factor (from table below)	1.6	
6.	Value at Time of Goal? (multiply item # 4 by item # 5)	$3,200	$
7.	Total Shortfall (subtract item # 11 from item # 7)	$9,800	$
8.	Monthly Amount You have to Invest? (multiply item # 7 by correct Automatic Savings Factor)	$63.11	$

FIGURE 23.3 - Inflation, Savings, and Future Value Calculators
Use the Below Table for Filling in the Above Table

Years to Reach Goal	Inflation Factor at 3%	Compound Interest Factor at 5%	Automatic Savings Factor at 5%
5	1.2	1.3	0.01470
10	**1.3**	**1.6**	**0.00644**
15	1.6	2.1	0.00374
20	1.8	2.7	0.00242
25	2.1	3.4	0.00167
30	2.4	4.3	0.00120
35	2.8	5.5	0.00088
40	3.3	7.0	0.00066

Note that in Appendix A & B of this book you will see a variety of Automatic Savings Factors and Inflation Factors should you want to be more conservative or aggressive in your assumptions.

Use for Step # 4 – Step # 5
Figure 23.4 – My Monthly Action Steps

Example from Figure 23.1

Goal	Investment Strategy: (Where you're putting your money and how it will be invested)	Cost per Month
Goal #1	Invest money in savings account #1	$289.72
Goal #2	Invest money in savings account #2	$529.20
Goal #3	401(k) plan contributions	$964.80

YOUR Turn

Goal	Investment Strategy: (Where you're putting your money and how it will be invested)	Cost per Month
Goal #1	_____	_____
Goal #2	_____	_____
Goal #3	_____	_____

Use for Step # 6 – Monitoring Your Plan

Date	Goal		Amount in Account	On Target? (Yes / No)
Month 1	#1	_____	$_____	_____
	#2	_____	$_____	_____
	#3	_____	$_____	_____
Month 6	#1	_____	$_____	_____
	#2	_____	$_____	_____
	#3	_____	$_____	_____
Month 12	#1	_____	$_____	_____
	#2	_____	$_____	_____
	#3	_____	$_____	_____
Month 18	#1	_____	$_____	_____
	#2	_____	$_____	_____
	#3	_____	$_____	_____

Chapter 24

Getting Some Help

Do You Need a Financial Planner?

Leaving our discussion between David and Mr. Mathers for a second, let's talk one-on-one. I realize that the information in this Secret might be tough for some people to understand and you might feel intimidated by filling out the last three charts or tables. My advice to you is don't sweat it too much. You can always get help via online calculators or from a certified financial planner.

I wanted to provide you with some information on financial planners, how to choose one, and what to expect when you first meet with your potential planner. There's a lot of ground to cover, but hopefully you'll come away from this chapter with a better understanding of what to ask a planner and how they can help you.

What Can a Planner Do for You?

Before we get into how to find a planner, let's talk about what they'll do for you.

What they'll do for you:
- Find out more about you and your needs
- Understand your goals and objectives
- Find out where you are currently (financial snapshot of assets/liabilities)
- Design a financial plan for you

What they should tell you:

You might have to ask some of these questions, but in general you should leave your initial interview with a planner with the following information:
- Tell you their investment philosophy
- Explain how they get paid
- Describe who their typical client is
- Tell you how often they'll contact you
- Show you the type of analysis they will provide you, what a plan would look like, and what kind of statements you can expect to receive
- Let you know the risks involved with investing

Where to Find Them?

The Institute of Certified Financial Planners
www.cfp-board.org
800-282-7526
The Institute of Certified Financial Planners are the keepers of the coveted CFP designate for planners. They certify their planners and make sure they're up to snuff. Check out their site for some great information on what to look for in a planner.

The Financial Planning Association
www.fpanet.org
800-322-4237
FPA is an organization of financial planners. It's a great site for finding a planner near you.

National Association of Personal Financial Advisors
www.napfa.org
www.cfp.net
888-237-6275
NAPFA is the largest association of Fee-Only financial planners in the US. NAPFA will definitely give you the dirt on your potential financial planner as long as they're a NAPFA member. Check out their "Resources and Products" section for a number of links to great sites.

There are a few other sites and organizations, but these are the big three that will answer all your questions. After cruising around these web-sites, you'll have a pretty good idea of the financial planning process and what to expect. Now before you go calling up financial planners, you need to determine if you really need one. Ask yourself the following questions:

Do I Really Need a Planner?

Am I Committed?
Before you throw down some money on the table, ask yourself if you're really committed to this whole wealth-building process. There's no sense in meeting with a planner, setting up an account, and not following through on putting the plan in motion. You need to realize that a planner can only do so much and they're not going to be able to force you to do anything. So, are you really committed to putting the Secrets of Wealth to work for you?

What Do You Want?
You need to start off by understanding what it is that you're looking for. Do you need everything or are you looking for advice in a specific area like insurance, estate planning, or investing? This is will be important information for your planner when you meet with them.

Why Do I Need a Financial Planner?
In short, why are you looking for a financial planner? What are your goals and aspirations? What are you trying to accomplish? How can an advisor help you put a plan together for you that's beyond the basics outlined in this book?

Finding Your Planner
Okay, you've answered the above questions and determined that you need a planner. Now what?

Get Referrals
If you've read *The Millionaire Next Door, you* know that the rich always have a great team of financial advisors and attorneys in their corner. The rich use planners to help them strategize and help them make their money work harder for them so they don't have to work hard all their life. The best way to find a planner is to ask a rich person. If you don't know any rich people, ask your accountant for the names of planners his or her rich clients use. Yes, it can be that simple. If you do happen to get a hold of a rich person, quiz them about their planner. Ask them what they like and dislike about their planner. How long they've been working together and how often they meet. You'll want to ask about the company they're affiliated with or whether they're operating on their own. Ask, ask, and ask some more. This person will be handling your money so you want to get all the dirt on them.

Finding a Planner on Your Own
If the referral route left you with no names, then it's time for you to do your own homework. Check out the web-sites I listed at the beginning of this chapter to find a planner near you.

Check Them Out Beforehand
You should see if the planners you are considering have ever had any disciplinary actions taken against them. The list at the end of this chapter will help you figure out where to go to do this.

Be Prepared
You should go to your meeting with your CASH FLOW CALCULATOR, Net Worth Statement, and goals list. Bring along last year's tax returns and brokerage account statements as well. Your potential planner might ask to see these.

Ask Before You Give
But before you hand over the above documents or answer questions the planner will ask you, you should ask some questions of your own. I tell people to interview the planner by asking the following:

Check List for Interviewing a Financial Planner

1. How long have you been a planner?

This great opening question will give you a sense for their level of experience. You should be looking for a planner with **a minimum of three years experience.**

2. What's your typical client look like?

Not what they physically look like, but what do they do, how much do they earn, etc. Does he/she have a large group of clients that are lawyers and doctors, or do they focus on other groups. Also ask how many clients they have. This question is important because you can get a feeling for whether you'll be a little fish in a big pond or the big fish among their clients. It's good if they have a number of clients and have been doing the planning thing for a while because they'll be recommending investments and options that they've implemented before for other clients.

3. Do you have any certifications or designations?

This will let you know if they have any licenses or certifications. You'll want to know if they're a CFP (Certified Financial Planner) or Certified Public Accountant (CPA), as well as any other designations. Ask them if they belong to any professional organizations as well. You can double-check the information at www.cfp.net after your interview, but you really should do this before your meeting.

4. What services do you offer?

Most planners can give you advice, but not all financial planners can sell insurance products or securities products (mutual funds, stocks, and bonds). They should be able to provide you with a brochure or pamphlet detailing the services they provide (retirement, financial, insurance, estate, and/or tax planning). You also want to know if the planner is going to be executing your trades and making your investments or whether it will be farmed out to some other division or company. Ask if they will be the only one you'll be working with.

5. What's your financial planning philosophy?

The person across from the desk could be managing your money one day and you're putting your financial future in their hands. With that in mind, it's critical to find out how they approach the financial planning process. Are they overly aggressive or too conservative?

6. How would we work together?

Does the planner just make recommendations, get your rubber stamp of approval, and execute trades? **Do they seek to educate you on the basics of the financial planning process** or do they dive right into putting the plan into action? Ask how often you would come in for meetings and portfolio reviews.

7. Do I get a written plan?

The company I used to work for provided its clients with an investment plan for a flat fee. It had all the bells and whistles and everything you needed to implement the program on your own if you chose to do so. Not every planner offers this, but if they do offer the service, **ask to see a sample plan.**

8. How do you get paid?

Planners can get paid in a number of ways:

- **Commissions:** Planners who work on commission typically get a base salary from their company and get a commission (expressed as a percentage of the amount you invest) from the mutual fund company or insurance company the product is purchased through.

- **Fee Only:** Fee-only planners will charge you by the hour for their services. You can pay anywhere from $50 to $400 an hour for planners, depending on the credentials and the type of plan/help you need. It's up to you to implement the plan through a brokerage house. This could be a good option for the do-it-yourselfer that wanted a second opinion.

- **Commission and Fees:** The planner gets a flat fee for developing the plan and commissions on any products they sell to you. They get a commission on your transactions/investments, but they also charge you a set fee for managing your money. A typical fee is around 1 to 1.5 percent of assets under management (ie, all the stocks, bonds, and other investments they're managing for you).

- **Fee-Based:** A fee-based planner will only charge you a flat fee based on the assets under management. The more money you have for them to manage, the less you'll pay. You don't pay commissions with these folks.

It's up to you to figure out which style and fee structure works best for you. Just realize that there might be a conflict of interest if the planner gets paid more the more you trade.

9. Have you ever been disciplined for unethical or unlawful activities at anytime in your career?

Of course you can find this out by going to a number of web-sites, but it's interesting to see their reaction. Of course you should have done your homework beforehand and eliminated offenders from your list, but you can always check up on them after your interview.

10. Ask for the names of three clients

I love this request and it never hurts to ask for the information. Just know that the people pulled out of the Rolodex™ will likely be their best or favorite clients.

Closing Comments

Your goal is to find someone that you're comfortable working with and who is also great at what they do. Make sure you pick someone who you can get along with and fits your personality type. You're going to be spending a lot of time with this person over the years and they're going to be managing your money, so choose wisely!

Invest in Your Education!

Regardless of whether you have the greatest planner on earth, you still have to know what's going on. What I mean is that you shouldn't simply hand over all your assets and do as your advisor says without asking questions and understanding the reasons behind their recommendations. You can't just turn over all control of your finances and your future to someone. If you've been in the Game of Life long enough, you already know that you're the only one who has your best interests in mind. You are the best financial planner for your money and your future. Stay involved. Ask questions. Make your advisor explain things and educate you in the process.

Advice on a Shoestring Budget

If you're concerned about the costs of a planner and you don't have a lot to invest, why not get some help up front and then take over the management of your accounts? Some well-known companies offer services whereby you sit with an investment consultant and they help build a diversified portfolio for you. Vanguard will charge you around $500 for a one-time consultation, while Schwab will charge you around $250 to $500 depending on your needs. You can also call your local Fidelity branch and see what the fee would be for a quick analysis of your needs. When I first started investing, I just walked into my local branch and got a quick portfolio of funds created at no charge. Just know that you don't get on-going help and be mindful that these planners might be pushing load funds on you because that's how they make their money.

In short, take the time to invest in yourself and learn the basics of investing. You'll find that you can manage to answer 90% of the questions on your own or with a little help from the Internet.

Check Out Your Planner Before You Sign on the Dotted Line

The below sites will let you know if your planner has all the credentials and experience they're claiming to have. You can also see if they've had any disciplinary actions against them in the past.

National Association of Securities Dealers
www.nasdr.com
800-289-9999
This should be tho starting point of your search since it has the most comprehensive database.

Certified Financial Planner Board of Standards
www.cfp-board.org
888-CFP-MARK
They set the standards for planners and will let you know who has the coveted Certified Financial Planner designation.

National Association of Insurance Commissioners
www.naic.org
816-842-3600
This group regulates insurance agents.

North American Securities Administrators Association
www.nasaa.org
888-84-NASAA
This is a voluntary association that is devoted to investor protection. They also can help entrepreneurs find valuable information on franchising and raising capital.

Securities and Exchange Commission
www.sec.gov
800-SEC-0330
You've probably heard about the SEC in the news after several high-profile insider trading busts, but the SEC does a whole lot more than police stock transactions. They oversee all the key agencies in the securities world, including the stock exchanges, brokers, dealers, mutual funds, and many, many more people and institutions.

"Do not wait for an opportunity to be all that you want to be. When an opportunity to be more than you are now is presented and you feel impelled toward it, take it. It will be the first step toward a greater opportunity."
  - Wallace D. Wattles, *The Science of Getting Rich*

"The three great essentials to achieving anything worthwhile are; first, hard work, second, stick-to-it-iveness, and third, common sense."
                                              - Thomas Edison

"Deciding to commit yourself to long-term results rather than short-term fixes is as important as any decision you'll make in your lifetime."
                                              - Anthony Robbins

Chapter 25

Time to Get Started

From Fear to Flight

"David, you now have in your possession the first ten Secrets of Wealth," Mr. Mathers said, putting his glasses on the table. "I hope you take the time and put in the effort to incorporate them into your life. They are simple ideas or lessons, but the rewards can be truly beyond your wildest imagination if you're willing to put the Secrets of Wealth to work for you."

"I'm sold Mr. Mathers. I can already see an improvement in my finances, as well as my mindset. It's like I already know I'm going to be wealthy one day because I know what I'm doing now and I know I have a plan that I can measure my progress against. I'm not going to be just throwing money into the stock market or spending my money on things I don't need or that don't add value to my future. I know the Secrets you gave me will help me achieve my goals."

"Good. It sounds like you've really taken the lessons to heart, which makes me feel good. Just remember that **the Secrets of Wealth will help you only as much as you're willing to stick to the plan that you have just created for yourself.** Work your plan and you'll have your money working hard for you in no time. Sit on your butt and procrastinate and well, you'll be right back where you started with only yourself to blame. **You MUST TAKE ACTION!**"

"Mr. Mathers I know I'll stick to the plan. It's so easy to follow. It's like I can't screw it up."

"David, you must stay the course. You're still young and have time on your side, so you don't have to sacrifice too much in the way of your current standard of living. For someone who is 10 or 20 years older than you, they have to take some drastic measures and at that stage of their lives, it becomes harder to change. For you, it should be relatively easy. Work that plan of yours and you're almost guaranteed to reach your goals without too much effort. Just put the plan in motion and get out of the way."

"I will Mr. Mathers. I promise and thank you again. Thank you for everything. I'll be forever grateful for what you have taught me."

He shook his head and waved his hands in front of me. "Don't start sounding like this is a good-bye," he said. "You'd better call me now and again when you need help and you will almost definitely need help. **You have the plan, but there will be speed bumps along the way and detours that can take you off course**. Just know that in advance and plan ahead for the inevitable roadblocks and curve balls that life throws at us and you'll be fine. Also, you know that I'll always be a phone call away if you need me, so don't hesitate to call me," he offered.

Pass on the Secrets of Wealth!

"And by the way, you can really **thank me by passing on the Secrets of Wealth on to others**. That's the most important thing you can do with the knowledge I have given you: pass it on."

"I'll do it. I promise," I replied.

With that, we both stood up and shook hands.

"I've got to stay behind today and do some research," he said. "You go on and enjoy the day before the summer is over and you haven't had a weekend that's filled with anything but finance and listening to boring old me," he said. There was a smirk on his face.

"I'd like to think I rather enjoyed the experience Mr. Mathers."

"Glad to hear it David," he said. "And again, don't sweat your future too much. With the Secrets of Wealth firmly in place, you're already on the fast track to Financial Freedom. Just remember to call me if you get off track or are about to make a major financial decision."

"I will. I promise," I said, then turned and left the library.

I would end up calling him to begin the next phase of my wealth-building program in three short years.

Chapter 26

Putting the Secrets of Wealth to Work for You

The "INGs" of Wealth

I've gone through a lot of information in this book and I've tried to give you the basics of saving, budgeting, investing, protecting, and living life in order to achieve Financial Freedom. **The original version of this book was over 700 pages long** and my publisher, as well as my early reviewers, thought I was nuts. In an effort to cut down the information, I've summarized the Secrets of Wealth as best I could given the constraints of pages. So to summarize even further, it can be said that you've learned the art of:

Dreaming
Saving
Budgeting
Managing
Living
Investing
Earning
Investing (in Your Home)
Guarding
Planning

What About Giving?

I know we didn't cover **GIVING**, one of the most important steps of wealth building, in this book. I did briefly touch upon this concept in Secret #9, but in a more self-serving way. I know that books like *The Richest Man in Babylon* or *Rich Dad's Guide to Investing* bring up the subject and say that everyone should get into the habit of giving their money away to worthy charities, regardless of their income or where they stand financially. Clason suggests that people set aside 10% of their income to give away. The "Ten Percent" mark comes up a lot in other books that you'll read.

So if I know why giving is so important to wealthbuilders, why didn't I cover giving? Because I think you would be better served by first taking care of your Financial House and going through the process of optimizing your cash flow. Once you realize that you can lead a fulfilling lifestyle despite "living below your means," you'll realize that you can fully fund your Financial Freedom Plan *and* have money left over. Once you're ready to make the jump from the Surviving to Striving Stage, I think it's important to start giving your money away to charity. But that doesn't mean you can't start giving if you're in the Struggling of Surviving Stages of the Game of Life. Let me explain.

3 Ways to GIVE!

I believe that there are three ways that you can give:

♥ **Giving Your Money**
♥ **Giving Your Time**
♥ **Giving Your Knowledge and Experience**

I'm not going to go into detail into what I mean by each of these areas because I think it's self-explanatory and I've already killed enough trees with this book. In short, if you're short on cash you can still give back to your community and others around you. I might not be lighting up the donation boxes yet, but I believe I'm giving back by donating my time to community events and charitable causes. I'm also giving away quite a bit of time, knowledge, and experience to others for FREE through my newsletter and those I'm helping via online chats, free conference calls, and one-on-one emails (drop me a line at fabman@fabmansecrets.com).

Again, I think that everyone should give back to their community and to others, but it doesn't necessarily have to involve money all the time. I'll discuss the concept of giving a bit more in my next book[67], but let's move on for now.

Everyone Can be Wealth, Even YOU!

I truly believe that every person is capable of becoming rich. It's just that most people quit even before they start down the path to Financial Freedom. They fail to take the necessary steps to change who they are, how they think, and the actions they take. Instead, they continue doing the same things over and over again, only to get frustrated because they're getting the same results over and over again.

I strongly believe that anyone who has the burning desire to change their circumstances can do so if they decide to change today and take focused action toward changing their lives forever. The moment you decide and resolve to succeed regardless of the roadblocks you will face, you're 90% of the way home.

---

[67] Unless you hate this book and so does everyone else and there's no demand and my publisher kicks me to the curb!

I beg you not to give up until you have achieved your goals. Be persistent and take consistent and MASSIVE ACTION toward your goals. Create that plan and work it harder than you've done anything else in your life. Don't stop just short of reaching your goals and definitely don't stop if you've had a few failures. Just because you have failed in the past doesn't mean you will fail in the future and if you do, so what? Pick yourself up, examine what worked and what didn't, adjust your sails and try again. Your future depends on your resolve and the fire in your belly.

Simple, Not Easy

Hey, getting rich IS as simple as I've made it sound in this book. You simply have to:

- Be Clear about Your Goals and Write them Down
- Save Ten Percent of Your Money (or more) on a Consistent Basis
- Get Out of (Bad) Debt and Stop Spending on consumer goods
- Budget Your Time and Your Money
- Spend Less than You Make – Live Below Your Means
- Start Investing Today, Not Tomorrow
- Invest in Yourself by Increasing Your Knowledge
- Your Home is for Shelter first, an Investment second
- Guard Your Wealth from Life, Others, Uncle Sam, and Yourself
- Plan for Your Brilliant Future TODAY!

There is NO Magic Pill

Simple right? But how many of you will actually step up to the plate and swing? Again, **the Secrets outlined in this book are simple and powerful, but they're not necessarily easy to put in place for the majority of people.** It drives me crazy to know this as fact because I've seen it happen right before my eyes dozens of times. I've attempted to help my friends, family members, and co-workers (as well as people I've met online), but the majority don't follow-through with the plan so they fail.

Are you wondering why they fail? Well, I think it's because they're looking for the magic bullet. They're looking for that "no money down" real estate deal. They want to start a business on a shoestring that costs $50 to start and doesn't require any effort on their part. **The moment you realize that THERE IS NO MAGIC PILL OR BULLET, you're on your way to Financial Freedom.**

> "You are searching for the magic key that will unlock the door to the source of power; and yet you have the key in your own hands, and you may make use of it the moment you learn to control your thoughts."
>
> - Napoleon Hill

The next step in the process is to actually make the simple changes that will pay huge dividends down the line. While there is no magic pill to what ails you, the truth is that most of the things you want to change in life are simple to change; yet you'll find it hard to change, for instance:

- Want to know how to lose weight? Eat less and exercise more.
- Want to know how to get rich it in the stock market? Buy Low and Sell High or Hold On.

How hard is that? Eat less and exercise more and you lose weight. No fat burners, no gimmicks, just a simple strategy and yet, millions of people shell out billions of dollars a year to take the short cut, when the answer is as simple as eating less and exercising more. But why won't they follow that strategy? Because it takes work and **the majority of people are lazy. They don't want to change their actions, but they want to change the results.** The definition of insanity has been said to be doing the same things over and over again, but expecting a different outcome every time. That's ludicrous. If you want to change your life, you've got to change your actions and behaviors.

Look, there is nothing complicated about the Secrets of Wealth. They really are just simple strategies that you can put into place with a minimal amount of effort. Yes, it requires work and effort up front, but the rewards are well worth the effort. Read any biography about a rich person and you'll be amazed at how simple their plan for getting rich was and how it required some effort up front, but then got easier over time. There will be speed bumps along the way, but once you've designed your plan and put it into action, it's practically smooth sailing the rest of the way.

Walk the Talk

The path to Financial Freedom has always been simple, just not easy to follow. Now I ask you, are you willing to take the next step? **Talk is cheap**. Ron LeGrand once said, **"When all is said and done, more is said than done."** No truer words were ever spoken. Take action, don't just talk about what you're going to do. Go and do it!

In the introduction and second chapter of this book I spoke about the reason for this book, mainly to help people get control of their financial lives and get their Financial House in order. Perhaps you always knew that you should have a financial plan or create a budget. You knew you should save more and invest more, but didn't have the tools you needed. Hopefully you have learned about the tools that have been building wealth for generations of millionaires in this country and abroad. I hope I was able to give you new tools and a new way of thinking about personal finance and your financial future. My hope is that you will have acquired the knowledge to start making smarter decisions with your money, your career, and your investments. If you're still uncertain, please seek out the advice of a competent financial advisor. They should be able to point you in the right direction.

Still Not Sure Where to Start?

There really are no Secrets of Wealth. It makes for an interesting title and story, but **wealth is more a result of discipline and patience than anything else**. Success in any endeavor is a habit that can easily be attained by anyone who truly wants it. All they have to do is believe they can achieve success and then pour their heart, their soul, and their mind into attaining it. At some point in every successful person's life they have encountered defeat have encountered what seemed like impossible odds. They simply chose to get started, forge ahead despite the odds, and get moving in the direction of their dreams.

There are many roads to wealth and financial security in life. There are Secrets that all of us can follow and use that will definitely have a positive impact on your financial future. Hopefully you've acted on some of the Secrets I have written about. If not, what are you waiting for? Just in case you're not sure of where to start, take a look below.

Start Dreaming – Take the time to think long and hard about what you want your life and your retirement to be like. Do you want to work at a part-time job? What kind of hobbies do you want to have? Where do you want to travel?

Stop Dreaming – That's right, stop dreaming about it and set some real goals for yourself. If you don't move from step one to step two (which so many people never do), you'll never retire in style, let alone retire on your own terms. You need to take responsibility for your financial future.

Set Goals - Goals will help focus your efforts and help you stick to your plan. The first step we talked about was dreaming about where you wanted to be 10, 20, and 30 years from now. Now you need to determine how much you need to put away on a monthly basis to reach those goals. It's important to figure out how much you have to save to meet those goals.

Stop Spending - Do you know where you're spending your dollars? Do a cash flow analysis to see where your money is going.

Start Saving - Start out by trying to save 10% of your salary. It's a benchmark, so put aside more if you can afford it and less if you're having trouble getting to that mark, but make sure you push yourself to save more money.

Start Paying - The first step after you've begun to save money (hopefully 10% or more) is to pay down your debt. You're never going to get ahead in life if you don't get rid of the burden of your bad debt.

Have a Plan - You're not going to be haphazardly investing or spending your money from now on. You will have created a Financial Freedom Plan for yourself that you will be working against.

Monitor Your Plan - Having a plan will help you track how you're doing versus the goals you've set for yourself. You need to make sure that your plan is on track and you're making progress toward your goals. Having a plan that incorporates your goals with checkpoints along the way is the best way to see how you're doing.

Start Learning – The more you know about investing and saving, the better off you will be today and tomorrow. Set aside a designated time each week (or day for you aggressive learners) where you read a book on budgeting, personal finance, or investing. Hit the library if you have to, but keep feeding your mind.

Build Your Emergency Fund - Emergencies happen. You must be able to deal with them when they do happen. Start putting aside a little money each week so you have a cushion to dip into in case something does happen (and it will)!

Start Saving for Your Retirement - Start investing in your retirement plans if you haven't done so yet. If you already are contributing, contribute a little more each month or two until you max out your contributions. In the meantime open up an IRA account, which type depends on your income and your financial situation. Consult your accountant or financial planner for help in deciding whether a traditional or Roth IRA makes the most sense. Regardless of which type you use, the earnings will grow tax-deferred even if you don't get a tax deduction for your contributions.

Get Automatic - Start making regular contributions to your savings and investments once you've picked your asset allocation and created your investment accounts.

Don't be Too Conservative - Retirement will cost you a lot more than you think. Plan on replacing 100 percent of your income during your retirement years. This means that you can't have the majority of your portfolio in bonds and expect to retire in style (nor does this mean you should be 100% invested in stocks). Use the appropriate mix for your age and stay focused. Review Secret #6 for more help with the asset allocation that's right for you.

Help Your Parents and Friends - Pass along your wisdom and help your family and friends. If your parents get the message, you'll be helping yourself as well. Why? Because you may end up supporting them years from now if they don't apply the Secrets of Wealth, but if they've built up a nest egg thanks to your wise words of advice, so much the better.   Besides, what's the use of retiring early if all your friends are hard at work while you're living the good life?

Give Back! - I covered this only briefly, but if you've mastered the first ten Secrets of Wealth, then you're well on your way to Financial Freedom. You probably have the resources and the time to give back to your community or help someone else by sharing the Secrets with them. Once you start giving, the joy and the sense of fulfillment that will overwhelm you will have you giving more and more. Trust me on this one. It's one of the best feelings in the world.

There, I'm done and I'm plain exhausted after going through everything in this book, but wanted to say one more thing…

"Whatever the mind of man can conceive
and believe, it can achieve."

- Napoleon Hill, *Think and Grow Rich*

CONCEIVE – BELIEVE – ACHIEVE

You can do anything you put your heart and mind to. If you sincerely love yourself and those around you, you will take that first step toward breaking free of the chains of debt and consumer spending. You will move with purpose from the Struggling stage of life to the Striving stage and beyond. The steps to get to those next stages in life have been outlined in this book, so start changing things NOW!!!

The Road Less Traveled

Maybe 5% of you will take action TODAY on the information contained in this book. My hope is that the number is higher. I know what a difference taking action can make in one's life. The information contained in this book gives you the ammunition you need to go and take back control of your life. The downside of a book like this is that you probably can read it faster than you can master the Secrets of Wealth and the lessons contained within these covers. I suggest you **take out a calendar and promise to reread this book in three months time**. Also mark on your calendar six months from now a total review of how you've progressed against your written goals. This is the best and only way to see if you've learned the Secrets of Wealth.

The moment I decided to stop procrastinating and get moving toward realizing my dreams, my life was changed forever. Just by taking action, I couldn't help but make progress. So get moving. Take action toward your dreams. Use the information in this book, but don't stop there. Read more on the subject of wealth-building (a book a month), find a mentor, but more importantly…get moving!

The losers, complainers, and whiners never get far in life because they follow the path that everyone before them has followed. As you know, 95% of people never do anything with the material they read. They just sit there and play the **Coulda, Shoulda, Woulda Game** that is prevalent among those in the Struggling and Surviving stages of life. They never take chances, never put forth the effort to change their circumstances and change their lives in the process. Don't be one of them.

Before you there are two paths. One is the beaten path of indifference, complacency, and cynicism. The other, less traveled path, is a winding road that requires a bit more effort to travel down, but it leads to every dream you can imagine. Which will you choose?

Start Walking Toward Financial Freedom TODAY…

Appendix A: Inflation Factor and Compound Interest Factor
(Future Value of $1 Calculator)

Yrs	3%	4%	5%	6%	7%	8%	9%	10%	11%
1	1.03	1.04	1.05	1.06	1.07	1.08	1.09	1.10	1.11
2	1.06	1.08	1.10	1.12	1.14	1.17	1.19	1.21	1.23
3	1.09	1.12	1.16	1.19	1.23	1.26	1.30	1.33	1.37
4	1.13	1.17	1.22	1.26	1.31	1.36	1.41	1.46	1.52
5	1.16	1.22	1.28	1.34	1.40	1.47	1.54	1.61	1.69
6	1.19	1.27	1.34	1.42	1.50	1.59	1.68	1.77	1.87
7	1.23	1.32	1.41	1.50	1.61	1.71	1.83	1.95	2.08
8	1.27	1.37	1.48	1.59	1.72	1.85	1.99	2.14	2.30
9	1.30	1.42	1.55	1.69	1.84	2.00	2.17	2.36	2.56
10	1.34	1.48	1.63	1.79	1.97	2.16	2.37	2.59	2.84
11	1.38	1.54	1.71	1.90	2.10	2.33	2.58	2.85	3.15
12	1.43	1.60	1.80	2.01	2.25	2.52	2.81	3.14	3.50
13	1.47	1.67	1.89	2.13	2.41	2.72	3.07	3.45	3.88
14	1.51	1.73	1.98	2.26	2.58	2.94	3.34	3.80	4.31
15	1.56	1.80	2.08	2.40	2.76	3.17	3.64	4.18	4.78
16	1.60	1.87	2.18	2.54	2.95	3.43	3.97	4.59	5.31
17	1.65	1.95	2.29	2.69	3.16	3.70	4.33	5.05	5.90
18	1.70	2.03	2.41	2.85	3.38	4.00	4.72	5.56	6.54
19	1.75	2.11	2.53	3.03	3.62	4.32	5.14	6.12	7.26
20	1.81	2.19	2.65	3.21	3.87	4.66	5.60	6.73	8.06
21	1.86	2.28	2.79	3.40	4.14	5.03	6.11	7.40	8.95
22	1.92	2.37	2.93	3.60	4.43	5.44	6.66	8.14	9.93
23	1.97	2.46	3.07	3.82	4.74	5.87	7.26	8.95	11.03
24	2.03	2.56	3.23	4.05	5.07	6.34	7.91	9.85	12.24
25	2.09	2.67	3.39	4.29	5.43	6.85	8.62	10.83	13.59
26	2.16	2.77	3.56	4.55	5.81	7.40	9.40	11.92	15.08
27	2.22	2.88	3.73	4.82	6.21	7.99	10.25	13.11	16.74
28	2.29	3.00	3.92	5.11	6.65	8.63	11.17	14.42	18.58
29	2.36	3.12	4.12	5.42	7.11	9.32	12.17	15.86	20.62
30	2.43	3.24	4.32	5.74	7.61	10.06	13.27	17.45	22.89
31	2.50	3.37	4.54	6.09	8.15	10.87	14.46	19.19	25.41
32	2.58	3.51	4.76	6.45	8.72	11.74	15.76	21.11	28.21
33	2.65	3.65	5.00	6.84	9.33	12.68	17.18	23.23	31.31
34	2.73	3.79	5.25	7.25	9.98	13.69	18.73	25.55	34.75
35	2.81	3.95	5.52	7.69	10.68	14.79	20.41	28.10	38.57
36	2.90	4.10	5.79	8.15	11.42	15.97	22.25	30.91	42.82
37	2.99	4.27	6.08	8.64	12.22	17.25	24.25	34.00	47.53
38	3.07	4.44	6.39	9.15	13.08	18.63	26.44	37.40	52.76
39	3.17	4.62	6.70	9.70	13.99	20.12	28.82	41.14	58.56
40	3.26	4.80	7.04	10.29	14.97	21.72	31.41	45.26	65.00

To use this chart, just find the rate of return (or inflation) that you want to use along the top and choose the number of years along the left-hand side. Where the two meet is your answer.

For example: If you want to find out how much a $1 will grow to over 10 years at 9%, the answer is $2.37. If you had a $1,000 and wanted to figure out how much it would be worth in 10 years at 9%, just multiply 2.37 by $1,000 and you'll know that you'll have $2,370 in 10 years' time.

Appendix B: Automatic Savings Factor
(Monthly Investment to Reach a $1 Calculator)

Yrs	3%	4%	5%	6%	7%	8%	9%	10%	11%
1	.08219	.08182	.08144	.08066	.08023	.07979	.07936	.07893	.07850
2	.04048	.04009	.03970	.03912	.03871	.03831	.03790	.03750	.03710
3	.02658	.02619	.02580	.02530	.02490	.02451	.02412	.02374	.02336
4	.01963	.01925	.01886	.01839	.01801	.01763	.01726	.01689	.01653
5	.01547	.01508	.01470	.01426	.01389	.01352	.01316	.01281	.01246
6	.01269	.01231	.01194	.01152	.01115	.01079	.01048	.01011	.00978
7	.01071	.01034	.00997	.00956	.00921	.00886	.00853	.00820	.00788
8	.00923	.00883	.00849	.00810	.00776	.00742	.00710	.00678	.00648
9	.00808	.00768	.00736	.00697	.00663	.00631	.00600	.00570	.00541
10	.00716	.00679	.00644	.00607	.00574	.00543	.00513	.00484	.00457
11	.00640	.00604	.00570	.00534	.00502	.00472	.00443	.00415	.00389
12	.00578	.00542	.00508	.00473	.00443	.00413	.00385	.00359	.00234
13	.00525	.00490	.00456	.00423	.00390	.00364	.00337	.00312	.00288
14	.00480	.00445	.00412	.00379	.00350	.00323	.00297	.00273	.00250
15	.00444	.00406	.00374	.00342	.00314	.00287	.00260	.00239	.00218
16	.00406	.00373	.00341	.00310	.00282	.00257	.00233	.00211	.00191
17	.00376	.00343	.00312	.00282	.00255	.00230	.00207	.00186	.00167
18	.00350	.00317	.00285	.00257	.00231	.00207	.00185	.00165	.00147
19	.00326	.00294	.00263	.00235	.00210	.00187	.00166	.00147	.00130
20	.00305	.00273	.00242	.00215	.00191	.00169	.00149	.00131	.00115
21	.00285	.00254	.00224	.00198	.00174	.00153	.00134	.00117	.00101
22	.00268	.00237	.00208	.00180	.00160	.00139	.00120	.00104	.00090
23	.00252	.00221	.00193	.00168	.00146	.00126	.00109	.00093	.00080
24	.00238	.00207	.00179	.00155	.00134	.00115	.00098	.00083	.00071
25	.00224	.00195	.00167	.00144	.00123	.00105	.00089	.00075	.00063
26	.00212	.00183	.00156	.00133	.00113	.00095	.00080	.00067	.00056
27	.00201	.00172	.00146	.00123	.00104	.00087	.00073	.00060	.00050
28	.00190	.00162	.00136	.00115	.00096	.00080	.00066	.00054	.00044
29	.00181	.00153	.00128	.00107	.00088	.00073	.00060	.00049	.00040
30	.00172	.00144	.00120	.00099	.00082	.00067	.00054	.00044	.00035
31	.00163	.00136	.00112	.00092	.00075	.00061	.00049	.00040	.00032
32	.00155	.00129	.00105	.00086	.00070	.00056	.00045	.00036	.00028
33	.00148	.00122	.00099	.00080	.00064	.00051	.00041	.00032	.00025
34	.00141	.00115	.00093	.00075	.00060	.00047	.00037	.00029	.00023
35	.00135	.00109	.00088	.00070	.00055	.00043	.00034	.00026	.00020
36	.00129	.00104	.00083	.00065	.00051	.00040	.00031	.00024	.00018
37	.00123	.00099	.00078	.00061	.00047	.00037	.00028	.00021	.00016
38	.00118	.00094	.00074	.00057	.00044	.00034	.00026	.00019	.00014
39	.00113	.00089	.00069	.00053	.00041	.00031	.00023	.00017	.00013
40	.00108	.00085	.00066	.00050	.00038	.00029	.00021	.00016	.00012

To figure out how much you have to set aside on a monthly basis to reach your goal, just find the rate of return you expect to receive along the top and choose the number of years along the left-hand side. Where the two meet is your answer.

For example: If you want to have $1 in 10 years and you expect a 9% rate of return, your answer is 0.00513. If you wanted to have $1,000 in 10 years, just multiply 0.00513 by $1,000 and you'll realize that you need to set aside $5.13 a month to reach your goal.

Appendix C: THE GAME OF LIFE — Where do your habits put you?

	STRUGGLING	SURVIVING	STRIVING
Goals	- No goals beyond making it through tomorrow or next week	- Major goal is to retire with enough money to live on - Pay for kids' college expenses - Pay off mortgage - Mostly financial goals	- Retire early - Become Financially Free by having passive income exceed monthly expenses - Have Achievement, Improvement and Financial goals
Savings	- No savings - Use credit cards for emergencies	- Might have 1 to 2 months of savings	- 3 to 6 months in savings set aside - Separate savings accounts for big purchases
Spending	- Living paycheck to paycheck - Spend first, think later - Constantly worrying about $ - No household budget	- No or little positive cash flow - Buy on impulse - No planning for big expenses, buy on credit	- Positive cash flow - Living below their means - Household budget dictates spending - Plan and save ahead for big expenses
Debt	- Credit cards are maxed and might not qualify for any or any more loans - Debt used to purchase necessities and luxuries	- Debt-to-Income ratio between 35% to 50% - Credit cards close to being maxed - Debt used to buy luxuries earlier than they can afford to buy them	- Little or no revolving debt - Pay off credit cards monthly - Debt used to buy appreciating assets that throw off a positive cash flow
Investing	- No investments - Savings accounts are only "investment" accts - Little or no retirement funds - Lottery tickets are their investments	- Small investment accounts - Not diversified: probably have the bulk of funds in 1-2 stocks - Try to time the market	- Large investment accounts - Proper asset allocation - Invest primarily in no-load, low-cost index funds - Buy the market instead of trying to time it
Education	- Don't invest in themselves after graduating from high school or college - Little or no money set aside for kids' college expenses	- May read a financial magazine or two per month - One of their biggest concerns is affording the cost of their kids' education, paying for weddings, etc.	- Spend between 1% to 3% on their education per year - Avid reader of magazines and "how to" books - Kids' college expenses are taken care of or a plan is fully in place to fund needs
Real Estate	- Rent and will probably never own - Can't afford a downpayment so they will rent for life	- Know the importance of owning real estate - Live above their means and buy a bigger house than they can afford. - Status seekers	- Know the importance of investment real estate and invest heavily in properties - Live below their means in an affordable house - Don't keep up with the Joneses

Appendix C: THE GAME OF LIFE – (cont'd)

	STRUGGLING	SURVIVING	STRIVING
Guarding	- Some or no life insurance - No or minimal health insurance - No disability insurance - No will, power of attorney or trusts	- Know the importance of life insurance, but don't have enough - Have health insurance through work - Short-term disability coverage only - No umbrella policies - Wills are out-of-date	- Have adequate life, home, and health insurance - Supplemental liability policy is more than adequate - Long-term disability insurance - Protect assets through trusts and corporations - Have an updated will and an estate plan
Taxes	- Little pre-tax investments - They're their best charity	- No tax planning - Get a large refund every year - Make investments without thinking of tax consequences - Contribute under 10% to pre-tax savings accounts - Some charitable contributions	- Meet with tax planners to develop tax plan - Make investments with tax consequences in mind - Have a tax-efficient investment plan in place - Max out pre-tax savings accounts - Use appreciated assets for charitable contributions
Planning	- Live for today attitude - No plan beyond next week's paycheck	- Don't really plan for major purchases or expenses beyond one or two months - May have a plan for kids' college expenses	- Have a plan and work that plan - Meet with a financial planner regularly

The above items and benchmarks are a matter of personal opinion in most instances, but if you read through them carefully, I think you'll agree that they are pretty fair and accurate. Don't be so concerned with making it to the next level in the Game right now. What you should be concerned about is getting your Financial House in order so that you have a firm foundation upon which to grow and then you'll find yourself moving quickly to the top of the Game of Life.

BIBLIOGRAPHY

Goals
Goals! by Brian Tracy

Save Ten Percent of What You Make
The Richest Man in Babylon by George Clason

Budget Your Time and Money
Believe and Achieve by W. Clement Stone

Get Out of (bad) Debt NOW!
Debt Free by 30 by Jason Anthony and Karl Cluck

Live Below Your Means
The Millionaire Next Door by Thomas Stanley and William Danko

Invest NOW, Not Tomorrow
All About Index Funds by Rick Ferri
Personal Finance for Dummies by Eric Tyson
The Only Investment Guide You'll Ever Need by Larry Swedroe
The Intelligent Asset Allocator by William J. Bernstein

Invest in Yourself
The Seven Habits of Highly Effective People by Stephen Covey
Think and Grow Rich by Napoleon Hill

Real Estate is Free
Ordinary People, Extraordinary Wealth, Ric Edelman
Rich Dad, Poor Dad, Robert T. Kiyosaki, Sharon Lechter
Creating Wealth by Robert G. Allen

Guard Your Wealth
Personal Finance for Dummies by Eric Tyson
Rich Dad, Poor Dad by Robert Kiyosaki and Sharon Lechter

Planning
Personal Finance for Dummies by Eric Tyson
(But mostly the CFP and other financial planning web-sites)

General
Conversations with Millionaires by Mike Litman and Jason Oman
Think and Grow Rich by Napoleon Hill

ACKNOWLEDGEMENTS

Especially Keith Agabob and Mike Litman

Mom and Dad, Teresa Agabob, Marc Allen, Michael Bastone, The entire staff at Central Plains Printing, Alfredo Chiappini, J. Collins Coyne, James C. Coyne, Kathy Coyne, Susan Coyne, Mark Farmer, Rick Ferri, Cathey Flickinger, Robert Fontaine, Seth Godin, Mary Goulet, Josh Hinds, Peter Hupalo, Jason Imperato, Joe Imperato, Tom Jacobs, Taylor Larimore, Mel Lindauer, Anna Marciano, Guy Marciano, Amy Paluskiewicz, Louis E. Rollano, Larry Swedroe, Phil Simonides, Brian Tracy

And lastly, but most importantly, to all loyal subscribers! Thank you!

DROP ME A LINE IF YOU WANT

IF THIS BOOK HAS BEEN HELPFUL AND HAS IN SOME WAY STEERED YOU TOWARD THE PATH OF FINANCIAL FREEDOM, THEN I HAVE DONE MY JOB. IT IS A HARD TASK TO TELL THESE SECRETS TO YOU AND I HOPE I HAVE DONE MY JOB WELL.

PLEASE LET ME KNOW ABOUT YOUR PROGRESS. SEND ME A LETTER OR EMAIL to: **fabman@fabmansecrets.com**.

**BEST OF LUCK ON YOUR JOURNEY,
BUT IF YOU'VE LEARNED ANYTHING FROM ME,
YOU'LL KNOW THAT LUCK HAS NOTHING TO DO WITH IT!**

www.fabmansecrets.com
Always check my site for new updates and FREE giveaways!

INDEX

The Yale Class of 53 Didn't Exist

Remember the story from Secret #1 about the Yale Class of 1953 that had that overachieving bunch of graduates that set goals for themselves? Well a Fast Company Magazine[68] author, Lawrence Tabak, did some research into that much used example of the importance of writing down your goals. He found out the story wasn't true. He even went to Yale to find out if the story was true. According to Research Associate Beverly Waters, "We are quite confident that the 'study' did not take place. We suspect it is a myth."

Tabak's story ends with this note: "Not that hard evidence like that has ever stopped a consultant. From his Solana Beach, California office, consultant Brian Tracy responded to Waters's findings. "Heard this story originally from Zig Ziglar. If it's not true it should be."

In my mind the story rings true to what I've seen and witnessed with my own eyes. Start setting goals for yourself and you'll soon find yourself achieving more than your peers could ever imagine for themselves or you for that matter.

This book is written with the intention of shifting your paradigm, as well as giving you insight into the basic tenets of wealth-building for the beginner. The world of personal finance and wealth-building could cover several books, workbooks, audio tapes, and seminars to be complete in nature. My hope is that this book will be equal parts motivational and instructional. If you have further questions, please do not hesitate to contact a professional for help regarding your specific situation.

---

[68] "If Your Goal Is Success Don't Consult These Gurus," by Lawrence Tabak, Fast Company, December 1996

Give the Gift of
FINANCIAL FREEDOM
to Your Loved Ones, Friends, and Colleagues

CHECK OUT YOUR LEADING BOOKSTORE OR ORDER HERE

❏ YES, I want ___ copies of *The Secrets of Wealth* at $19.95 each, plus $4 shipping per book (New York residents please add $1.40 sales tax per book). Canadian orders must be accompanied by a postal money order in U.S. funds. Allow 15 days for delivery.

Name _____

Organization _____

Address _____

City/State/Zip _____

Phone _____ Email _____

Please make your check payable and return to:

The Wealthy Pauper, LLC
P.O. Box 676
Harrison, NY 10528

For more information on orders and
ordering **multiple copies at a discount**,
please visit our web-site at:
www.thewealthypauper.com